THE ABCs OF LEARNING

DISABILITIES

Second Edition

THE ABCs OF LEARNING

DISABILITIES

Second Edition

BERNICE Y. L. WONG

Faculty of Education
Simon Fraser University
Burnaby, British Columbia
Canada

LORRAINE GRAHAM

School of Educational Studies
University of New England
Armidale, Australia

MAUREEN HOSKYN

Faculty of Education
Simon Fraser University
Burnaby, British Columbia
Canada

JEANETTE BERMAN

Communications and Education Department
University of Canberra
ACT, Australia

AMSTERDAM • BOSTON • HEIDELBERG • LONDON
NEW YORK • OXFORD • PARIS • SAN DIEGO
SAN FRANCISCO • SINGAPORE • SYDNEY • TOKYO
Academic Press is an imprint of Elsevier

Cover Design: Joanne Blank
Cover Images: © iStockphoto, Jupiter Images

Elsevier Academic Press
30 Corporate Drive, Suite 400, Burlington, MA 01803, USA
525 B Street, Suite 1900, San Diego, California 92101-4495, USA
84 Theobald's Road, London WC1X 8RR, UK

This book is printed on acid-free paper. ∞

Library of Congress Cataloging-in-Publication Data
The ABCs of learning disabilities / editors, Bernice Y.L. Wong ... [et al.]. – 2nd ed.
  p. cm.
Rev. ed. of: The ABCs of learning disabilities / Bernice Y.L. Wong. c1996.
  Includes bibliographical references.
  ISBN-13: 978-0-12-372553-0 (hardcover : alk. paper) 1. Learning disabled children–Education. 2. Learning
disabilities. 3. Learning disabilities–Research. 4. Language arts. 5. Mathematics–Study and teaching.
I. Wong, Bernice Y. L. II. Wong, Bernice Y. L. ABCs of learning disabilities.
LC4704.W645 2008
  371.9–dc22
  2007043978

British Library Cataloguing in Publication Data
A catalogue record for this book is available from the British Library

ISBN 13: 978-0-12-372553-0

For all information on all Elsevier Academic Press publications
visit our Web site at www.books.elsevier.com

Printed in the United States of America
08 09 10 9 8 7 6 5 4 3 2 1

This book is dedicated to Sorcha and Jamie Harrop; Joy (Lorraine's mother); Tom, Corri, and Krysta Hoskyn; Kyle, Evan, and Rhianna Berman; Rod and Kristi Wong.

CONTENTS

2

LANGUAGE AND LEARNING DISABILITIES   37

3

WORKING MEMORY AND LEARNING DISABILITIES   63

4

SOCIAL DIMENSIONS OF LEARNING DISABILITIES   89

5

SELF-REGULATION AND LEARNING DISABILITIES   133

6

ASSESSMENT FOR LEARNING   153

7

READING   175

8

MATHEMATICS   197

9

WRITING INSTRUCTION   217

PREFACE

I wish to thank Nikki Levy for her persistence and persuasion in getting me to attempt a revised edition of *The ABCs of Learning Disabilities*. If not for Nikki, I would not have had the marvelous opportunity to gather three friends to contribute chapters to the revised edition of the book or the great enjoyment of thinking and writing.

It is with deep gratitude and appreciation that I list my contributors: Lorraine Graham, Maureen Hoskyn, and Jeanette Berman. Without them, this book would not have been completed. Each of them brought her individual expertise and perspective to the book. Words cannot express my appreciation of their concerted efforts to meet the deadline, especially Lorraine, who wrote while battling an ear infection that made her feel as if the room was spinning around.

The four of us enjoyed a division of labor. Maureen wrote Chapters 2, 3, and 8 on language and learning disabilities, memory and learning disabilities, and mathematics, respectively. Lorraine and Jeanette collaborated on Chapters 5, 6, and 7: self-regulation and learning disabilities, assessment, and reading. I wrote Chapters 1, 4, and 9: the history of learning disabilities, social dimensions of learning disabilities, and writing. Our writing has been facilitated by the fact that we wrote on areas that we enjoyed or in which we conducted research.

In writing the chapter on language and learning disabilities, Maureen had benefited from Tomasello's literature. In her chapter on working memory and learning disabilities, Maureen profited much from Lee Swanson's noted research on working memory. Similarly, Lorraine wishes to acknowledge the usefulness of Swanson, Harris, and Graham's book *Handbook of*

Learning Disabilities. In writing the chapter on the history of learning disabilities, I benefited much from three books: Mercer and Pullen; Hallahan, Lloyd, Kauffman, Weiss, and Martinez; and Hallahan and Mock. Jeanette thanks Carol Lidz for her ongoing inspiration, and Lorraine thanks Anne Bellert for their previous collaborative research on reading comprehension.

We also greatly appreciate the help of Nikki Levy of Elsevier, who has always been helpful, informative, and positive. Barbara Makinster (senior developmental editor with Elsevier) has always been understanding, patient, and helpful. And we thank Julie Ochs in the production department at Elsevier Academic Press and the copyeditor, Deborah Prato, for doing such a wonderful job with our book. Last but not least, we thank the following individuals for their help: Paul Yeung, a doctoral student at Simon Fraser University, and Devi Pabla, secretary to the associate dean in the faculty of education at Simon Fraser University.

To the student

In this revised edition of *The ABCs of Learning Disabilities,* you see the combined efforts of four authors, each writing on areas of her expertise. More important, we bring to our writing tasks much experience in teaching undergraduate students. The breadth of our teaching experience gives us a shrewd sensitivity to your instructional needs, and this sensitivity guides our writing.

In the chapters on reading, mathematics, and writing, you will notice the absence of the words *and learning disabilities*. This omission is deliberate. We wanted to emphasize that the instructional materials given in those chapters are designed for use in inclusive classrooms, with clear and specific pointers on adaptations for use with students with learning disabilities.

We have tried to smooth out differences in our individual writing styles, while maintaining a sense of humor and efforts to stimulate you to think about what you are reading. We hope you find this revised edition reader-friendly and useful.

Cheers and best wishes,

Bernice Wong

LEARNING DISABILITIES:
FROM PAST TO PRESENT

This chapter traces the history of the learning disabilities field and presents the standard gamut of topics subsumed in the history of the field. These include, but are not limited to, the origins of the learning disabilities field, the influential definitions of learning disabilities, the characteristics of individuals with learning disabilities, the condition of attention deficit hyperactivity disorder, and the etiology of learning disabilities. The chapter concludes with an assessment of the current hot topic of the response to instruction model as an alternative to the IQ-achievement discrepancy model of diagnosing learning disabilities and boldly raises the question of the contributions of the research of response to instruction (RTI standard-protocol approach) to the learning disabilities field.

Since the beginning of the learning disabilities field, two primary issues—that did not shape but must be dealt with—have maintained their prominence: (1) the need to validate the hypothetical notion that learning disabilities are neurologically based and thus represent a genuine handicap and (2) the need to devise methods of effective identification, diagnosis, and intervention for individuals with learning disabilities (Torgesen, 1993). In tracing the history of the learning disabilities field, we follow the lead of Hallahan and Mock (2003) and divide it into several distinguishable periods that reflect diverse sources of influence on the development of the field.

THE INFLUENCE OF EUROPE (1800–1920)

During this period, European doctors and researchers began to investigate the relationship between brain injury and speech disorders. We focus only on the legacies of those who had an impact on the learning disabilities field.

In the first decade of the nineteenth century, Franz Joseph Gall, a physician, made the assertion that separate areas of the brain controlled specific functions—in other words, that brain functions are localized. He based his assertion on the observations of his patients who had brain injury. Gall's notion of localization of brain functions was confirmed by the work of Bouillaud in the 1820s. Broca furthered Bouillaud's work through the use of autopsies and drew the conclusion that speech functions lie in the inferior frontal lobe. This area was subsequently called Broca's area. Moreover, Broca's name is linked to a specific type of speech dysfunction called Broca's aphasia: "a slow, laborious, dysfluent speech" (Hallahan & Mock, 2003, p. 17).

Another disorder called "sensory aphasia" was named by Wernicke based on his case studies of ten brain-injured patients with language disorders. In this type of aphasia, patients would talk fluently, but what they said was meaningless. Wernicke believed that the area responsible for this particular speech disorder was the left temporal lobe, the area that now bears his name. Wernicke published his case studies in 1874.

The relevance of the preceding work to the learning disabilities field is that they show unequivocally that brain damage to specific areas of the brain can result in specific kinds of mental/cognitive impairment. The progress made in research in language disorders spilled over to interest in disorders related to reading (Hallahan & Mock, 2003).

In 1896, the first case study of a child with congenital word-blindness (reading disability) was published by an English physician W. Pringle Morgan. Morgan's work inspired a Scottish ophthalmologist, Sir Cyril Hinshelwood, to study specific reading disabilities. He reported the first systematic clinical studies of this disorder in 1917. Some of his patients were adults who had suddenly lost their reading ability, while their other mental or cognitive abilities remaining intact. Hinshelwood studied a number of such cases and attributed this loss of reading ability to damage in specific regions of the brain. His opinion paralleled those about patients who lost their speech through brain damage of, say, Broca's area or Wernicke's area.

Hinshelwood also examined cases of children with severe difficulties in learning to read. His descriptions of these cases were careful, detailed, and compelling (see Torgesen, 2004, p. 9). He called such conditions "congenital word blindness" and believed it resulted from damage to a particular area in the brain in which visual memories for words and individual letters were stored. His speculation that damage to that region was the cause of congenital word blindness turned out to be wrong. But his contributions to the learning disabilities field are still relevant because he pointed out that these children's inability to learn to read juxtaposed with normal abilities in other intellectual skills, such as arithmetic. Moreover, Hinshelwood thought the occurrence of cases of word blindness to be very rare, with an incidence rate of less than one in a thousand.

In summary, the twentieth century witnessed clinical research that showed connections between types of brain damage and specific loss of various speech and language functions in adults. Interest in these connections spilled over to children who had extreme difficulties in learning to read. Hinshelwood was the first to report cases of children with this congenital word blindness. Although some dispute Hinshelwood's relationship to the development of the learning disabilities field (see Torgesen, 2004), Hinshelwood made a very important contribution. He maintained that such children had intact cognitive functions outside of the reading domain, and it is this specificity of cognitive malfunction that is at the heart of learning disabilities!

THE INFLUENCE OF AMERICA (1920–1960)

Beginning in the late 1930s, before the field of learning disabilities was formally established, two separate but parallel strands of clinical and research interests emerged that left indelible marks on interventions or remediation of children with learning disabilities. One strand emphasized general cognitive abilities that are presumed to underlie successful performance on a wide range of tasks. This emphasis originated from the research of Goldstein and was continued by Werner and Strauss. The other strand emphasized auditory and language processes and focused more narrowly or specifically on reading. The individuals associated with it were Helmer Mykelbust and Samuel Kirk. We examine the work of these two strands of clinical research in the next few sections.

Kurt Goldstein, a physician, was the director of a hospital for soldiers who sustained head injuries from World War I. He observed these brain-injured soldiers and noticed a group of particular behaviors that included hyperactivity, indiscriminate reaction to stimuli, confusion with figure-ground perception, concrete thinking, perseveration, meticulosity, and emotional lability. At the Wayne County Training School for children with mental retardation, Werner and Strauss became interested in applying and extending Goldstein's clinical research to children. Strauss was a neuropsychiatrist, and Werner was a developmental psychologist.

Strauss and Werner divided the children in their training school into two groups: those with mental retardation resulting from a brain injury (exogenous mental retardation) and those with familial mental retardation (endogenous mental retardation). They found that compared to children with endogenous mental retardation, children with exogenous mental retardation showed more indiscriminate reactions to auditory and visual stimuli. They tended to be more impulsive, erratic, and socially unacceptable. Such findings led them to conclude that the special education category of mental retardation is not a homogenous group. Their conclusion was supported by an additional finding that after four to five years of training at the Wayne County Training School, children with endogenous mental retardation gained by an average of four points in IQ, whereas children with exogenous mental retardation did not show any gains. This discovery of no gains in children with exogenous mental retardation to the given training spurred Strauss and Werner and their associates to design an educational environment that aimed to reduce their behavioral problems and promote better attention focusing. Consequently, they engineered educational environments that reduced irrelevant stimuli while enhancing relevant stimuli in learning for children with exogenous mental retardation. Their efforts culminated in the publications of two books: *Psychopathology and Education of the Brain-Injured Child* (Strauss & Lehtinen, 1947) and *Psychopathology and Education of the Brain-Injured Child: Progress in Theory and Clinic* (Vol. 2; Strauss & Kephart, 1955).

Strauss and Werner's influence in the learning disabilities field lies in providing a general orientation to teaching children with special needs. This general orientation subsumes three premises: (1) Individual differences in children's learning should be understood through analyzing the cognitive processes that facilitate or hinder learning, (2) instructional procedures should match the individual child's processing strengths and weaknesses, and (3) by strengthening their deficient processes, children with deficient processes might be helped to learn adequately (Hallahan & Cruickshank, 1973; Torgesen, 2004). After the inception of the learning disabilities field, these premises of the general orientation to educating exceptional children assumed special significance as the field attempted to stake out identity as a separate category within special education that would qualify children with learning disabilities for funding for special education services. The premises provided the necessary rationale and assertion that learning disabilities constitute a separate entity alongside other categories within special education.

Werner and Strauss's work was continued and extended by their associate Kephart, who elaborated on their theory that perceptual-motor skill development provides the foundation to higher mental learning—for example, conceptual learning. A logical consequence derived from this theory is that training in perceptual-motor skills should help children experiencing learning difficulties in school. Kephart (1960) subsequently wrote the book *Slow Learner in the Classroom,* which contains educational procedures for use in learning disabilities classrooms.

After Kephart, William Cruickshank became connected with the work of Werner and Strauss. He worked with children with cerebral palsy and observed that they showed the same kind of characteristics as children with exogenous mental retardation in the clinical research of Werner and Strauss.

Specifically, Cruickshank found that children with cerebral palsy showed more indiscriminate reaction to background in figure-ground perception studies than children without cerebral palsy. Thus, he recommended creating a similar educational environment for children with cerebral palsy where distractions were minimized. He went on to test the efficacy of his recommendation in a pilot study in Montgomery County, Maryland (the Montgomery County Project). Cruickshank and his associates (Cruickshank, Bentzen, Ratzeburg, & Tannhauser, 1961) published the pilot study in a book, *A Teaching Method for Brain-Injured and Hyperactive Children*. Hallahan and Mock (2003) wrote that under current diagnostic criteria, many children in the case studies in Cruickshank's pilot study would qualify as children with learning disabilities or children with comorbidity of learning disabilities and Attention Deficit Hyperactivity Disorder (ADHD).

Cruickshank has a special place in the history of learning disabilities because he provided the bridge between mental retardation and learning disabilities (Hallahan & Mock, 2003). Through him, the educational treatment of children with learning disabilities embodied Werner and Strauss's emphasis: reduction of environmental distraction and salience of relevant dimensions and tight structure. The academic instructional part of the treatment consisted of "readiness training, perceptual, perceptual-motor exercises, homework, and arithmetic" (Hallahan & Mock, 2003, p. 21). The educational program, however, neglected the cultivation of reading skills.

Auditory and language processes were the clinical and research interest of individuals in the separate but parallel strand, such as Helmer Mykelbust and Samuel Kirk, who were contemporaries of the preceding individuals. Mykelbust's background was research of the hearing-impaired, but he also alerted people's attention to children and adults who have auditory verbal comprehension problems. Kirk, in contrast, played a very important role in the development of the learning disabilities field.

Kirk was strongly influenced by the work of Orton and Monroe. In 1937, 20 years after Hinshelwood published his case studies on adults, Orton, an American child neurologist wrote about his theory of reading disability. Recall that Hinshelwood coined the term *congenital word blindness* for his case studies of children who could not read. He believed that damage to a localized area of the brain where visual memories for words and individual letters were stored caused congenital word blindness. In contrast, Orton proposed a theory that posits a delay or failure in establishing cerebral dominance as cause for a child's reading disability. He coined the term *strephosymbolia* to describe reversals (e.g., b/d, was/saw) that are commonly observed in oral reading of children with reading disability. Neither Orton's theory nor his focus on reversal being the prime characteristic of dyslexia (severe reading disability) had any foundation, but clinics and educational treatments similar to Hinshelwood's (Torgesen, 2004, p. 10) were successful.

Marion Monroe's work was influential in the early 1930s for developing a reading index, a practice of calculating the discrepancy between actual and expected levels of reading achievement; keeping meticulous records on case studies of children with reading disabilities; and advocating for a focus on patterns of reading errors rather than on the sum total or end score on a test. In short, she emphasized qualitative analysis of reading errors that could lead to remediation rather than quantitative analysis of test scores.

According to Hallahan and Mock (2003), Kirk's doctoral thesis showed the influence of both Orton and Monroe. After finishing his degree, Kirk went to work at the University of Illinois, where he set up the first experimental preschool for children with mental retardation. Recognizing the need for assessment tools, Kirk embarked on a test development with an ambitious goal: He wanted to develop an assessment tool that would not only pinpoint problems but would also lead directly into remedial programming and treatment. Thus was born the Illinois Test of Pyscholinguistic Abilities (ITPA; Kirk, McCarthy, & Kirk, 1961). The ITPA tested discrete processes. Children were given training in areas of deficiencies. The test enjoyed much popularity and widespread use in the 1970s, but the underlying theoretic assumption was flawed. The subtests test discrete cognitive processes, which suggests the test developers assumed areas in the brain function independently. The brain, however, does not function that way, but rather, interconnections appear to be the modus operandi. More important, research clearly showed that process training as advocated by Kirk and his associates did not transfer to reading achievement (Hammill and Larsen, 1974a; 1974b).

Kirk basically reinforced the notions of intraindividual differences in children with learning disabilities and discerning these children's strengths and deficits and to remediate the latter. These ideas hark back to Werner and Strauss.

To summarize, before the field of learning disabilities emerged in 1963, two separate but parallel strands of clinical research interests existed. One strand emphasized more general processes in learning and was represented by Werner and Strauss, whose research findings established the heterogeneous nature of children with mental retardation and the characteristics of brain-injured children. These included distractibility, peseveration, concreteness, indiscriminate response to stimuli, emotional lability, and figure-ground perceptual problems. Their work was subsequently extended by Kephart, a research associate, and Cruickshank, a researcher who was involved with children with cerebral palsy. The other strand emphasized auditory and language processes, which were represented by Mykelbust and Kirk. The legacies from these two strands of clinical research consisted of three principles in the education of children with learning disabilities and the need to balance attention to perceptual, perceptual-motor processes in training with attention to auditory and language processes. The three educational principles include analyzing the cognitive bases of the intraindividual differences in a child's learning and performance, pinpointing strengths and weaknesses in the child's learning and performance so as to attain a match between them and the instructional program; and focusing on strengthening the child's weak areas. The introduction of structured educational environments that minimized distractions for hyperactive and brain-injured children was timely and useful. But the introduction of process training based on the ITPA did not bear fruit regarding the desired outcomes of gains in reading for children with learning disabilities.

THE RISE AND CONSOLIDATION OF THE LEARNING DISABILITIES FIELD (1963–1985)

Before the learning disabilities field obtained its name in the first national conference organized by parents in 1963, the condition that we now label as learning disabilities had long been recognized by medical and educational professionals and especially parents of children who experienced inordinate difficulties in learning to read. However, because the disorder did not fit into extant categories of special education, these children could not receive government-funded support services in schools. So the obvious goal of parents of these children was to force the federal government to recognize this as a medical disorder that would be covered by state funds. The disorder, however, had to be named to distinguish it from the extant categories in special education. Samuel Kirk fulfilled this need by suggesting *learning disabilities*. This label was enthusiastically received by the parents at the first national conference in 1963 because it pinpointed what characterized these children in their reading acquisition and, more important, it distinguished them from children with mental retardation. The latter differentiation is important because these children had average to above average intelligence. Prior to this label, children with learning disabilities were called children with learning difficulties.

Finding an appropriate name for this cognitive disorder was the first step in establishing the field, but the next step proved to be very difficult— namely, to define the disorder. Defining learning disabilities is necessary because the parameters of this cognitive disorder must be clearly recognized and measurable for the purposes of diagnosis and remediation. If it is not defined, it cannot be recognized, assessed, or diagnosed, or distinguished from other cognitive disorders. Therefore, there had to be a consensus on its definition among interdisciplinary professionals who worked with individuals with learning disabilities.

Although it may seem tedious, it is important to examine the many definitions of learning disabilities. The commonalities and differences among definitions and how these definitions are shaped can be very revealing.

DEFINITIONS OF LEARNING DISABILITIES

Four definitions of learning disabilities include the Federal Registrar 1977, the National Joint Committee on Learning Disabilities, the Association of Children with Learning Disabilities, and the Interagency Committee on Learning Disabilities.

The definition issued by the U.S. Office of Education (1968), the 1977 Federal Registrar, is essentially the same as that incorporated into Public Law 91-230, the Specific Learning Disabilities Act of 1969. This definition was originally drafted by members of the National Advisory Committee on Handicapped Children (NACHC), which was chaired by Samuel Kirk. He provided the leadership in developing the definition of *learning disabilities*. To make it acceptable to interdisciplinary professionals who were involved with children with learning disabilities, the definition included terms such as *perceptual handicaps*, which appealed to those associated with the work of Werner and Strauss and Cruickshank, and *minimal brain damage*, the term used by medical professionals. The definition is as follows:

> Children with specific learning disabilities exhibit a disorder in one or more of the basic psychological processes involved in understanding or in using spoken or written languages. These may be manifested in disorders of listening, thinking, talking, reading, writing, spelling, or arithmetic. They include conditions which have been referred to as perceptual handicaps, brain injury, minimal brain dysfunction, dyslexia, developmental aphasia, etc. They do not include learning problems which are due primarily to visual, hearing or motor handicaps, to mental retardation, emotional disturbance, or to environmental disadvantage. (p. 34)

Subsequent to being in the Federal Registrar, which also included the regulations for the definition and identification of students with learning disabilities under Public Law 91-230 in 1977, this same definition was incorporated into Public Law 101-476, Individuals with Disabilities Education Act (IDEA) in 1990. In 1992 and 1997, IDEA was reauthorized with amendments that saw increased emphasis on early preschool interventions and parental influence. According to Mercer and Pullen (2005), at present this definition is used in the administration of programs for individuals with learning disabilities. However, this definition came under fire for certain components—for example, "basic psychological processes" and "perceptual handicaps, brain injury, minimal brain dysfunction, dyslexia, developmental aphasia."

Out of dissatisfaction with the 1977 Federal Registrar definition of learning disabilities, the National Joint Committee on Learning Disabilities (NJCLD) created another definition of *learning disabilities*. This committee was formed by representatives from the American Speech-Language Hearing Association (ASHA), the Association for Children and Adults with Learning Disabilities (ACLD), now formally known as Learning Disabilities Association of America (LDA, an organization of parents), the Council of Learning Disabilities (CLD), the Division for Children with Communication Disorders (DCCD), the International Reading Association (IRA), and the Orton Dyslexia Society. Representatives of these organizations considered the term *psychological processes* to be too vague and elusive to operational measurement, and terms such as *perceptual handicaps, minimal brain dysfunction, dyslexia,* and *developmental aphasia* are confusing to professionals in educational domains. Consequently, they came up with the following definition:

> Learning disabilities is a generic term that refers to a heterogeneous group of disorders manifested by significant difficulties in the acquisition and use of listening, speaking, reading, writing, reasoning, or mathematical abilities. These disorders are intrinsic to the individual and presumed to be due to central nervous system dysfunction. Even though a learning disability may occur concomitantly with other handicapping conditions (e.g., sensory impairment, mental retardation, social and emotional disturbance) or environmental influences (e.g., cultural differences, insufficient/inappropriate instruction, psychogenic factors), it is not the direct result of those conditions or influences. (Hammill, Leigh, McNutt, & Larsen, 1981)

As we can see in the wording, the NJCLD definition removed terminology from the Federal Registrar's 1977 definition with which the representatives of NJCLD disagreed. In 1988, NJCLD (1988) revised the definition to keep apace with advances in knowledge of learning disabilities.

Specifically, NJCLD acknowledged the lifespan nature of learning disabilities and disagreed with LDAC/LDA's inclusion of social competence problems as learning disabilities. The revised definition states that learning disabilities "may occur across the life span" and "problems in self-regulatory behaviors, social perception, and social interaction may exist with learning disabilities but do not by themselves constitute a learning disability" (NJCLD, 1988, p. 1).

Interestingly, NJCLD's 1981 definition was spurned by the ACLD. This is an organization of parents of children with learning disabilities. ACLD/LDA rejected the NJCLD definition because the organization felt the need to emphasize the lifelong nature of the condition of learning disabilities—that learning disabilities are manifest not only in children but also adolescents and adults. ACLD/LDA also considers learning disabilities to go beyond academics and extend into the social and emotional domains. Hence, ACLD/LDA produced its own definition of learning disabilities that reads as follows:

> Specific Learning Disabilities is a chronic condition of presumed neurological origin that selectively interferes with the development, integration, and/or demonstration of verbal and or nonverbal abilities. Specific Learning Disabilities exists as a distinct handicapping condition and varies in its manifestations and in degrees of severity. Throughout life, the condition can affect self-esteem, education, vocation, socialization, and/or daily living activities.

The last definition is the one proposed by the federal Interagency Committee on Learning Disabilities (ICLD) in 1987. This committee was composed of representatives from 12 agencies within the Departments of Education and Health and Human Services. The ICLD members found fault with the NACHC (1967) definition and pinpointed four specific problematic areas. The first concerned a lack of clarity on the heterogeneity of learning disabilities. The second related to the failure in that definition to acknowledge that learning disabilities are a lifelong condition. The third had to do with the lack of clear specificity of the inherent changes in processing information in individuals with learning disabilities. The fourth was the lack of recognition that learning disabilities can co-occur in individuals with other kinds of handicap—for example, hearing impairment (Torgesen, 2004).

Although the ICLD's definition is a modification of the NJCLD definition, it differs importantly from it in that it endorses social skills as one type of learning disability:

> Learning disabilities ... refers to a heterogeneous group of disorders manifested by significant difficulties in the acquisition and use of listening, speaking, reading, writing, reasoning, or mathematical abilities, or social skills. (ICLD, 1987, p. 222)

Research informs us of the diverse social problems experienced by children, adolescents, and adults with learning disabilities (Wong & Donahue, 2002). However, problems in social competence are not ubiquitous among individuals with learning disabilities. Specifically, Kavale and Forness (1996) found that three out of four individuals with learning disabilities have social relational problems. Thus, not all individuals with learning disabilities have social relational problems. For social competence problems to qualify as a universal characteristic and hence a defining attribute, *all* individuals with learning disabilities must manifest it. We therefore do not think social competence problems justify as a type of learning disability. To date, the 1988 NJCLD definition appears to be the one that has the broadest endorsement in the learning disabilities field (Hammill, 1993).

SOME ADDITIONAL POINTS

Now that we have seen four influential definitions of learning disabilities and examined their commonalities and differences, we will conclude with seven more points for you to think about.

1. Each of the definitions by NJCLD (1988), ACLD/LDA (1986), and ICLD (1987) came into existence because they were critical of the 1977 Federal Registrar's definition of *learning disabilities* and with one another! Dwell on and weigh the respective proponents' mutual criticisms of one another's definitions. Then consider one definition that you would support and justify your support.

2. All three definitions (NJCLD, ACLD/LDA, and ICLD) include social skills. Both the ACLD/LDA and ICLD definitions include social skills as constituting one type of learning disability, but the NJCLD definition does not countenance such consideration even though it mentions it.

Why do all three definitions acknowledge social skills problems in individuals with learning disabilities? The answer is straightforward: These definitions bow to the influence of research findings. In 1978, one of the five research institutes funded to research learning disabilities focused on social skills in children with learning disabilities. Spearheaded by Tanis Bryan at the University of Illinois at Chicago, programmatic research on social rejection and communications problems in children with learning disabilities began. Together with her research associates, Mavis Donahue and Ruth Pearl, Bryan collected instructive and interesting data. The impact of their research on the learning disabilities field is reflected in social skills being included in the definitions of learning disabilities and in shifting professionals' focus from one of exclusive attention to the academic domain to include a focus on the nonacademic domain—namely, the social domain.

Similarly, the NJCLD (1988) definition mentions "self-regulatory behaviors." This too reflects the influence of research. The 1980s witnessed the heydays of cognitive strategy research in cognitive psychology and education. In learning disabilities, much research was done on cognitive strategy training designed to enhance learning in students with learning disabilities (Wong, Harris, Graham, & Butler, 2003). Such training was paired up with self-regulating steps usually designed to enable students with learning disabilities to self-monitor and self-evaluate progress in their own strategy learning, to regulate their on-task focus, and to give themselves self-reinforcement (a pat on the back for a job well done!). Self-regulation is part and parcel of cognitive strategy training and has been amply documented by empirical research to play a cardinal role in students' effective learning. So not surprisingly, "self-regulatory behaviors" find a place/niche in the 1988 NJCLD definition of learning disabilities. You see how advances in research play a part in the formulations of learning disabilities definitions!

3. Increase in knowledge about the condition of learning disabilities led to the realization among professionals in learning disabilities that the condition is lifelong and that it not only occurs in children but in adolescents and adults as well. This realization has been properly acknowledged in the definitions of the NJCLD (1988), the ACLD/LDA (1986), and the ICLD (1987).

4. The term psychological processes appears in the definition of the Federal Registrar 1977, and this definition remains intact in the definition of IDEA. The usage of this term is understandable when we recall the context and main person responsible for drafting the definition: It was Samuel Kirk, who chaired the committee for NACHC (1968), and under his leadership, the committee wrote the definition that was subsequently used in the

Federal Registrar 1977. Kirk was influenced by contemporary thinking that embraced the prominence of general cognitive processes. According to Werner and Strauss, these cognitive processes were thought to underlie learning (Torgesen, 2004). Kirk's own test, the ITPA, exemplified the role of psychological processes in successful performance of his test. Thus, it is understandable that in a definition of learning disabilities that was developed under his leadership, the term *psychological processes* would appear. This term, however, does not appear in the NJCLD (1988) definition because the representatives of the various associations in NJCLD do not find it useful for assessment purposes. How do you measure a psychological process? What test can you use? Nevertheless, Torgesen (2004) staunchly defends the consideration of psychological processes.

5. One component found in all the definitions is the mention of neurological impairment or *central nervous system dysfunction* (Mercer & Pullen, 2005, p. 18). This simply refers to the acknowledgement that some form of brain dysfunction or delayed development causes learning disabilities. You may wonder how such a notion arises. Well, recall that in the nineteenth and twentieth centuries, many clinical researchers reported cases of adults losing their previously normal language functions after they suffered brain damage. More important, through autopsies, clinical researchers (mainly physicians) were able to pinpoint specific locations of brain areas responsible for loss of language functions. Hinshelwood was responsible for bringing to light cases of children who experienced enormous difficulties in learning to read. Interestingly, these children had little difficulty in learning other school subjects such as arithmetic. Extrapolating from research information on adults who lost their language functions because of localized brain damage, clinical researchers such as Hinshelwood and, later, Orton, implied the inference of similar causes of brain damage in children who could not learn to read readily.

In light of this and the research on children with exogenous and endogenous mental retardation by Strauss and Werner and their associates and later Cruickshank with children with cerebral palsy, and Kirk with his experimental preschool for children with mental retardation, it is easy to see why interdisciplinary professionals who worked with children with learning disabilities would tacitly assume that some form of brain dysfunction caused their learning disabilities.

6. Learning disabilities are a unique form of handicap, distinct from existing forms of handicaps recognized in the various categories of special education. This point is clearly stated in the ACLD/LDA definition but not so in the others. You must infer this point from the other definitions. Notice, for example, that both the Federal Registrar 1977 definition and the NJCLD definition state that learning disabilities can co-occur with other kinds of handicaps, such as mental retardation, social or emotional disturbance, and environmental problems such as inappropriate or

insufficient instruction, but are not caused by them. These definitions only state in a more indirect way that learning disabilities constitute a unique condition.

7. A singular missing component in the four definitions is that they do not state the discrepancy component. Children with learning disabilities stand out in the early grades because their extreme difficulty in learning to read is out of character with their general learning capacity. Teachers do not expect them to have so much difficulty in learning to read because they have adequate intelligence and they learn other subjects, such as arithmetic, without difficulty. There is thus a notable discrepancy between their specific reading difficulty or disability and their general intelligence or performance in other subjects such as arithmetic. In light of this criticism, the developers of the definitions discussed in this section have been indeed remiss. Why do you think they are mum on this important component in defining learning disabilities? Well, it may be because measuring the discrepancy is a big headache. We will pick up on this point in a later section.

ETIOLOGY

There is a general consensus among researchers in the learning disabilities field that phonological processing difficulties are the core deficit in reading disabilities. This appears to be the majority view, although some feel that visual processing deficits deserve more attention (Willows, 1995). The neurological correlates thought to underlie the cognitive deficits in severe reading disabilities center around the left temporal-parietal region. Specifically, research findings spotlight differences in asymmetry of the planum temporale that have been consistently found in association with reading disabilities.

Geschwind and Levitsky (1968) first reported findings from a postmortem examination of one hundred brains from nondyslexics. They found that 65 percent had a larger left planum temporale, 11 percent a larger right planum temporale, and the residual 24 percent were of equal size. Subsequently Galaburda and Kemper (1979) found symmetrical plana with polymicrogyri in a postmortem examination of a young male dyslexic. Polymicrogyri are considered to be an anomaly of neurological ontogeny. They are a collection of numerous atypical or unusually small gyria. Galaburda and his associates further observed symmetrical plana in three other dyslexic males in a follow-up study (Galaburda, Sherman, Rosen, Aboitiz, & Geschwind, 1985). A similar finding of symmetrical plana were found in postmortem examinations of three female dyslexics (Humphreys, Kaufman, & Galaburda, 1990). These studies provided further information about the nature of the brain of dyslexics. But researchers realized the need for a more specific protocol or standard procedure to measure the planum temporale and, more important, to measure it in living individuals. Fortunately, researchers have available tools of magnetic resonance imaging (MRI) and functional magnetic resonance imaging (fMRI) to achieve that goal.

Using MRI scans on clinically identified dyslexic children, Hynd, Semrud-Clikeman, Lorys, Novey, and Eliopulos (1990) observed a pattern of smaller left plana in relation to the right plana (reversed symmetry). Larsen, Hoien, Lundberg, and Odegaard (1990) found dyslexic individuals tended to have a larger right plana, and this asymmetry was linked to phonological processing problems. These two studies highlighted deviations from normal patterns of plana asymmetry in the dyslexic participants.

Research has been conducted into other regions of the brain, such as the corpus callosum and the perisylvian region. However, we choose not to cover this research because of the paucity of studies or conflicting findings that make coherent summarization of them difficult.

In summary, the research findings from postmortem studies, brain imaging studies, family studies, and genetic studies (see Thomson & Raskind, 2003) support a neurobiological basis of the etiology of reading disabilities. The brain structures implicated in the neurobiological basis of reading disabilities are structures known to be involved in the processing of language and/or visual information. Hence, it is perfectly conceivable that damage or abnormal development of these structures would be associated with language and/or visual deficits in reading disabilities. A caveat for readers is that reading disabilities is the area that has been the focus of much of the preceding research and where the neurobiological basis of this cognitive disorder may be best understood (Miller, Sanchez, & Hynd, 2003). Further research is called for regarding other areas in learning disabilities, such as learning disabilities in mathematics.

GENETIC CONTRIBUTIONS TO READING AND WRITING DISABILITIES

There now exists a sizeable amount of evidence on the genetic contribution to the development of reading and writing disabilities. This evidence comes mainly from studies of twins, both identical (monozygotic, MZ) and fraternal (dizygotic, DZ). However, it is important to remember that environmental variables still play a role in the development of reading and writing disabilities. This is because the concordance rate of reading and writing disabilities among MZ twins is less than complete, suggesting the role of the existence of nongenetic variables in the development of reading and writing disabilities. According to Thomson and Raskind (2003), "Concordance means the presence of some trait in a set of individuals, such as a pair of twins" (p. 266). In this case, the trait would be reading and/or writing disabilities. That in addition to genetic variables, nongenetic variables should figure in reading and writing disabilities makes sense given the complex interactions between genetic background and environmental variables. Hence, it is unlikely that genetic information alone can serve as the definitive diagnostic test for reading and writing disabilities. Nevertheless, genetic information can inform educators of children at high risk for developing reading and/or writing disabilities so that these children can receive timely early intervention (Thomson & Raskind, 2003).

ATTENTION DEFICIT HYPERACTIVITY DISORDER (ADHD)

In classrooms with children with confirmed ADHD, the teachers would freely admit frustrations in their attempts to get these children to focus and stay focused on their tasks and complete given assignments. Such children characteristically are constantly off-task and readily distractible. They frequently leave their seats when they are expected to be seated to complete given tasks. Currently, three types of ADHD are recognized: ADHD predominantly Inattentive, ADHD predominantly Hyperactive-Impulsive, and ADHD, Combined Type. For diagnostic purposes, most professionals involved with ADHD depend on the American Psychiatric Association's (APA) *Diagnostic and Statistical Manual of Mental Disorders* (DSM). The diagnosis follows stringent conditions. Specifically, for a professional, such as a psychiatrist, to diagnose the first type of ADHD predominantly Inattentive type, the child must show at least six particular behavioral characteristics that pertain to inattention. For example, the first three indices of inattentive behaviors under the list of Criterion 1: Inattention in the DSM-IV (1994) are (1) "Fails to give close attention to details or makes careless mistakes in schoolwork, work, or other activities"; (2) "Has difficulty sustaining attention in tasks or play activities"; and (3) "Does not seem to listen when spoken to directly." Similarly, the first three behavioral indices under Criterion 2: ADHD Hyperactivity-Impulsivity in DSM-IV (1994) are (1) "Fidgets with hands or feet or squirms in seat"; (2) "Leaves seat in classroom or in other situations in which remaining seated is expected"; and (3) "Runs about or climbs excessively in situations in which it is inappropriate (in adolescents or adults, may be limited to subjective feelings of restlessness)." Children with at least six of the behaviors in the list under Criterion 1 for Inattention and at least six of behaviors in the list under Criterion 2 for Hyperactivity-Impulsivity are considered to fit the Combined Type of ADHD.

Apart from examining how a child fits the behavioral criteria for each of the three types of ADHD, the diagnostician also ascertains that the child has shown the particular behaviors persistently for at least six months and that their onset occurred no later than age seven. Moreover, the criterial behaviors must occur in two or more environmental contexts, such as home and school (Mercer & Pullen, 2005). Hence, the diagnosis of any of the three types of ADHD involves a very careful process and follows stringent criteria.

According to the majority of authorities on ADHD, the chief characteristic of those with ADHD is difficulty with behavioral inhibition. Barkley (2000a & b) is credited with conceptualizing ADHD as a difficulty in behavioral inhibition, which has three components: (1) postpone a response, (2) abruptly terminate an ongoing action if one notes that the action is inappropriate because of unexpected changes in task demands, and (3) ability to maintain response production (put differently, stay on task) and ward off distractions or competing/interfering stimuli (Hallahan et al., 2005). Because of the problem in behavioral inhibition, individuals with ADHD have a problematic sense of time awareness and management. Barkley observes that individuals with ADHD have problems in executive functions. Executive functions underlie certain self-directed behaviors, including working memory, inner speech, and self-regulated emotions (Hallahan et al., 2005).

Why is it important to diagnose ADHD in a child with learning disabilities? The reason is that children with ADHD need proper diagnosis and educational treatment because they are either characterized by inattention (the first type of ADHD) or hyperactivity-impulsivity (second type of ADHD) or both (combined type), which likely leads them to miss out on at least parts of the teachers' instructions.

To illustrate, they may miss parts of the mathematic calculation procedures in regrouping that are commonly taught in grade two. These bouts of inattention and hyperactivity-impulsivity may cumulate in knowledge gaps that bode ill for academic learning and achievement. Therefore, children with ADHD need appropriate diagnosis and educational treatment.

Hallahan et al. (2005) described three components that are recommended in a diagnosis of ADHD: a medical examination, a clinical interview, and the use of rating scales. The medical examination is necessary to eliminate physical causes for ADHD such as disorder of the thyroid or presence of a brain tumor. The clinical interview allows the examiner to collect information on the child and his or her family. However, the clinical interview is subjective and must be balanced with more objective information gathering. This is where the use of teacher rating scales comes in. One of the rating scales used is the Connors's (1997) Teacher Rating Scale-Revised (S).

Hallahan et al. (2005) illustrated how a diagnosis of ADHD (first type: Inattention) was arrived at concerning a girl named Shannon. The psychiatrist asked the girl's parents to check the behaviors listed under Criterion 1: Inattention and Criterion 2: Hyperactivity-Impulsivity in DSM-IV and note the behaviors their daughter consistently displayed. The psychiatrist also asked the classroom teacher to do the same and found the same behaviors on the parents' and the teacher's lists. Then the psychiatrist asked the teacher to complete part of the Connors's rating scale. Medical examination and clinical interview had been conducted. Hallahan et al.'s (2005) description of the diagnosis process is exemplary in its instruction.

Concerning prevalence rates of ADHD, the picture is rather murky. This is largely due to the inconsistencies in the findings of various studies and to the overlap between ADHD and learning disabilities. However, it is now known that the most common type of ADHD is the Combined type followed by the Inattentive type and finally the Hyperactivity-Impulsivity type. Moreover, boys with ADHD appear to be more prevalent than girls (Hallahan et al., 2005).

Causes of ADHD involve neurological factors, and hereditary factors have also been suggested in some research studies (Hallahan et al., 2005). Regardless of causal factors, the prime concern should be the education of children with ADHD. Educational treatment of children with ADHD tends to favor structuring environments with the least amount of distraction for their learning. Stimulus reduction appears to be the key and harkens back to Cruickshank's original ideas for teaching hyperactive children.

When a child is diagnosed with both ADHD and learning disabilities, the classroom teacher and the resource room or special education teacher need to collaborate closely to devise appropriate teaching approaches for the child. Hallahan et al. (2005) provide very useful ideas for teaching children with ADHD.

CHARACTERISTICS OF CHILDREN, ADOLESCENTS, AND ADULTS WITH LEARNING DISABILITIES

In writing a section like this, authors in learning disabilities wrestle with a dilemma. Should they eschew listing characteristics of individuals with learning disabilities and focus on describing observable behaviors in specific case studies of students with learning disabilities, or should they stay with a more traditional/standard approach that provides university and college students with a litany of characteristics that can be readily memorized for a midterm exam? The former approach has the merit of presenting characteristics of learning disabilities in the flesh, and student teachers and other undergraduate readers can easily relate to them, especially when these observed behavioral characteristics are accompanied by comments from the classroom teacher, the resource room teacher, or the special educational consultant and parent(s). The obvious limitation of this approach is that it does not allow for portraying the tremendous heterogeneity of individuals with learning disabilities. However, because of the heterogeneity of learning disabilities, to give a modicum of sufficient portrayal of the heterogeneous nature of the combinations of characteristics of learning disabilities in students with learning disabilities, one would need to compile a huge volume of case studies! The heterogeneity of learning disabilities means no two students with learning disabilities would have precisely the same profile of academic and nonacademic strengths and weaknesses. But such a behavioral approach to describing or identifying characteristics of students with learning disabilities helps teachers to deal with the tangible and avoid more abstract definitions of learning disabilities.

The second approach of providing broad guidelines on the characteristics of learning disabilities has the merit of sensitizing student and novice teachers to students with learning disabilities. Such sensitization may put them at an advantage as to when to seek out more experienced and skilled teachers for mentoring or guidance in dealing with students with learning disabilities. Thus, if student and novice teachers are mindful that what they are given are broad guidelines and not a litany of characteristics of learning disabilities set in stone, and that students with learning disabilities are tremendously heterogeneous, then learning about the characteristics of students with learning disabilities can benefit them. Moreover, it gives us perspective on the issue of characteristics of students with learning disabilities when we realize that children with learning disabilities are very aware of their academic deficiencies, attention problems, and their social-emotional problems (Rashkind, Margalit, & Higgins, 2006).

Concerning students with learning disabilities—particularly children—problems in phoneme awareness (phoneme segmentation and blending) appear to be a notable characteristic. This comes as no surprise because of the ample research that attests to phoneme awareness problems in at-risk children and in children with learning disabilities (Wong, 1996). Academic problems, especially in reading and mathematics, and language problems are also major characteristics. Others include social-emotional problems (Margalit & Al-Yagon, 2002), working memory problems (Swanson, Cooney, & McNamara, 2004), and self-regulation problems (Harris, Reid, & Graham, 2004).

Although students with learning disabilities are heterogeneous in their characteristics, like students without learning disabilities, they benefit from instruction that is well researched, such as direct instruction or explicit explanation, learning strategies in reading and writing (Graham & Bellert, 2004; S. Graham, Harris, & MacArthur, 2004), cooperative learning (Mercer & Pullen, 2005), and behavioral interventions such as response cost (Hallahan et al., 2005).

We end this section on the characteristics of students/individuals with learning disabilities by selectively summarizing several insightful and instructive pointers from Mercer and Pullen (2005, p. 24). Mercer and Pullen remind readers the cardinal point of heterogeneity among individuals with learning disabilities and for them to avoid forming or holding any stereotypical notions of such individuals. Instructions should be designed to suit the particular needs of a student with learning disabilities. Moreover, it is important for us not to lose sight of areas of strengths of any individual with learning disabilities. We must not be mired in awareness of the academic problems of students with learning disabilities to the extent that we forget they are capable individuals in certain areas. It is their assets of which we must remind themselves and ourselves!

Concerning prevalence rates of learning disabilities, Hallahan and Mock (2003) reported an overrepresentation of learning disabilities among African-Americans and American Indians. Mercer and Pullen (2005) reported a prevalence rate of 4.50 percent of American children and young adults aged 6–21 from the U.S. Department of Education (2001). Apparently the prevalence rate fluctuates among the various American states, from a low of 2.36 percent to a high of 7.29 percent. Because the prevalence rate of learning disabilities, at least in the United States, appears to change owing to how it is measured and what definitional criteria of learning disabilities prevail, we should expect different prevalence rates in the future. Hence, the present information on them should be considered to be subject to change.

ACHIEVEMENTS IN THE LEARNING DISABILITIES FIELD

When we think about and compare the past and present states of the learning disabilities field, we marvel at its achievements! First and foremost is the fact that in the early 1960s, the field of learning disabilities struggled for legal status in the United States. Now the study of learning disabilities has a firm legal status in the U.S. legislation. Although in Canada learning disabilities do not have similar legal status, the condition is recognized by the support services in schools. Education ministries in Canadian provincial governments allocate funding for those services. In Australia, as in Canada, learning disabilities do not have a legal status. Instead, students with learning disabilities constitute a subset within a broader term of (students with) learning difficulties. Students with learning difficulties consist of those with mild intellectual disabilities, with language difficulties, and who are low achievers for various reasons. These students with learning difficulties receive help from a learning support teacher (LST) who collaborates closely with the classroom teacher in informal assessments and teaching of students with learning difficulties in the inclusive classroom (see *Journal of Learning Disabilities* special issue in September/October 2007). There are two Australian organizations involved with learning disabilities: the Learning Disabilities Association (LDA) and Specific Learning Disabilities (SPLD). The Australian LDA organization produces a journal entitled *Australian Journal of Learning Disabilities.*

Second, learning disabilities initially did not receive public recognition. But now, there is public awareness of learning disabilities, not only in North America but in Europe and Scandinavia as well. In America, this awareness is prominently sustained by various organizations. There is the ACLD/ LDA that was formed in 1964 and now has over 40,000 members and almost 300 local affiliates in 50 U.S. states. The Learning Disabilities Association of Canada adds to it another 10,000 members. The latter organization was incorporated in 1971 (Torgesen, 2004). Other organizations also promote the course of learning disabilities by disseminating research findings and development or use of effective teaching approaches through annual conferences. These include the Division of Learning Disabilities (DLD) within the Council of Exceptional Children (CEC). DLD has the largest number of members within the CEC. Additionally, there are the Council of Learning Disabilities (CLD) and the International Academy of Research on Learning Disabilities (IARLD). The latter IARLD encourages participation of European researchers by alternately hosting its yearly conference in Europe and the United States.

Third, the learning disabilities field now has at least three journals that publish peer-reviewed papers: *The Journal of Learning Disabilities*, which has an international readership, the *Learning Disabilities Quarterly*, and *Learning Disabilities Research and Practice*. Researchers, however, also publish their papers elsewhere—for example, the *Journal of Educational Psychology*. By publishing articles that contain current research findings and practice information, journals that focus exclusively on learning disabilities benefit researchers, university/college instructors, graduate and undergraduate students in learning disabilities, and interdisciplinary professionals who are interested in or working with individuals with learning disabilities.

Fourth, since 1995, multidisciplinary researchers at the Interdisciplinary Research Center on Learning Disabilities at the University of Washington have been engaging in brain research involving dyslexic children (dyslexic readers see the letters transposed). They have found structural differences between the brains of dyslexic and nondyslexic children (Berninger, 2004). Such recent findings provide much needed research-based support to the long-held notion that children with learning disabilities have some form of brain dysfunction. Moreover, this research is important because the information has been collected from live participants, not autopsies.

The fifth achievement in the learning disabilities concerns intervention research. A notable advance has been made here! Research by various early-intervention research groups has shown that it is possible to effect reading in children with learning disabilities. Space restricts us to mention only one of them. Torgesen and his research associates have produced theory-based interventions with children with learning disabilities who show one particular type of reading disability—namely, decoding problems. By centering their intervention on building phoneme awareness, with the exception of a small group of children, Torgesen and his associates were able to teach children with a reading disability to read, and they narrowed the gap between that group and children with no reading disability (Torgesen et al., 2000). Phoneme awareness has been consistently found to be a critical component in children's learning to read (Wong, 1996).

Sixth, an area of learning disabilities that has seen substantial increase in research interest is the social domain. Here, researchers have struck out into new areas for their inquiries. They no longer pursue the same research paths that had been explored in the 1970s and early 1980s, where research focused on cognitive and language problems thought to underlie the extraordinary unpopularity of children with learning disabilities (Wong, 1996). Instead, contemporary research in social dimensions of learning disabilities focuses on peer relations/interactions to better understand the rejection of children and adolescents with learning disabilities. Researchers also attend to contextual factors, individual differences in friendship formation, and maintenance among children and adolescents with learning disabilities (Wong & Donahue, 2002).

Last but not least, in line with the trend of inclusion, researchers investigate effective collaborations between classroom and resource room teachers who team-teach in the classroom. Tacitly forming a community of practice, facilitated by researchers, teachers collaborate to effect successful learning for all the students in the class. Interesting work is being done by many, and we will mention only a few: Janette Klingner and her associates at the University of Colorado, Lorraine Graham and her associates at the University of Armidale in Australia, Deborah Butler and Nancy Perry at the University of British Columbia, and Bernice Wong, Maureen Hoskyn, and their associates at Simon Fraser University in Canada.

WINDS OF CHANGE

The IQ-achievement discrepancy model has guided the diagnosis of learning disabilities since the field began. This reflects directly the fact that the notion of discrepancy is rooted in the historical beginnings of the field. It was the discrepancy between the child's apparent normalcy in measured intelligence and sensory functions on the one hand and his or her unexpected and enormous difficulties in learning to read on the other that triggered the groundswell among parents with such children for attention from public educators and local and federal governments in the United States. Subsequent political recognition of the plight of such children led to the development of the learning disabilities field with desired legislation that secured special education for them. But the use of the IQ-achievement discrepancy model was also influenced by the findings of Rutter and Yule's (1975) large-scaled epidemiological study. Based on their data, Rutter and Yule theorized the existence of two subgroups of poor readers. One of these was described as having "specific reading retardation," defined by a significant discrepancy between observed and expected reading achievement in the absence of general learning problems. The other was described as having "general reading backwardness" defined by general learning problems and an absence of a significant discrepancy between observed and expected reading achievement. Rutter and Yule's finding was shown by later research to be a result of floor and ceiling effects of the reading measures used. Nevertheless, the use of the IQ-achievement discrepancy model to diagnose learning disabilities had prevailed and eventually became incorporated into legislation for individuals with learning disabilities (see PL-142).

However, across the years the diagnostic use of the IQ-achievement discrepancy model has garnered increasing dissatisfaction in the learning disabilities field. This discontent occurs at two fronts: research and practice. In research, Siegel (1989) pointed out that her findings indicated that children with and without IQ-achievement discrepancy did not differ either in reading achievement or in tests of cognitive abilities presumed to underlie reading acquisition, such as phonological awareness, short-term verbal memory, word retrieval, orthographic coding, and visual analysis. Fletcher et al. (1994) independently found similar findings in their study. Together, these findings by Siegel (1989) and Fletcher et al. (1994) seriously undermined the IQ-achievement discrepancy model.

In practice, the discrepancy model has been adopted by most of the state departments of education in the United States. But they chose to define it the way they wanted, resulting in definitions of discrepancy that varied according to its computation, size of discrepancy, and the intelligence and achievement tests used. Such variations inevitably resulted in huge inconsistencies in the prevalence rates of learning disabilities in the various U.S. states (Fuchs, Mock, Morgan, & Young, 2003). A direct result of such inconsistencies is over- and/or underidentification of learning disabilities. For example, if the size of discrepancy were small (e.g., 1.0 SD), there would be a high likelihood of overidentification of learning disabilities. The reverse occurs if the discrepancy were big (e.g., 2.0 SD)—that is, underidentification of learning disabilities would most likely occur.

More important, among the children without a discrepancy between IQ and achievement are those in need of reading enrichment or remediation. These children come from low-SES homes, with relatively low IQ scores that do not differ sufficiently from their low achievement scores to warrant special education services under the IQ-achievement discrepancy model. Regarding these children, some have clamored that the discrepancy diagnostic model practices class bias and denies them access to needed education services with long-term negative consequences for their future career options and success. Devoid of competent literacy skills, as adults, they will be denied access to good job opportunities, disproving the claims of equal opportunity in the U.S. workforce (Artiles, 2004; Connor, 2005; Neufeld & Hoskyn, 2005; Reid & Valle, 2004).

An additional source of discontent with the IQ-achievement discrepancy model is that it does not consider the child's preschool and educational history. Hence, it does not differentiate between reading difficulties arising from experiential and instructional deficiencies and reading difficulties arising from more deep-seated biologically based deficiencies in reading-related cognitive abilities such as phonological processes (Vellutino, Scanlon, Small, & Fanuele, 2006). Finally, test information from the IQ-discrepancy model does not inform instruction (Vaughn & Fuchs, 2003; Vellutino, Scanlon, & Lyon, 2000).

The preceding explains the discontent with the IQ-achievement discrepancy model that has always simmered in the learning disabilities field. But the catalyst that finally uproots the precariously ensconced discrepancy model is the continual overidentification of children with learning disabilities with the concomitant costs in special education. Public educators and politicians finally lost patience with the amazing exponential rise (read: overidentification) in the number of children identified with learning disabilities and the soaring costs in the special education budget for them. They demand an alternative to the discrepancy model in identifying learning disabilities and the response to instruction (RTI) model appears to be the forerunner (Fuchs et al., 2003).

Why is the RTI model the forerunner? One reason appears to be what RTI research studies using the standard-protocol approach have achieved—namely, enhancing reading achievement in young at-risk children while isolating a core of potentially reading-disabled children. Three well-designed studies using standard treatment of fixed duration yielded excellent data showing that giving at-risk children in kindergarten, grade one, and grade two intervention in reading-related cognitive processes embedded in a comprehensive and well-balanced early literacy instruction appreciably increased their reading achievements (Vaughn, Linan-Thompson, & Hickman, 2003; Vellutino et al., 1996; Vellutino et al., 2006). Both of Vellutino et al.'s studies included more reading-related cognitive processes than have been validated in prior research to play a critical or causal role in children's learning to read (Vellutino, Fletcher, Snowling, & Scanlon, 2004).

What is the RTI model? In their scholarly review, Fuchs et al. (2003) expounded on the two RTI models: the problem-solving approach and the standard-protocol approach. They highlighted the major strengths and weaknesses of both. Specifically, the problem-solving approach appears to be more sensitive to individual differences, and the standard-protocol approach more rigorous in its control of intervention procedures. Moreover, the problem-solving approach lacks empirical support, whereas the standard-protocol approach has strong empirical support.

We will focus on the RTI model with the standard-protocol approach because it has stronger empirical support. However, this should not be construed as a negative stand toward the problem-solving RTI model or approach. We openly acknowledge and commend the strengths of the latter model—in particular the feature of flexibly individualizing instruction to suit the particular child's learning needs.

Now we turn to the basic design and intervention procedures in an RTI study using the standard-protocol approach. In such a study, the researchers identify the at-risk population for intervention. This is done either through a battery of standardized tests (e.g., Vaughn et al., 2003) or through an experimental test backed up by additional tests in phonological awareness (Vellutino et al., 2006). The entire sample of at-risk children then receives the intervention for a fixed duration or period. The intervention is given by trained staff members who often are certified teachers. To ensure treatment fidelity, the intervention is closely monitored. At the end of the first intervention period (Tier I treatment), at-risk children who do well on the posttests or meet a priori exit criteria return to join the regular class. Those who do not do well or fail to meet exit criteria receive more intensive, small-group (group size ranges from two to six children per group) intervention for another fixed duration or period. By providing more intensive, small-group instruction to children who do not respond to the first treatment (Tier I treatment), more children would profit and be able to rejoin the regular classroom. At the end of this second intervention (Tier II treatment), the at-risk children are again assessed for their progress. Those who do well or meet exit criteria now join the regular class. For the at-risk children who still do not do well or meet exit criteria, some researchers would press on to give them another dose of intervention (Tier III treatment as in Vaughn et al., 2003), but researchers can choose to stop the intervention cycle after Tier II treatment and recommend referring the remaining at-risk children for further testing and potential special education placement. As Reschly (2005) pointed out, the number of tiers varies. The positive note from extant RTI studies using the standard-protocol approach is that the residual number of at-risk children who show insubstantial progress after Tier II or Tier III treatment is typically small. These are the ones that are considered to be very likely to develop reading disabilities (see Vellutino et al., 2006, pp. 165–167).

Three RTI studies using the standard protocol approach or model appear to be frequently cited in the nascent research literature on RTI, Vaughn et al. (2003); Vellutino et al. (1996; 2006). Researchers interested in conducting meta-analyses on the efficacy of such studies have to wait for more cumulative work or a richer data base. But we are confident that more RTI research studies with the standard protocol model will grace the journals in the coming years. To provide readers with a flavor of RTI research studies using the standard protocol model, we describe and summarize the findings of Vellutino et al. (2006). We single out this study because the findings afforded a more fine-grained difference among the at-risk children with reading problems.

The purpose of Vellutino et al.'s (2006) study was to attempt to separate children whose reading problems stem from experiential or instructional deficiencies from children whose reading problems stem from more deep-seated biological causes. The children who received the intervention were randomly assigned to the intervention, whereas the children in the comparison condition received no treatment in their home schools.

Screening of the kindergarten children for the intervention consisted of administration of a test of letter-name knowledge. From the results of this screening, 30 percent were identified as at-risk. To back up the children's at-risk status, the researchers further administered four tests: (1) phonological awareness (specifically sensitivity to rhyme and alliteration), (2) rapid automatized naming (RAN) of objects, (3) counting by ones, and (4) number identification.

The intervention consisted of a small group (two or three children) being taught by a qualified teacher trained by the research staff, twice per week, with 30 minutes per instructional session. The instruction focused on emergent literacy skills that included knowledge of print concepts, print awareness, letter recognition, letter identification, phonological awareness, letter-sound mapping, sight word learning, shared and guided reading, and listening to and reading stories. Intervention began in the fall of kindergarten and lasted throughout kindergarten.

To evaluate the outcome of intervention, the children were readministered the letter identification and phonological awareness tests from screening in December, March, and June. Additionally, the children were re-administered the experimental tests on print concepts, word identification (primary identification), knowledge of letter sounds, letter-sound decoding (primary decoding), and two extra phonological awareness skills—phonological blending and segmentation.

With the exception of performance of print concepts, rhyme detection, rhyme alliteration, and phonological blending, the children in the intervention or treatment condition surpassed substantially the children in the comparison condition. Thus, they did significantly better than children in the comparison condition on phonologically based literacy skills, especially in phoneme segmentation, knowledge of letter names, knowledge of letter sounds, word identification, spelling, and letter-sound decoding.

After kindergarten intervention, the children from the whole sample were tested to see who still required remedial intervention. The "whole sample" refers to children who received the kindergarten intervention as well as children who did not receive any intervention in their home schools. The researchers found that "50 percent of the kindergarten project treatment group qualified as poor readers. However, 60 percent of the children from the kindergarten school-based comparison group qualified as poor readers when the entire group was considered, and 80 percent qualified when we considered only children from schools that did not offer their own kindergarten intervention" (Vellutino et al., 2006, p. 160).

All the children in the entire sample were given the Letter Identification, Word Identification, and Word Attack subtests from the Woodcock

Reading Mastery Tests-Revised (WRMT-R; Woodcock, 1987) and measures that were given in kindergarten: letter-sound knowledge, word identification, and letter-sound decoding skills. To provide normative standards for further comparison with the at-risk children, the researchers added a normal reader group that was divided into children with average IQ and above-average IQ. These children had not been identified as at-risk at the kindergarten screening but were entering grade one as the at-risk children. They too were given the same evaluative tests as the at-risk children. We now summarize and discuss the findings.

Of interest and most important is the finding that among the current grade one at-risk children who received intervention throughout kindergarten, one group of children performed so well at the re-evaluation (subtests of Woodcock Reading Mastery Tests and kindergarten screening tests as just detailed) that the researchers dubbed them "children no longer at-risk (NLAR)." Relative to the normal readers with average IQ, the test performance of this group of NLAR children was firmly in the average range. More important, the performance trend of these NLAR children was maintained at the end of grade three!

In contrast to the NLAR children, on the bases of the same tests given at the start of grade one, Vellutino et al. found that there was a group of children who needed further remedial assistance. Based on the responsiveness to instruction, some of these at-risk children were found to be more responsive or less difficult to remediate (LDR), whereas others were less responsive to the additional intervention in grade one. These latter children were dubbed "difficult to remediate" or "DR." The test performances of the LDR children were superior to those of the DR children. In fact, the LDR children's performances in grade three were very close to the performances of the NLAR children (see Vellutino et al., 2006, Table 5, p. 163). The LDR children were doing just as nicely as the NLAR children in Word Attack by grade two! In striking contrast, the test performances of the DR children remained poor in grades two and three. However, these DR children did well at the end of grade one, with the exception in reading comprehension, where they fell to the low average range. But their gains in Word Identification and Word Attack were not maintained at the end of grades two and three.

Clearly the findings of Vellutino et al.'s (2006) study have cardinal implications. The findings point to the critical importance of early screening and intervention for at-risk children. Both the design of the screening tests and criteria in at-risk designation framed the intervention. Of special commendation in Vellutino et al.'s study is the efficient use of a simple experimental screening test backed up by additional tests in ascertaining children's at-risk status. Moreover, the design of intervention contents, designated trained instructors, and duration of intervention register as nonnegotiable factors in effective early intervention.

The finding of various groups of children with gradated responsiveness to remedial instruction is interesting, significant, and poignant with implications. It points to the expected, but hitherto undocumented, diversity among poor readers. Most important, it points to the need to differentiate them effectively for appropriate intervention. Clearly, Vellutino et al. (2006) highlight the usefulness of a carefully designed and executed RTI approach in differentiating among the various groups of at-risk children who will benefit from gradated remedial instruction. The DR children represented in Vellutino et al.'s study may well be children with severe learning disabilities who will need long-term, sustained, and intensive one-on-one instruction that is torqued to the particular individual child's remedial needs.

CRITIQUE OF RTI

Our critique of RTI comprises two areas: (1) The immediate problems concerning moving RTI from research to practice and (2) the broader context of conceptual and definitional problems.

PROBLEMS IN MOVING RTI FROM RESEARCH TO PRACTICE

RTI standard-protocol research studies attest unequivocally to the efficacy in isolating a hard core of children at risk for developing reading problems through its two- or three-tiered intervention approach. The rub now lies in moving RTI from research to practice. To put in place the RTI standard protocol model in primary schools, several pressing problems must be addressed.

The first problem concerns identifying children who are nonresponsive to given instruction in early reading and thus require more intensive instruction. Some researchers suggest using performance standards; for example, Good, Simmons, and Kame'enui (2001) suggested benchmark goals for all grade one children to read at the end of grade one at or above 40 words per minute on grade-level material using curriculum-based measurements (CBM) oral fluency procedures. Moreover, Good, Simmons, Kame'enui and Chard (2003) promote the idea that a score below 20 on the CBM oral reading fluency (ORF) in the spring of first grade signals the need for more intensive instructional support. They recommend using a continuum of oral fluency indicators of foundational early-reading skills, such as on the Dynamic Indicators of Basic Early Literacy Skills (DIBELS), to inform instructional decisions on when to increase intervention intensity for the at-risk children. The advantage in using performance standards appears to lie in alleviating decision making by teachers. But the disadvantage is that it does not have the flexibility in accommodating factors such as low SES and English Language Learners (ELL). Additional serious problems arise when the benchmark cutoff scores do not work consistently across schools in various school districts, rural and urban regions, and states (see Compton, 2006; see also L. Fuchs's 2003 insightful comments on the criterion for signaling learning to be insufficient). One alternative selection criterion is to model on Vellutino et al. (2006) and use an empirically validated screening procedure that nets a larger proportion of at-risk children, such as 30 percent. This proportion effectively guards against false negatives and thus increases accuracy of prevalence rate of children who have a high probability of being diagnosed as reading-disabled in the future. However, screening at kindergarten may be too costly for school districts' budgets and may net many false positives. Hence, screening children at entry to grade one may be a more economically viable alternative.

The second problem pertains to the need in training teachers to provide research-based instruction. This is a tall order if advocates of RTI want widespread national implementation of the standard protocol model. To fulfill this order, RTI advocates would need to coordinate with administrators and instructors of teacher training programs at universities and colleges to oversee additions to the curricula with the goal of producing new primary teachers who could implement the RTI standard-protocol model and research-based instruction in early literacy under this model. RTI standard protocol researchers themselves can train local schoolteachers to use the model and to use research-based instruction in early grades. They may need to negotiate with their own faculties and universities to make such school-based inservice part of tenure and promotion requisition. It is commonplace for university researchers in education faculties or Colleges of Education to give inservice to schools. Long before RTI came into existence, many noted education researchers have engaged in constant inservice to teachers regarding evidence-based instruction—to name a few, Don Deshler and his associates (Jean Schumaker, Keith Lenz, Ed Ellis, Janet Bulgren); Margo Mastropieri and Tom Scruggs; Karen Harris and Steve Graham; Doug and Lynn Fuchs; Annemarie Palincsar; Carol-Sue Englert; Taffy Raphael; Sharon Vaughn; the late Candy Bos; Janette Klingner; Lorraine Graham; and Deborah Butler.

Third, RTI standard protocol researchers must consider the nature of instruction for at-risk children who are considered unresponsive after Tier II instruction (Compton, 2006). Surely these children should not receive more of the same kind of instruction, since they have not been responsive to it in Tier II! Perhaps these children may need more individually tailored versions of the instruction they have been receiving? Here they may consider experimenting with the instructional flexibility in the problem-solving model of RTI (Fuchs et al., 2003; Reschly, 2005).

Fourth, how long should Tier II and post–Tier II instruction be given? In the research studies, Tier II instruction typically has a fixed duration of "X" weeks. In the real world application of the RTI standard protocol model, is it realistic to be so fixed? School instruction is often interrupted by public holidays, school vacations, teachers' conferences, and so on. It seems more reasonable and realistic to let teachers decide on the length of Tier II and post–Tier II instruction because well-trained or good teachers recognize and understand the instructional problems and learning needs in the children they teach and how much more instruction they might need. Similarly, the duration of Tier I treatment too may need to be thoroughly reconsidered. Vaughn et al. (2003) found in their study that the at-risk children attained maximal gains in the first ten weeks of intervention. Based on this finding, it may be feasible for Tier I intervention to last ten weeks. At any rate, this ten weeks' Tier I intervention duration merits an empirical trial.

Fifth, what should be the exit criteria for children in post–Tier II instruction? Perhaps here we may consider use of some form of performance standards that provides room for input from the teachers in their application. In the school context, well-trained or good teachers would be able to ascertain when an at-risk child can be returned to regular class with continual support. We assume that post–Tier II instruction would be given in the resource room where the child receives one-on-one instruction, if not small group instruction. The teacher's knowledge here should play a role in applying any performance standards developed by researchers. Otherwise, the performance standards may prove to be too rigid or narrow.

Finally, for children who successfully return to the regular classrooms after Tier II, provision of continual instructional support and monitoring may be necessary. Such provision appears to be warranted from data in Vaughn et al.'s (2003) study that indicated some of these children regressed in grade three. For more astute and complete analyses of practical implementation problems of RTI, readers are strongly encouraged to read Mastropieri and Scruggs (2005).

The preceding problems concern the immediate move of RTI from research to practice. But there are additional problems that lie in the conceptual and definitional realm. First and foremost is the nagging question of whether children unresponsive to Tier II instruction have learning disabilities. Vaughn and Fuchs (2003) suggested further diagnostic testing to ascertain if this is the case. This suggestion is sensible, but the real question is, what diagnostic tests should be used in the absence of the assessment guiding framework of IQ-achievement discrepancy? The latter has been soundly knocked down by the rise of the RTI models (standard protocol and problem-solving). This question has not been addressed.

The second conceptual/definitional problem is that reading disability does not equate a learning disability! Although the majority of individuals with learning disabilities have a reading disability, learning disabilities are not exclusively centered in reading disability. Specifically, equating reading disability with a learning disability and focusing early effective instruction exclusively on reading neglects those with arithmetic/math problems. Siegel and Ryan (1988) found seven-year-olds whose word identification on the Wide Range Achievement Test (WRAT) was adequate but whose arithmetic/math was very poor. Subsequently, Siegel and Shaffrir (1994) found similar findings in adolescents and adults. Moreover, as children with learning disabilities grow older, the manifestations of learning disabilities change (Torgesen, 2003). These changes reflect in part changing instructional foci and curricular demands from grades 1 to 12. Some of the children with learning disabilities will display writing problems (Graham et al., 2004). It is important for those connected or interested in the learning disabilities field to bear in mind that learning disabilities and reading disability are not interchangeable entities or conceptual/definitional terms. To ignore this fact ill serves individuals with learning disabilities and the field of learning disabilities! For an astute perspective on the conceptual problems of RTI, readers are strongly encouraged to read Gerber (2005).

In conclusion, it may be premature, albeit legitimate, to ask, "What has the RTI research with the standard-protocol approach contributed to the learning disabilities field?" To answer this question, let us think back to what the accidental founding father of learning disabilities, Sam Kirk, and his associates conceptualized about learning disabilities in the early sixties. In the days of Kirk, at the heart of learning disabilities, there were three basic issues. The first was the notion of discrepancy. Children with learning disabilities were of normal intelligence and sensory functions, yet they encountered unexpectedly enormous difficulties in learning to read. The second was that children with learning disabilities need special education. By this we mean education that differs from the education that is given in the regular classroom. However, we do not think Kirk and his associates had any clear notion of the nature of this special form of education that would meet the instructional needs of children with learning disabilities. This is understandable because in the 1960s, the learning disabilities field was so new that one can hardly expect either researchers or teachers to produce instruction that would suit such children! The third issue was that children with learning disabilities differed from low achievers, students who achieve poorly in school because of a variety of problems such as low intelligence and behavioral, emotional, and motivational problems.

We believe the contributions of the RTI standard-protocol research to the learning disabilities field are (1) RTI standard-protocol research has clearly demonstrated that at-risk children can benefit from research-based instruction in early reading; and (2) RTI standard-protocol research studies have shown that when implemented properly, we can isolate a core of at-risk children for more intensive instruction and monitoring so that they may not develop reading disability. As a by-product, these research studies have shown how low achievers can effectively be separated from at-risk children who may have learning disabilities. These low achievers were shown to have reading problems arising from experiential and/or instructional deficiencies.

Thus, in the context of the three basic conceptual/definitional issues that arose at the beginning of the learning disabilities field, the RTI standard-protocol research has successfully dealt with the second and third issues. RTI standard-protocol research studies have shown that indeed children who are likely to have learning disabilities need a different kind of instruction than given in regular classrooms. They need instruction the intensity of which is not typically found in regular classrooms (Torgesen, 2000). And RTI standard protocol research studies have effected the separation of what Keith Stanovich called a "garden variety" of poor readers from those who may develop a reading disability.

We end this section by declaring first our view on the discrepancy model and second our stand on the RTI standard-protocol research. In our view, the current status and evolvement of the learning disabilities field is such that perhaps we should consider treating the discrepancy notion as a distinct characteristic of students with learning disabilities and cease attempting to measure it! The grounds for dismissing the IQ-achievement discrepancy "formula" have already been covered. Continuing to be mired in debates over how to reshape measurements of this discrepancy in students with learning disabilities appears to be analogous to efforts spent on pursuing the Holy Grail! We may do better with our cognitive juices and efforts on devising instruction for at-risk children post–Tier II!

Regarding RTI standard-protocol research, we think indeed that it has the potential of being "a first cut" in the diagnostic process of learning disabilities, as coined by Vellutino et al. (2006). Specifically this "first cut" differentiates between garden variety poor readers and those at-risk for developing reading disability. Its merits lie therefore in early identification and prevention. But the RTI standard-protocol model itself may not be realized on a national scale because of the serious problem in training sufficient numbers of teachers who not only must deliver research-based instruction but who must also have the ability and savvy to identify nonrespondents to the given instruction. We think RTI, the standard-protocol model, is much more likely to be realized in regional pockets across the United States where there is local leadership provided by veteran researchers experienced in school-based interventions and collaborative research with teachers. Direct experience with RTI standard-protocol research may be an advantage but is not essential. Last but not least, we repeat that conceptual/definitional problems need to be addressed by RTI proponents.

SUMMARY

This chapter presented the history of the learning disabilities field with most of the topics found in textbook chapters on the history of the field and an introduction of a new topic of RTI. We highlight several aspects of this chapter.

• We have covered the rise of the RTI movement and given a fair assessment of the strengths of RTI standard-protocol research, the weaknesses in implementing RTI, and boldly addressed the contributions RTI standard-protocol research studies make to the field.

• We have focused readers on the forces that shaped the four influential definitions of learning disabilities covered in our chapter: social political forces, as well as cumulative knowledge of research and practice.

• On the topic of characteristics of individuals with learning disabilities, we point out to readers the two common approaches taken by textbook authors in dealing with this topic and the advantages and disadvantages associated with them. In so doing, we believe readers are guided to a more enlightened understanding of this topic of the characteristics of individuals with learning disabilities.

• Finally, on the contemporary research on brain structures of dyslexic children, we remind readers that there is still much to be accomplished with future research. The area in which there are sufficient research data is the planum temporale, and that as Miller, Sanchez, and Hynd (2003) observed, research has concentrated for the most part on reading disability and the neurobiological basis of reading disability. Further research is called for regarding other areas in learning disabilities, such as mathematics.

REFERENCES

Artiles, A. (2004). The end of innocence: Historiography and representation in the discourse practice of learning disabilities. *Journal of Learning Disabilities*, 37(6), 550–555.

Barkley, R.A. (2000a). *A new look at ADHD: Inhibition, time, and self-control* (video manual). Baltimore: Guiford Press.

Barkley, R.A. (2000b). *Taking charge of ADHD: The complete, authoritative guide for parents* (rev. ed.). New York: Guilford Press.

Berninger, V.W. (2004). The reading brain in children and youth: A systems approach. In Bernice Wong (Ed.), *Learning about learning disabilities* (3rd ed.). (pp. 199–248). San Diego, CA: Elsevier Academic Press.

Compton, D.L. (2006). How should learning disabilities "unresponsiveness" to secondary interventions be operationalized? It is all about the nudge. *Journal of Learning Disabilities*, 39(2), 170–173.

Connor, D.J. (2005). Studying disability and disability studies: Shifting paradigms of learning disabilities—A synthesis of responses to Reid and Valle. *Journal of Learning Disabilities*, 38(2), 159–174.

Connors, C.K. (1997). *Connors' Teacher Rating Scale-Revised (S)*. North Tonawanda. NY: Multi-Health Systems.

Cruickshank, W.M., Bentzen, F.A., Ratzeburg, F.H., & Tannhauser, M.T. (1961). A teaching method of brain-injured and hyperactive children. Syracuse, NY: Syracuse University Press.

Fletcher, J.M., Shaywitz, S.E., Shankweiler, D.P., Katz, L., Liberman, I.Y., Stuebing, K.K., Francis, D.J., Fowler, A.E., & Shaywitz, B.A. (1994). Cognitive profiles of reading disability: Comparisons of discrepancy and low achievement definitions. *Journal of Educational Psychology*, 86:6–23.

Fuchs, D., Mock, D., Morga, P.L., & Young, C. (2003). Responsiveness-to-instruction: Definitions, evidence, and implications for the learning disabilities construct. *Learning Disabilities Research and Practice*, 18(3), 157–171.

Fuchs, L.S. (2003). Assessing intervention responsiveness: Conceptual and technical issues. *Learning Disabilities Research & Practice*, 18(3), 172–186.

Galaburda, A.M., & Kemper, T.L. (1979). Cytoarchitectonic abnormalities in developmental dyslexia: A case study. *Annals of Neurology*, 6:94–100.

Galaburda, A.M., Sherman, G.F., Rosen, G.D., Aboitiz, F., & Geschwind, N. (1985). Developmental dyslexia: Four consecutive patients with cortical abnormalities. *Annals of Neurology*, 18:222–233.

Gerber, M.M. (2005). Teachers are still the test: Limitations of response to instruction strategies for identifying children with learning disabilities. *Journal of Learning Disabilities*, 38(6), 516–524.

Geschwind, N., & Levitsky, W. (1968). Human brain: Left-right asymmetries in temporal speech region. *Science*, 161:186–187.

Good, R.H., Simmons, D., & Kame'enui, E. (2001). The importance and decision-making utility of a continuum of fluency-based indicators of foundational reading skills for third-grade high-stakes outcomes. *Scientific Studies of Reading*, 5:257–288.

Good, R.H., Simmons, D., Kame'enui, E., & Chard, D. (2003, Dec.). *Operationalizing response to intervention in eligibility decisions*. Paper presented at the National Research Center on Learning Disabilities Responsiveness to Intervention Symposium, Kansas City, MO.

Graham, L., & Bellert, A. (2004). Difficulties in reading comprehension for students with learning disabilities. In B.Y.L. Wong (Ed.), *Learning about learning disabilities* (3rd ed.). (pp. 251–279). San Diego, CA: Elsevier Academic Press.

Graham, S., Harris, K.R., & McArthur, C. (2004). Writing instruction. In B.Y.L. Wong (Ed.), *Learning about learning disabilities* (3rd ed.). (pp. 281–313). San Diego, CA: Elsevier Academic Press.

Hallahan, D.P., & Cruickshank, W.M. (1973). *Psychoeducational foundations of learning disabilities*. Engelwood Cliffs, NJ: Prentice Hall.

Hallahan, D.P., Lloyd, J.W., Kauffman, J.M., Weiss, M.P., & Martinez, E.A. (2005). *Learning disabilities: Foundations, characteristics, and effective teaching* (3rd ed.). Boston: Pearson Education, Inc.

Hallahan, D.P., & Mock, D.R. (2003). A brief history of the field of learning disabilities. In H. Lee Swanson, Karen R. Harris, & Steve Graham (Eds.), *Handbook of learning disabilities*, (pp. 16–29). New York: The Guilford Press.

Hammill, D.D. (1993). A timely definition of learning disabilities. *Family Community Health*, 16(3), 1–18.

Hammill, D.D., & Larsen, S.C. (1974a). The relationship of selected auditory perceptual skills and reading ability. *Journal of Learning Disabilities*, 7(7), 429–435.

Hammill, D.D., & Larsen, S.C. (1974b). The effectiveness of psycholinguistic training. *Exceptional Children*, September, 5–15.

Hammill, D.D., Leigh, J.E., McNutt, G., & Larsen, S.C. (1981). A new definition of learning disabilities. *Learning Disability Quarterly*, 4:336–342.

Harris, K.R., Reid, R.R., & Graham, S. (2004). Self-regulation among students with learning disabilities and ADHD. In B.Y.L. Wong (Ed.), *Learning about learning disabilities* (3rd ed.). (pp. 167–195). San Diego, CA: Elsevier Academic Press.

Humphreys, P., Kaufman, W.E., & Galaburda, A. (1990). Developmental dyslexia in women: Evidence for a subgroup with a reversal of cerebral asymmetry. *Annals of Neurology*, 28:727–738.

Hynd, G.W., Semrud-Clikemen, M., Lorys, A., Novey, E., & Eliopulos, D. (1990). Brain morphology in developmental dyslexia and attention deficit hyperactivity disorder. *Archives of Neurology*, 47:919–926.

Kavale, K.A., & Forness, S.R. (1996). Social skills deficit and learning disabilities: A meta-analysis. *Journal of Learning Disabilities*, 29:226–237.

Kephart, N.C. (1960). *Slow learner in the classroom*. Columbus, OH: Merrill.

Kirk, S.A., McCarthy, J.J., & Kirk, W.D. (1961). *Illinois Test of Psycholinguistic Abilities* (Experimental ed.). Urbana: University of Illinois Press.

Larsen, J.P., Hoien, T., Lundberg, I., & Odegaard, H. (1990). MRI evaluation of the size and symmetry of the planum temporale in adolescents with developmental dyslexia. *Brain and Language*, 39:289–301.

Margalit, M., & Al-Yagon, M. (2002). The loneliness experience of children with learning disabilities. In Bernice Wong and Mavis Donahue (Eds.), *Social dimensions of learning disabilities: Essays in honor of Tanis Bryan* (pp. 53–75). Mahwah, NJ: Erlbaum.

Mastropieri, M.A., & Scruggs, T.E. (2005). Feasibility and consequences of response to instruction: Examination of the issues and scientific evidence as a model for the identification of individuals with learning disabilities. *Journal of Learning Disabilities*, 38(6), 525–531.

Mercer, C.D., & Pullen, P.C. (2005). *Students with learning disabilities* (6th ed.). Upper Saddle River, NJ: Pearson Education, Inc.

Miller, C.J., Sanchez, J., & Hynd, G.W. (2003). Neurological correlates of reading disabilities. In Lee Swanson, Karen R. Harris, & Steve Graham (Eds.), *Handbook of learning disabilities* (pp. 242–255). New York: Guiford Press.

Neufeld, P., & Hoskyn, M. (2005). Learning disabilities and the new reductionism: A response to Reid and Valle. *Journal of Learning Disabilities*, 38(2), 183–187.

Pearl, R. (2002). Students with learning disabilities and their classroom companions. In Bernice Wong & Mavis Donahue (Eds.), *Social dimensions of learning disabilities: Essays in honor of Tanis Bryan* (pp. 77–91). Mahwah, NJ: Erlbaum.

Rashkind, M.H., Margalit, M., & Higgins, E.L. (2006). "My LD": Children's voices on the Internet. *Learning Disability Quarterly*, 29:253–268.

Reid, D.K., & Valle, J.W. (2004). The discursive practice of learning disabilities: Implications for instruction and parent-school relations. *Journal of Learning Disabilities*, 37(6), 466–481.

Reschly, D.J. (2005). Learning disabilities identification: Primary intervention, secondary intervention, and then what? *Journal of Learning Disabilities*, 38(6), 510–515.

Rutter, M., & Yule, W. (1975). The concept of specific reading retardation. *Journal of Child Psychology and Psychiatry*, 16:181–197.

Shafrir, U., & Siegel, L.S. (1994). Subtypes of learning disabilities in adolescents and adults. *Journal of Learning Disabilities*, 27(2), 123–134.

Siegel, L.S. (1989). IQ is irrelevant to the definition of learning disabilities. *Journal of Learning Disabilities*, 22:469–478.

Siegel, L.S., & Ryan, E.B. (1988). Development of grammatical sensitivity, phonological and short-term memory skills in normally achieving and learning-disabled children. *Developmental Psychology*, 24(1), 28–37.

Strauss, A.A., & Kephart, N.C. (1955). *Psychopathy and education of the brain-injured child,* Vol. II: *Progress in theory and clinic*. New York: Grune & Stratton.

Strauss, A.A., & Lehtinen, L.E. (1947). *Psychopathy and education of the brain-injured child*. New York: Grune & Stratton.

Swanson, H.L, Cooney, J.B., & McNamara, J.K. (2004). Learning disabilities and memory. In B.Y.L. Wong (Ed.), *Learning about learning disabilities* (3rd ed.). (pp. 41–92). San Diego, CA: Elsevier Academic Press.

Thomson, J.B., & Raskind, W.H. (2003). Genetic influences on reading and writing disabilities. In H. Lee Swanson, Karen R. Harris, and Steve Graham (Eds.), *Handbook of learning disabilities research*, (pp. 256–270). New York: Guilford Press.

Torgesen, J.K. (1993). Foreword. In Lynn J. Meltzer (Ed.). *Strategy assessment and instruction for students with learning disabilities: From theory to practice* (pp. xiii–xvii). Austin, TX: Pro-Ed.

Torgesen, J.K. (2000). Individual differences in response to early interventions in reading: The lingering problem of treatment resisters. *Learning Disabilities Research & Practice*, 15(1), 55–64.

Torgesen, J.K. (2003, December). Operationalizing the response to intervention model to identify children with learning disabilities: Specific issues with learning disabilities children. Paper presented at the National Research Center on Learning Disabilities Responsiveness-to-Instruction Symposium, Kansas City, MO.

Torgesen, J.K. (2004). Learning disabilities: A historical and conceptual overview. In Bernice Wong (Ed.), *Learning about learning disabilities* (3rd ed.). (pp. 3–40). San Diego, CA: Elsevier Academic Press.

U.S. Department of Education. (2001). *To assure the free appropriate public education of all children with disabilities: Twenty-third annual report to congress on the implementation of the Individuals with Disabilities Education Act.* Washington, DC: U.S. Department of Education.

Vaughn, S., & Fuchs, L.S. (2003). Redefining learning disabilities as inadequate response to instruction: The promise and potential problems. *Learning Disabilities Research & Practice*, 18(3), 137–146.

Vaughn, S., Linan-Thompson, S., & Hickman, P. (2003). Response to instruction as a means of identifying students with reading/learning disabilities. *Exceptional Children*, 69(4), 391–409.

Vellutino, F.R., Fletcher, J.M., Snowling, M.J., & Scanlon, D.M. (2004). Specific reading disability (dyslexia): What have we learned in the past four decades? *Journal of Child Psychology and Psychiatry*, 45(1), 2–40.

Vellutino, F.R., Scanlon, D.M., & Lyon, G.R. (2000). Differentiating between difficult-to-remediate and remediated poor readers: More evidence against the IQ-achievement discrepancy definition of reading disability. *Journal of Learning Disabilities*, 33(3), 223–238.

Vellutino, F.R., Scanlon, D.M., Sipay, E.R., Small, S.G., Chen, R.S., Pratt, A., & Denckla, M.B. (1996). Cognitive profiles of difficult to remediate and readily remediated poor readers: Early intervention as a vehicle for distinguishing between cognitive and experiential deficits as basic causes of specific reading disability. *Journal of Educational Psychology*, 88:601–638.

Vellutino, F.R., Scanlon, D.M., Small, S., & Fanuele, D.P. (2006). Response to intervention as a vehicle for distinguishing between children with and without reading disabilities: Evidence for the role of kindergarten and first-grade interventions. *Journal of Learning Disabilities*, 39 (2), 157–169.

Wiener, J. (2002). Friendship and social adjustment of children with learning disabilities. In Bernice Wong & Mavis Donahue (Eds.), *Social dimensions of learning disabilities: Essays in honor of Tanis Bryan* (pp. 93–114). Mahwah, N.J: Erlbaum.

Willows, D.M. (1995). Visual processing in learning disabilities. In B.Y.L. Wong (Ed.), *Learning about learning disabilities* (3rd ed.) (pp. 203–236). San Diego, CA: Academic Press.

Wong B., & Donahue M. (Eds.) (2002). *The social dimensions of learning disabilities: essays in honor of Tanis Bryan*, Mahwah, NJ: Erlbaum

Wong, B.Y.L. (1996). *The ABC's of learning disabilities* (1st ed.). San Diego, CA: Academic Press.

Wong, B.Y.L, Harris, K.R., Graham, S., & Butler, D.L. (2003). Cognitive strategies instruction research in learning disabilities. In H. Lee Swanson, Karen R. Harris, Steve Graham (Eds.), *Handbook of learning disabilities* (pp. 383–402). New York: The Guilford Press.

Woodcock, R.W. (1987). *Woodcock Reading Mastery Tests—Revised.* Circle Pines, MN: American Guidance Services.

2

LANGUAGE AND LEARNING
DISABILITIES

In this chapter, we explore the relationships among language, language development, and learning disabilities within the context of a social-pragmatic view of language acquisition. Acquiring a language is a complex process that involves both acquisition of knowledge about language tools and language use. As we illustrate here, to fully understand the origins and maintenance of learning disabilities, one must consider influences associated with both the child and the social and academic environments in which the child lives and develops, and, in particular, the language development of the child.

The process of interpreting and using language for children in all cultures of the world is a complex, multifaceted process that begins early in infancy and extends well into adolescence. An extensive body of research shows that by the time children reach school age, they will have acquired proficiency in one or more language systems, regardless of the complexity of the sounds or grammatical systems they hear around them (Bates, 1976; Bates, Camaioni, & Volterra, 1975; Tomasello, 1998, 1999, 2003). They will also have increased capacities to read the intentions of others, to self-regulate their emotions, and to problem solve and plan when presented with social or academic challenges. With increasing age, children become metalinguistically aware of complex language forms and structures and how they are used in spoken and written communication. What is remarkable about this process is that language develops for all children, but in a rhythm unique to the individual, and along multiple trajectories defined by interactions between genes and experience. Culture also matters, for it is the wisdom of generations that provides the tools to guide and shape social relations and the social networks from which linguistic meanings are constituted (Searle, 1998). Given this complexity, it is not surprising that teasing apart biological, cultural, or ontological processes that together contribute to the ebb and flow of language development over time is difficult.

Nevertheless, one of the more robust findings from language acquisition research suggests that although all children learn the language of their culture, there is a wide scope of variation in the ways that language is used by children of different ages. Further, young children's emerging capacity to use language in communication with others is predictive of long-term academic and social outcomes (Girolametto et al., 2001). However, not all children with delayed language acquisition in the years prior to school entry are later diagnosed with learning disabilities (Paul, 1996). Further, for some children with learning disabilities, their progression of language development appears stable in the years prior to school entry but slows or becomes irregular when they are faced with the language demands of reading and writing in school curriculums and forming lasting friendships with peers. In short, although atypical or unusual language development for children at any age serves as a marker for the possible expression of learning disabilities, several questions remain: What language abilities are critical for children's academic and social success? Why do some children with delayed or uneven language development eventually become diagnosed with learning disabilities and others do not? How does a "specific language impairment" differ from a "specific learning disability"? The purpose of this chapter is to address these and other questions about the relations between children's language acquisition and learning disabilities. We begin the chapter by providing a brief overview of a social-pragmatic view of language acquisition (Bates, 1976; Tomasello, 1999, 2003). This theoretical approach is helpful to guide understanding about how children's knowledge and use of language may influence their learning within the social milieu of a classroom or school culture. Then, we review how children's development of language may influence learning and the expression of learning disabilities in academic and social domains. The chapter concludes with a summary of important research findings.

WHAT IS LANGUAGE?

The discussion of language and learning disabilities in this chapter is informed by social-pragmatic theories of language acquisition that emphasize the reciprocal relations between mediated action and language use (Tomasello, 1998, 1999, 2003). Such theories are mutually reinforcing of a strand of thought in philosophy that is concerned with action-oriented approaches to language and language use, identified with such authors as Wittgenstein (Wittgenstein & Waismann, 2003), Austin (1962), and Searle (1998).

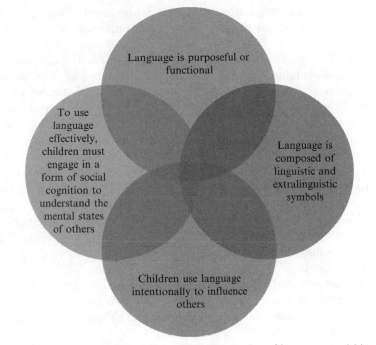

FIGURE 2.1   Features of the social pragmatic view of language acquisition.

A social-pragmatic perspective of language acquisition has four main components, which are illustrated in Figure 2.1. First, a language system is *functional*. Children accomplish things with their words as they speak: They describe, question, state a position, criticize, and so on, and the function or purpose of such language is to facilitate social contact and influence others. As early as eight to ten months of age, children learn to track goal states of those with whom they interact (Buresh & Woodward, 2007), and they use language as a symbolic resource to mediate these social experiences (Bates, Camaioni, & Volteraa, 1975, Kryatzis, 2004).

Second, as they grow and learn to use words and linguistic constructions in the manner of adults, children become sensitive to the use of *linguistic and extralinguistic symbols* (i.e., words, word combinations, and gestures) to express different perspectives; that is, they see that the exact same phenomenon may be construed in many different ways for different communicative purposes, depending on the context in which the communication takes place (Tomasello, 1999). For example, a mother who exclaims, "Look at all the toys!" to a young child in a toy store directs the child's attention to an array of toys on a shelf, but when the very same words are shouted to a child playing at home, it is signaling that it is time for the child to put away the toys strewn about the floor. Children learn to use additional linguistic symbols (e.g., tone of voice, prosody, facial expressions) to accurately interpret the intention of the speaker making the same utterance in different contexts.

Finally, it is within this dynamically changing, flexible communicative architecture that children actively engage in a kind of *social cognition* where they interpret and *intentionally* manipulate the mental states of others in complex ways (Tomasello, 1999, 2003). Consider the child who responds to his mother's request to clean up the toys ("Look at all the toys!") by handing her a book, climbing on her knee, and, with a wide smile, asking "Time for a story?" By using this topic shift in speech and with gestures, the child is intentionally redirecting the mother's attention to a more pleasant activity than cleaning up the toys. As this social exchange illustrates, *communication* occurs when messages are intentionally expressed and interpreted, ideas are co-constructed, and feelings are expressed. To communicate effectively and successfully interact in social environments, children must grow to understand and produce *speech* that adheres to the grammar or rules of a language, and they must develop proficiency in the use of extra-linguistic gestures and actions that have meaning in their culture. It is through the use of this complex symbolic code that children learn to both interpret the intentional states of others and make their own intended goals known to others.

HOW DOES CHILDREN'S LANGUAGE DEVELOP?

Children's acquisition of language begins at birth. Studies have shown that even very young infants are perceptually sensitive to the human sound system they hear about them, and they can distinguish these sounds from those of unfamiliar languages (Werker, Pons, & Dietrich, 2007). In the absence of sound, infants can discriminate subtle differences in mouth movements among speakers of languages different from their own (Soto-Faraco, Navarra, & Weikum, 2007). They can also use other cues (e.g., prosody of voice and content of speech) to determine whether their mothers are addressing them or someone else and what it is that is being referred to in conversation (Saffran, Werker, & Werner, 2006). As they grow older, infants respond to the initiations of adults with a stream of babble that increasingly comes to sound more like the tones and intonations of adult speech. This babbling and cooing has starts and stops, much the same way as listeners and speakers stop to listen or formulate a response in adult conversation.

Infants quickly begin to acquire the linguistic tools for such functions as meeting their material needs, communicating experiences, or telling others about something (Halliday, 1975). It is generally accepted that by the age of ten months, most infants have developed the capacity to read the intentions of others by attending to gestures, facial expressions, and overall body posture, and they begin to imitate these same linguistic tools to make their own intentional goals known to others. This use of linguistic tools occurs long before children have acquired the neurological prerequisites to control physical movements to produce speech that accurately reproduces the sound patterns of a language. By 18 to 24 months, children use language to not only have their basic needs met but also to interact in a form of triadic communication with another about shared objects in their environment (Hobson, 2006). For example, a mother and an infant may be engaging in communication over a ball; the mother looks at the infant, then the ball, then back to the infant, and says, "Let's make the ball bounce!" Then the ball is bounced. By participating in this exchange, the infant has learned that eye contact and joint attention on the object supports communication. If the child's mother had not looked at the child and waited for the child to follow her gaze, the infant may have missed the purpose of the communication entirely. It is through communicative exchanges such as these that young children begin to learn meanings of words and combinations of words that have meaning in their culture. Not surprisingly, children's lexical knowledge increases exponentially during this time period. Research has shown that on average, children produce about 50 words at 18 months and 300 words at 24 months of age; however, the standard deviation (175) is very large, indicating that there is considerable variability in lexical knowledge for infants aged 24 months. Further, children differ markedly in the size of their lexicons of known words throughout the early years (Rescorla, Alley, & Christine, 2001).

Between the ages of three and four years, children develop a sensitivity to the cognitive (reference to thoughts and beliefs) and emotional (reference to feelings and desires) states of others in their conversations; however, this sensitivity varies as a function of social context. For example, in a study of children's reference to mental states in their conversations, Claire Hughes and her colleagues (Hughes, Lecce, & Wilson, 2007) found that young children referred to inner states more frequently with their siblings than with friends and that there was a greater proportion of references to their own feelings and emotions with their siblings than with friends. Girls spoke more frequently about their emotional states than did boys; however, there were no gender differences in the amount of references to children's own inner states relative to those of others. These differences in inner-state talk are a consequence of what Hughes and her colleagues refer to as a "partner effect" and highlight the importance of context in guiding social cognition and the way that even very young children communicate with each other.

When they enter school, children must learn to monitor the cognitive and emotional states of a multitude of new conversation partners they meet in the classroom and on the playground. This increased sensitivity is reflected in the way that they effectively vary their speech rate and tone to emphasize emotions and feelings in their communication with others (Gleason, 2005). Children at this age also have a variety of linguistic tools available to them to access in their interactions with others in their social worlds: They understand and have the ability to speak thousands of words, and they can put these words into sentences that are grammatically correct, without any direct knowledge of grammatical concepts such as plurals, verbs, subjects, objects.

Most children are well prepared to handle the challenge of learning the language and communication contexts of the school: vocabulary (e.g., teacher, homework, recess); social routines (eating lunch with others; lining up for assemblies); and social rules for communication (turn taking; working quietly while others are talking). Instruction in reading and writing adds another dimension to children's growing inventory of language tools. They systematically learn that letters (in an alphabetic language) can be used to represent the sounds of the language they speak, and they begin to use this symbolic code to communicate their own ideas in printed form. Children must also learn to shift between spoken and written language with ease and to recognize the subtle differences between these language systems. With such linguistic tools, children acknowledge and manipulate the perspectives of others in ways that are necessary for them to benefit from spoken instruction from teachers and to form lasting friendships with peers.

Children's awareness of language continues to develop during the elementary school years and well into adolescence (Berman, 2007), but language acquisition for older children occurs at a somewhat slower rate than that observed in infancy and early childhood (Nippold, 2000). By the age of 11 years or so, most young adolescents understand and use complex syntactic structures such as embedded clauses ("My grandmother *who is visiting us from Toronto* enjoys playing chess. *When I play with her*, I usually win") and adverbial connectives ("*Nevertheless*, she will ask me to play chess again tomorrow") in their speech and in their written language (Nippold, Ward-Lonergan, & Fanning, 2005). According to a social pragmatic view of language acquisition, these advanced structures and forms of language are used for their potential to sharpen communication of complex ideas and concepts in academic and/or social contexts. They do not emerge as a result of an innate linguistic acquisition device available to all children (e.g., Chomsky, 1965), nor do they emerge simply from imitating adult models to obtain reinforcement (Skinner, 1957). Language development from a social-pragmatic perspective is a complex process that requires a speaker or writer to act purposefully to understand and influence others, to engage in a complex form of social cognition (sensitivity to mental states of others), and to consciously access known symbols (spoken and printed words, gestures) and the rules that govern their use in a specific social context. For older children and adolescents, this means that they increasingly think consciously about language and they begin to actively talk about their use of language in meaningful ways.

Learning to use the linguistic tools within a language community to achieve one's intended goals is a remarkable feat, and it is not surprising that for some children, this process presents unique challenges. As mentioned previously, young children whose language development is pervasively slow or uneven and older children who have difficulty managing the linguistic challenges presented when communicating in academic and/or social contexts at school may eventually become diagnosed with language-learning disabilities. However, not all young children with language delays are diagnosed with learning disabilities when they reach school age, and not all children with learning disabilities have difficulties in language. Early detection of language-learning disabilities among children and adolescents are topics of interest to many researchers. In the following section, we discuss the research findings that have contributed to our current knowledge of how language develops for children with language-learning disabilities.

EARLY LANGUAGE DEVELOPMENT
AND LEARNING DISABILITIES

Children with language-learning disabilities are children whose academic achievement and/or social competence falls well below age- or grade-level expectations due to their lack of knowledge of linguistic tools and/or their ability to use such tools effectively in communication with others. Although learning disabilities are assumed to be lifelong and theoretically identifiable at any age, the label is rarely applied to describe children's problems with learning prior to school entry. One problem facing diagnosticians interested in the early expression of learning disabilities is that research on the long-term outcomes of young children with observable language delays have reported findings that are somewhat equivocal.

Five groups have investigated the issue in longitudinal studies (Girola-metto, Wiigs, & Smyth, 2001; Lyytinen, Eklund, & Lyytinen, 2005; Paul, 1996; Rescorla, 2000, 2001, 2002, 2005; Whitehurst, Fischel et al., 1991). In a study of 31 late talkers, Paul (1996) found that by the age of three years, the majority of children had increased the number of words in their lexicons to age-appropriate levels; however, children continued to have difficulty on language tasks that required them to apply knowledge of the phonology or syntax to formulate responses. By the age of four years, the only difficulty that persisted for this group of children was with expressive syntax, and by school age, all children performed within the average range on standardized measures of general language (inventory of vocabulary words, knowledge of phonology, syntax). Eight children in the sample performed below the 10th percentile on a measure of syntax calculated from performance on a more challenging narrative task; however, this difficulty did not translate to literacy problems when the children entered school. Rescorla and her colleagues (Mandhart & Rescorla, 2002; Rescorla, 2000, 2001, 2002, 2005) also studied language development of 33 children who were late talkers over a number of years and found that by the age of four years, the majority of the children (71 percent) produced utterances with a mean length (MLU) that fell above the 10th percentile rank relative to the utterances made by typically developing children. By the time the children were five years of age, 87 percent scored within the average range for all measures, but four children (15 percent) continued to have difficulty on measures of expressive grammatical ability. A year later, when the children were six years of age, these scores had improved and fell within the average range, relative to age peers. Whitehurst and Fischel (1994) found that by the age of five and a half, children earlier identified as late talkers performed in the average range on standardized measures of general language ability. Other studies have reported positive psychosocial outcomes for children with language delays that had resolved by five and a half years, but an increased incidence of attention and social difficulties was found among children whose language difficulties persisted through the school years (Snowling et al., 2006).

At first glance, these findings suggest that children who have histories of language delay appear to catch up to their typically developing peers by the age of five years. However, there are several reasons to suggest that this general assumption may be premature. First, there is evidence to suggest that when the language development of late talkers is monitored by having children perform on language tasks that require more advanced forms of social cognition, difficulties in language use become more apparent. Girolametto, Wiigs, & Smyth (2001), the fourth research group who investigated the long-term outcomes of 21 children who had expressive language delays at the age of two years, found that only three children continued to score below the average range on standardized measures of vocabulary and syntax at five years of age; however, the majority of children in the sample continued to have difficulty on narrative and perspective-taking language tasks, such as retelling a story in their own words and telling a story from a wordless picture book. Children also reportedly had difficulty performing on a standardized measure that assessed children's knowledge of language tools typically used in academic settings.

Girolametto and colleagues' finding that differences in children's performance on norm-referenced general language tests abate by the age of five and a half years affirms findings reported in previous studies of late talkers. It is possible that standardized general language tasks do not tap children's ability to use language to express complex ideas or to attend to and manipulate the intentions of others through communication. Rather, they measure children's ability to understand and produce discrete language symbols (e.g., "Show me the dog" or respond to "What is this?" when presented with an array of pictures, one of which is a dog). These tasks are also presented in a social context where the purpose for communicating meaning may be arbitrary to the child (i.e., the reason for communication is simply to please the examiner). It is also important to note that although late-talking children typically achieve within age and/or grade level norms on standardized measures of language and achievement when tested at school entry, their performance falls at the extreme end of the low average range and may decline further with increasing age (Rescorla, 2005).

There are other reasons why the conclusion that late talkers eventually "catch up" to their typically developing peers is not warranted. Scarborough and Dobrich (1990) propose that language for typically developing children occurs in spurts of growth separated by extended plateaus, and it is during these plateaus that preschool-aged children with language delays appear to catch up with their peers. According to Scarborough and Dobrich, the gains observed by late talkers at school entry are best conceived as *illusory recovery*, for when children with typical language development spurt forward again, children with language problems remain stalled.

A related concern with the research on late talkers has to do with the way that children with language delays are identified. A late talker at the age of two years is identified on the basis of the number of words in his or her lexicons. However, we know with some certainty that by the age of four years, children have increased ability to form multiword utterances and to communicate their intended goals by adjusting their language use to the perspectives of others (Slade & Ruffman, 2005). It may be that assessing the number of words children use at the age of two years is not a robust predictor of their ability to engage in more complex forms of communication later in childhood and at school.

Together, these findings suggest that some but not all children with early language delays will have language difficulties that persist into the school years and contribute to language-learning disabilities; however, the prediction of learning disabilities is made stronger when measures of children's language knowledge and use are evaluated by their response to complex social and cognitive tasks. The reasons for variation in academic outcomes among children who are identified as late talkers are not entirely clear at this time. However, there is some indication from studies conducted by Lyytinen and her colleagues in Finland that late-talking children who are at familial risk for dyslexia have poorer outcomes than children not at risk. Lyytinen, Eklund, and Lyytinen (2005) studied the reading and spelling outcomes of groups of children identified as late talkers at the age of two and a half years with and without familial risk of dyslexia. Study findings showed that by the age of three and a half, late talkers in the not-at-risk group were performing near levels attained by typically developing peers; whereas late talkers in the at-risk group continued to perform below their peers on measures of language when five and a half years of age and on measures of spelling and reading in the second grade.

Although early language difficulties or delays may eventually result in a diagnosis of language-learning disability, the terminology used most frequently to describe the language difficulties of young children that persist throughout the early years includes *severe language impairment, specific language disability, language delay, language disorder*, and *slow expressive language disorder*. The wide range of terms in usage to describe the language problems of children prior to school entry and during the school years leads to much confusion for both parents and professionals. A more fruitful approach to ensure clarity about the nature of children's language-learning disabilities may be to consider individual differences in language on a continuum. And difficulties in language manifest in ways that vary with the children's age and the social-cognitive demands of the context in which they interact with others. In this way, children vulnerable to language-learning disabilities can be identified early and intervention provided to families of young children long before they are faced with the academic and social challenges within a school language community. Research on learning disabilities has rarely taken the role of social context into consideration to understand children's language learning problems; rather, the emphasis has been on learning about the specific nature of the language system that underlies individual differences in children's academic and social competence. Although this research has a narrow focus, study findings have contributed significantly to our understandings of the origins of language-learning disabilities among children and a review of the important findings from this body of research follows.

COMMUNICATION OF CHILDREN WITH LEARNING DISABILITIES

Although children with language-learning disabilities could potentially have problems with understanding the function of language, with reading the intentions of others, or with the cognitive demands of managing linguistic and social information in social settings, the focus of research on language-learning disabilities has traditionally been on the linguistic knowledge that is necessary for children to communicate in academic and/ or social contexts. Linguistic knowledge here refers to rules within a language community that govern word *forms* and that govern the *syntactic structure* (combination words into sentences). In the social-pragmatic view of language, linguistic symbols (i.e., words and rules) are socially constructed and maintained through language practices in a cultural community. These linguistic tools include knowledge of phonology (i.e., the sound system of language), morphology (i.e., the system for combining the smallest units of language that have meaning), syntax (i.e., the system for combining words into grammatical structures within a language), and the lexicon (i.e., an inventory of stored words that provide information about morphological variants and grammatical usage of words in a language community).

Children with language-learning disabilities may have varying proficiencies in any or all of these language systems. They also may have varying *metalinguistic knowledge* of the ways these language systems contribute to their spoken and written communication. The most common way for school-aged children to learn to reflect upon language constructions is through reading. Therefore, children with language-learning disabilities are at a disadvantage to develop knowledge of such linguistic tools as lexical organization (e.g., categories of similarities and differences), metaphor, irony, and humor. They may also be less likely to engage in reflection to clarify meanings gleaned from the syntactical constructions in the text they read (e.g., after reading "Mary said he hit her," the child asks "Who is hurt: Mary or her friend, Susan?") or to edit their own constructions in their writing (e.g., the child self-corrects "He is suppose to go to school today" to "He is supposed to go to school today").

The idea that a single "deficit" underlies the language of children with language-learning disabilities seems somewhat simplistic given the complexity of the language systems that children must use in everyday communication at home and at school. Rather than conceptualizing the variations in their language use among children with learning disabilities as "deficits" or missing skills, a more fruitful approach may be to consider them as constraints within the scope of language tools children have available to them for communication in social and academic contexts. For all children, these constraints operate to arrest development and to inhibit further growth in knowledge of language symbols and their use; however, the extent to which this is considered problematic is determined by the age of the child and the context in which children are required to communicate. In the following discussion, we describe how children's knowledge and use of language tools influence the expression of learning disabilities among school-aged children of different ages in academic and social contexts.

PHONOLOGY

Phonology represents the sound system of language. As previously discussed, from birth onward, children are remarkably sensitive to the human sounds they hear about them. This sensitivity is important for children to recognize the speech sounds that are used reliably to communicate with others in their language community. Sounds of speech that are used in a specific linguistic community to form words are called phonemes.

Children's sensitivity to the phonemes used in their language community is thought to be essential to allow for efficient storage of words in their lexicons (Metsala, 1999; Metsala & Walley, 1998; Walley, Metsala, & Garlock, 2003). As young children hear and repeat words that effectively meet their communicative aims (e.g., "please cookie" to request a cookie from their mother), they likely perceive and use this word or combination of words as a holistic sound pattern (i.e., /pleaskUkI/). Young children with very few words in their lexicons have no need to isolate or to segment each word into its constituent sounds (Chiat, 2001; Newman et al., 2006). However, as the size of their lexicon expands, children are faced with the problem of storing similar-sounding words that have different meanings (e.g., *cook, cookie, cooking*) and consequently begin to construct more precise phonological representations of words from the speech they hear around them. A number of researchers have pointed out that the acoustic signal corresponding to a phoneme may sound different depending on the sounds that are adjacent to it within a word (e.g., compare the vowel sounds in *car* and *cat* to see how the open vowel /a/ changes when followed by /r/). Clearly, discriminating the speech signal is not a straightforward task (Liberman, 1997). This finding has led Lyytinen and his colleagues (Lyytinen, Ahonen, & Eklund, 2001) to suggest that speech perception difficulties identifiable early on in infancy affect word reading in the school years. In support of their hypotheses, Lyytinen and his colleagues compared the developmental pathways of infants with and without familial risk for dyslexia and found that group differences in speech perception (as measured by event-related potential responses [ERP] to speech sounds and in head-turn responses) could be found as early as when infants were six months of age. Molfese (1989) also showed that variation in speech perception of words could be documented in ERP responses of infants by the age of 14 months. In a subsequent study, Molfese and his colleagues (Molfese, Molfese, Key, & Kelly, 2003) showed that variation in ERP response to acoustic stimuli among young children is associated with environmental influences. Parent interviews about parenting practices and family activities, as well as observations of the physical aspects of the home, were conducted when children were three and eight years of age. Different ERP responses were associated with groups of children who had relatively more access to learning materials, warmth and acceptance from adults, academic stimulation, modeling, variety of experiences compared to children with less access to these influences. This research sets the stage for further investigation of the processes within children's early experiences that mediates development of speech perception.

An alternative view, and one that has dominated much of the research on learning disabilities, suggests that phonemes available to infants during speech perception and production are functionally identical to the phonemes accessed by older children during reading or writing. However, a conscious awareness of these phonemic units is not thought to emerge until children learn to read an alphabetic script (Bowers & Newby-Clark, 2002) that makes the segmental structure of spoken syllables (i.e., consonants and vowels) more transparent (Dale, Crain-Thoreson, & Robinson, 1995; Ehri, 1997). This view is supported by findings that show when children are provided with instructional activities in the orthography of an alphabetic language, their awareness of phonemes in their language improves (e.g., Juel & Minden-Cupp, 2000), and phoneme awareness seems to stabilize for the majority of children once they enter school and reading instruction begins (Burgess, 2002). A growing body of research suggests that additional factors related to health (e.g., sleep patterns) and early experience (e.g., attachment, modeling) may also mediate children's learning of orthography and the sounds that the orthographic symbols represent (Molfese et al., 2007).

The research on phoneme awareness development clearly shows that without the ability to form precise phonological representations from spoken words, children have difficulty learning the phonic skills (e.g., that the consonant and vowel sounds of a word can be represented by letters) that are prerequisite skills to single-word reading and spelling. Countless studies have shown that children with poor phonological skills have difficulties reading words and that although children's phonological skills can become compensated through early intervention and/or remedial instruction, their word reading remains slow and labored, which in turn constrains their ability to construct meanings from the text they read.

Whether children must learn to segment speech into its constituent sounds or whether children's awareness of the phonological structure of their language emerges only after they are faced with print is a matter of theoretical debate; however, in each case, children's difficulty with language learning and subsequent reading and writing is assumed to be a consequence of inadequately formed phonological representations of the sound system of their language in memory. Children are forced to repeatedly check the sounds they hear and use in speech against partially formed representations they have stored and available for matching. This consumes valuable cognitive resources, ones that could be used for other aspects of social cognition, such as attending to the intents of others with whom they are conversing through speech or written communication.

THE TIMING HYPOTHESIS

Although the phonological processing account of language-related learning disability has gained acceptance among scholars in the field, there are competing views available in the research. One possibility that has been proposed by Paula Tallal and her colleagues (1997) suggests that children with language-learning disabilities are unable to discriminate speech sounds because of the rapid, temporal dimensions of incoming auditory signals. In over 20 years of research using both behavioral and neuroimaging methods, Tallal found that children with dyslexia had greater difficulty recognizing distinct sounds when they were presented together in quick temporal order than when the sounds were separated by several milliseconds. In later studies of infant development, slowness in temporal processing of auditory signals was shown to be predictive of later language impairments (Benasich & Tallal, 2002). This difficulty with temporal processing appears to extend beyond the phonological system to the visual system for the majority of children in Tallal's studies also had difficulty discriminating shapes presented at a rapid pace. She therefore hypothesized that the underlying mechanism that explained children's inability to process phonological information was a general inefficiency in temporal processing.

Support for Tallal's hypothesis also comes from research that has established that children's performance on rapid naming tasks—such as naming serially presented letters, colors, numbers, and objects—contributes to the variance in the prediction of word recognition beyond that attributable to phonological awareness (Bowers, 1995; Bowers & Newby-Clark, 2002; Wolf & Bowers, 1999) and that this prediction is significant both for young, elementary school–aged children, as well as for children in the middle school grades (Scarborough, 1998). However, not all researchers agree that children who perform poorly on rapid naming tasks have inefficiencies in temporal processing. Some researchers argue that the problem has to do more with children's general processing speed rather than temporal processing (Catts et al., 2002; Kail, Hall, & Caskey, 1999), and others suggest that weaknesses in children's ability to attend to phonological or visual information influences the rate of processing (Neuhaus, Foorman, Francis, & Carlson, 2001).

How would a phonological processing constraint influence children's growth in language knowledge or use? Imagine a young infant who calls his father /tata/; in this case, the infant's father would likely be delighted with the child and would not worry that the infant's articulation of the voiced alveolar sound /d/ has become the unvoiced alveolar /t/. This is because although the infant may be able to distinguish a /t/ from a /d/ sound in spoken speech, the child may not have learned the physical mechanism necessary to make a voiced alveolar. However, consider a school-aged child who writes in his journal, "The dog barkt and jumpt in a puttle" (The dog barked and jumped in a puddle). In this case, it appears that the child hears an unvoiced, alveolar /t/ at the end of the words "barked" and "jumped" and has represented this sound with the letter "t." However, when a voiced alveolar /d/ is spoken in the middle of a word, /pUdl/, the child seems to have difficulty distinguishing the voiced from the unvoiced alveolar (i.e., /d/ = /t/) and therefore continues to use the letter "t" to represent a voiced /d/. For a child who is learning to map the alphabet to the sounds of language in the primary grades, this sentence may reflect increasing but not complete proficiency in the use of the alphabetic principle; however, for a fifth grader, the sentence is more likely representative of a phonological constraint that has influenced or stalled the child's emerging ability to both understand print and to express himself in written communication.

MORPHOLOGY

More recently, researchers have turned their attention to children's morphological awareness and the ways that children's understandings of morphology may contribute to difficulties in spoken and written communication, particularly in the mid- to late elementary grades (Nagy, Berninger, & Abbott, 2006; Singson, Mahoney, & Mann, 2000) and in the high school years (Carlisle, 2000). All words are constituted from morphemes, which are defined as the smallest units of meaning in a language. For example, the word *unhappiest* is composed of three morphemes: *un-happy-est*. *Happy* is a *free morpheme* because it can be used independently of other morphemes, whereas *est* is an *inflectional morpheme* and *un* is a *derivational morpheme*. Inflectional and derivational morphemes must be attached to free morphemes in words.

There are seven inflectional morphemes in the English language that are found only at the end of words and change the function of the word (e.g., -*s* (plural) and -*s* (possessive) are noun inflections; -*s* (third person singular), -*ed* (past tense), -*en* (past participle), and -*ing* (present participle) are verb inflections; -*er* (comparative) and -*est* (superlative) are adjective and adverb inflections. Children as early as two years of age begin to use inflectional morphemes to categorize words more efficiently within their lexicons, and children's use of inflectional morphemes accounts for much of the rapid expansion in lexical and syntactic growth during the preschool years (Gleason, 2005). One of the more frequently observed language difficulties of children in the preschool years is the ability to consistently mark verbs for tense and number; particularly with regular (e.g., played) and irregular (e.g., ate) past tense (Rice, Wexler, Marquis, & Hershberger, 2000). For example, children typically use an infinitive form of a verb instead of a finite verb with a tense marker (e.g., "The girl jump" instead of "The girl jumped").

Two alternate hypotheses are found in the literature to explain difficulties that children may have using morphological tense markers. One explanation that is somewhat complementary to Tallal's timing hypothesis is the *surface account* (Leonard, McGregor, & Allen, 1992).

In this view, morphemes that mark verb tenses are difficult for children to process because they have shorter phonetic durations in connected speech than adjacent free morphemes. Further, these morphemes are unstressed and may be spoken at a lower pitch and softer than surrounding morphemes. This means that children may be inefficient processors of very brief presentations of sound, and this inefficiency interferes with their ability to recognize the grammatical function of the morpheme. A second hypothesis, the *extended optional infinitive account* (Rice & Wexler, 1996; Rice et al., 2000) explains children's inconsistent or unstable marking of verb tense and number results because young children are unaware that this rule of language is obligatory in their language community. By the age of five years, most children have learned that they must mark tense on finite verbs rather than treat them as infinitives; however, some children may know about the concepts of present and past but continue to mark tenses inconsistently. Rice and her colleagues report that children who mark tenses inconsistently in early childhood may do so far less often at the age of eight years (i.e., 10 to 15 percent of the time); however, this frequency remains high in comparison to age-peers who have typically developing language abilities.

Older school-aged children are expected to expand their language systems as they encounter more complex language forms used in the texts they read and in the instructional discourse they hear around them. The rule system that governs the use of *derviational morphemes* is complex because they can be attached to the beginning or the end of the word and can change the word's meaning or alter the syntactic category of the attached base (e.g., *function* is a noun, *functional* is an adjective, *familiar* is an adjective, *familiarize* is a verb). Children's understanding and use of derviational morphemes has been linked to individual differences in word recognition and reading comprehension (Mahoney, Singson, & Mann, 2000; Nagy, Berninger, & Abbott, 2006) among school-aged children. Several theoretical explanations have been proposed to account for children's lack of knowledge about the function and use of derviational morphemes. These include children's (1) basic insensitivity to the grammatical rules that govern morpheme structures (i.e., similar to Rice's *extended optional infinitive account*); (2) inefficient phonological processing (i.e., similar to Leonard's *surface account*); or (3) inadequate conceptual understanding of when and where to use complex morphological units to expand and/or refine word meaning. Conceptual understandings of derivational morphemes are created from experiences reading texts that include these forms. It follows that poor readers may be missing the reading experiences that are critical to facilitate development of an awareness of morphological distinctions (Bryant, Nunes, & Bindman, 1998).

LEXICAL KNOWLEDGE AND ACCESS

Children with language-learning disabilities have been shown to have smaller lexicons than children without learning disabilities. That is, when communicating with others, their speech is bereft of descriptive vocabulary; when reading and writing words in texts, they misunderstand the lexical meanings of words. A number of studies in different countries have shown that children's word knowledge is a robust predictor of literacy outcomes (for a review, see Lonigan, 2007; Walley, Metsala, & Garlock, 2003); however, the relations between word knowledge and literacy development are reciprocal. Sénéchal and LeFevre (2002) found that preschool-aged children's experiences listening to stories in books predicted the word knowledge, which in turn was a predictor of reading comprehension ability in grade 3. A similar finding is reported by Dufva and her colleagues (Dufva, Niemi, & Voeten, 2001), who studied the early literacy development of Finnish children in preschool and found that children's understandings of words in the stories they heard predicted reading performance in second grade. Among adolescents and young adults, Braze and his colleagues (Braze, Tabor, Shankweiler, & Mencl, 2007) suggest that accessing lexical meanings in speech may be easier than accessing the same knowledge in printed form. Readers do not have access to coarticulation and prosodic information that supports lexical access in speech; therefore, the quality of the lexical representation in printed symbols is less salient than when in spoken form. In a study of reading among 16- to 24-year-olds, the authors report that lexical knowledge (i.e., interpreted as the quality of lexical representation and the efficiency of lexical access from printed symbols) accounts for significant variance in reading comprehension beyond decoding and comprehension of speech.

Children's difficulties with forming adequate lexical representations may originate from multiple sources: They may confuse semantically related words such as antonyms (*up-down*) and synonyms (*run-jog-sprint*), and they may have difficulty associating words that have structural similarities (e.g., *happy, happiness, happily, unhappy*). They may confuse meanings of phonetically similar words (e.g., *horse, hoarse*), or they may have difficulty associating words where meaning varies as a result of change in a single phoneme (e.g., *pen, pin, pan*). As a result of these confusions at the phonetic and semantic levels, storage of words in memory may be inefficient. Neuroimaging studies show that children as young as 20 months are sensitive to the organization of semantic meanings of words in memory (Torkildsen et al., 2006), and it follows that children (and adults) whose lexicons are poorly organized may not be able to access or retrieve words efficiently for academic or social purposes.

SYNTAX

Limitations in children's lexical knowledge has clearly been linked to difficulties in social communication and their language comprehension (Catts, Fey, & Tomblin, 2002; Nation & Snowling, 1998; Stanovich & Siegel, 1994). However, having a large inventory of known words in a mental lexicon is not sufficient for children to communicate effectively in academic or social contexts. The academic and social competence of children is also reliant upon their knowledge about how words are integrated into complex syntactic structures (Craig, Connor, & Washington, 2003; Vos & Friederici, 2003) and the ways in which these syntactic structures are used to convey subtle meanings within a linguistic community. For example, children may have difficulty understanding and using abstract, figurative language tools such as metaphor, idioms, and proverbs (Nippold & Taylor, 2002). These language forms are interpretable only through knowledge of language use in a specific social and/or cultural context. We provide two examples of figurative language: one example that may be more easily interpreted by an adolescent and one that is more likely understood by an elderly person in today's world:

"That big mogul is just begging for a kicker."

(Translation: That mound in the snow is going to send a snowboarder high in the air.)

"The early bird catches the worm."

(Translation: Those who work hard and with effort reap rewards.)

In both examples, the figurative language has both a literal meaning that could be derived from the relations between individual words in a syntactic structure and a socially determined, metaphorical meaning, in which the words are interpreted together as a single unit. When children (or adults) encounter metaphorical expressions in spoken or written communication, they must inhibit acceptance of the literal meaning in favor of a metaphorical interpretation, based on their experiences with others in a linguistic community (e.g., snowboarders) as well as previous cues in the conversation or text (Glucksberg, Newsome, & Goldvarg, 2001).

Earlier in this chapter, we suggested that children's language-learning disabilities are best conceived as constraints that result in the temporary arrest of language acquisition rather than specific skill deficits in language abilities. Further evidence in support of this view comes from Nation and Snowling's (2000) study of the knowledge and use of syntax among good and poor readers, matched on age, nonverbal ability, and decoding ability. Nation and Snowling asked participants to first listen to a sentence with a jumbled word order and then to put the words in the correct order. Poor readers were less able than good readers to formulate sentences with active or passive constructions. Passive sentences were more difficult than active sentences for both groups of readers; however, the magnitude of difficulty was greater for children with reading comprehension problems. This finding led the authors to conclude that children with language-learning disabilities (associated with reading comprehension) process language in much the same way as children without language problems; therefore, the authors argue that the problems of syntax observed among poor readers is best conceived as an arrest in the acquisition of language rather than a deficit.

DISCOURSE

As children mature socially and linguistically, they develop the ability to comprehend spoken and written discourse constructed in more complex genres (e.g., persuasion) and for a variety of audiences (teachers, peers, parents, community members) in several social contexts (e.g., at home, on the playground, in classrooms, at the grocery store). Children with language-learning disabilities have been shown to have difficulty accessing words, initiating and maintaining a topic, and adjusting their language use to cope with the language demands of social interaction or academic tasks. A recurrent finding in the research is that the narratives of children with language-learning disabilities contain few references to the internal states of others (such as anger, surprise, fear; Gillam & Carlile, 1997). They retell stories using shorter utterances and less information that was provided in the original narrative (Humphries, Cardy, Worling, & Peets, 2004); they are better at making inferences from narratives they hear than those they read (Wright & Newhoff, 2001); they rarely seek clarification for stalls, repairs, or dropped utterances in their conversations (Thordardottir & Weismer, 2002); and they have writing difficulties that stem from their inability to make connections between various language forms (Berninger et al., 2002). These constraints in social and academic language contribute to a general passivity in children's interactions with others (Bryan, Donahue, & Pearl, 1981) that in turn have been shown to negatively influence children's self-concept and their social acceptance with peers (Erlbaum & Vaughn, 2003).

SUMMARY

In this chapter, we attempted to frame research on children's language-learning disabilities within a social-pragmatic view of language acquisition. This is important for a number of reasons: First, language does not exist in isolation of social context. Language evolves as a means to interpret the mental states and influence others in our linguistic communities. Second, without such language tools, children are at a disadvantage to participate fully in the activities valued in a society or culture. Third, when children's knowledge or use of language tools is constrained in some way, it is useful to conceptualize and research how these constraints affect children's language systems at different ages and in various social and academic environments. The impact of constraints on children's social and academic competence may vary over time, but intervention is required long before the full effects are realized by others in the child's social world. Specifically, in this chapter, we summarized and highlighted the following research findings:

• Approximately 1 to 15 percent of children who are late talkers at the age of two years continue to have delays in language that persist into the school years. However, these language difficulties are not detected by standardized, norm-referenced measures of general language abilities. Rather, language tasks that require knowledge of more complex language tools (e.g., narrative story retelling or generation) are required to detect children's pervasive language problems.

• Language-learning disabilities and language disorders have similar origins, and different terms have been used to describe children with language problems: *specific language impairment, severe language impairment, language delay, learning disabled,* and *language-disabled.* The language and learning problems that contribute to these diagnoses are pervasive over time.

• Children's phonological processing is assumed to be either a consequence of inadequately formed phonological representations of the sound system of their language in memory or from a deficit in temporal processing of auditory (and visual) information.

• There are two hypotheses to explain children's difficulties processing inflectional and derivational morphemes: the *surface account* (Leonard, McGregor, & Allen, 1992) and the *extended optional infinitive account* (Rice & Wexler, 1996; Rice et al., 2000).

• Children with language-learning disabilities often have fewer words in their lexicons, either due to a lack of lexical knowledge or inefficient organization of words within the lexicon.

• The quality of lexical representations in the lexicon affects children's and adult's ability to access the meanings of words efficiently.

• Children with language-learning disabilities frequently interpret figurative language forms (e.g., metaphor, idioms, proverbs) literally. One explanation of this finding is that children must inhibit use of the literal interpretation derived from knowledge of word structures to accept figurative interpretations, which are constructed as linguistic units within a cultural community.

• Both understanding and production of structurally complex and cohesive narratives and expository discourse are problematic for children with language-learning disabilities.

• Children with language-learning disabilities are passive in their interactions with others, and this sometimes leads to low rates of social acceptance from peers.

These understandings about the nature of language-learning disabilities within a social-pragmatic view of language acquisition still require much research and revision. However, this approach holds much promise in the future as a means to not only understand the current constraints in language knowledge and use observed among school-aged children with language-learning disabilities but also their developmental origins and the social and academic contexts in which they are most problematic over time.

REFERENCES

Austin, J.L. (1962). *How to do things with words*, Oxford: Clarendon Press.

Bates, E. (1976). *Language, thought, and culture: The acquisition of pragmatics*. New York: Academic Press.

Bates, E., Camaioni, L., & Volterra, V. (1975). The acquisition of performatives prior to speech. *Merrill-Palmer Quarterly*, 21:205–224.

Benasich, A., & Tallal, P. (2002). Infant discrimination of rapid auditory cues predicts later language impairment. *Behavioural Brain Research*, 136(1), pp. 31–49.

Berman Ruth, A. (2007). Developing linguistic knowledge and language use across adolescence. In E. Hoff, & M. Shatz (Eds.), *Malden Blackwell handbook of language development*, (pp. 347–367). Malden, MA: Blackwell Publishing.

Berninger, V.W., Abbott, R.D., Abbott, S.P., Graham, S., & Richards, T. (2002). Writing and reading: Connections between language by hand and language by eye. *Journal of Learning Disabilities*, 35(1), 39–56.

Bishop, D.V.M. (2000). How does the brain learn language? Insights from the study of children with and without language impairment. *Developmental Medicine and Child Neurology*, 42:133–142.

Bowers, P.G. (1995). Tracing symbol naming speed's unique contributions to reading disability over time. *Reading and Writing: An Interdisciplinary Journal*, 7:189–216.

Bowers, P.G., & Newby-Clark, E. (2002). The role of naming speed within a model of reading acquisition. *Reading and Writing: An Interdisciplinary Journal*, 15:109–126.

Braze, D., Tabor, W., Shankweiler, D.P., & Mencl, E. (2007). Speaking up for vocabulary: Reading skill differences in young adults. *Journal of Learning Disabilities*, 40(3), 226–243.

Bryan, T., Donahue, M., & Pearl, R. (1981). Learning disabled children's peer interactions during a small-group problem-solving task. *Learning Disability Quarterly*, 4.13–22.

Bryant, P., Nunes, T., & Bindman, M. (1998). Awareness of language in children who have reading difficulties: Historical comparisons in a longitudinal study. *Journal of Child Psychology and Psychiatry and Allied Disciplines*, 39:501–510.

Buresh, J.S., & Woodward, A.L. (2007). Infants track action goals within and across agents. *Cognition*, 104(2), 287–314.

Burgess, S.R. (2002). The influence of speech perception, oral language ability, the home literacy environment, and pre-reading knowledge on the growth of phonological sensitivity: A one-year longitudinal investigation. *Reading and Writing: An Interdisciplinary Journal*, 15:709–737.

Carlisle, J.F. (2000). Awareness of the structure and meaning of morphologically complex words: Impact on reading. *Reading and Writing: An Interdisciplinary Journal*, 12:169–190.

Catts, H.W., Fey, M.E., & Tomblin, J.B. (2002). A longitudinal analysis of reading outcomes in children with language impairments. *Journal of Speech, Language, & Hearing Research*, 45:1142–1157.

Catts, H.W., Gillespie, M., Leonard, L., Kail, R., & Miller, C. (2002). The role of processing, rapid naming, and phonological awareness in reading achievement. *Journal of Learning Disabilities*, 35:510–535.

Chiat, S. (2001). Mapping theories of developmental language impairment: Premises, predictions and evidence. *Language and Cognitive Processes*, 16(2–3), 113–142.

Chomsky, N. (1965). *Aspects of the theory of syntax*. Cambridge, MA: MIT Press.

Craig, H.K., Connor, C.M., & Washington, J.A. (2003). Early positive predictors of later reading comprehension for African American students: A preliminary investigation. *Language, Speech and Hearing Services in Schools*, 34:31–43.

Dale, P.S., Crain-Thoreson, C., & Robinson, M. (1995). Linguistic precocity and the development of reading: The role of extralinguistic factors. *Applied Psycholinguistics*, 16:173–187.

Dufva, M., Niemi, P., & Voeten, M. (2001). The role of phonological memory, word recognition, and comprehension skills in reading development: From preschool to grade 2. *Reading & Writing: An Interdisciplinary Journal*, 14:91–117.

Ehri, L.C. (1997). Learning to read and learning to spell are one and the same, almost. In C. Perfetti, L. Rieben, & M. Fayol (Eds). *Learning to spell: Research theory and practice across languages* (pp. 237–269). Mahwah, NJ: Lawrence Erlbaum.

Erlbaum, B., & Vaughn, S. (2003). For which students with learning disabilities are self-concept interventions effective? *Journal of Learning Disabilities*, 36(2), 101–108; discussion 149–150.

Gillam, R., & Carlile, R.M. (1997). Oral reading and story retelling of students with specific language impairment. *Language, Speech, and Hearing Services in the Schools*, 28:30–42.

Girolametto, L., Bonafacio, S., & Visini, C. (2002). Mother-child interactions in Canada and Italy: Linguistic responsiveness to late-talking toddlers. *International Journal of Language & Communication Disorders*, 37(2), 151–171.

Girolametto, L, Hoaken, L, Weitzman, E., & van Lieshout, R. (2000). Patterns of adult-child linguistic interaction in integrated day care groups. *Language, Speech, and Hearing Services in the Schools*, 31:155–158.

Girolametto, L., Wiigs, M., & Smyth, R. (2001). Children with a history of expressive vocabulary delay: Outcomes at 5 years of age. *American Journal of Speech-Language Pathology*, 10(4), 358–369.

Glucksberg, S., Newsome, M., & Goldvarg, Y. (2001). Inhibition of the literal: Filtering metaphor-irrelevant information during metaphor comprehension. *Metaphor & Symbol*, 16:277–293.

Halliday, M.A.K. (1975). *Learning how to mean*. London: Edward Arnold.

Hobson, P. (2006). From feeling to thinking (through others). In R. Menary (Ed.). *Radical enactivism: Intentionality, phenomenology and narrative: Focus on the philosophy of Daniel D. Hutto* (pp. 179–184). Amsterdam, Netherlands: John Benjamins Publishing Company.

Hughes, C., Lecce, C., & Wilson. (2007). "Do you know what I want?" Preschoolers' talk about desires, thoughts, and feelings in their conversations with sibs and friends. *Cognition and Emotion*, 21(2), 330–350.

Humphries, T., Cardy, J.O., Worling, D.E., & Peets, K. (2004). Narrative comprehension and retelling abilities of children with nonverbal learning disabilities. *Brain and Cognition*, 56(1), 77–88.

Juel, C., & Minden-Cupp, C. (2000). Learning to read words: Linguistic units and instructional strategies. *Reading Research Quarterly*, 35:458–492.

Kail, R., Hall, L., & Caskey, B.J. (1999). Processing speed, exposure to print and naming speed. *Applied Psycholinguistics*, 20:303–314.

Kryatzis, A. (2004). Talk and interaction among children and the co-construction of peer groups and peer culture. *Annals of Behavioural Anthropology*, 33:625–649.

Leonard, L.B., McGregor, K.K., & Allen, G.D. (1992). Grammatical morphology and speech perception in children with specific language impairment. *Journal of Speech and Hearing Research*, 35:1076–1085.

Liberman, A.M. (1997). How theories of speech affect research in reading and writing. In Benita A. Blachman (Ed.), *Foundations of reading acquisition and dyslexia: Implications for early intervention*, (pp. 3–19). Mahwah, NJ: Lawrence Erlbaum Assoc.

Lonigan Christopher, J. (2007). Vocabulary development and the development of phonological awareness skills in preschool children. In R.K. Wagner, A.E. Muse, & K. Tannenbaum (Eds.), *Vocabulary acquisition: Implications for reading comprehension* (pp. 15–31). New York: Guilford Press.

Lyytinen, H., Ahonen, T., & Eklund, K. (2001). Developmental pathways of children with and without familial risk for dyslexia during the first years of life. *Developmental Neuropsychology*, 20(2), 535–554.

Lyytinen, P., Eklund, K., & Lyytinen, H. (2005). Language development and literacy skills in late-talking toddlers with and without familial risk for dyslexia. *Annals of Dyslexia*, 55(2), 166–192.

Mahoney, D., Singson, M., & Mann, V. (2000). Reading ability and sensitivity to morphological relations. *Reading and Writing: An Interdisciplinary Journal*, 12:191–218.

Mandhart, J., & Rescorla, L. (2002). Oral narrative skills of late talkers at ages 8 and 9. *Applied Psycholinguistics*, 23:1–21.

Metsala, J.L. (1999). Young children's phonological awareness and nonword repetition as a function of vocabulary development. *Journal of Educational Psychology*, 81:3–19.

Metsala, J.L., & Walley, A.C. (1998). Spoken vocabulary growth and the segmental restructuring of lexical representations: Precursors to phonemic awareness and early reading ability. In J.L. Metsala, and L.C. Ehri (Eds.), *Word recognition in beginning literacy*, (pp. 89–120). Mahwah, NJ: Lawrence Erlbaum Assoc.

Molfese, D.L. (1989). Electrophysiological correlates of word meanings in 14-month-old human infants. *Developmental Neuropsychology*, 5:79–103.

Molfese, V.J., Beswick, J., Molnar, A., Jacobi-Vessels, J.J., & Gozal, D. (2007). The impacts of sleep duration, problem behaviors and health status on letter knowledge in pre-kindergarten children. *Child Health and Education*, 1(1), 1–13.

Molfese, D.L., Molfese, V.J., Key, A.F., & Kelly, S.D. (2003). Influence of environment on speech-sound discrimination: findings from a longitudinal study. *Developmental Neuropsychology*, 24(2–3), 541–558.

Nagy, W., Berninger, V.W., & Abbott, R.D. (2006). Contributions of morphology beyond phonology to literacy outcomes of upper elementary and middle-school students. *Journal of Educational Psychology*, 98(1), 134–147.

Nation, K., & Snowling, M.E. (2000). Factors influencing syntactic awareness skills in normal readers and poor comprehenders. *Applied Psycholinguistics*, 21:229–241.

Nation, K., & Snowling, M.E. (1998). Semantic processing and the development of word-recognition skills: Evidence from children with reading comprehension difficulties. *Journal of Memory and Language*, 39:85–101.

Neuhaus, G., Foorman, B., Francis, D.J., & Carlson, C.D. (2001). Measures of information processing in rapid automatized naming (RAN) and their relation to reading. *Journal of Experimental Child Psychology*, 78:359–373.

Newman, R., Ratner, N.B., Jusczyk, A.M., Jusczyk, P.W. & Dow, K.A. (2006). Infants' early ability to segment the conversational speech signal predicts later language development: A retrospective analysis. *Developmental Psychology*, 42(4), 643–655.

Nippold, M.A. (2000). Language development during the adolescent years: Aspects of pragmatics, syntax, and semantics. *Topics in Language Disorders*, 20(2), 15–28.

Nippold, M.A., & Taylor, C.L. (2002). Judgments of idiom familiarity and transparency: A comparison of children and adolescents. *Journal of Speech, Language, and Hearing Research*, 45(2), 384–391.

Nippold, M.A., Ward-Lonergan, J.M., & Fanning, J.L. (2005). Persuasive writing in children, adolescents, and adults: A study of syntactic, semantic, and pragmatic development. *Language, Speech, and Hearing Services in Schools*, 36(2), 125–138.

Paul, R. (1996). Clinical implications of the natural history of slow expressive language development. *American Journal of Speech-Language Pathology*, 5(2), 5–21.

Pruden, S., Hirsh-Pasek, K., & Golinkoff, R.M. (2006). The social dimension in language development: A rich history and a new frontier. In P.J. Marshall & N.A. Fox (Eds.), *The development of social engagement: Neurobiological perspectives* (pp. 118–152). New York: Oxford University Press.

Rescorla, L. (2000). Vocabulary growth in late talkers: Lexical development from 2.0 to 3.0. *Journal of Child Language*, 27(2), 293–311.

Rescorla, L. (2001). Conversational patterns in late talkers at age 3. *Applied Psycholinguistics*, 22(2), 235–251.

Rescorla, L. (2002). Language and reading outcomes to age 9 in late-talking toddlers. *Journal of Speech and Hearing Research*, 45(2), 360–371.

Rescorla, L. (2005). Age 13 language and reading outcomes in late-talking toddlers. *Journal of Speech, Language, and Hearing Research*, 48(2), 459–472.

Rescorla, L., Alley, A., & Christine, J. (2001). Word frequencies in toddlers' lexicons. *Journal of Speech, Language, and Hearing Research*, 44(3), 598–609.

Rescorla, L., & Roberts, J. (2002). Nominal versus verbal morpheme use in late talkers at ages 3 and 4. *Journal of Speech, Language, and Hearing Research*, 45(6), 1219–1231.

Rice, M.L., & Wexler, K. (1996). Toward tense as a clinical marker of specific language impairment in English speaking children. *Journal of Speech and Hearing Research*, 39:1239–1257.

Rice, M., Wexler, K., Marquis, J., & Hershberger, S. (2000). Acquisition of irregular past tense by children with specific language impairment. *Journal of Speech, Language, and Hearing Research*, 43:1126–1145.

Saffran, J.R., Werker, J.F., & Werner, L.A. (2006). The infant's auditory world: Hearing, speech, and the beginnings of language. In D. Kuhn, R.S. Siegler, & W. Damon (Eds.), *Handbook of child psychology: Vol 2, Cognition, perception, and language.* (6th ed.). (pp. 58–108). Hoboken, NJ: John Wiley & Sons Inc.

Scarborough, H., & Dobrich, W. (1990). Development of children with early language delay. *Journal of Speech and Hearing Research*, 33:70–83.

Searle, J. (1998). *Mind, language, and society: Philosophy in the real world.* New York: Basic Books.

Sénéchal, M., & LeFevre, J. (2002). Parental involvement in the development of children's reading skill: A five-year longitudinal study. *Child Development*, 73:445–460.

Singson, M., Mahoney, D., & Mann, V. (2000). The relation between reading ability and morphological skills: Evidence from derivation suffixes. *Reading and Writing: An Interdisciplinary Journal*, 12:219–252.

Skinner, B. (1957). *Verbal behavior.* Englewood Cliffs, NJ: Prentice Hall.

Slade, L., & Ruffman, T. (2005). How language does (and does not) relate to theory of mind: A longitudinal study of syntax, semantics, working memory and false belief. *British Journal of Developmental Psychology*, 23:117–141.

Snowling, Margaret, J., Bishop, D.V.M., Stothard, S.E, Chipchase, B., & Kaplan, C. (2006). Psychosocial outcomes at 15 years of children with a preschool history of speech-language impairment. *Journal of Child Psychology and Psychiatry*, 47(8), 759–765.

Soto-Faraco, S., Navarra, J., & Weikum, W.M. (2007). Discriminating languages by speech reading. *Perception & Psychophysics*, 69(2), 218–231.

Stanovich, K.E., & Siegel, L.S. (1994). Pheonotypic performance profile of children with reading disabilities: A regression based test of the phonological-core variable difference model. *Journal of Educational Psychology*, 86:24–53.

Tallal, P., Miller, S.L., Jenkins, W.M., & Merzenich, M.M. (1997). The role of temporal processing in developmental language-based learning disorders: Research and clinical implications. In B. Blachman (Ed.), *Cognitive and linguistic foundations of reading acquisition*, (pp. 49–66). Hillsdale, NJ: Erlbaum.

Thordardottir, E.T., & Weismer, S.E. (2002). Content mazes and filled pauses in narrative language samples of children with specific language impairment. *Brain and Cognition*, 48(2–3), 587–592.

Tomasello, M. (1998). Emulation learning and cultural learning. *Behavioural and Brain Sciences*, 21:703–704.

Tomasello, M. (1999). *The cultural origins of human cognition*. Cambridge, MA: Harvard University Press.

Tomasello, M. (2003). *Constructing a language: A usage-based theory of language acquisition*. Cambridge, MA: Harvard University Press.

Torkildsen, J., Sannerud, T., Syversen, G., Thormodsen, R., Simonsen, H., Moen, I., Smith, L., & Lindgren, M. (2006). Semantic organization of basic-level words in 20-month-olds: An ERP study. *Journal of Neurolinguistics*, 19(6), 431–454.

Vos, S., & Friederici, H. (2003). Intersentential syntactic context effects on comprehension: The role of working memory. *Cognitive Brain Research*, 16:111–122.

Walley, A.C., Metsala, J.L., & Garlock, V.M. (2003). Spoken vocabulary growth: Its role in the development of phoneme awareness and early reading ability. *Reading and Writing*, 16(1–2), 5–20.

Werker, J.F., Pons, F., & Dietrich, C. (2007). Infant-directed speech supports phonetic category learning in English and Japanese. *Cognition*, 103(1), 147–162.

Whitehurst, G.J., Fischel, J.E., Lonigan, C.J., Valdez-Menchaca, M.C., Arnold, D.S., & Smith, M. (1991). Treatment of early expressive language delay: If, when, and how. *Topics in Language Disorders*, 11:55–68.

Whitehurst, G.J., & Fischel, J.E. (1994). Early developmental delay: What if anything should the clinician do about it? *Journal of Child Psychology and Psychiatry*, 35:613–648.

Whitehurst, G.J., & Fischel, J.E. (2000). Reading and language impairments in conditions of poverty. In D.V. Bishop, & L.B. Leonard (Eds.), *Speech and language impairments in children: Causes, characteristics, intervention and outcome* (pp. 53–71). New York: Psychology Press.

Wittgenstein, L., & Waismann, F. (2003). *The voices of Wittgenstein*. England: Routledge.

Wolf, M., & Bowers, P. (1999). The question of naming-speed deficits in developmental reading disabilities: An introduction to the double-deficit hypothesis. *Journal of Educational Psychology*, 19:1–24.

Wolf, M., Goldberg O'Rourke, A., Gidney, C., Lovett, M., Cirino, P., & Morris, R. (2002). The second deficit: An investigation of the independence of phonological and naming-speed deficits in developmental dyslexia. *Reading and Writing: An Interdisciplinary Journal*, 15:43–72.

Wright, H.H., & Newhoff, M. (2001). Narration abilities of children with language-learning disabilities in response to oral and written stimuli. *American Journal of Speech-Language Pathology*, 10:308–319.

3

WORKING MEMORY AND
LEARNING DISABILITIES

In this chapter, we discuss the impact of working memory on the expression of children's learning disabilities. We describe Constructivist and Information Processing accounts of working memory development. Also, we summarize research findings on the development of working memory among children with learning disabilities. We then expand on ideas introduced in Chapter 2.

WORKING MEMORY AND LEARNING
DISABILITIES

Memory problems have long been associated with slow rates of learning for school-aged children with learning disabilities. Since the late 1960s and early 1970s, researchers have conducted studies that compare the memory abilities of children with learning disabilities with their nondisabled peers, and findings generally confirmed that the performance of children with learning disabilities on memory measures is depressed relative to their non-disabled peers (see Swanson, Cooney, & McNamara, 2004, for a historical review). Another avenue of research that has dominated the field for over 40 years has focused on children's understanding and use of memory strategies to support their storage and recall of information. Findings show that in general, children with learning disabilities do not readily engage in mnemonic strategies such as clustering, elaboration, and rehearsal (Scruggs & Mastropieri, 2000; Swanson & Sache-Lee, 2000), and they appear to be less aware that strategies can be used to improve their efficiency of recall

(Wong & Jones, 1982). However, when provided with direct instruction in strategy understanding and use, school-aged children with learning disabilities can learn to identify memory strategies and the conditions under which they are most helpful. Unfortunately, despite having gained this knowledge about strategies and strategy use, their performance on memory tasks remains depressed relative to nondisabled peers in the academic domains that the strategies are meant to improve (e.g., reading comprehension, writing, mathematics). In more recent years, research attention has shifted and focused on the role of working memory on the learning of school-aged children with learning disabilities. Working memory is defined generally as a limited attentional capacity that temporarily stores and manipulates information in the face of distraction and/or attention shifts (Baddeley & Logie, 1999; Just & Carpenter, 1992; Turner & Engle, 1989). For example, imagine that you receive a phone call from a friend who provides the URL of an interesting website that you would like to see, but before you can enter the URL in the browser of your computer, you must do the following: search for a laptop, check the battery light, possibly use an adapter (because the battery light indicates there is no power available), wait several seconds while the computer begins the startup sequence, address any error messages or possibly incoming e-mail, and open the browser. During the time that these events are occurring, the URL of the website is being maintained in your working memory; and for some individuals, this process can be effortful and cognitively demanding.

It is probably not surprising that academic and social outcomes of children with learning disabilities is reliably associated with limitations in working memory capacity. However, there are several questions that arise: How does a child's working memory develop? What is the relationship between early working memory development and language acquisition? What is the relationship between development of working memory and other executive systems? Does working memory of young children influence later academic and/or social outcomes? Can children be taught strategies to compensate for age or individual constraints in working memory capacity? The purpose of this chapter is to review research on these issues. The chapter is divided into four parts: The first three sections each describe a somewhat different view of working memory and working memory development and how each perspective informs the field of learning disabilities. In the fourth section, we discuss approaches to intervention for children with learning disabilities associated with working memory. The chapter concludes with a summary of the important research findings.

THE CONSTRUCT OF WORKING MEMORY

One problem faced by researchers who are interested in learning about the emergence of working memory early in childhood is the lack of conceptual clarity about the nature of working memory for young children.

Working memory is but one of several memory processes that develop in early childhood, and distinguishing working memory as separate from other forms of memory has been historically controversial (Brown & Hulme, 1992; Cantor, Engle, & Hamilton, 1992; Conway et al., 2005). Second, working memory is not an isolated cognitive skill. Rather, it operates in tandem with other developing executive processes and cognitive skills that support children's language and social endeavors (to be discussed; Rothbart, Posner, & Kieras, 2006). Third, although working memory tasks are thought to be universal and performance differences rest within the constitution of the individual, it is possible that, like other developmental tasks, measures of working memory can be solved differently in different social and cultural environments (Greenfield, Keller, Fuligni, & Maynard, 2002).

Another frequently overlooked but important consideration for developmental theorists is that age-related changes in working memory capacity coincide in time with children's developing understandings of language structure and use (Heimann et al., 2006). As described in the previous chapter, this path of inquiry is gaining importance as an increasing number of studies show that near the latter part of the first year of life, infants begin to use linguistic symbols to communicate with others about objects and/or events in their social worlds (Liszkowski et al., 2004; Meltzoff, 1995; Woodward, 1998; Woodward & Sommerville, 2000). By the age of four years, most children engage in communicative exchanges in which they not only position sounds, gestures, objects, events, and intentional actions of agents but also the mental states of others (Frith & Frith, 1999). The ability to keep track of thoughts in working memory becomes increasingly important as young children participate in these complex, communicative transactions. Most broadly, working memory is thought to afford infants and young children rich communicative experiences, the interactivity of which is critical to the emergence of language (Tomasello, 2003) and for developing social understandings (Carpendale & Lewis, 2004) and social competence (Keller, 2003). Active engagement in these activities is considered crucial to children's academic and social success in school.

THEORIES OF WORKING MEMORY AND WORKING MEMORY DEVELOPMENT

In general, descriptions of working memory and working memory development have evolved from either constructivist or information processing paradigms. Briefly, constructivist theories such as Pascual-Leone's theory of silent operators conceptualize working memory as the simultaneous activation of knowledge (schemes) held in long-term memory and a mechanism for integrating knowledge from these many different kinds of knowledge states. Alternatively, information processing models view working memory as an interrelated system of processes that operate together as a separate structure (De Ribaupierre & Bailleux, 2000). Baddeley and Hitch's (1974) multicomponent model of working memory has dominated the research from this perspective; however, recently a number of single-mechanism neural network models of working memory have been proposed in the literature. A complete discussion and critique of constructivist versus modular or unitary information processing views of working memory is well beyond the scope of this chapter. What is important to our discussion is the relative emphasis that each perspective places on the mental representations (or schemes) that constitute the content of working memory and on the executive (or attentional) control mechanism that serves to coordinate operations necessary for participation in social and cognitive activities. It is these core processes that either individually or in combination appear to be important to developmental change in working memory capacity, to social pragmatic theories of early childhood language acquisition (i.e., Tomasello, 2003), and to the emergence of self-control, emotion regulation, and planning in toddlers and preschool-aged children (Rothbart, Posner, & Kieras, 2006; Rueda, Posner, & Rothbart, 2005), which in turn is predictive of later academic and social outcomes.

CONSTRUCTIVIST THEORIES OF WORKING MEMORY DEVELOPMENT

Pascual-Leone (1987, 1989) proposed the "field of working memory" to represent the combination of figurative, operative, and executive schemes that become activated during effortful processing (Pascual-Leone & Ijaz, 1989). Figurative knowing refers to constructing symbols that imitate a world of objects and events. Silent operators activate these figurative schemes within a subset of working memory that Pascual-Leone called the "field of attention."

Pascual-Leone developed a mathematical model to explain age-related increases in the number of schemes activated within the field of attention. Total capacity for mental energy (or working memory) is symbolized as $(e + k)$, where e is the space to *store* information necessary for the performance of tasks across cognitive domains, and k is the space allocated to the *processing* of information specific to the task at hand. The value of e is thought to be epigenetic and largely invariant, whereas k is flexible and increases systematically as children develop. These increments in units of activation of task-relevant schemes (represented mathematically as $k + 1, k + 2 \ldots k + 7$) are associated with Piagetian stages that occur every second year between the ages of 3 and 16 years. In short, as illustrated in Figure 3.1, as children's attentional capacity increases, more schemes and

Working Memory Capacity (child aged 4 years)

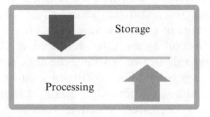

Working Memory Capacity (child aged 8 years)

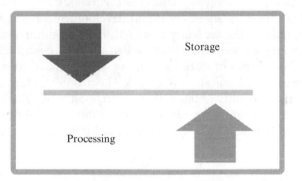

FIGURE 3.1   Pascual-Leone's view of working memory development.

structures become activated, and children are able to participate in increasingly complex cognitive and social activities.

Pascual-Leone and his colleagues conducted several studies to test their hypothesis that attentional capacity increases with age. In one study (Case, 1972), children were shown numbers that were sequenced in order but had gaps in the sequence (e.g., 3, 8, 12). Children were given a number (e.g., 4) and asked to find the place where it belonged in the sequence. When children showed that they understood the task, the numbers were presented to them one at a time instead of in an array. The last number was out of sequence, and children were asked to indicate where that number belonged. This task is representative of most working memory span tasks in research today because the children were required to (1) selectively attend to a series of operations (i.e., sequencing numbers); (2) store the partial products of this processing while interfering information was present (i.e., each time a number was spoken, it interfered with the child's ability to remember the previous number); and (3) elicit a response that took into account the temporal order of the operations (i.e., the child had to place the number in its correct place in the sequence; Case, 1995). The findings were generally supportive of Pascual-Leone's model: a maturational increase in span of 1 to 3 units was found between the ages of four and seven years, the number of units processed accurately slowed after the age of eight years, and an asymptotic performance was reached at ten years, which coincides with Piaget's formal operational stage of cognitive development.

Case (1985) and his colleagues (Case, Kurland, & Goldberg, 1982) later suggested that the overall size of working memory capacity remains constant over time; however, growth in performance on working memory tasks occurred, since as children's knowledge becomes more automatized, the demand on processing decreases, which in turn frees up more working memory capacity for the storage of the partial products of processing. In this view, processing demands are determined by the cognitive complexity of the task and are modality specific (see Figure 3.2).

Recent findings from studies of infant development suggest that the prerequisite cognitive skills necessary to constitute the figurative knowledge of working memory are met at a much earlier age than described in Pascual-Leone's or Case's views of working memory. By the age of six months, most infants show deferred imitation (Collie & Hayne, 1999; Herbert, Gross, & Hayne, 2006), a cognitive ability that is originally thought to emerge at stage 5 of the sensorimotor stage, when infants are approximately 18 months of age (Piaget, 1962). Deferred imitation refers here to an infant's

Working Memory Capacity (child aged 4 years)

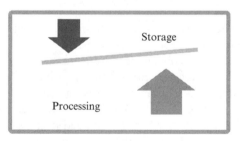

Working Memory Capacity (child aged 8 years)

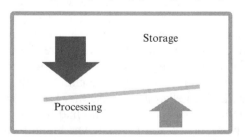

FIGURE 3.2   Case's view of working memory development.

ability to construct and maintain a mental representation of an action over time and then imitate the action based on recall (Bauer & Kleinknecht, 2002). Infants with deferred imitation are able to show the goal of the behavior they have observed, as well as the specific actions that brought about that goal (Tomasello, 1998). For example, deferred imitation occurs when an infant observes an adult intentionally pulling apart a toy and then imitates this action. The infant has placed himself/herself in the action sequence in the place of the adult (much like placing a number in a sequence on Pascal-Leone's sequencing task) and then recreates the sequence of events to have the same goal met. By the age of 11 months, most infants are able to recall and reproduce multistep action sequences up to a month after watching an adult perform them (see Bauer & Kleinknecht, 2002, for a review).

One explanation of this developmental change in infants' performance on deferred imitation tasks is that as they mature, infants have an increased ability to form figurative schemes of the actions they observe. A second view holds that increases in the overall attentional capacity of the infant, rather than symbolic capacity, mediates recall of cause-effect action sequences. For infants to perform on a deferred imitation task, they must show both figurative and operative aspects of knowing. However, Bates (1976) argues that for infants to communicate about this knowledge, the content must first be objectified into symbolic communicative schemes (i.e., mental representations of communicative acts). When an infant prepares such communicative schemes, instead of just knowing, the infant groups this knowledge into a set of schemes that they know are functional in their social communication with others. A selected portion or "chunk" of this set of schemes is then "transferred" to be operated on to produce the concatenation of sounds that constitute linguistic symbols known as words. Bates suggests that the number of words produced in an utterance is a function of developmental constraints in this "chunk-and-transfer capacity" (p. 94), and although not directly stated, this capacity appears to be synonymous with the age-defined bounds of the attentional space of working memory described in Pascual-Leone's theory. In this sense, working memory may function in a biological way to prepare infants for participation in social activities that require the use of linguistic symbols. Although somewhat speculative, it also seems reasonable to propose that working memory is important to track attentional states in infancy and to attend to more complex mental states of others in early childhood (e.g., anger, sadness, happiness); however, further research is needed to confirm this hypothesis.

Constructivist views of working memory, such as those of Pascual-Leone and Case, are developmental in orientation in that they attempt to account for age-related change in children's working memory capacities. These views have rarely been applied to further understandings of slow or uneven growth trajectories of children, such as those that characterize school-aged children with learning disabilities. To further our understandings of relations between age or individual differences in working memory for children's learning disabilities, researchers have relied primarily on models of information processing. In the next section, we briefly review two approaches that have dominated research in the field. One view originates from the work of Baddeley and his colleagues and the second from connectionist accounts of working memory systems.

INFORMATION PROCESSING MODELS AND LEARNING DISABILITIES

BADDELEY'S MODEL

Baddeley and Hitch's (1974) tri-component model of working memory includes a central executive that interacts with two auxiliary slave systems: the phonological loop and the visual-spatial sketchpad. The phonological loop temporarily stores the products of phonological processing, whereas the visual sketch pad is responsible for the storage of visual-spatial information. Both systems are under control of the central executive, a supervisory attentional resource that coordinates activities within a general cognitive system and also allocates resources to the two subsystems (Baddeley, 1986; Baddeley & Logie, 1999). An issue that has been historically controversial is whether processing within the phonological loop and the visual-spatial sketchpad is synonymous with short-term memory; a passive, temporary storage buffer, the capacity of which is measured by simple memory span tasks and mediated by efficiency of memory strategies, such as rehearsal and chunking (Brown & Hulme, 1992). Despite a long history of debate, recent studies report findings that suggest short-term memory operates in part independently of the phonological loop and/or visual-spatial sketchpad in working memory (Cantor, Engle, & Hamilton, 1992; Conway et al., 2005; Engle, 2002; Swanson & Ashbaker, 2000). A fourth component is included in the most recent version of Baddeley's working memory model: an episodic buffer that is responsible for the integration of information from several sources (including long-term memory, the phonological loop, and the visual-spatial sketchpad) through conscious awareness (Baddeley, 2000). Although Baddeley's model is static and not developmental in orientation, it has been used repeatedly in research to describe the nature of the working memory system for children of different ages and for children with learning disabilities. One view holds that differences in children's working memory capacity, either due to age or individual variation, stems from inefficient processing within the phonological loop. A second view suggests that working memory capacities of younger children or children with learning disabilities is constrained by limitations in attentional control within the central executive.

PROCESSING EFFICIENCY

A *processing efficiency* view parallels the ideas of Case (1985) and predicts that age or individual differences in working memory capacity are a function of the efficiency and speed with which children retrieve phonological information from long-term memory and rehearse subvocal, speech-based information in the phonological loop (Roodenrys, Hulme, & Brown, 1993). As processing demands increase (i.e., among young children who are less proficient in retrieval of phonological codes), fewer resources are available in working memory for the storage of partial products of processing. Inefficiencies in phonological retrieval creates a bottleneck that restricts the flow of information upward through the system, and constrains overall working memory capacity.

Baddeley (2003) argues that the phonological loop "evolved to facilitate the acquisition of language" (p. 832). Evidence to support this claim comes from studies that show phonological working memory is positively correlated with vocabulary acquisition (Gathercole, Tiffany, Briscoe, & Thorn, 2005). Further, linguistic manipulations such as articulatory suppression, word length, and phonological similarity interrupt processing in the phonological loop (see Baddeley, 2003, for a review). As discussed in the previous chapter on language and learning disabilities, the linguistic tools available to a child (i.e., phonology, morphology, vocabulary, syntax) are an important component of a social-pragmatic view of language acquisition. A child's ability to interpret, store, and retrieve phonological representations of the speech signal is necessary to interpret the linguistic tools that are functional in communicative activities in their social worlds. However, phonological processing is necessary but not sufficient for language acquisition to occur. Children must also match the phonological input they hear with the intentions and the goal states of the person with whom they must take this information into consideration when they generate their own phonological symbols to convey their own intentional states to others. The simultaneous attention to and control of these activities represents the *executive* component of Baddeley's model.

A large body of research evidence currently exists to support the idea that learning disabilities of older, school-aged children may stem from deficiencies in processing related to the phonological loop. As discussed in the previous chapter on language and learning disabilities, children's difficulties forming accurate phonological representations from spoken words translate to problems learning the prerequisite phonic skills (e.g., that the consonant and vowel sounds of a word can be represented by letters) necessary for single-word reading and spelling. When the phonetic representations formed in a child's long-term memory are unstable (i.e., they are not precise in their formation), accessing phonetic information becomes inefficient and may require activating multiple traces before sufficient phonological information is accessed for processing spoken or written language. The overall result is that phonological processing in the phonological loop is slow and labored, and valuable resources are consumed from the executive that could be allocated to other functions, such as interpreting or constructing meaning from the words decoded or spelled.

THE ROLE OF THE CENTRAL EXECUTIVE

A *general capacity model* assumes that age and individual differences in working memory capacity coincide with variation in the central executive that serves to divide and shift and to control attention. In this view, the executive shares resources with lower-level component systems; however, the flow of information is unidirectional, top-down, from the executive to subcomponent systems that for the most part operate independently of the executive. Thus, for older children or for children without learning disabilities, the executive resource pool is larger and is not deleted to the same extent as the pool of resources available to younger children or children with learning disabilities. In this view, performance differences on measures of working memory are not an outcome of variation in phonological processing skills but rather are attributable to changes in a working memory executive that facilitates performance across a wide range of cognitive tasks, not all of which are specific to phonological aspects of language (Swanson, 1999; Swanson & Ashbaker, 2000).

WORKING MEMORY IN INFANCY AND EARLY CHILDHOOD

Executive processes within a working memory system may be operational even in infancy. Evidence in support of this view comes from studies that have linked infant performance on delayed response or "A not B" tasks to emerging prefrontal cortical activity (Pushina, Orekhova, & Stroganova, 2005; Reznick, Morrow, Goldman, & Snyder, 2004). In this task, an infant is shown a preferred toy that is repeatedly hidden in one of several locations (position "A"). After a delay of a few seconds, a distraction is provided, and the infant is told to search for the toy. When the toy is hidden in a new location, "B," in full view, the infant usually responds by reaching for the toy in the position where it was first hidden and makes an "A not B" error. The ability to flexibly adapt to a changing environment is an essential component of human cognition and infants as young as five and a half months are successful on A not B delayed response tasks, provided that they are searching for a person instead of an object and they respond using eye gaze instead of reaching (Reznick, Morrow, Goldman, & Snyder, 2004). As infants mature, performance on delayed response tasks improves. At 12 months, infants are able to manage increasingly longer delays from the time that an object is hidden and the search begins without making an A not B error (Diamond, 1991). Perseveration of reflexive actions such as observed on A not B delayed response tasks in infancy has also been observed on card sorting tasks in three-year-olds. Children at this age can sort cards easily on one dimension—color or shape—but when asked to switch the rule for sorting, children of this age tend to perseverate on the rule that they used first (Zelazo, Frye, & Rapus, 1996). Theoretically, children with relatively larger working memory capacities make fewer perseveration errors on A not B or card-sorting tasks because they have more executive resources available to selectively attend to relevant information in the current rule for sorting cards while disregarding irrelevant information contained in a previously rewarded, old rule (O'Reilly, Braver, & Cohen, 1999; Goldman-Rakic, 1987).

Relationships between working memory and inhibitory control during early childhood have also been investigated with conflict tasks (Hanauer & Brooks, 2005; Rennie, Bull, & Diamond, 2004). For example, on the Day-Night Stroop task, children say "night" when they see a picture of a sun and "day" when they see a picture with a moon and stars (Diamond, Kirkham, & Amso, 2002; Gerstadt, Hong, & Diamond, 1994; Simpson & Riggs, 2005). Performance on conflict tasks such as the Day-Night task is assumed to consume attentional resources (from working memory) to resist prepotent responses and has been linked to young children's ability to form theories of mind, to self-regulate emotions, and to manage conflict in everyday social situations (Carlson, Moses, & Breton, 2002; Rueda, Posner, & Rothbart, 2005). When children reach school age, they are faced with cognitively demanding activities that influence their ability to suppress irrelevant information, and this is a source of difficulty for many children with learning disabilities (Chiappe, Hasher, & Siegel, 2000; Swanson & Cochran, 1991).

WORKING MEMORY IN SCHOOL-AGED CHILDREN

Another executive function within a working memory system that has been linked to school-aged children with learning disabilities is updating. As children perform on tasks that involve working memory, they must actively monitor, constantly revise, and update information. To illustrate this relationship, researchers have developed tasks to directly assess children's ability to update information under increasingly challenging processing conditions. One example, used mostly in the cognitive neuroscience literature, is the *n-back* task. Children are shown a series of stimuli (e.g., objects, letters, numbers) in order and asked to indicate by a button press whether they have seen the object *n-back*. The researcher determines whether the *n-back* task is 1-back, 2-back, or possibly 3-back. Each condition involves a different working memory load that increases in difficulty. To perform on this task, the child must constantly update the information they have previously viewed. Performance on the *n-back* task has been associated with differences in neural functioning of children with brain injury (Chapman et al., 2006) and Tourette's syndrome (Crawford, Channon, & Robertson, 2005).

In the behavioral literature on learning disabilities, Swanson and others (Swanson, 1999; Swanson & Ashbaker, 2000; Swanson & Kim, 2007; Swanson & Sache-Lee, 2001) developed a series of working memory tasks administered under three conditions that vary in terms of demands on processing and storage. In the first condition, children complete a working memory task without cues or support to improve processing (i.e., the task requires both processing and storage of information). In the second condition, cues are provided to improve performance to the child's maximum ability (i.e., the task minimizes the demands on storage and estimates a child's processing efficiency), and in the third condition, the task is readministered without cues (i.e., the task estimates the child's ability to maintain or store the products of the asymptotic performance obtained with cues over time). In a series of studies, Swanson and his colleagues have used these tasks to tease out the nature of the relations between different components of a working memory executive system and learning disabilities of school-aged children. In general, the findings indicate that most children with learning disabilities perform worse than their nondisabled peers under all three conditions, and these relations were stable across tasks that varied with respect to the amount of verbal, visual-spatial, or semantic information.

Baddeley's model has been used extensively to investigate the components of a working memory system that underlie learning disabilities of school-aged children in language (Gathercole, Pickering, Ambridge, & Wearing, 2004), reading (Berninger, Abbott, Thomson et al., 2006; Gathercole & Alloway, 2006; Swanson & Ashbaker, 2000; Swanson & Sache-Lee, 2001), mathematics (Geary et al., 2007; Swanson & Kim, 2007), and attention (Budson & Price, 2005). In the following discussion, we highlight the ways that capacity constraints in working memory are thought to contribute to children's learning disabilities and the important research findings that help to clarify these relations.

WORKING MEMORY AND LANGUAGE-LEARNING DISABILITIES

There are several reasons to believe that working memory may play a significant role in the expression of language-learning disabilities among older, school-aged children. Recall that working memory, according to Baddeley, facilitates the organization of sounds into words (i.e., Baddeley, 2003) within the phonological loop. Inefficient processing in the phonological loop may contribute to inefficient storage and/or retrieval of words from a child's lexicon, which in turn may constrain growth of children's syntactical and discourse abilities. As discussed in the previous chapter on language acquisition, this bottom-up perspective focuses on the acquisition of knowledge about the structure of language and has dominated research on practices to support children with language-learning disabilities. However, an alternative view, and one that is consistent with a social pragmatic view of language acquisition, suggests that a working memory executive is also important for children to both engage in social cognition and to use language tools effectively. We provide two specific examples of ways in which limitations in a working memory executive may influence interpretation and use of linguistic tools in different social and academic contexts. First, consider the spoken words *Unfortunately, this book is ruined because each page is torn with the enormous tears of the little child who could not stop crying.* The word that is ambiguous in this spoken utterance is *tears*, meaning either rips in the page or teardrops from the child's eyes. One way that the listener may process this sentence is to listen to it in its entirety and then backtrack to clarify the meaning of the ambiguous word. Another possibility is that both meanings of the word may be simultaneously activated (Foss & Cairns, 1970) as the listener hears the word and then, after hearing the remainder of the sentence (and we would argue, after also taking into consideration the intentional goals and aims of the speaker), the listener makes a choice to the appropriate meaning. Working memory is thought to facilitate the access of semantic information (in either case), for the listener must keep the ambiguous word in mind while simultaneously processing the remaining words in the sentence and the context in which it is used. It follows that children with language-learning disabilities may have difficulty understanding this sentence, not because they have little knowledge of the two interpretations of the word *tear* but because they have trouble accessing and maintaining the semantic meanings (Wiig & Semel, 1984) in working memory while they are simultaneously processing other information in speech.

Consider another example: *Susan's mother says that it is raining, and when Susan goes to school, she is going to wear her boots and take an umbrella.* In this spoken sentence, there are several pronouns: *her, it,* and *she.* To find the referents to which these pronouns refer, the listener must refer either back (e.g., *her, she* refers to *Susan*) or forward (e.g., *it* refers to *raining*). Some children with language-learning disabilities have difficulty tracking the referents of multiple pronouns, particularly when pronouns are embedded in complex clauses and/or separated from their referents by other utterances in long stretches of connected discourse (Fayne, 1981). Moreover, all conversations break down at times and, as listeners, children with learning disabilities may not always ask for clarification when they lose track of the association between pronouns and referents. As speakers, children with language-learning disabilities also tend to be less effective at reformulating their message in a way that is functional for them (Knight-Arest, 1984).

Demands on working memory are thought to be lessened when significant cues from the social context are available to assist in the interpretation or the expression of the meaning in utterances. For example, a child's interpretation of the utterance *Susan's mother says that it is raining, and when Susan goes to school, she is going to wear her boots and take an umbrella* is supported when it is spoken by her mother (the speaker) as she hangs up the receiver of a phone, gestures to a pair of boots and an umbrella nearby, looks at her daughter (the listener), motions with her eyes to the boots and umbrella, and then looks back to the child. In this example, the child is provided with multiple social and attentional cues to interpret her mother's communicative goal (i.e., that she put on her boots and take an umbrella to school). Cues from a social setting can be used to scaffold and assist communication among listeners and speakers in conversation; however, when language tools are in printed form, the only cues available to the child are situated in the text that is being read or constructed. For some children with learning disabilities, reading and writing are more problematic for them than communicating with others in conversation, possibly because they do not have the added support of social context to guide their understandings of the linguistic symbols on a page of text.

WORKING MEMORY AND LEARNING DISABILITIES WITHIN DIVERSE ACADEMIC DOMAINS

As mentioned previously, a substantive body of research is currently available to show that limitations in the phonological loop and/or in a working memory executive contributes to achievement in reading comprehension (Swanson & Ashbaker, 2000; Swanson & Sache-Lee, 2001; Turner & Engle, 1989) and mathematics reasoning (Geary et al., 2007; Swanson & Kim, 2007) among older children and adolescents with learning disabilities. Inefficiencies in processing in the phonological loop have been associated with immature word identification, spelling, and reading comprehension of children learning to read and write in the primary grades (Berninger et al., 2006). Whether constraints in a working memory executive also contribute to the depressed academic achievement of children in the primary grades has not been clearly established, in part because, as previously discussed in this chapter, opinions differ among researchers about the nature of the developing working memory system for young children (Kail, 1997). One possibility is that because a working memory executive develops and consolidates with age, reading, and writing difficulties among young children may arise more from deficiencies in phonological skills and other memory (i.e., phonological short-term memory) or specialized executive systems (i.e., attention, set shifting, inhibition) that develop earlier than a working memory system (Hanauer & Brooks, 2005; Rennie, Bull, & Diamond, 2004). Alternatively, it can be argued that beginning reading for such children is a cognitively demanding activity and as such requires the involvement of working memory, even though their overall working memory capacities are relatively small in comparison to older children and adults (Gathercole et al., 2005). Initial findings from cross-sectional studies within our longitudinal program of research (Hoskyn, 2004; Hoskyn & Tzoneva, 2006; Hoskyn, Tzoneva, & Yeung, 2004) support the view that growth in a working memory executive during the preschool years facilitates the emergence of early reading and writing skills of children when they are in kindergarten and first grade. After controlling for variation in IQ, verbal ability, and articulation speed, performance on measures of processing efficiency and storage within working memory were found to be moderately and positively associated with individual variation in children's early use of bound morphemes and complex sentences in their speech and written language and in the legibility of their printing on writing tasks.

CONNECTIONIST MODELS OF WORKING MEMORY

Resource-sharing models such as the one proposed by Baddeley and Hitch (1974) have been challenged on a number of grounds, the most critical of which is that a domain-free ability to control attention is common to performance on working memory span tasks, irrespective of the specific domain the measure is designed to tap (see Barrett, Feldman, Tugade, & Engle, 2004, for a review). This has led a number of theorists to propose unitary, computational models in which working memory functions as a general attentional resource to activate representations stored in long-term memory (Cantor & Engle, 1993). Developmental or individual variations in capacity are a function of the total amount of activation available on a neural net. Assuming a one-to-one correspondence between neurons in a neural net and the mental representations that they encode is clearly an oversimplification of the workings of the brain. Further, because information is stored economically, the complexity of social activity from which meanings are constituted is ignored. For example, intentionality within social interaction in a connectionist sense does not need to involve the subjective experience of control; instead, it refers broadly to controlled and automatic processes that are triggered by environmental stimuli (Bargh & Ferguson, 2000) and maintained by the executive in working memory (Barrett et al., 2004). Modeling conceptual and perspectival understandings within communicative interactions or while learning in complex academic activities is well beyond the scope of current connectionist approaches.

Nevertheless, connectionist models have been helpful in illustrating how the developmental progression of working memory, attentional control, and neural connectivity are inextricably linked. Connectionist models have also been used in neuroimaging studies to model neural networks activated during children's performance on working memory tasks. Findings from this growing body of research suggest that children activate similar regions of the brain as do adults when performing on working memory tasks (Klingberg, Forssberg, & Westerberg, 2002; Munakata, 2004; Nelson et al., 2000). For example, studies show involvement of the prefrontal cortex during the delay part of the delayed performance task; which suggests the prefrontal region is important for stable memory without interference in infants (Bell & Wolfe, 2007), children (Bell & Fox, 1992; Diamond, 1991), and adults (Leung, Gore, & Goldman-Rakic, 2005). Two explanations of activation in the prefrontal cortex during performance on working memory tasks have been proposed. One group of models posit that the prefrontal cortex is divided into two areas that are specialized to the contents of working memory: The ventrolateral prefrontal regions (BA 45/47) activate on tasks that require object working memory (i.e., the "what" of a visual task), and dorsolateral regions (BA 46/9) activate when spatial working memory is recruited (i.e., the "where" of a visually guided action; Goldman-Rakic, 1987; Wilson, O'Scalaidhe, & Goldman-Rakic, 1993). Kaldy and Sigala (2004) provide preliminary evidence that these two brain regions are integrated in infants by six and a half months of age for one object and nine months for two objects. Another group of models posits that the prefrontal region is important for stimulus selection and a wide range of brain activities that are not specific to content (Mecklinger et al., 2000; Stedron, Sahni, & Munakata, 2005). Research that compares developing prefrontal cortex in children and adults is limited; however, there is some evidence that white matter maturation in the frontal lobe regions is associated with working memory development (for a review, see Klingberg, 2006) and with learning disabilities related to attention (Olesen, Macoveanu, Tegnér, & Kingberg, 2007).

Although connectionist models of neural activity have potential to explain the circuitry of a working memory system in the brain for groups of children with learning disabilities, these models fall well short of describing how working memory develops for this group of children or how working memory supports the social activities in which linguistic meanings are constituted relationally between children and adults. By analogy, knowing the ways that mechanisms in a bicycle can operate to allow a rider to go faster, to slow down to accommodate bumps in the road, or to brake entirely has little do with how riders engage in activities with the bike, such as during mountain biking, riding through a park, or riding on a busy roadway. Similarly, caution must be exercised when applying findings from brain research to education. Teachers, parents, and child care providers are well acquainted with the term *brain-based learning*, and despite the gap between current science and direct classroom application, a plethora of commercial programs and packages based on this construct are available for use in educational contexts. Use of these programs and materials is usually justified by the publishers from prevailing "neuromyths," information that is presented to teachers inaccurately as scientific fact (for a review, see Goswami, 2006).

One neuromyth is that increases in brain activity in regions associated with working memory after intervention are stable and correspond to growth in learning activities associated with working memory. It is largely unknown whether the neural systems associated with working memory in humans are plastic (Olesen, Westerberg, & Kingberg, 2004); most of the work that has attempted to alter neural activity associated with working memory has been conducted in studies with nonhuman primates. For example, Rainer and Miller (2002) trained macaques with increasingly more difficult delayed response tasks over several weeks; task difficulty was controlled by gradually degrading the salience of the visual stimulus. Findings showed that repeated practice of the tasks led to change in the receptive neuronal characteristics in the regions near the principal sulcus in the prefrontal cortex. Among human adults, there is some limited experimental evidence to suggest that increased activity in the prefrontal and parietal regions occurs after repeated practice on working memory tasks over a five-week period (Olesen, Westerberg, & Kingberg; 2004). What is often overlooked by educators and practitioners interested in such findings is that any type of repeated practice or training will be reflected in changes in brain activity; the question is whether increases in neural circuitry translate to meaningful change domains that are theoretically linked to working memory.

A study conducted by Rueda and her colleagues (2005) on the effects of training of working memory and attention in preschoolers is illustrative of this issue. The training exercises used in the study were modeled after those used to train rhesus macaques for space travel to improve stimulus discrimination, anticipation, and conflict resolution. On one working memory task, children were asked to pick the larger of two arrays of digits presented on a computer screen; interference was included by using smaller digits in the larger array. On another computer task that tapped working memory, children manipulated a cat character in a game of tag with a duck. The duck presented challenges for the child such as diving into a pond that required the child to recall the ducks trajectory and anticipate where it would surface. Difficulty of the task was manipulated by controlling the delay between the duck's disappearance and resurfacing and the relative speed of each of the characters. A conflict task was administered at each session before and after training. Children also completed tasks on an intelligence test prior to intervention and five days later, after intervention. Control children did not received matched computer training, but they watched videos for five sessions in the research laboratory. Even when compared to a no-treatment control, the effects of the training on attention were not statistically detectable. Only the four-year-old children in the study performed better on the measures of nonverbal intelligence test after training (Ravens Matrices and Kauffman nonverbal IQ); however, since the tests were administered only five days apart, these gains in performance are likely attributable to item familiarity and a practice effect. Subsequent EEG data showed that the training changed brain activity of the six-year-olds in the anterior cingulate for children in a way that matched that of adults; for four-year-olds, the effect was marginal. On the basis of these results, the authors argue that "training improves executive attention in a way that also generalizes to aspects of intelligence" (Posner & Rothbart, 2005, p. 101). We would argue that this claim is premature in light of the study's methodological limitations. Moreover, it seems unlikely that the effects of repeated practice on a limited number of working memory tasks will generalize to all situations where working memory plays a role any more than the effects of repeated practice of lists of vocabulary words translates to native-like proficiency in a language. Having said this, continued research on the plasticity of the biological processes that underlie working memory may be helpful to guide educators with respect to optimal times in children's development when engagement in social activities will result in optimal intersubjective understandings that are needed to facilitate further language and social development.

APPROACHES TO COMPENSATE FOR WORKING MEMORY LIMITATIONS

Throughout this chapter, we have emphasized that working memory, whether viewed from a constructivist or an information processing perspective, involves a capacity to attend to mental representations stored in long-term memory, to inhibit irrelevant information, and to either prereflexively or reflexively monitor the products of processing. Coordination of these core executive processes resides within the psychology of the individual and is thought to contribute to planning, inductive reasoning, and flexible, strategic problem solving, all of which support children as they attempt to read the intentions of others and/or to achieve future-orientated goals (Welsh, Friedman, & Spieker, 2006) in social interaction and as they engage in activities to support academic learning.

Much of the intervention work to date is compensatory in nature and has focused on instructing older, school-aged children to reflect upon their use of strategies to improve memory performance. As discussed briefly at the beginning of this chapter, this line of research has yielded somewhat disappointing results, largely because successful recall of information cannot be attributed to simply learning a strategy. Rather, a child's performance on a memory task is the result of a combination of factors including the child's knowledge of the strategy, the child's ability to self-monitor the efficacy of the strategy, and whether the child is motivated to use the strategy (see Pressley, 1994, for a discussion).

Another approach that is preventative in orientation and that is consistent with both constructivist theories that attempt to explain working memory development and with social pragmatic views of language acquisition emphasizes scaffolding and self-scaffolding during social interaction and communication. Scaffolding is usually conceived as supportive behaviors used by an adult to facilitate the learning of a child so that the child is able to perform a task that, without support, would not be accomplished (Bruner, 1975; Cole, John-Steiner, Scribner, & Souberman, 1978). Bickhard (1992) proposes another form of scaffolding that is functional in nature and that promotes development in young children. In this view, scaffolding and self-scaffolding refer to the situation where a young child uses and must learn to use resources available to help him or her to reduce the cognitive (or in this case, working memory) demands of a problem for the sake of solving a problem (Bickhard, 1992). Scaffolding in this sense is functional and occurs through the communicative activities of both the child and the adult with whom the child interacts. However, the goal of the scaffolding is not to improve communicative abilities per se but to improve the child's self-scaffolding to minimize working memory demands and to access the language tools necessary for social communication. When viewed from this perspective, the impact of working memory capacity constraints on children's learning is age- and situation-specific. Arguably, alterations in children's social and learning environments may serve to help the child learn about and engage in self-scaffolding, which in turn improves cognitive performance and reduces later negative academic and social outcomes. Although the idea that functional scaffolding can support children's development has garnered significant attention from theorists interested in infant and early child development, there are few studies in natural contexts to support the claim that this approach minimizes the long term effects of working memory capacity or other cognitive constraints on school-aged children's academic and social learning. For the moment, this theory remains untested and is an issue for further research.

SUMMARY

In this chapter, we highlighted current views on working memory, working memory development, and its relationship to learning disabilities:

• Historically, memory problems have been associated with depressed academic performance of children with learning disabilities relative to nondisabled peers.

• Children with learning disabilities can learn about a strategy and when to use it; however, this increase in strategy use does not typically improve performance on memory task to age-norms.

• Working memory is defined as a limited, attentional capacity that temporarily stores in the face of distraction of attention shifts.

• Working memory capacity constraints are associated with learning difficulties in reading, math, language, and attention.

• Pascal-Leone and Case provide two models of working memory development based on constructivism.

• Working memory may be used by infants as young as six months of age to solve deferred imitation tasks.

• Information processing models (i.e., Baddeley's model and connectionist accounts) have been used more often to describe the working memory system that underlies the academic achievement (across domains of reading, writing, mathematics) of children with learning disabilities.

• Working memory is associated with other executive systems such as inhibitory control and updating or monitoring of information.

• The phonological loop in Baddeley's model has been used extensively to describe the origins of reading and writing problems among children with learning disabilities.

• Children with learning disabilities have also been shown to have limitations in the executive component of working memory.

• Connectionist models of working memory describe working memory as a unitary executive system (i.e., without component systems as in Baddeley's model).

• Connectionist models have been used to describe brain activity of children and adults while performing working memory tasks.

• Two explanations of activation in the prefrontal cortex during performance on working memory tasks have been proposed.

• Training studies to support working memory development report results that, at best, are considered inconclusive.

• Further research is needed to explore ways to both prevent academic and social problems due to working memory limitations among young children and to compensate for working memory capacity constraints among older children and adolescents with learning disabilities.

REFERENCES

Baddeley, A.D. (1986). *Working memory*. Oxford: Clarendon.

Baddeley, A.D. (2000). The episodic buffer: A new component of working memory? *Trends in Cognitive Sciences*, 4:417–422.

Baddeley, A.D. (2003). Working memory: Looking back and looking forward. *Nature Reviews*, 4(10), 829–839.

Baddeley, A.D., & Hitch, G.J. (1974). In G.A. Bower (Ed.), *Recent Advances in Learning and Motivation* (pp. 47–89). New York: Academic Press.

Baddeley, A.D., & Logie, R.H. (1999). The multiple-component model. In A. Miyake & P. Shah (Eds.), *Models of working memory: Mechanisms of active maintenance and executive control* (pp. 28–61). Cambridge, England: Cambridge University Press.

Barrett, L. Feldman, Tugade, M., & Engle, R.W. (2004). Individual differences in working memory capacity and dual-process theories of the mind. *Psychological Bulletin*, 130(4), 553–573.

Bargh, J.A., & Ferguson, M.J. (2000). Beyond behaviorism: On the automaticity of higher mental processes. *Psychological Bulletin*, 126:925–945.

Bates, E. (1976). *Language and context: The acquisition of pragmatics*. New York: Academic Press.

Bauer, P.J., & Kleinknecht, E.E. (2002). To "ape" or to emulate? Young children's use of both strategies in a single study. *Developmental Science*, 5(1), 18–20.

Bell, M., & Wolfe, C.D. (2007). Changes in brain functioning from infancy to early childhood: Evidence from EEG power and coherence during working memory tasks. *Developmental Neuropsychology*, 31(1), 21–38.

Bell, M., & Fox, N.A. (1992). The relations between frontal brain electrical activity and cognitive development during infancy. *Child Development*, 63:1142–1163.

Berninger, V.W., Abott, R.D., Thomson, J., Wagner, R., Swanson, H.L., Wijsman, E.M., & Raskind, W. (2006). Modeling phonological core deficits within a working memory architecture in children and adults with developmental dyslexia. *Scientific Studies of Reading*, 10(2), 165–198.

Bickhard, M.H. (1992). Scaffolding and self-scaffolding: Central aspects of development. In L.T. Winegar & J. Valsiner (Eds.), *Children's development within social context* (pp. 33–52). New Jersey: Lawrence Erlbaum.

Brown, G.D., & Hulme, C. (1992). Cognitive psychology and second language processing: The role of short term memory.

Bruner, J.S. (1975). The ontogenesis of speech acts. *Journal of Child Language*, 2:1–19.

Budson, A.E., & Price, B.H. (2005). Memory dysfunction. *The New England Journal of Medicine*, 352(7), 692–699.

Cantor, J., & Engle, R.W. (1993). Working memory capacity as long-term memory activation: An individual differences approach. *Journal of Experimental Psychology: Learning, Memory, and Cognition*, 19:1101–1114.

Cantor, J., Engle, R.W., & Hamilton, G. (1992). Short-term memory, working memory and verbal abilities: How do they relate? *Intelligence*, 15:229–246.

Carlson, S.M., Moses, L., & Breton, C. (2002). How specific is the relation between executive function and theory of mind? Contributions of inhibitory control and working memory. *Infant and Child Development*, 11:73–92.

Carpendale, J.I.M., & Lewis, C. (2004). Constructing an understanding of mind: The development of children's social understanding within social interaction. *Behavioral and Brain Sciences*, 27(1), 79–151.

Case, R. (1972). Validation of a neo-Piagetian capacity construct. *Journal of Experimental Child Psychology*, 14:287–302.

Case, R. (1985). *Intellectual development: Birth to adulthood*. New York: Academic Press.

Case, R. (1995). Capacity-based explanations of working memory growth: A brief history and reevaluation. In F.E. Weinert & W. Schneider (Eds.), *Memory performances and competencies: Issues in growth and development* (pp. 23–44). Mahwah, NJ: Lawrence Erlbaum.

Case, R., Kurland, D.M., & Goldberg, J. (1982). Operational efficiency and the growth of short-term memory span. *Journal of Experimental Child Psychology*, 33:386–404.

Chapman, S.B., Gamino, J.F., Cook, L.G., Hanten, G., Li, X., & Levin, H.S. (2006). Impaired discourse gist and working memory in children after brain injury. *Brain and Language*, 97:178–188.

Chiappe, P., Hasher, L., & Siegel, L.S. (2000). Working memory, inhibitory control, and reading disability. *Memory and Cognition*, 28(1), 8–17.

Cole, M., John-Steiner, V., Scribner, S., & Souberman, E. (1978). In L.S. Vygotsky (Ed.). *Mind in society: The development of higher psychological processes*. Oxford: Harvard University Press.

Collie, R., & Hayne, H. (1999). Deferred imitation by 6- and 9-month-old infants: More evidence for declarative memory. *Developmental Psychobiology*, 35(2), 83–90.

Conway, A.R., Kane, M.J., Bunting, M.F., Hambrick, D.Z., Wilhelm, O., & Engle, R.W. (2005). Working memory span tasks: A methodological review and user's guide. *Psychonomic Bulletin & Review*, 12(5), 769–786.

Crawford, S., Channon, S., & Robertson, M.M. (2005). Tourette's syndrome: Performance on tests of behavioral inhibition, working memory and gambling. *Journal of Child Psychology and Psychiatry*, 46(12), 1327–1336.

De Ribaupierre, A., & Bailleux, C. (2000). The development of working memory: Further note on the comparability of two models of working memory. *Journal of Experimental Child Psychology*, 77:110–127.

Diamond, A. (1991). Neuropsychological insights into the meaning of object concept development. In S. Carey & R. Gelman (Eds.), *The epigenesis of mind: Essays on biology and cognition* (pp. 67–110). Hillsdale, NJ: Lawrence Erlbaum.

Diamond, A., Kirkham, N., & Amso, D. (2002). Conditions under which young children can hold two rules in mind and inhibit a prepotent response. *Developmental Psychology*, 38:352–362.

Engle, R. (2002). Working memory capacity as executive function. *Current Directions in Psychological Science*, 11:19–23.

Fayne, H. (1981). A comparison of learning disabled adolescents with normal learners on an anaphoric pronominal reference task. *Journal of Learning Disabilities*, 14:597–599.

Foss, D.J., & Cairns, H.S. (1970). Some effects of memory limitation upon sentence comprehension and recall. *Journal of Verbal Learning and Verbal Behavior*, 9(5), 541–547.

Frith, C.D., & Frith, U. (1999). Interacting minds—A biological basis. *Science*, 286:1692–1695.

Gathercole, S.E., & Alloway, T.P. (2006). Practitioner review: Short-term and working memory impairments in neurodevelopmental Disorders: Diagnosis and remedial support. *Journal of Child Psychology and Psychiatry*, 47(1), 4–15.

Gathercole, S.E., Pickering, S.J., Ambridge, B., & Wearing, H. (2004). The structure of working memory from 4 to 15 years of age. *Developmental Psychology*, 40(2), 177–190.

Gathercole, S.E., Tiffany, C., Briscoe, J., & Thorn, A., ALSPAC team. (2005). Developmental consequences of poor phonological short-term memory function in childhood: A longitudinal study. *Journal of Child Psychology and Psychiatry*, 46(6), 598–611.

Geary, D.C., Hoard, M.K., Bryd-Craven, J., Nugent, L., & Numtee, C. (2007). Cognitive mechanisms underlying achievement deficits in children with mathematical learning disability. *Child Development*, 78(4), 1343–1359.

Gerstadt, C.L., Hong, Y., & Diamond, A. (1994). The relationship between cognition and action: Performance of children 3½ to 7 years old on a Stroop-like day-night test. *Cognition*, 53(2), 129–153.

Goldman-Rakic, P.S. (1987). Circuitry of primate prefrontal cortex and regulation of behaviour by representational memory. In F. Plum (Ed.), *Handbook of physiology, the nervous system, higher functions of the brain*: Vol. 5 (pp. 373–417). Bethesda, MD: American Physiological Society.

Goswami, U. (2006). Neuroscience and education: From research to practice? *Nature Reviews Neuroscience*, p. 2.

Greenfield, P.A., Keller, H., Fuligni, A., & Maynard, A. (2002). Cultural pathways through universal development. *Annual Review of Psychology*, 54:461–490.

Hanauer, J.B., & Brooks, P.J. (2005). Contributions of response set and semantic relatedness to cross-modal Stroop-like picture-word interference in children and adults. *Journal of Experimental Child Psychology*, 90:21–47.

Heimann, M., Strid, K., Smith, L., Tjus, T., Ulvund, S.E., & Meltzoff, A.N. (2006). Exploring the relation between memory, gestural communication, and the emergence of language in infancy: A longitudinal study. *Infant and Child Development*, 15:233–249.

Herbert, J., Gross, J., & Hayne, H. (2006). Age-related changes in deferred imitation between 6 and 9 months of age. *Infant Behavior & Development*, 29(1), 136–139.

Hoskyn, M.J. (2004). Working memory and emergent writing: What develops? Paper presented at American Psychological Association Annual Conference, Honolulu, Hawaii. Working memory and emergent writing: What develops?

Hoskyn, M.J., & Tzoneva, I. (2006). Mathematical abilities of children in kindergarten: The role of working memory. Paper presented at the American Psychological Association 114th Annual Conference, New Orleans, LA.

Hoskyn, M.J., Tzoneva, I., & Yeung, P. (2004). Working memory development in preschool-aged children. Paper presented at: International Conference on Executive Function and Socialization, Vancouver, B.C.

Just, M., & Carpenter, P.A. (1992). A capacity theory of comprehension differences in working memory. *Psychological Review*, 99:122–149.

Kail, Robert (1997). Phonological skill and articulation time independently contribute to the development of memory span. *Journal of Experimental Child Psychology*, 67:57–68.

Kaldy, Z., & Sigala, N. (2004). The neural mechanisms of object working memory: What is where in the infant brain? *Neuroscience and Biobehavioral Reviews*, 28:113–121.

Keller, H. (2003). Socialization for competence. *Human Development*, 46:288–311.

Klingberg, T. (2006). Development of a superior frontal-interparietal network for visuo-spatial working memory. *Neuropsychologia*, 44:2171–2177.

Klingberg, T., Forssberg, H., & Westerberg, H. (2002). Increased brain activity in frontal and parietal cortex underlies the development of visuospatial working memory capacity during childhood. *Journal of Cognitive Neuroscience*, 14(1), 1–10.

Knight-Arest, I. (1984). Communicative effectiveness of learning disabled and normally achieving 10–13 year old boys. *Learning Disability Quarterly*, 7:237–245.

Leung, H., Gore, J.C., & Goldman-Rakic, P. (2005). Differential Anterior Prefrontal Activation during the Recognition Stage of a Spatial Working Memory Task. *Cortex*, 15(11), 1742–1749.

Liszkowski, U., Carpenter, M., Henning, A., Striano, T., & Tomasello, M. (2004). Twelve-month-olds point to share attention and interest. *Developmental Science*, 7(3), 297–307.

Mecklinger, A., Bosch, V., Gruenwald, C., Bentin, S., & von Cramon, D.Y. (2000). What have klingon letters and faces have in common? An fMRI study on content-specific working memory systems. *Human Brain Mapping*, 11:146–161.

Meltzoff, A.N. (1995). Understanding the intentions of others: Re-enactment of intended acts by 18-month-old children. *Developmental Psychology*, 31:838–850.

Munakata, Y. (2004). Computational cognitive neuroscience of early memory development. *Developmental Review*, 24:133–153.

Nelson, C.A., Monk, C.S., Lin, J., Carver, L.J., Thomas, K.M., & Truwit, C.L. (2000). Functional neuroanatomy of spatial working memory in children. *Developmental Psychology*, 36:109–116.

Olesen, P.J., Macoveanu, J., Tegnér, J., & Kingberg, T. (2007). Brain activity related to working memory in children in adults. *Cerebral Cortex*, 17(5), 1047–1054.

Olesen, P.J., Westerberg, H., & Kingberg, T. (2004). Increased prefrontal and parietal activity after training of working memory. *Nature Neuroscience*, 7(1), 75–79.

O'Reilly, R.C., Braver, T.S., & Cohen, J.D. (1999). A biologically based computational model of working memory. In A. Miyake & P. Shah (Eds.), *Models of working memory: Mechanisms of active maintenance and executive control* (pp. 375–411). New York: Cambridge University Press.

Pascual-Leone, J. (1987). Organismic processes for neo-Piagetian theories: A dialectical causal account of cognitive development. *International Journal of Psychology*, 22:531–570.

Pascual-Leone, J. (1989). An organismic process model of Witkin's field-dependence-independence. In T. Globerson & T. Zelniker (Eds.), *Cognitive style and cognitive development* (pp. 36–70). Norwood, NJ: Ablex.

Pascual-Leone, J., & Ijaz, I. (1989). Mental capacity testing as a form of intellectual-developmental assessment. In R.J. Samuda, S.L. Kong, J. Cummins, J. Pascual-Leone, & J. Lewis (Eds.), *Assessment and placement of minority students* (pp. 143–171). Toronto: C. J. Hogrefe.

Piaget, J. (1962). *Play, dreams, and imitation in childhood*. New York: Norton.

Posner, M.I., & Rothbart, M.K. (2005). Influencing brain networks: implications for education. *Trends in Cognitive Sciences*, 9(3), 99–103.

Pushina, N.N., Orekhova, E.V., & Stroganova, T.A. (2005). Age-related and individual differences in the performance of a delayed response task (the A-not-B task) in infant twins aged 7–12 months. *Neuroscience and Behavioral Physiology*, 35(5), 481–491.

Pressley, M. (1994). Embracing the complexity of individual differences in cognition: Studying good information processing and how it might develop. *Learning and Individual Differences*, 6:259–284.

Rainer, G., & Miller, E.K. (2002). Timecourse of object-related neural activity in the primate prefrontal cortex during a short-term memory task. *European Journal of Neuroscience*, 15 (7), 1244–1254.

Rennie, D., Bull, R., & Diamond, A. (2004). Executive Functioning in Preschoolers: Reducing the Inhibitory Demands of the Dimensional Change Card Sort Task. *Developmental Neuropsychology*, 26(1), 423–443.

Reznick, J.S., Morrow, J.D., Goldman, B.D., & Snyder, J. (2004). The onset of working memory in infants. *Infancy*, 6(1), 145–154.

Roodenrys, S., Hulme, C., & Brown, G. (1993). The development of short term memory span: Separable effects of speech rate and long-term memory. *Journal of Experimental Child Psychology*, 56:431–442.

Rothbart, M.K., Posner, M.I., & Kieras, J. (2006). Temperament, attention and the development of self-regulation. In K. McCartney & D. Phillips (Eds.), *Handbook of early childhood development* (pp. 167–187). New York: Blackwell.

Rueda, M.R., Posner, M.I., & Rothbart, M. (2005). The development of executive attention: Contributions to the emergence of self-regulation. *Developmental Neuropsychology*, 28(2), 573–594.

Scruggs, T.E., & Mastropieri, M.A. (2000). The effectiveness of mnemonic instruction for students with learning and behavior problems: An update and research supported thesis. *Journal of Behavioral Education*, 10:163–173.

Simpson, A., & Riggs, K. (2005). Inhibitory and working memory demands of the day-night task in children. *British Journal of Developmental Psychology*, 23:471–486.

Stredron, J.M., Sahni, S.D., & Munakata, Y. (2005). Common mechanisms for working memory and attention: The case of perseveration with visible solutions. *Journal of Cognitive Neuroscience*, 17(4), 623–631.

Swanson, H. Lee (1999). What develops in working memory? A lifespan perspective. *Developmental Psychology*, 35(4), 986–1000.

Swanson, H.L., & Ashbaker, M.H. (2000). Working memory, short term memory, speech rate, word recognition, and reading comprehension in learning disabled readers: Does the executive system have a role? *Intelligence*, 28(1), 1–30.

Swanson, H.L., & Cochran, K. (1991). Learning disabilities, distinctive encoding and hemispheric resources. *Brain and Language*, 40:202–230.

Swanson, H.L., Cooney, J.B., & McNamara, J.K. (2004). Learning disabilities and memory. In B. Wong (Ed.), *Learning about Learning Disabilities* (3rd ed.), pp. 41–92. San Diego, CA: Academic Press.

Swanson, H.L., & Kim, K. (2007). Working memory, short-term memory, and naming speed as predictors of children's mathematical performance. *Intelligence*, 35:151–168.

Swanson, H.L., & Sache-Lee, C. (2001). A subgroup analysis of working memory in children with reading disabilities: Domain-general or domain-specific deficiency? *Journal of Learning Disabilities*, 34:249–263.

Tomasello, M. (1998). Emulation learning and cultural learning. *Behavioural and Brain Sciences*, 21:703–704.

Tomasello, M. (2003). *Constructing a language: A usage-based theory of language acquisition*. Cambridge, MA: Harvard University Press.

Turner, M.L., & Engle, R.W. (1989). Is working memory capacity task dependent? *Journal of Memory and Language*, 28:127–154.

Welsh, M.C., Friedman, S., & Spieker, S.J. (2006). Executive functions in developing children: Current conceptualizations and questions for the future. In K. McCartney & D. Phillips (Eds.), *Handbook of early childhood development* (pp 167–187). New York: Blackwell.

Wiig, E., & Semel, E. (1984). *Language assessment and intervention for the learning disabled* (2nd ed.). New York: Merrill/Macmillan.

Wilson, F.A.W., O'Scalaidhe, S.P., & Goldman-Rakic, P.S. (1993). Dissociation of object and spatial processing domains in primate prefrontal cortex. *Science*, 260:1955–1958.

Wong, B.Y.L., & Jones, W. (1982). Increasing metacomprehension of learning disabled and normal achieving students through self-questioning training. *Learning Disabilitiy Quarterly*, 5:228–240.

Woodward, A. (1998). Infants selectively encode the goal object of an actor's reach. *Cognition*, 69:1–34.

Woodward, A., & Sommerville, J.A. (2000). Twelve-month-old infants interpret action in context. *Psychological Science*, 11(1), 73–77.

Zelazo, P.D., Frye, D., & Rapus, T. (1996). An age-related dissociation between knowing rules and using them. *Cognitive Development*, 11:37–63.

4

SOCIAL DIMENSIONS

OF LEARNING DISABILITIES

INTRODUCTION

This chapter summarizes contemporary research in the social dimensions of learning disabilities. The foci taken by contemporary researchers in this area indicate new directions of research. Hence, we deem it more instructive and refreshing to focus on their achievements than recapturing previous work. This is, however, not to be construed as lack of appreciation and valuing of past research. On the contrary, it bears reminding that the present research achievements build on what the pat research has so richly achieved.

THE BEGINNING

The social relational problems in students with learning disabilities came to the fore in the learning disabilities field and caught the attention of researchers in 1974 with the publication of Tanis Bryan's landmark study on the social unpopularity of children with learning disabilities. She asked the children in grades 3, 4, and 5 to nominate classmates who were and were not desired as friends, neighbors in classroom seating, and guests at a party. Additional questions included "Who is handsome or pretty?" and "Who finds it hard to sit still in class?" Bryan found that female children with learning disabilities and white children with learning disabilities were most unpopular. In a follow-up study, Bryan (1976) replicated her earlier findings. In this study, the children with learning disabilities were attending new classes and had mostly new classmates. Nevertheless, Bryan found that the children with learning disabilities continued to get fewer positive and more negative nominations.

With her 1974 study, Bryan heralded research in the social relational problems in children/adolescents with learning disabilities and provided leadership in founding the research area of social dimensions of learning disabilities. The period of 1975–1986 could be considered the heyday of research in that area. The research auspiciously began with Bryan's (1974) study that upstaged the traditional areas of research into neurological problems and cognitive processing deficits (Donahue & Wong, 2002). But why did it take Bryan's 1974 study a good eight years after the initial start of the learning disabilities field to launch this research area?

The answer lies in the fact that in 1962 professionals and parents involved with children with learning disabilities were struggling to establish learning disabilities as a legitimate category in special education, distinct from extant categories such as mental retardation. Success here would guarantee funding for special education services for these children. Since the primary characteristic of children with learning disabilities is their inexplicable but real and substantial difficulties in learning to read despite apparent normalcy in sensory functions and measured intelligence, it was and remains understandable that their advocates focused on these children's learning/academic problems in the early years of the field. Moreover, there were pressing concerns on developing appropriate assessments and remedial approaches for children with learning disabilities. It should, however, not be construed that teachers were unaware of social relational problems in children with learning disabilities.

Bryan's trail-blazing research lifted the floodgate of research studies in the area of social relational problems of children with learning disabilities. Eager to explore causes for the social unpopularity of children with learning disabilities, researchers in the early 1980s to the mid-1990s investigated a variety of areas. These included social perception, role/perspective-taking, comprehension of social mores, social problem solving, comprehension of nonverbal cues, lack of motivation or social discrimination, and communication problems (Wong, 1996). Results of the research indicated that none of these problems provided a complete explanation to the social unpopularity of children with learning disabilities. From the mid-1990s to the time of this writing, research on social dimensions of learning disabilities appears to have been overshadowed by the rise of early intervention research and the conceptual debate and research on response-to-instruction as an alternative to the IQ-performance discrepancy formula in defining and diagnosing learning disabilities. Essentially early intervention research is a natural sequence to the ample research pinpointing the critical role of phoneme awareness in children's learning to read. Innumerable early intervention research studies that provided training packages centered on phoneme awareness had graced the pages of *Journal of Learning Disabilities* and

Learning Disabilities Research and Practice from the mid-1990s to the start of the twenty-first century. In turn, as part of the push toward getting teachers to use research-based instruction, early intervention research has turned beneficially into practice. Researchers' embrace for having research-based instruction in schools is one factor that spawned the notion of using response-to-instruction as an alternative approach to diagnosing and defining learning disabilities. The twenty-first century opened with heated debates on this notion in learning disabilities (see special issue in *Journal of Learning Disabilities*, 2003). All of this: early intervention research, research-based instruction, and response-to-instruction have taken center stage in the learning disabilities field. Hence, not surprisingly, interest in research on social dimensions of learning disabilities has taken a back seat as evidenced in the marked decrease in the amount of publications on the topic. Nevertheless, there is a core of researchers dedicated to uncovering the causes for the social unpopularity of children/adolescents with learning disabilities. Informed of the findings of prior research these researchers no longer seek unitary factors as answers to the question. Rather, they acknowledge contextual and transactional variables in the social relational problems of children and adolescents with learning disabilities, forge new directions in research, and seek new theoretical frameworks to guide their research and interpret their data. Specifically, they look to friendship formation in students with learning disabilities: peer relations (number of friends, number of reciprocal or mutual friends), quality of friendships, the nature of the friends of children and adolescents with learning disabilities, and family support for answers to the question of unpopularity among these children and adolescents. But they are also mindful of the need to research the consequences of being unpopular: the loneliness of children with learning disabilities. Moreover, they explore areas that may enhance understanding and ameliorate social relational problems of children and adolescents with learning disabilities such as social cognition and self-understanding (Wong & Donahue, 2002). These researchers provide the bright lights of contemporary research in the social dimensions of learning disabilities, and summarizing their research is the focus of this chapter.

PEER STATUS

The extent to which children are liked or disliked by peer groups that they meet regularly—for example, classmates—defines peer status (Schneider, Wiener, & Murphy, 1994). Children may be judged in terms of the extent to which they are liked or disliked. Using nomination sociometrics in which children are asked to nominate a designated number of children whom they either like or dislike, researchers assess affective evaluations. Typically researchers find children who receive many positive nominations are the popular ones and children who receive many negative nominations are the unpopular ones. However, in between these two categories are children who receive very few nominations in both categories. These children are called *neglected* (Coie, Dodge, & Coppotelli, 1982).

Peer status in children with learning disabilities constitutes an important area of research because children who are rejected are at risk for various disorders in childhood and adulthood (Bagwell, Newcomb, & Bukowski, 1998). A prominent and sustained finding is that children and adolescents with learning disabilities are more likely to be socially rejected or neglected by peers than those without learning disabilities.

STABILITY OF PEER STATUS

Two studies found a decline in the peer status of children with learning disabilities over the course of a school year. Specifically, many children with learning disabilities who enjoyed average social status at the start of the school year became neglected or rejected by the end of the school year (Kuhne & Wiener, 2000; Vaughn, Elbaum, & Schumm, 1996). Peer rejection of children with learning disabilities had been reported to be high in studies of children in contained special education classes (Wiener, Harris, & Shirer, 1990), of children in mainstreamed classrooms who are pulled out for resource room services (Stone & La Greca, 1990), and of children in full inclusion classes (Vaughn, Elbaum, & Schumm, 1996). Peer neglect is most commonly found for children with learning disabilities in self-contained special education classes (Coben & Zigmond, 1986; Wiener, Harris, & Duval, 1993). Last, Wiener and Tardiff (2004) found that peer acceptance is lower in children with learning disabilities who receive special education help in a resource room than those who receive instruction from a special education teacher in the regular education classroom.

The studies summarized in the preceding paragraph examined the peer status of children with learning disabilities for the duration of one school year. More recently, Estell, Jones, Pearl, Van Acker, Farmer, and Rodkin (in press) investigated peer status of children with learning disabilities when they were in the third grade to the sixth grade. They also assessed peer status using multiple measures, thereby obtaining more comprehensive data and providing a broader picture of peer status of children with learning disabilities.

Estell et al.'s (in press) study reported the following findings. First, children with learning disabilities joined peer groups at a comparable rate as the children without learning disabilities. Second, there was no difference between the within-group status of children with and without learning disabilities. Third, children with learning disabilities joined peer groups of similar size and status in the classroom social network as the children without learning disabilities. Fourth, and this is a key finding, children with learning disabilities had inferior status among the peers in the classroom.

To elaborate, children with learning disabilities had a lower number of best-friend nominations than their nondisabled classmates, were marginally lower in peer-nominated popularity, and in social preference were rated as much lower. (Rating of popularity was done by the children nominating three children who were "liked by a lot of kids in the class." Social preference was obtained by asking the child to nominate up to three children from the class list whom they liked the best and three whom they liked the least.) More important, the differences regarding lower peer status among the children with learning disabilities were found at the start of the study when they were in the spring semester of grade 3 and persisted to the fall of grade 6! This means that despite having membership in peer groups, the children with learning disabilities nevertheless consistently enjoyed lower peer status across later childhood from grade 3 to 6 in inclusive classrooms.

On the surface, Estell et al.'s (in press) study appears to question the effect of inclusive classrooms on promoting social relations or friendship formation between children with and without learning disabilities. But this would be an invalid conclusion because (1) there was no comparison condition where the children with learning disabilities were not in an inclusive setting, and (2) the children's social (peer) status did not deteriorate across the grades. They simply maintained similar lower peer status. Thus, one may argue that being in inclusive classrooms might have prevented further lowering or deterioration of the peer status among the children with learning disabilities. Estell et al.'s study points to the need for teachers' active involvement in creating a social environment of acceptance of diversity among the children and to promote friendship formation among children with learning disabilities and with disabilities other than learning disabilities and children without disabilities.

FRIENDSHIP

Bukowski and Hoza (1989) defined friendship as the relationship between two persons who possess positive feelings towards each other.

Number of Friends. If one does not consider whether the friend named or nominated by the child with learning disabilities reciprocates the friendship, then there is no difference between the number of friends reported by children with learning disabilities and children without learning disabilities. The picture changes when one takes into account the reciprocity of the relationship. Here we find conflicting research data. On the one hand, several studies found no difference in the number of reciprocal friendships between children with and without learning disabilities (Bear, Juvonen, & McInerney, 1993; Vaughn & Haager, 1994; Vaughn et al., 1993). On the other hand, there are studies that found a difference. Wiener & Sunohara (1998) found that children with learning disabilities had fewer mutual or reciprocal friends. Vaughn et al. (1996) found that in the fall, 26 percent of elementary children with learning disabilities had reciprocal friendships compared to 63 percent of average/high-achieving students. Even though the percentage of children with learning disabilities with reciprocal friendships more than doubled in the following spring of the school year, they still had fewer reciprocal friendships than the average/high achievers (53 percent compared to 72 percent).

Nature of Their Friends.   Who are these individuals that children and adolescents with learning disabilities call friends? The large majority of friends of children with learning disabilities are same-sex peers. Wiener and Schneider (2002) found that they tend to have friends who are two or more years younger than themselves than children without learning disabilities. Similarly, Wiener (2002) found that children with learning disabilities named younger children as friends more often than did children without learning disabilities, despite most of the friends named by them were same-aged. However, one study found that children with learning disabilities had friends a year older (Fleming, Cook, & Stone, 2002).

Also, according to their teachers, children with learning disabilities more often have friends who also have learning problems than do children without learning disabilities. However, these friends do not necessarily have learning disabilities. There are two possible explanations for the choice of such children as friends among children with learning disabilities. First, children may choose friends who are like themselves, with problems in academic achievement. Second, they may choose friends who are in the same instructional grouping as themselves.

Stability of Friendship.   Consistently, research findings indicate that children with learning disabilities had less stable friendships than children without learning disabilities. Tur-Kaspa, Margalit, and Most (1999) found that the friendships of children with learning disabilities deteriorated over the school year. Specifically, the researchers found that more students with learning disabilities had no reciprocal or mutual friends at the start of the school year compared to their non-learning-disabled peers (31 percent of student with learning disabilities versus 20 percent of students without learning disabilities). By spring, the difference increased to 39 percent of children with learning disabilities with no mutual friends versus 17 percent of children without learning disabilities. More disturbing is the finding that by the end of the school year, more children with learning disabilities had developed a mutual hostility toward a classmate! To the question of "Which of the boys and girls in your class would you least like to have as your friend?," 56 percent of children with learning disabilities named someone who also reciprocated (who named *them*) compared to 27 percent of the nondisabled classmates.

Quality of Friendship.   Friends serve important functions. Specifically, friends validate one another—for example, "You have a real strong kick in your swimming!" They comfort one another in distress, such as when adolescent girls surround and support the girl who's been dumped by her boyfriend. Friends share secrets. They protect one another and are loyal, and never betray one another.

Researchers have found the quality of friendships in children and adolescents with learning disabilities to be poor compared to the friendships of children and adolescents without learning disabilities. Wiener (2002) studied friendship in dyads of children: 15 of these dyads had one member with learning disabilities and the other without learning disabilities. Wiener found that compared to children without learning disabilities, the children with learning disabilities felt they were less validated by their friends. The children with learning disabilities also had more conflicts with their best friends. For example, they reported that they and their best friends got mad at each other a lot, argued a lot, and fought and annoyed one another a lot. At the same time, these children with learning disabilities reported more trouble reconciling with their best friends after a spat—in other words, they had more difficulties in repairing relationship. Moreover, compared to dyads where both members did not have learning disabilities, Wiener found that the child with learning disabilities in dyads with one child being learning disabled "was more likely to report that their best friend (in the dyad) was less likely to provide companionship at school." School companionship was assessed by statements such as "My friend and I always sit together at lunch ... play together at recess ... pick each other as partners ... help each other with schoolwork." Wiener also found that the child with learning disabilities in dyads where one member had learning disabilities had a higher probability of reporting more disclosures than did dyads without a member with learning disabilities. Disclosure was assessed by items or statements such as "My friend and I always tell each other about our problems" or "I can think of lots of secrets my friend and I have told each other." These dyad members with learning disabilities showed a tendency to report more disclosure, help and sharing, and trust and caring than did the member without learning disabilities in the same dyads. Help and sharing were assessed by items or statements such as "My friend and I help each other with chores or other things a lot" or "We do special favors for each other." In addition, there were items that could possibly be seen as involving a unidirectional relationship such as "When I'm having trouble figuring out something, I usually ask my friend for help and advice" or "My friend often helps me with things so I can get done quicker." Trust and caring items were "My friend would still like me even if all the other kids didn't like me" or "My friend cares about my feelings." Wiener (2002, p. 101) speculated on why the children with learning disabilities in the dyads with one member who had no learning disabilities and who was their best friend(s) would report higher disclosure, trust, and caring than their mutual best friends in the same dyads. She concluded that the children with learning disabilities were "engaged in wishful thinking." Hence, they distorted the reality of their friendships with their best friends.

Vaughn and Elbaum (1999) also found lower levels of intimacy and support for self-esteem in the friendships of students with learning disabilities than in the friendships of students without learning disabilities. Similarly, in Geishthardt and Munsch's (1996) study, students with learning disabilities reported having fewer friends to turn to for support in dealing with a stressful event than their normally achieving peers. Elementary children with learning disabilities were found to perceive their friendships to be of lower quality than children without learning disabilities. Sadly, although the quality of friendships of the children without learning dsiabilities increased through high school, the quality of friendships of the children with learning disabilities did not (Vaughn et al., 2001).

Research on parental perspectives on friendships in children and adolescents shows parents' insights, concerns, and efforts in problem solving in the friendship problems of their sons and daughters with learning disabilities. Wiener and Sunohara (1998) conducted telephone interviews of parents of 16 preadolescents and adolescents with learning disabilities who were receiving therapy at a government-funded mental health center for emotional social needs. Hence, the sample of preadolescents and adolescents with learning disabilities was not random. Consequently, the generalizability of the findings appear to be compromised.

Wiener and Sunohara (1998) asked the 16 parents seven questions:

1. How do you see Robert's friendships?
2. You indicated that _____, _____, and _____ were Robert's friends. Can you tell me about these relationships?
3. Robert also identified _____ as his friend, whereas you didn't. Can you tell us about Robert's relationship with _____?
4. What are your expectations regarding Robert's friendships?
5. Are you satisfied with Robert's friendships?
6. Who do you see as more concerned about Robert's friendships? You or him? Please explain.
7. How do you see your role and that of your spouse in the area of Robert's friendships? (Wiener & Sunohara, 1998, p. 244)

From the telephone interviews data, Wiener and Sunohara distilled seven themes. The first theme was about the discrepancy between how parents and children conceptualize friendship. Nine out of 16 parents said that at least one child who was identified as a friend by their children was not really a friend. These parents conversed about how their children did not understand what a *friend* really is: "He doesn't quite understand that a friend is someone that you talk to. Well, to me anyhow, a friend is someone you talk to on a regular basis, go out with on a regular basis. He thinks because he knows 20 different kids, they're all his friends." Clearly, the parents had a very clear and definite criterion of a friend: constant companionship beyond the context of school. When this companionship with particular acquaintances is absent, they disregarded these individuals as friends of their children.

The second theme centered on social immaturity. Seven of the parents considered their children socially immature on the basis that they choose friends who are much younger than themselves: "The friends he does have, generally, are younger than himself. His best friend at the moment is a little boy who lives next door, and he's two years and about five months younger than Billy. And he spends most of his time with him right now."

The third theme is social skills deficits. Thirteen parents think that their children's problems in peer relationships reflect social skills deficits. The parents pointed out that their children had difficulties initiating or maintaining conversations when they met someone they knew. Making small talk did not seem to be a social skill that they possessed: "You're friendly, and you know, you talk, and people listen, and you talk and you listen, and before you know it, you have a friend. But it's not that easy for a kid like Adam. When he feels very new, he just doesn't know how to connect, how to meet somebody. You know, 'Hi, how are you? What's your name? What school do you go to?' He doesn't know how to do that."

Another expression of social skills deficits appears to come from children with learning disabilities who inadvertently said things that were mean or inappropriate: "And you know how they (children with learning disabilities) kind of interact with their friends, strangely—they have strange reactions. He (child with learning disabilities) would walk up to somebody in his class and instead of saying, 'Hi, how are you?' he'd say 'Hi, you hate me, don't you?'" Two other parents found their children with learning disabilities to be domineering and self-centered: "She can be quite moody with a friend. I've seen it happen here. She'll want to do one thing and the friend won't and then she'll just put her back up and that's it and like 'OK, Mum, they might as well go home, if they don't want to do what I want to do.'"

Three of the parents attribute the inappropriate statements and behaviors of their children with learning disabilities to problems in reading social cues. Also, three of the children with learning disabilities had difficulties with self-control. They caused peer rejection because of their low frustration tolerance, a quick temper, and aggression.

The fourth theme is compatibility. Seven out of 16 parents reported that their children had at least one close mutual friend. Five of the parents accounted for this through compatibility in temperament and interests: "Adam and Bob are very much alike.... They're both stubborn, they both wanted to do things their way, which was great, and it gave them both a way of compromising or an opportunity to compromise, and they did it,

you know, it was terrific." But two parents accounted for compatibility arising from personality differences. One boy, Ian, is very academic, whereas
the other, Jeff, was not. Moreover, the mother of Jeff observed that the boys
had different personalities. So the boys' friendship really baffled Jeff's
mother: "So it's a very peculiar relationship to me, but they get along
famously. And I think Ian has a very calming effect on Jeff...." Similarly,
two parents were puzzled that non-LD children who were more able and
mature befriend their children with LD. The answer appears to lie in the fact
that the more able and mature children found the company of the children
with LD relaxing because the latter children were accepting and not threaten-
ing: "Well, I think Greg's very nonthreatening, very accepting, and very
loyal. He never says a bad word about anybody.... I think that he's just a
very safe friend in a lot of ways. He's a friend they can really relax with and
be themselves; they don't have to be on edge, or be competitive. So I think
for, especially for his friend Ralph, who's very competitive and finds himself
with gifted children and very athletic children, that it's actually quite a relief
to be with Greg. And he's said that, 'It's very relaxing to be with Greg.'"

Nine parents thought that the compatibility in a relationship arose from
the commonality of learning disabilities among the children: "I guess the
two of them, both with learning disabilities, just can relate to each other,
and they can bring out the best in both of them."

The fifth theme is satisfaction with relationships. Several parents indicated that they had to modify their expectations of their children's friendships. For example, five parents said it suffices for their children with
learning disabilities to have just one good friend or just to be included.
But the parents showed many varied concerns. These concerns included
their children with learning disabilities showed little interest in social relationships, their children's unhappiness and depression about their problems
in peer relationship, the potential vulnerability to bad company or exploita-
tion: "I have worries about what high school will be like. I also know that
children who are having difficulties who have learning disabilities sometimes
end up hanging around other children who are having difficulties, and they
won't necessarily be doing socially acceptable things. So I worry if she'll get
into the wrong crowd."

The sixth theme is barriers and facilitators. Mothers identified barriers
to friendship formation for their children with learning disabilities, such
as friends moving away, scarcity of children in their neighborhood, insufficient supervision at friends' homes that render visits difficult, or difficulties
in getting together with friends because the latter are too preoccupied with
responsibilities (Wiener & Sunohara, 1998, p. 249). Facilitators include
proximity such as friends being neighbors and special education classes that
could also act as barriers. Special education classes served as facilitators for
friendship formation when the skilled teacher fostered social relationships
and a sense of community that scaffold friendships. But special education

classes served as barriers to friendship formation when the children with learning disabilities had to be bused to a school away from the neighborhood where their friends attended a different school and distance made visiting their special education classmates difficult.

The last (seventh) theme concerns parents' role in facilitating the development and maintenance of the friendships of their children with learning disabilities. Thirteen mothers assumed an active role in encouraging their children to phone and visit their friends and talked of the need for emotional support. Six parents coached their children on how to interact with others in different social situations. Four mothers made their homes welcoming to other children so that their children with learning disabilities would have children to be friends with or "be included." Two parents reported trying to do fun things together as a family when their children had no friends to interact with. One father would take the son to the movies and play Nintendo with him: "It's really good that he's (the father) been like that because all those years when he (the son with learning disabilities) didn't have a friend, at all, he had a dad."

The perspectives of parents with children and preadolescents with learning disabilities (they were from 10 to 14 years old) in Wiener and Sunohara's (1998) study underscore the findings of researchers on the poor quality of friendships among children and adolescents with learning disabilities. Among adolescents with learning disabilities, the desire for friends and quality friendships may inadvertently lead to unprofitable ends. One parent, it is recalled, feared that when her daughter entered high school, she might come under the influence of bad company because of her need for friends.

Ruth Pearl (2002) and her research associates investigated the nature of the company of adolescents with learning disabilities. Pearl researched the hypothesis that adolescents with learning disabilities may be especially vulnerable to bad peer influence. She based the hypothesis on several reasons First, adolescents with learning disabilities crave being accepted because of their poor social/peer status and lack of friends. This immense need makes them liable to respond indiscriminately to friendly overtures. Second, they have substantial problems in social cognition, role-taking, and comprehension of implicit and ambiguous social cues. Third, they appear to have different experiences with the real world that render them less wary of deliberate deception and ploys engaged in by others to ensnare people for illegal ends. Fourth, they have linguistic and pragmatic problems that put them at a disadvantage in situations where they are led into mischief such as shoplifting.

In a series of experiments, Pearl and her research associates tested the hypothesis. Pearl, Bryan, and Herzog (1990) investigated expectations among high school students with and without learning disabilities regarding different situations in which one teenager attempted to involve or recruit another in misconduct such as shoplifting or stealing a car. The researchers were interested to find out if adolescents with learning disabilities would be as knowledgeable as adolescents without learning disabilities about how such a situation would evolve. Specifically, they focused on what the adolescents would expect the recruiter would say, what would ensue if the recruiter's request was accepted or refused, and what would motivate the adolescent to accept or refuse the request.

The results indicated that adolescents with learning disabilities differed from their nondisabled counterparts in three ways. (1) The adolescents with learning disabilities expected the recruiter to couch the request to engage in misconduct in a straightforward, exhortative way. In contrast, adolescents without learning disabilities were more savvy in that they expected the recruiter to use persuasive ploys to entice them to join in the misconduct, such as "We'll have fun." They also expected the recruiter to minimize the negative aspects of the misconduct of, say, stealing a car: "We'll bring the car right back." (2) The adolescents with learning disabilities were less likely to consider the consequences of the misconduct if they were to accept the request. They were more likely than adolescents without learning disabilities to be concerned that the recruiter would feel bad should they refuse the request. (3) They showed less insight regarding these situations and provided fewer alternative scenarios for potential consequences if the requests were accepted or refused.

These results were replicated in a follow-up study by Pearl and Bryan (1992) in which they controlled for oral language problems in adolescents with learning disabilities. Instead of asking them questions and having them respond orally in the previous study, Pearl and Bryan asked the participating adolescents with and without learning disabilities to choose as their responses one statement from two given statements.

Another study by Pearl, Bryan, Fallon, and Herzog (1991) investigated the detection of deception. Adolescents with and without learning disabilities listened to tape-recorded stories of interactions between two characters, with one character making a concluding statement per story. In some of these stories, the story content indicates that the concluding statement was deliberately deceptive. Pearl et al. (1991) found that adolescents with learning disabilities were much more naive than adolescents without learning disabilities when it came to detecting deception. Upon further data analyses, Pearl et al. were amazed to discover that the adolescents with learning disabilities did recognize the deception in the final statements of the manipulated stories, but despite this realization, they were more likely to think that the speaker was sincere and that the deception was not deliberate!

Last, Bryan, Werner, and Pearl (1982) investigated the willingness to conform to peer activities among junior high students with and without learning disabilities. The students were given a questionnaire that described various hypothetical situations in which they are pressed to join in activities by their friends, activities that they had no wish to join. The researchers predicted that adolescents with learning disabilities would be more willing to acquiesce than adolescents without learning disabilities because of their low social status and eagerness to win peer approval.

The results showed that although no between-groups differences were obtained in prosocial activities, adolescents with learning disabilities were more likely to agree to participate in situations involving misconduct. More disconcerting is the finding that adolescents with learning disabilities reported feeling less concerned when engaged in misconduct. A follow-up study by Bryan, Pearl, and Fallon (1989) replicated the findings here.

Clearly, this series of studies by Pearl and her associates on adolescents with learning disabilities showed how vulnerable they were to negative peer influence. They bear out the anxiety of the parents in Wiener and Sunohara's (1998) study. This particular parent understood the potential risk of falling into bad company in high school in her daughter with learning disabilities because of her low social status and friendless state. The susceptibility of students with learning disabilities to negative peer influence is coupled with their lack of concern for engaging in misconduct. Moreover, they showed more willingness to agree with friends' requests to become involved in misconduct. They also were more likely than adolescents without learning disabilities to expect negative feelings in the recruiter for refusing the latter's request to participate in misconduct.

Pearl (2002) interpreted the preceding findings to highlight what needs to be done for adolescents with learning disabilities. She suggests that many of these adolescents are not aware when they are being led astray. They seem to lack the knowledge and savvy astuteness that are shown by adolescents without learning disabilities in situations where they are being recruited for misconduct. Adolescents without learning disabilities realize the kind of language typically used when someone tries to entice them into misconduct, and they can successfully deflect such attempts. They also realize the negative consequences of being caught in misconduct. In short, adolescents without learning disabilities are more wary and judicious when confronted with temptation to participate in illegal activities such as stealing a car or shoplifting. They do not succumb readily to immediate gain or short-term pleasure. Of course, they do not have the pressure to agree to participate as the adolescents with learning disabilities possess out of low social status and eagerness to have friends. Pearl's alternate lens highlights what adolescents with learning disabilities need to learn.

SOCIAL COGNITIVE PROBLEMS

Part of the vulnerability to bad peer influence among adolescents with learning disabilities appears to stem from their social cognitive problems. This has been hinted at in the research of Pearl and her associates.

We now turn to the research on social cognitive problems in students with learning disabilities with the view of understanding why these problems may contribute to the social-relational problems in students with learning disabilities.

Why should we suspect social cognitive problems to contribute to the social-relational problems in students with learning disabilities? The answer is straightforward. Because social cognition is believed to mediate social behavior, researchers consider it reasonable to explore social cognitive problems in students with learning disabilities so as to understanding their social-relational problems. Although there have been numerous studies on social cognitive problems in students with learning disabilities and all reported findings of such problems, they examined only single aspects of social cognition. They had not researched the multiple aspects of social cognition (Tur-Kaspa, 2002). With the advance of Dodge's (1986) model, researchers are provided with a model that assesses social cognition and social problem solving in a substantially more comprehensive manner.

Tur-Kaspa and Bryan (1994) used Dodge's (1986) model to investigate social cognitive skills in students with learning disabilities, low-achieving (LA) students, and above-average (AA) students from the third, fourth, seventh, and eighth grades. Dodge's (1986) model assesses social skills in a very comprehensive way. According to Dodge's model, children come to any social situation or task with response capabilities that are biologically determined. As well, the children bring with them memories of past experiences and goals. Children process social cues from the environment, and how they respond to them corresponds to how they process them. In Dodge's model, the children process social cues sequentially. Hence, each step in the model is an essential part of competent social responding, but the children may not act on them consciously.

In Dodge's (1986) model, the first step in social information processing involves the child's encoding the social cues in the environment. Hence, the child must acquire skills of attending to appropriate social cues, devises ways of organizing or chunking information, and uses rehearsal and mnemonic strategies to store the information. The second step is to form a mental representation of the social cues once they have been encoded. Put differently, the child must understand the social cues and interpret them accurately. To do so, the child integrates the social cues with prior experiences. The third step involves the child in a search for appropriate social response. After the child has encoded and understood the social cues, she begins to generate possible behavioral responses to the social cues. In the fourth step, ideally the child learns to evaluate the likely outcome of each response generated and in particular to estimate the likelihood of positive outcomes while simultaneously considering the environmental context and his own social behavioral capabilities. This processing step is a response decision step. In the fifth or last step, the child has chosen a response and proceeds to enact it. This last step also involves the child's self-monitoring the effects of her behavioral response to the social cues in the environment and self-regulating it.

Using five vignettes created by themselves, Tur-Kaspa and Bryan (1994) assessed the students with learning disabilities, the LA students, and AA students in the five steps of Dodge's (1986) model. They also measured the students' expressive and receptive vocabulary and teachers' ratings of students' social competence and school adjustment.

The researchers found several interesting differences among the students with learning disabilities, LA students, and AA students. But we focus only on findings that appear to shed some light on the vulnerability to bad peer influence in students with learning disabilities. Specifically, Tur-Kaspa and Bryan (1994) found that students with learning disabilities were less competent at encoding social cues than LA and AA students. Second, students with learning disabilities chose self-generated solutions of a poorer quality to resolve problems in social situations than did LA and AA students. In sum, students with learning disabilities in Tur-Kaspa and Bryan's (1944) study were socially incompetent in the first and fourth stages of Dodge's (1986) model.

The preceding findings enable us to understand, at least in part, why adolescents with learning disabilities appeared to be so vulnerable to bad peer influence in the research of Pearl and her associates. If adolescents with learning disabilities were deficient in encoding social cues accurately, and if they were substantially less competent in choosing good self-generated solutions to problematic social situations, then the possibility would be high for them to be duped by bad peers into misconducts such as stealing a car or shoplifting.

One important note is that the findings in Tur-Kaspa and Bryan (1994) cannot be accounted for by low academic status in the students with learning disabilities or by language problems. The researchers found that the students with learning disabilities were academically significantly poorer than the LA students. Moreover, there were no differences in expressive or receptive vocabulary between the students with learning disabilities and the LA students. But the researchers cautioned that they focused only on semantics and not pragmatics. Thus, there may be differences in pragmatics between students with and without learning disabilities.

Meadan and Halle (2004) ran an exploratory study on whether children with learning disabilities who varied in social status would have different social perceptions of the same events. Accordingly, they found three children with learning disabilities who enjoyed high social status and three with low social status. All of them were boys with learning disabilities. Each child viewed a six-minute videotape of two children (one boy and one girl) putting together a puzzle and was interviewed three times. In the first interview, the child with learning disabilities was asked after viewing the videotape to talk about what he saw. He was asked a broad, open-ended question: "Tell me everything you remember about this videotape we saw." This was followed by questions that target more information about what the child saw in the videotape such as "Who did what?" Moreover, questions were posed to elicit the child's interpretations of what was seen—for example, "How did they (the boy and girl in the videotape) feel? How do you know they felt that way?" The child was also asked to talk about his experiences in similar contexts. After an interval of a week to two weeks, a second interview was held. In the second interview, the child with learning disabilities was asked to look at five still pictures taken from the videotape. The purpose of using still photos was to draw more specific information on the social perceptions of the child with learning disabilities. The child was asked to describe what was occurring in the photos and then to choose two to talk about. Questions similar to those used in the first interview were posed. The last interview occurred about 8 to 11 weeks after the end of the second interview, the purpose of which was for the interviewer to have an opportunity to ask clarifying questions of the child.

Because they were primarily interested in social perception in children with learning disabilities, Meadan and Halle (2004) used only the first two stages of Dodge's (1986) model in their study. These two steps/stages were (1) encoding social cues and (2) representation (understanding) and interpreting social cues. In their study, Meadan and Halle used their own definition of *social perception*. For them, the term encompasses both social cognition (i.e., encoding and interpreting) and social experience.

Meadan and Halle (2004) distilled three themes from their qualitative data and found similarities and differences between the children with high and low social status. The three themes included encoding and interpreting social situations, the experience of being labeled as having learning disabilities and having academic difficulties, and the characteristics of friendship relationships and "best friend." On the first theme of encoding and interpreting social situations, the similarities between the two groups of boys with high and low social status consisted of their attention to facial expressions and the use of encoded cues and their own social experiences to interpret the social situation. The differences between the boys with learning disabilities with high and low social status on this theme pointed to less sensitivity to facial expression among two out of three of the boys with learning disabilities with low social status and to different interpretations of the pictures. This interpretive difference was a function of the differences in their social experiences in similar situations.

On the second theme of the experience of having the learning disabilities label and having academic difficulties, the similarities between boys with learning disabilities high in social status and their counterparts with low social status lie in their fondness in going to the resource room and their negative experiences or emotions about their disabilities. The differences on this theme lie in how the boys with learning disabilities feel about themselves as compared with normally achieving classmates. The boys with learning disabilities who enjoyed high social status did not feel differently from their normally achieving classmates. This was not true of the boys with learning disabilities with low social status. Two out of three of them felt different from their classmates.

On the last theme of the characteristics of friendship and relationship and "best friend," the similarities lie in the following findings: (1) Each of the six boys with learning disabilities had "a number of friends" and "at least one best friend"; (2) characteristics of friendship relations (play, help, share); and (3) reasons for friendship relations ("same as me," known for a long time). The differences on this theme include boys with learning disabilities with high social status and indicated that they tried to be generally well behaved and self-controlled, boys with learning disabilities with low social status indicated that they tended to be aggressive to others who are not their friends, and that they have difficulties controlling their behaviors when they are very angry.

The preceding findings in Meadan and Halle (2004) are interesting and useful. However, caution is in order with the data for several reasons. First, the number of participants is very small. There were only three boys with learning disabilities with high social status and three boys with low social status. (Social status was obtained through peer nominations.) Second, there is the problem of nonrandomness. Out of 15 children with learning disabilities, only seven parents gave consent for their children's participation in the study. Third, at times, only two out of three of the boys show a particular behavior pattern. Hence, uniformity of response was not consistently obtained, at least from the boys with learning disabilities with low social status. Fourth, the study did not attend to the reciprocity or mutuality of friendships when the boys with learning disabilities were asked about the number of friends they had. Fifth, parental perspectives were not considered. These limitations of the study are serious and remind us to best consider Meadan and Halle's (2004) study as exploratory. However, the merit of the study is that the investigators highlight the need for us to stop viewing children with learning disabilities who have social relational problems as a homogeneous group, that not all of them have social relational problems. It is opportune to recall the study by Kavale and Forness (1996) in which they found three out of four individuals with learning disabilities to have social relational problems. Hence, one out of four does *not* have these problems in the social realm!

Bauminger, Edelstein, and Morash (2006) investigated social cognition and the understanding of complex emotions in children with and without learning disabilities. They used the six stages in Dodge's (1986) model to research social information processing (SIP) in children with and without learning disabilities. Moreover, they added an innovative step or stage of linking goal generation and selection of solution to Dodge's six stages. Although subsequent data did not yield significant relations here between goal generation and selection of solution, the addition per se had merit.

To investigate understanding of complex emotions, Bauminger et al. (2005) measured emotional recognition and emotional knowledge. Under emotional recognition, the researchers used stories and pictures. In the emotional recognition in stories, Bauminger et al. adapted for use the Emotional Comprehension Task, which originally consisted of 18 different stories portraying six different emotions: sadness, happiness, anger, fear, shame, and interest. In the adapted or modified version, the researchers kept the two original stories on happiness and developed two new stories for the emotions embarrassment, loneliness, pride, and guilt. There were thus a total of ten stories. Each child was seen individually and was asked to tell how the girl or boy in the story felt. Additionally, the child had to explain the relevance of his or her response.

For emotional recognition from pictures, Bauminger et al. (2006) used the Affective Matching Measure developed by Feshbach (1993). Again, the researchers adapted the original, which consisted of 19 different pictures of six different emotions. Four of the six emotions were basic emotions such as happiness, fear, anger, and sadness. The remaining two were complex emotions such as loneliness and pride. Bauminger et al.'s adaptions of the original contained more pictures of complex emotions. There were 12 pictures of eight different emotions. Specifically, there was one for each basic emotion as in the original, and two for each of four complex emotions of loneliness, pride, embarrassment, and guilt. Each child was seen individually and assessed on his or her accuracy of the identification of the emotion in the picture. Also, as in assessment of emotional recognition from stories, the child was asked to explain the relevance of his or her answer.

To measure emotional knowledge in children with and without learning disabilities, Bauminger et al. (2006) used the Kusche Affective Interview (Kusche, Greenberg, & Beilke, 1988). First, children had to define five emotions (happiness, loneliness, embarrassment, pride, and guilt), and their definitions were coded as correct or incorrect. Second, they recounted a time they had experienced each emotion. Their responses were also coded as correct or incorrect examples of the emotion. Third, they were asked about clues to recognize emotions in oneself or in others—for example, "How do you know when you are feeling (happy)? How do you know when other people are feeling (happy)?" The children's responses were coded as (1) bodily signs (smile, facial expression); (2) situational signs (e.g., for loneliness, "when he sits alone and no one pays attention to him"); (3) internal signs (e.g., for happy, "when I feel good inside"); and (4) verbal signs (e.g, for pride, "he's happy and he tells everyone so"). Fourth, children were measured on their knowledge of mixed emotions—specifically, the simultaneity of emotions, such as "Can someone feel _____ and _____ (sad/mad, happy/sad, love/anger) at the same time?" If the children responded that it is possible, they were asked to provide an example of a time when they experienced both feelings at the same time. Children's responses were coded on a scale of 1 to 5 where 1 equated not possible and 5 possible with the feelings being directed to the same individual. "I was happy that my picture looked so good, but I was sad that it wasn't perfect." A score of 2 indicates the child said feeling simultaneously two feelings is possible but as a sequential experience, such as "mad when he broke my watch/happy he got into trouble for it." A score of 3 means such experience is possible, but the feelings were directed toward separate individuals, such as "I am sad I can't go to the game, and I am mad at my mom." A score of 4 indicates the child said feeling two emotions is possible but without indicating with certainty that the emotions were directed at the same individual or object.

We summarize the results on the SIP (social information processing) of the children with and without learning disabilities in Table 1 of Bauminger et al.'s (2005) study. The researchers had presented the data according to the six steps in Dodge's (1986) model. In step 1 of encoding, the children with LD recalled significantly fewer core information units than the children without learning disabilities. In step 2 of interpretation of information, in context attribution, the children with learning disabilities considered significantly less the social context of the vignettes. In step 3 of clarification of goals, the children with LD generated fewer goals than the children without learning disabilities. In step 4 of response search, the children with learning disabilities generated much fewer solutions than their normally achieving counterparts. Their solutions were also significantly less competent than those generated by the children without learning disabilities. However, the children with learning disabilities generated substantially more aggressive solutions and were more passive-avoidant. As well, they had generated more other ineffective solutions. There were no significant differences between the children with and without learning disabilities in step 5 (response decision), step 6 (competency of solution), and the researchers' added step of concurrency between goal generation and selection of solution.

If students with learning disabilities are incompetent in encoding social cues and choosing appropriately self-generated solutions to socially problematic situations, how can we help them to improve here? Would helping them realize or understand their social incompetence in these areas be the suitable first step? But what must develop prior to insightful understanding of their own social incompetence? Perhaps the first step may involve self-understanding of their own learning disabilities that cause their academic problems and indirectly lead to their social relational problems.

SELF-UNDERSTANDING

Research on self-understanding of one's learning disability is an important area because the individual with learning disabilities may well feel liberated when he realizes that his cognitive disability is not global but circumscribed, is limited to one specific cognitive area of reading or mathematics, can be ameliorated but not eliminated, and does not necessarily cause a stigma. More important, research on successful and unsuccessful adults with learning disabilities suggests that the former adults possess self-understanding of their learning disabilities. Such understanding has led them to accept their learning disability and reflect on their own cognitive assets and deficits. In turn the self-reflections lead them to set realistic educational or career goals and fuel them to fulfill these goals with perseverance and self-regulated focus on goal attainment (Spekman, Goldberg, & Herman, 1992).

Self-understanding interests researchers because conceivably it may impact on an individual's sense of self-efficacy and positive self-esteem. High self-efficacy and self-esteem affect an individual's choice of goals and tasks. Self-understanding of learning disabilities has been the research focus of Merith Cosden and her research associates.

Using Heyman's test of self-perception of a learning disability (SPLD), Rothman and Cosden (1995) researched the relationship between self-perception of a learning disability and self-concept and social support. Earlier Heyman (1990) had observed that acknowledgement of the presence of a learning disability and understanding the circumscribed nature of its impact on other dimensions of the individual's life have a positive effect on self-esteem. She hypothesized that students who perceived their learning disability as having a widespread impact on many dimensions of their lives would have a lower self-esteem than those who considered that their learning disability was more circumscribed and modifiable. Heyman developed the SPLD Scale to test her hypothesis. The SPLD measures the degree to which students feel that their learning disability has a permanent and negative impact on their lives. The test scores are based on student answers to questions about the extent to which they see their learning disability as circumscribed or global, modifiable or permanent, and stigmatizing or socially accepted. Using SPLD, Heyman (1990) found in an initial study that students' self-perceptions of their learning disability were significantly related to their academic and general (global) self-concept. Students who had a more positive perception of their learning disability—that is, that it is circumscribed, modifiable, and not stigmatizing—had higher academic and general self-concepts than students with a more negative perception of their LD—that is, that it is global in impact, permanent (unmodifiable), and stigmatizing. The findings explain the variation in the global self-concept of students with learning disabilities. The within-group variation all comes down to the meaning to which students with learning disabilities give to their learning disability.

Rothman and Cosden (1995) gave 56 third to sixth graders with learning disabilities Heyman's SPLD and Renick and Harter's (1988) What I Am Like test to measure general and domain-specific self-concept and Harter's (1985) People in My Life test to measure perceived social support. They found a significant correlation between the students' scores on the SPLD and global self-concept. Moreover, the students' scores on the SPLD correlated significantly with their self-perceptions of ability, writing competence, behavior, and social acceptance. Students' SPLD scores were further significantly correlated with support from parents, classmates, and friends. Put differently, students with perceptions of higher levels of support from parents and peers reported more positive perceptions of their learning disability.

Thus, Rothman and Cosden's (1995) findings supported Heyman's (1990) earlier findings of a relationship between self-perception of a learning disability and academic and general (global) self-concept. Additionally, students with a more positive perception of their learning disability (ties) met with fewer serious achievement problems, specifically in math, in Rothman and Cosden's study. These students with learning disabilities did not view their learning disability (ties) as having a global or general effect on their lives, as one that can be ameliorated, and one that is nonstigmatizing.

In Rothman and Cosden's (1995) study, they found the students with learning disabilities who had more positive views of their learning disability to score higher in math than students with learning disability with a more negative view of their learning disability. Hence, in the context of their study, these students with learning disabilities who did relatively well in math did have one strong academic area. Against this academic strength, they accurately perceived their learning disability to be less "encompassing and negative" (Rothman & Cosden, 1995). In light of the findings of the students with learning disabilities who had more positive perceptions of their LD and who did relatively well in math, Rothman and Cosden think students with learning disabilities with lower math achievement may be more likely to harbor negative emotions about their learning diability. The researchers appear to be justified in their concern because they found that the students with learning disabilities who had negative views of their learning disability also perceived themselves as less competent cognitively. But the perception of lower cognitive competence was not substantiated by their achievement test scores outside of math.

The findings from Rothman and Cosden's (1995) study are interesting and have important implications for educators and counselors. However, the findings are correlations and do not permit the researchers to draw causal relations. Nevertheless, they point to areas for further empirical explorations—for example, the finding that students with learning disabilities who have specific areas of academic strength may be more disposed to view their learning disability in a more constructive light.

Cosden, Elliott, Noble, and Kelemen (1999) were interested in exploring how elementary children and junior high students with learning disabilities were informed about their learning disability, their knowledge of it, and how this self-understanding is related to self-esteem and global self-concept. They administered two tests to 23 grade 3 to grade 6 elementary and 72 junior high students as well as a structured interview. The tests given were Heyman's (1990) SPLD and Harter's (1985) What I Am Like.

The results showed that the biggest proportion of elementary and junior high students with learning disabilities received the information of their learning disability from the teacher, while others received it from their parents. Of concern is that over one-third of the elementary children and over 20 percent of the junior high students reported that no one informed them about their learning disability. Moreover, children told by teachers about their learning disability fell into two extreme categories: either they reported receiving no information or accurate information that enabled an accurate understanding of learning disability. These findings point to the inconsistency in teacher training programs and strike a somber note on what should be included in the curricular of these training programs in education faculties of colleges and universities.

Junior high students were more able to articulate their understanding of learning disability than the elementary children. A majority of the elementary children were unable to explain clearly what a learning disability is. Among junior high students, one-third were able to define *learning disability* in a way that shows they understood the circumscribed nature of a learning disability (e.g., "Where you're smart and everything, but you have something where you're not good, like English or spelling"). However, one-third of junior high students stated that learning disabilities were general problems (e.g., "It's that you can't do things that other people can, so you're either special or not normal or stupid"). Also, a majority of the students believed that they would outgrow their problems (Cosden, Elliot, Noble, & Kelemen, 1999).

Because the elementary children were not able to articulate an understanding or explanation of a learning disability, the researchers had to use only the verbal explanations of the junior high students in analyzing the data from the structured interview. Although the adolescents' verbal descriptions were not found to correlate with SPLD scores, they were significantly correlated with their global self-esteem. Curiously, the researchers found that junior high students who could not articulate a definition of learning disabilities had higher self-esteem scores than junior high students who described their learning disability as either global or circumscribed/delimited. Hence, the hypothesis that student's ability to explain what it means to have a learning disability would be related to a higher self-esteem

was not substantiated. Rather, ironically, the ability to articulate the meaning of learning disabilities was found to be associated with lower self-esteem
among junior high students!

Cosden et al. (1999) did find students' cognitive and achievement scores
were related to their scores on the SPLD. Students who had higher tested
cognitive abilities and academic achievement felt better about their learning
disabilities. But cognitive and achievement scores were not significantly
related to global self-esteem. Achievement was associated with self-perceptions of learning disabilities but not to global self-esteem. The researchers
found an association between students' global self-esteem and perceptions
of nonacademic competencies, especially social acceptance, physical attrac-
tiveness, and behavioral conduct. These associations had previously been
found by Kloomok and Cosden (1994) and Renick and Harter (1989) and
had been used to support the compensatory hypothesis. Thus, students with
learning disabilities who had positive self-ratings in nonacademic domains
also reported higher self-esteem.

In addition, there was an association between the global self-esteem
measure and SPLD. How children perceive their learning disabilities
impacts their self-esteem, and children with higher self-esteem tend to perceive their learning disabilities more positively. Cosden et al. (1999) concluded that perceptions of learning disabilities were related to actual and
perceived academic performance, but global self-esteem was related with
perceived competence in nonacademic areas. They emphasized the importance and interrelations of both sets of perceptions in children with learning
disabilities.

Cosden et al.'s (1999) study highlights the need to attend to helping
children and adolescents with learning disabilities understand their learning
disability. In particular, they need to realize that their learning disability is
not global but delimited/circumscribed, that it can be ameliorated through
effective remediation; and that they should not feel stigmatized with a
learning disability. More important, there should be a reliable source where
this information should ensue. It seems that teachers, either classroom or
resource room teachers, should have the responsibility to provide accurate
information to students with learning disabilities on what a learning disability is about. In turn, for this instrumental step to materialize, university programs in teacher preparation must train student teachers to fulfill this
momentous responsibility. Students with learning disabilities should not
be kept ignorant about their learning disability.

There is, however, a caveat. At issue is when such enlightenment on a
learning disability should be given to students with LD. It is recalled that
Cosden et al. (1999) found that elementary children (grades 3–6) were
unable to explain what a learning disability is. They rightly considered the
finding to reflect a developmental problem. However, self-understanding
involves metacognition, and according to the late Ann Brown (who

conceptualized the link between metacognition and reading), metacognition is late in development. Hence, it may be that information on what a learning disability is would be better understood by students with learning disabilities in adolescence. Regarding children with learning disabilities, some form of developmentally appropriate information may be attempted, perhaps with an emphasis that having a learning disability does not detract from the children's other positive assets as individuals.

Finally, Cosden et al. reported the disconcerting finding that adolescents with self-understanding of learning disabilities had lower self-esteem than those without! Hence, not only do we need to research the optimal age(s) for enlightening students with learning disabilities on what a learning disability is, but we also need to research the ways in which we can do and still maintain self-esteem in the students with learning disabilities. Because successful adults with learning disabilities possess self-understanding of a learning disability, they must somehow have developed coping strategies that enable them to overcome a potential initial depression or lowered self-esteem upon discovering that they have a learning disability. It may profit researchers to interview successful adults with learning disabilities with the purpose of discovering how they overcome the initial depression or lower self-esteem upon learning about the nature of their learning disability, if they should have experienced either. These research questions in self-understanding of a learning disability are tall orders and deserve serious attention from researchers in learning disabilities.

Self-understanding in children with LD was researched in a strikingly innovative way by Raskind, Margalit, and Higgins (2007). Through studying and reviewing the contents of e-mails sent by children with learning disabilities, the researchers were able to show multiple aspects of their self-understanding, including the awareness of having a learning disability, self-understanding that one has academic problems stemming from a learning disability, and emotional and social stresses from having a learning disability in children with learning disabilities. The children's e-mails were sent to an extant and free website that had been designed for children with learning and attention problems. Specifically, this website, SparkTop.org had been developed by SchwabLearning, which is a program of the Charles and Helen Schwab Foundation. The website was launched in 2003 and is designed for children aged 8 to 12 with learning and attention problems. The goals of the website are "to provide an online experience and create a virtual community where children could connect with other children, build self-esteem, develop self-awareness, enhance self-advocacy, gain knowledge of learning strategies, create art, play games, as well as receive information about learning and attention" (Rashkind et al., 2007, p. 257). The site is available to all children, despite that the target users are supposedly those with learning and attention problems. The researchers' purpose in their study was to let children with learning disabilities give voice to issues that are important to them. They wanted the perspectives of the children with learning disabilities on issues that profoundly affect them.

The participants consisted of 164 children aged 9 to 18 who had self-identified themselves with learning disabilities. Of these, 108 were female and 56 male. This gender ratio was in line with gender preferences in research on children's messages online.

Thus, the three researchers studied the e-mails of the 164 participants sent to three kinds of participants: (1) participants who also self-identified themselves as having learning disabilities, (2) registered website users who did not self-identify as having learning disabilities, and (3) guests that included registered and nonregistered users who might have signed on as guests. The researchers also studied e-mails sent to four animated fictionalized characters. These characters were based on three actual adolescents, "the teen mentors," and a doctoral "Learning Disabilities" expert. Moreover, all four characters were described as having learning and attention problems.

The analyses of the e-mails yielded seven themes. The first theme involved the learning disabilities identity. (The researchers cautioned that not all of the children but many in their e-mails self-identified as those who belonged to a group of children with learning disabilities.) The children with learning disabilities perceived their learning disability(ies) as part of their identity, part of their self-definition. Samples of relevant quotes include "Why do we have learning disabilities?" and "Dyslexia here, too." They also view having a learning disability as a liability as well as an identity.

The second theme involves disclosures of academic problems that show the children with learning disabilities are very aware of such problems. "My learning disability is MATH." "My learning disability is reading." "I had attention deficit disorder." The third theme involves disclosure of emotional attitudes. "I don't like what can I do?" "Sometimes I feel stupid because I have...." Loneliness was voiced: "Sometimes I feel like I am the only one with a learning disability." "I have no friends." To these children with learning disabilities, teachers assume enormous importance and influence. The teachers' attitudes toward these children can really affect the quality of their lives. "Will ... teachers get really harsh on you if you have a learning disability?"

The fourth theme involves disclosure of social or interpersonal issues. The children with learning disabilities revealed social relational problems amply covered in the research literature. The rejection and difficulties in making and keeping friends are shown in the following quotations: "People don't want to be around me or hang out with me!" "I'm an outcast and don't have a lot of friends and always called retarded and dumb." "This girl at school keeps teasing me because I have a learning disability. I told teachers and their parents but she keeps bugging me about it. What should I do?" "They don't want me on their team."

The fifth theme involves asking for help. "Hi, Kyle, I'm not good at reading or spelling or writing. What should I do?" "I get bad grades even when I study really hard. What should I do?" "What should I do in class when I try so so so so hard to pay attention, but I can't.... I wander off, thinking about things totally off subject. How can I stay focused?"

The last theme involved a positive outlook of learning disabilities. Here the researchers were hoping to find some positive signs or expressions of learning disabilities. They found that only a few children expressed positive sentiments toward their learning disability: "I have dyslexia. I am overcoming it though." "I can read a lot better in fifth grade, thanks." "You can still get good grades if you have learning disabilities." In addition to the scarcity of such positive statements, the researchers thought the statements were "subdued."

The findings of Rashkind et al. (2007) have given us the welcome voice of children with learning disabilities on issues closest to their hearts. Most important, these children with learning disabilities made us realize their astounding self-understanding of the academic problems that they have stemming from their learning disabilities and attention problems. They also revealed the undesirable by-products of having a learning disability—namely, the social rejection and loneliness resulting from social rejection and the need for discerning teacher support and help with bullies. Last but not least, these children with learning disabilities enlighten us on their self-perception of a learning disability as being part of their identity and self-definition.

LONELINESS

One of the sad consequences of the social relational problems in children and adolescents with learning disabilities is the loneliness that they experience. We are unsure that self-understanding of learning disabilities would guarantee children and adolescents freedom from loneliness. Only improved social relational skills that would increase successful friendship making and maintaining may free children and adolescents from loneliness. The stark reality of loneliness in the children and adolescents with learning disabilities has been systematically investigated in the programmatic research of Malka Margalit. We focus on her research because she has provided the most comprehensive and integrative research on this topic.

Margalit used Peplau and Perlman's (1982) definition of loneliness to frame her research. They defined it as "the unpleasant experience when individuals perceive a discrepancy between the desired and accomplished pattern of their social network." Loneliness reveals an individual's subjective experience of stress. But Valas (1999) claimed that the study of individuals with learning disabilities showed that their loneliness experience frequently reflects real social difficulties that results in their poor social network, low social status, and peer rejection.

Three chief factors have been frequently identified as predictors of social difficulties and loneliness in children with learning disabilities: (1) knowledge deficiency (Pearl, 1992); (2) performance deficits (Vaughn & La Greca, 1992); and (3) taking on the behavioral style of rejected and lonely children, accepting the reputation of socially isolated individuals and beliefs as to how lonely children frequently behave (Margalit, 1994). We now summarized Margalit's interesting programmatic research on loneliness.

Margalit and Al-Yagon (2002) investigated the consistency of the loneliness experience in children with and without learning disabilities. Three hundred and seventy-nine preschool children (238 at risk for developing learning disabilities and 141 normally developing children) were compared on the loneliness measure of Asher et al. (1990) at both the beginning and end of one academic year. The researchers found that at the end of the school year, both groups of children felt less lonely, but the loneliness of the at-risk children remained substantially higher. Moreover, the correlation between the loneliness measures at the start and end of the school year was moderate and significant.

The loneliness of three groups of children in different kinds of instructional settings was investigated in Margalit's (1998) study. Full inclusion was the instructional setting for the first two groups of children. In this setting, the regular class and special education teachers team-taught. These two groups of children were from the same school, and each group had ten children categorized as at risk for developing learning disabilities. The third and last group of children was recruited from 17 different preschools and the at-risk members received remedial help in a municipality-supported after-school center. Margalit (1998) found higher levels of loneliness in the children at risk for developing learning disabilities. However, instructional setting made no impact on the at-risk children. Put differently, there was no significant difference in loneliness between the groups of children in full inclusion or regular education system with municipality-supported remedial help.

Pursuing further the investigations on the parameters of loneliness, Margalit, Tur-Kaspa, and Most (1999) researched the effect of "identified enemies" on children's loneliness experience. An identified enemy is defined as someone in the class of the child with learning disabilities whom the latter dislikes and vice versa. The findings indicated that children with learning disabilities who had at least one identified enemy in class felt lonelier and less coherent than children with learning disabilities who had no class enemies. Interestingly, similar within-group findings were not found in the children without learning disabilities. The researchers interpreted the findings to suggest social-emotional vulnerability in children with learning disabilities to the social distress of having an identified enemy in class.

What does it mean that the children with learning disabilities felt less coherent? It means that they felt their internal and external worlds are less organized or orderly and predictable. The construct of the sense of coherence originated with Antonovsky (1979, 1987). This construct refers to "a generalized worldview, reflecting the extent to which an individual has dynamic confidence that his or her internal and external environments are structured and predictable, and that there is a high probability that life situations will work out as well as can be expected. An inclination to perceive the world as orderly and explicable enables the individual to develop a cognitive assessment of the difficulties stemming from stressors and facilitates the active search for appropriate coping strategies" (Margalit, 2000, p. 60).

Weissberg's (2002) master's thesis suggested the important role of computers in predicting lower levels of loneliness for children with learning disabilities. In that thesis, three factors were found to predict the loneliness experience: personal (sense of coherence), interpersonal (expressed by peer nominations), and instrumental (the attitude toward computers). A common loneliness model was identified for both groups of children with and without learning disabilities. Separate use of the model to analyze data from each group of children with and without learning disabilities yielded contrasting findings. For the children without learning disabilities, all five predictors turned out to be significant: age; gender; personal, including attitudes; and interpersonal variables. For the children with learning disabilities, only personal perceptions (in terms of sense of coherence) and attitudes toward computers were significant. The findings were interpreted as highlighting the role of computers in predicting lower levels of loneliness for students with learning disabilities.

Margalit and Ben-Dov (1995) investigated loneliness in adolescents with and without learning disabilities in two settings: Israeli kibbutz and the city social system. Two opposing hypotheses were posed. The kibbutz researchers expected the children to experience less loneliness because the kibbutz environment is saturated by social relations. The opposite expectation was proffered by the city researchers who anticipated higher levels of loneliness in the adolescents with learning disabilities in the kibbutz environment. This is because they thought these adolescents with learning disabilities were expecting to develop social relations when they were too immature to do so. Hence, they would experience social pressure and in turn more loneliness.

The findings were surprising! Adolescents with learning disabilities in both settings, kibbutz and the city social system, reported higher levels of loneliness than adolescents without learning disabilities. The finding is particularly puzzling or remarkable with the kibbutz adolescents with learning disabilities because their peers rated them to have more friends, and their teachers thought they had better self-control!

Al-Yagon and Margalit (2006) investigated self-reported loneliness and sense of coherence and perception of the homeroom teacher as a secure base in third graders with reading difficulties. The unique feature of this study lies in the fact that the researchers studied the children prior to formal diagnostic assessment, so they had controlled for the possible impact of diagnosis.

The dependent outcomes included: (1) children's feelings of loneliness as indicated by their experience of peer relations and social alienation, (2) children's perception of their own coping resources as shown in their sense of coherence, and (3) children's perception of their teacher as a security base, as indicated by the children's close relationships with a significant adult. In line with prior research, Al-Yagon and Margalit's study explored teacher-child relationships from the perspective of an attachment theory.

Al-Yagon and Margalit (2006) posed five predictions. We focus on the first three because the last two are more suitably discussed in the context of the theoretical framework of risk and resilience in a later section. First, they predicted higher loneliness and a lower sense of coherence in children with reading difficulties. Second, compared to children without reading difficulties, they predicted these children would report a less secure relationship with their teacher. Third, they predicted a positive correlation between the children's perception of the teacher as a secure base and loneliness and sense of coherence. That is, a higher perception of the teacher as a secure base would correlate with lower loneliness and a higher sense of coherence in the children. The results substantiated all three predictions and were interpreted to indicate the possible role of children's reading difficulties as a vulnerability factor for the development of social emotional maladjustment and impairment of the quality of teacher-child relationship. Despite perceiving the teachers to be providing sufficient instrumental care, such as giving additional help and instruction, the children with reading difficulties perceived their teachers as more rejecting than their normally achieving peers.

Margalit (2002, p. 72) concluded her chapter with this thought-provoking position: "Everyone experiences loneliness at some time, and the goals of loneliness research are not to prevent the aversive yet basic human experience, but to increase understanding of the alienation affect and to promote coping strategies through skill training and identifying moderating ecological factors."

THE RISK AND RESILIENCE THEORETICAL FRAMEWORK

What is this theoretical framework and how did it originate? And why does this theoretical framework appeal to researchers in the social domain of learning disabilities? Essentially the risk and resilience theory holds that concerning an individual at risk, such as an individual with learning disabilities, the ultimate outcome of his or her prospects as a successful citizen in the society is by no means predetermined to be negative simply because of the learning disability. This is because how the learning disability plays out depends on the presence or absence of factors that may ameliorate the adverse effects of a learning disability. These are the so-called protective factors. More formally defined, a protective factor is one that likely promotes successful adaptation of a child who is at risk. Protective factors may range from constitutional characteristics such as a child's pleasing temperament or above-average intelligence to environmental factors such as a cohesive family and supportive school (Garmezy, 1983). Protective factors foster the resilience in children with learning disabilities that enables successful adaptation despite their vulnerability to academic and nonacademic failures stemming from their having a learning disability.

Risk factors are "negative or potentially negative" conditions that thwart or threaten to thwart normal development (Keogh & Weisner, 1993). A learning disability is a risk factor because it impedes the child's successful reading acquisition.

The risk and resilience theoretical frame was first applied by Werner and Smith (1982) to account for their longitudinal data on a group of 22 adults with learning disabilities. These adults constituted a subgroup within a cohort of 72 whom Werner and Smith had tracked since birth in 1955 on the island of Kauai in their longitudinal study. All 72 had perinatal problems and grew up in appalling conditions of poverty. All were tracked in their cognitive and psychological developments at birth, and at ages of 1, 2, 10, 18, 31/32, and 40. At each age of testing, the investigators found different stressors/risks as well as protective factors. Concerning the adults without learning disabilities in this cohort of 72, at ages 31/32, they were all employed, mostly in skilled trade or technical and managerial jobs. About 10 percent were semiskilled. Additionally, they were happy (satisfied) with themselves, their marriages, and their jobs. At age 40, this positive trend was found to have continued for them. Specifically, the women anticipated more opportunities in employment, and the men were more reflective about families and children. The important and provocative theme from these findings is that growing up in adverse conditions does not implacably lead to adverse adult outcomes.

Werner and Smith (2001) reported that 60 percent of the males and 70 percent of the females of this cohort group (minus the 22 adults with learning disabilities) had job and marital satisfaction, a sense of self-efficacy, and a general sense of psychological well-being. Such positive adult outcomes in these individuals despite growing up in "grinding poverty" speak to the powerful role of protective factors in the environment, chief of which is sustained emotional support from caregivers and significant others such as teachers or ministers and concerned adults who served as mentors and gatekeepers. These protective factors effectively buffered the adverse conditions (Werner & Smith, 2001).

The intriguing part of Werner and Smith's longitudinal data concerns the 22 adults with learning disabilities. Of these, 25 percent indicated the familiar profile of the adult with learning disabilities, one of unemployment and dissatisfaction with themselves and poor social lives. But the remaining bucked the familiar and negative profile of the adult with learning disabilities!

To begin with, all 22 of these adults with learning disabilities were diagnosed with learning disabilities at the age of ten by a diagnostic team composed of a pediatrician, a psychologist, and a public health nurse. The diagnosis of learning disabilities was based on the following: (1) a serious reading problem as shown by below-grade reading achievement (more than one grade below), despite average or above-average intelligence as measured by the Wechsler Intelligence Scale for Children (WISC; Wechsler, 1974); (2) much scatter on the subtest's performance on the WISC suggesting erratic performance, with a large discrepancy between verbal and performance IQ; (3) substantial errors on the Bender-Gestalt Visual-Motor Test; and (4) reported by mothers, teachers, and diagnosticians to be persistently hyperactive, unable to concentrate, and highly distractible.

Among these 22 adults with learning disabilities, there were more males (14) than females (8). Moreover, a high percentage of them (64 percent of the males and 36 percent of the females) came from very poor families. Twenty-three percent of them came from middle and upper middle class. Between the ages of 10 and 18, these individuals with learning disabilities did very poorly in the cognitive and psychological assessments. More important, between the ages of 10 and 18, more than four-fifths (80%) of the youths had reportedly had some brush with the law. Of this 80%, specifically 27 percent had come into contact with the police. This rate was almost twice that of the total 1955 cohort. Half of these were repeated contacts that resulted in referrals to the family court. These repeated contacts were caused by "car accidents, malicious injury, larceny, burglary, running away from home, repeated truancy, curfew violations, and trespassing and unlawful hunting" (Werner & Smith, 2001, p. 134). At 18, these 22 young adults with learning disabilities did very poorly in their academic (reading and writing) and psychological (self-acceptance, sociability, socialization) tests. Compared to a control group of adults without learning disabilities, these young adults with learning disabilities had a significantly higher external locus of control. Put differently, they perceived themselves not to be in control of what occurs to them. The control group was composed of randomly selected individuals from the original 698 individuals born in 1955, excluding the individuals from the focal cohort group of 72. Werner and Smith (2001) carefully matched the participants in the control group with the adults with learning disabilities on gender, socioeconomic, and ethnic backgrounds. The young adults in the control group had no learning disabilities or behavior problems.

The intriguing part of the data in Werner and Smith's (2001) longitudinal study came when the 22 adults with learning disabilities turned 32. At this point, the researchers were able to locate 18 of them. These 18 adults with learning disabilities were all gainfully employed, albeit in blue-collar work. They enjoyed a similar rate of marital success as the nondisabled control group. Moreover, they were self-accepting and satisfied with themselves, their jobs, and marriages. Why did these 18 adults with learning disabilities show a profile that differs sharply and dramatically from the more familiar negative profile of the unsuccessful adult with learning disabilities? To account for the turnaround of these adults with learning disabilities from the expected and continual downward spin of young adulthood at 18, Werner and Smith (1993) proffered five clusters of protective factors.

Cluster 1 referred to the presence of a pleasingly easy temperament that elicited positive responses from parents, peers, teachers, and spouses. Cluster 2 referred to ethics/values and skills that enabled the individual to put to good use whatever natural aptitudes he or she possessed. Such individuals felt they could overcome problems. Put differently, they exhibited a strong sense of self-efficacy. Additionally, they had realistic plans in learning and career. They demonstrated responsibility and self-regulation toward household tasks at home. Cluster 3 referred to parents with effective parenting skills. Specifically, they provided the child with structure, support, and emotional stability at home and promoted self-esteem in the child. In these homes, the mothers had education beyond high school and held good jobs. Hence, the mothers were well educated. Cluster 4 referred to the presence of nurturing adults, in particular a mentor who served as the "gatekeeper" for the future. The child's grandparent, or a youth leader, or a church minister could fulfill the role of such a mentor. The special attribute of this mentor is his or her unwavering confidence in the individual with learning disabilities. Cluster 5 referred to opportune chances for the individuals with learning disabilities at crucial life transition junctures, such as from high school to job employment, or joining the army, that charted a positive course or trajectory to adulthood for these individuals with learning disabilities.

The contents of these clusters indicate both internal and external factors to the individual with learning disabilities. The internal factors include the individual's pleasing or easy temperament, resourcefulness, awareness of his or her own cognitive potential and planful self-regulation to put it to good use (metacognition), and availing himself or herself of opportunities such as apprenticeships at school leaving. The external factors include the widespread and sustained social network of emotional support from home and significant others and effective parents who not only provided structure at home and emotional support but also good role models. Most important of all, these parents saw to it that the child with learning disabilities sustained a healthy global self-concept despite the learning disability. Gatekeepers or mentors and timely opportunities at important transition points complete the list of external protective factors. Although Werner and Smith's (2001) protective clusters distinctly present a more optimistic outlook for the plight of adults with learning disabilities, a caveat is in order. It is important to point out that these successful adults with learning disabilities in Werner and Smith (2001) represented 75 percent of the individuals that they studied. The remaining 25 percent, unfortunately, exhibited the more typical profile of the adult with learning disabilities: unemployed and unsuccessful in social relations. Understandably, these more typical adults with learning disabilities were dissatisfied with themselves.

Werner and Smith's use of the risk and resilience theoretical frame has heralded increasing interest in its use among researchers in the social domain of learning disabilities, such as Cosden, Margalit, and Wiener. As pointed out by those who share an interest in it, the risk and resilience framework appeals to researchers because it moves us away from the hackneyed "deficit" model that pits individuals with learning disabilities against their nondisabled counterparts in between-groups research designs. In its stead, the risk and resilience framework focuses on studying the interactions between the child and contextual factors *within* the groups of individuals with and without learning disabilities. Using designs of longitudinal studies, we can track how risk and protective factors play out across different samples and at different developmental points (Keogh, 2002). In short, we can better understand individual differences within respective samples of persons with and without learning disabilities in longitudinal studies using the risk and resilience framework. Better understanding of how risk and protective factors interplay would in turn lead eventually to the designs of interventions that could on the one hand, minimize risk factors and on the other hand, maximize protective factors. But first, we need to encourage more longitudinal research so as to identify risk and protective factors the way Werner and Smith (2001) had done.

SOCIAL COMPETENCE INTERVENTIONS

In this section, we deliberately eschew coverage of social skills interventions in the 1980s and 1990s because they have been widely covered in many textbooks (Wong, 1996). Instead, we focus on describing a more recent attempt at social competence intervention. Researchers who attempt social competence interventions face substantially more challenges than those who attempt academic interventions. This is because the fluid and dynamic nature of social interactions makes it difficult for the deployment of specifically trained social competencies. There are no definite, hard and fast rules in social interactions. Successful social interactions involve in part, accurate reading of social cues and body language between two or more individuals. Moreover, occasionally successful social interactions may involve additional role-taking skills. Hence, obtaining generalization of learned social competencies among trainees can present a serious challenge. One way to promote generalization of learned social competencies appears to be through a whole-school approach in fostering such skills. We focus on describing one example of this approach.

In 2002, the state of Victoria in Australia launched a statewide initiative that acknowledged the interconnections among students' academic learning, their social functioning, and their well-being. The Victorian government considers successful educational outcomes serve as an important preparation for students' taking on active roles in society. More important, the government looks upon social competence as essential to that preparation.

The reason the Victorian state government promoted the inculcation of social competence parallel to academic competence is that research indicates that development of social competence in children helps them to better buffet stresses and decrease future likelihood of social problems. Research also indicates that when children's uncooperative and aggressive behaviors are not attended to and redressed, these behaviors could eventuate in antisocial behavior and/or violence in later years.

Thus, under the aegis and within the context of the statewide initiative was developed the concept of a whole-school approach to foster social competence with emphasis on linking it to students' learning and to students' well-being. Six principles underlie a whole-school approach to social competence. The first principle states, "Students learn best when they experience a sense of belonging and significance." Three points elaborate on this first principle. Students' sense of connection or relatedness is strengthened in a culture of inclusiveness. When students are connected with one another, they will develop resilience to social stressors. Students feel a sense of significance or empowerment when they feel they have a contribution to make (to the class or to a project).

The second principle states, "Schools are a major social learning environment." Relevant elaborative points are that it is important for teachers to model and teach prosocial behaviors and that students can make long-term social goals such as behavior management and discipline procedures.

The third principle states, "Well-being is intrinsic to learning." This principle is elaborated in the following points. "A safe, supportive and engaging environment" promotes better preparation for student learning. A student's relationship with at least one concerned adult can foster his or her resilience to social stressors.

The fourth principle states, "Students' learning occurs mainly in the context of social relationships." This principle focuses on the role social mediation plays in students' learning.

To elaborate, "peer relations contribute significantly to social and cognitive development. . . . Learning is enhanced through positive social and emotional dynamics betweens students."

The fifth principle states, "Cognitive, emotional, and behavioral domains are interlinked." This principle is self-explanatory and elaborations are unnecessary.

The sixth and last principle states, "Schools can contribute to social capital." To elaborate, when teachers foster friendships among students with those who are similar to them as well as different from them, they contribute to social inclusiveness or social cohesion.

We now look at selective examples of implementations in schools that had launched a whole-school approach to fostering social competence. These implementations reflect the premise among the school personnel (the principle and teachers and support staff) that the best way for students to learn social competencies is when they see their environment (school) demonstrates, actively teaches, and embodies ("live out") social competence.

In grade 2, the children contributed to making a class book called "Everyday Problems and How to Solve Them" by working on their individual pages. This activity sought to develop a range of social competencies that connect the thinking, feeling, and behavioral domains. The children write down what concerns them as a social problem and draw a picture to accompany what they have written. Then they are helped to find options to resolve the problem. These options show respect and helpfulness and are purposed to foster positive peer relations. Figures 4.1 and 4.2 show what two children wrote and drew. The figures also show options that were developed to redress the problem. The teacher helps with generating the solutions.

Figure 4.1 portrays a problem that we can all empathize with: being blamed for something we did not do! This second grader expressed his emotions when he was blamed for something he did not do: "I feel awful." We can imagine the child's sense of bewilderment, his desire for justice, and his anxiety over clearing his name. The boy's options for solving the problem included explaining what occurred and seeing if he could participate in sorting out the situation.

In Figure 4.2, the child discloses the hurt of being dumped unceremoniously by a friend. The child feels hurt because this friend has just asked her to be her playmate. But when the friend's other friend turned up, she immediately dumped the child. In the figure, the second grader revealed her feelings in this incident of thoughtlessness in a specific context. Such incidents of wanton abandonment by playmates may be frequently experienced by young children. By writing it down and drawing it, the child was able to vent her frustrations and resentment and, more important, was helped to solve the problem. Her two options in solving the problem included asking the friend to put herself in the forsaken child's shoes and/or choosing a new playmate next time so her feelings would not get hurt again.

FIGURE 4.1   The Innocent. Copyright owned by the State of Victoria (Department of Education). Used with permission.

In Figure 4.3, a sixth grade girl filled out a specific form after she had defaced a classmate's desktop. The cause for her behavior was displacement of her anger from being called a name that she resented. In getting this sixth grader to fill out the particular form, the teacher's goal was to foster the child's reflection on what classroom rule was broken, why the child broke it, and for the child to realize that retaliation per se is not the logical solution to the offense of being called a

FIGURE 4.2 The Abandoned. Copyright owned by the State of Victoria (Department of Education). Used with permission.

name. What is positive about logical solutions in the context of the whole-school approach to social competence is that a logical solution differs from punishment and is based on goodwill. It is focused on the present and future behavior. Based on Nelson, Lott, and Glenn (2000), a logical solution has four essential attributes: "(a) it relates to the behavior, (b) it is respectful of all participating parties, (c) it contains reasonable expectations, and (d) it aims to build relationships."

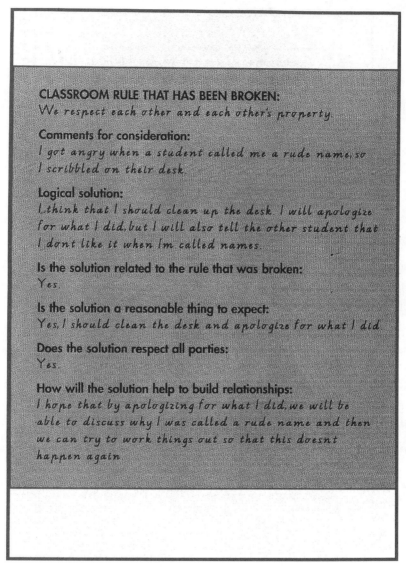

CLASSROOM RULE THAT HAS BEEN BROKEN:
We respect each other and each other's property.

Comments for consideration:
I got angry when a student called me a rude name, so I scribbled on their desk.

Logical solution:
I think that I should clean up the desk. I will apologize for what I did, but I will also tell the other student that I don't like it when I'm called names.

Is the solution related to the rule that was broken:
Yes.

Is the solution a reasonable thing to expect:
Yes, I should clean the desk and apologize for what I did.

Does the solution respect all parties:
Yes.

How will the solution help to build relationships:
I hope that by apologizing for what I did, we will be able to discuss why I was called a rude name and then we can try to work things out so that this doesn't happen again

FIGURE 4.3 Respect for Other's Property. Copyright owned by the State of Victoria (Department of Education). Used with permission.

Other examples of implementation of a whole-school approach to fostering social competencies are voluntary helpers in the classroom where those students who arrive early automatically tidy up the classroom (e.g., tidy up the sports sector and set up sports equipment to be ready for use). When they have completed their voluntary task, they sign the volunteer card so there is a record of what has been done. Another example involves older students mediating between conflicts in younger students. A sixth grader who serves as a buddy to a younger student helps the latter to resolve the problem of being left out in a game on the school grounds. Another older student serving as peer mediator helps resolve a problem of sharing a soccer ball between two younger students.

We end with two examples of implementation from the high school. The first concerns how a group of high school students dealt with a school-yard incident. The group listened to and recorded the various perspectives of those involved in the incident. They also noted how the incident was resolved and the consequences attached. The group analyzed the incident and explored other alternative options for resolving the incident and potential consequences for each option. They then chose the options that had a higher possibility of positive outcomes and presented them to the class.

The second example concerns another group of high school students who used survey data from the school to help resolve health issues arising from students carrying heavy backpacks. From the survey data, the students realized several reasons why students choose to carry such heavy bags with them. Apparently, they did so for self-protection against locker thefts and vandalism, as well as the lack of time between classes for trips back to their respective lockers for change of books and notepads. The time intervals between classes were just too short for such locker visits. The students in the group brainstormed ideas for options to help in resolving the issue of carrying around excessively heavy backpacks that are a health hazard for the back and shoulders.

This whole-school approach to social competence development was the brainchild of a gifted teacher, Sandra Mahar, and an able clinical psychologist, Lyndall Cameron. They oversaw pilot projects in 18 schools. What they had was vision in social competence training. The implementation activities as shown in the selective examples attest to their ingenuity in social competence training and relatedness to elementary school children and high school students. It is our understanding that they would be helped in evaluative research on the school projects. However, sadly, the programs are no longer funded. We hope, however, that by describing their exciting and refreshing social competence training program, you, our undergraduate readers, will engage in pursuing and extending the work of Mahar and Cameron upon returning as graduate students in future!

FUTURE DIRECTIONS FOR RESEARCH

We proffer some suggestions for future research. Wiener's (2002) study on friendship formation and maintenance in dyads of children with and without learning disabilities represents a new approach to studying social relation problems in children with learning disabilities in that researchers probed perceptions and perspectives of friendship from these children, beyond studying their social status. It seems to us a profitable follow-up to this research avenue would be to conduct interview studies with children without learning disabilities to seek answers to why the majority of them would not befriend children with learning disabilities. More specifically, researchers may probe possibilities that contribute to the social rejection of children with learning disabilities. For example, children with learning disabilities may be perceived as academic losers, and thus to be avoided at all cost. Another possibility may be that children with learning disabilities are not aware that they can irritate children without learning disabilities. For example, one mother related how her son with learning disabilities would approach a peer or a new classmate with an extraordinarily inappropriate and puzzling greeting: "Hi, I'm (name of child). You must hate me, don't you?" Or as another mother observed, the child with learning disabilities may be excessively self-centered and only wants friends who let her have her way (Wiener & Sunohara, 1998). Interviewing children without learning disabilities on reasons for rejecting children with learning disabilities may provide us with new insights on this complex phenomenon of social unpopularity of children with learning disabilities. We may begin to see in some cases that perhaps unwittingly children with learning disabilities may elicit or even provoke their own social rejection.

On the research on self-understanding, the central issue is when and how best a learning disability can be explained to children with learning disabilities. Because self-understanding involves metacognition, and, according to the late Ann Brown, the originator of and authority on metacognition and reading, metacognition is late in developing. Given that, it is understandable that Cosden and her associates found cultivating self-understanding of learning disabilities was easier in adolescents with learning disabilities and more problematic in children with learning disabilities. Thus, researchers must consider the factor of development of metacognition as they struggle with the issue of when best to foster self-understanding of learning disabilities in children with learning disabilities.

Raskind et al.'s (2006) study showed us how studying e-mail contents of children with learning disabilities gave us access to their perspectives on having a learning disability. Their study sparks research interests and ideas in using the Internet or e-mails to foster friendships among children with learning disabilities and friendships among children with learning disabilities with those without learning disabilities. It would be instructive to research use of this avenue of e-mails to reduce loneliness among children, adolescents, and adults with learning disabilities. Moreover, we could research the stability and quality of friendships that are born from e-mails and electronic networking.

Last but not least, we need to confront the issue of whether social relation problems should be included in the definition of learning disabilities.

We know and understand the sentiment of those who wish to see it as a definitional component. But we also know the findings of Kavale and Forness's (1996) study that three out of four individuals with learning disabilities have social relation problems. However, one out of four does not. For social relation problems to be included in any definition of learning disabilities, we maintain that every individual with learning disabilities must have social relation problems. That is not the case, at least according to Kavale and Forness (1996). Until research findings attest to the universality of social relation problems in individuals with learning disabilities, we cannot support its inclusion in any definition of learning disabilities. Researchers in the social dimensions of learning disabilities need to grapple with and resolve this important issue.

SUMMARY

This chapter focuses on summarizing contemporary research in the social dimensions of learning disabilities. We highlight several aspects of it:

• Moving beyond social status per se of students with learning disabilities, the research makes an important distinction between the number of friends versus the number of reciprocal/mutual friends that students with learning disabilities have.

• The role of parents, as shown in the parental perspectives on the nature of friendships among their adolescent sons and daughters, presents a new and significant area of research.

• The perspectives of children with learning disabilities on their own learning disabilities, social and emotional consequences of having a learning disability not only contain new questions for research but also reaffirm the importance of researching self-understanding in individuals with learning disabilities.

• The research underscores the relevance of the risk and resilience framework for research in learning disabilities.

• There is a strong suggestion for a change in the direction in social skills interventions where a whole-school approach is advocated. This potential change fits the ensconced inclusive school practice in North America and Australia.

REFERENCES

Al-Yagon, M., & Margalit, M. (2006). Loneliness, sense of coherence and perception of teachers as a secure base among children with reading difficulties. *European Journal of Special Needs Educaion*, 21(1), 21–37.
Antonovsky, A. (1987). *Unravelling the mystery of health.* San Francisco: Jossey-Bass.

Antonovsky, A. (1979). *Health, stress and coping*. San Francisco: Jossey-Bass.

Asher, S.R., Parkhurst, J.T., Hymel, S., & Williams, G.A. (1990). Peer rejection and loneliness in childhood. In S.R. Asher & J.D. Coie (Eds.), *Peer rejection in childhood* (pp. 253–273). Cambridge, England: Cambridge University Press.

Bagwell, C.L., Newcomb, A.F., & Bukowski, W.M. (1998). Preadolescent friendship and peer rejection as predictors of adult adjustment. *Child Development*, 69:140–153.

Bauminger, N., Edelstein, H.S., & Morash, J. (2005). Social information processing and emotional understanding in children with learning disabilities. *Journal of Learning Disabilities*, 38(1), 45–61.

Bear, G.G., Juvonen, J., & McInerney, F. (1993). Self-perceptions and peer relations of boys with and boys without learning disabilities in integrated setting: A longitudinal study. *Learning Disability Quarterly*, 16:127–136.

Bryan, T. (1974). Learning disabilities: A new stereotype. *Journal of Learning Disabilities*, 7:304–309.

Bryan, T. (1976). Peer popularity of learning-disabled children: A replication. *Journal of Learning Disabilities*, 9:307–311.

Bryan, T., Pearl, R., & Fallon, P. (1989). Conformity to peer pressure by students with LD: A replication. *Journal of Learning Disabilities*, 22:458–459.

Bryan, T., Werner, M., & Pearl, R. (1982). Learning-disabled students' conformity responses to prosocial and antisocial situations. *Learning Disability Quarterly*, 5:344–352.

Bukowski, W.M., & Hoza, B. (1989). Popularity and friendship: Issues in theory, measurement, and outcome. In T.J. Berndt, & G.W. Ladd (Eds.), *Peer relationships in child development*, (pp. 15–45). New York: Wiley.

Coben, S., & Zigmond, N. (1986). The social integration of learning-disabled children from self-contained and mainstreamed elementary school settings. *Journal of Learning Disabilities*, 19:614–618.

Cosden, M., Brown, C., & Elliott, K. (2002). Development of Self-Understanding and Self-Esteem in Children and Adults with Learning Disabilities. In Bernice Y.L. Wong & Mavis Donahue (Eds.), *Social Dimensions of Learning Disabilities* (pp. 33–52). Mahwah, NJ: Erlbaum.

Cosden, M., Elliott, K., Noble, S., & Kelemen, E. (1999). Self-understanding and self-esteem in children with learning disabilities. *Learning Disability Quarterly*, 22:279–290.

Dodge, K.A. (1986). A social information processing model of social competence in children. In M. Perlmutter (Ed.), *Minnesota Symposium on Child Psychology*, 18, 77–125. Hillsdale, NJ: Erlbaum.

Estell, D.B., Jones, M.H., Pearl, R., Van Acker, R., Farmer, T., & Rodkin, P. (2006). Peer groups, popularity, and social preference: Trajectories of social functioning among students with and without learning disabilities. *Journal of Learning Disabilities*, in press.

Feshbach, N. (1993). The affective matching measure.Unpublished manuscript, University of California: Los Angeles.

Fleming, J.E., Cook, T.D., & Stone, C.A. (2002). Interactive influences of perceived social contexts on reading achievement of urban middle schoolers with learning disabilities. *Learning Disabilities Research & Practice*, 17:47–64.

Garmezy, N. (1983). *Stressors of childhood*. Minneapolis, MN: McGraw-Hill.

Harter, S. (1985). *Manual for the Social Support for Children*. Denver, CO: University of Denver.

Heyman, W.B. (1990). The self-perception of learning disability and its relationship to academic self-concept and self-esteem. *Journal of Learning Disabilities*, 23:472–475.

Kavale, K.A., & Forness, S.R. (1996). Social skills deficit and learning disabilities: A meta-analysis. *Journal of Learning Disabilities*, 29:226–237.

Keogh, B. (2002). Models of longitudinal research: Implications for the study of the social dimensions of learning disabilities. In Bernice Y.L. Wong & Mavis Donahue (Eds.), *Social Dimensions of Learning Disabilities* (pp. 215–226). Mahwah, N.J: Erlbaum.

Keogh, B., & Weisner, T. (1993). An ecocultural perspective on risk and protective factors in children's development: Implications for learning disabilities. *Learning Disabilities Research & Practice*, 8:3–10.

Kloomok, S., & Cosden, M. (1994). Self-concept in children with learning disabilities: The relationship between global self-concept, academic "discounting," nonacademic self-concept, and perceived social support. *Learning Disability Quarterly*, 17:140–153.

Kuhne, M., & Wiener, J. (2002). Stability of social status of children with and without learning disabilities. *Learning Disability Quarterly*, 23:64–75.

Kusche, C.A., Greenberg, M.T., & Beilke, B. (1988). *The Kusche affective interview*. Unpublished manuscript, University of Washington, Seattle, Department of Psychology.

Margalit, M. (1994). *Loneliness among children with special needs: Theory, research, coping and intervention*. New York: Springer-Verlag.

Margalit, M. (1998). Sense of coherence and loneliness experience among preschool children with learning disabilities. *Journal of Learning Disabilities*, 31(2), 173–180.

Margalit, M., & Al-Yagon, M. (2002). The loneliness experience of children with learning disabilities. In Bernice Y.L. Wong & Mavis Donahue (Eds.), *Social Dimensions of Learning Disabilities* (pp. 53–76). Mahwah, NJ: Erlbaum.

Margalit, M., & Ben-Dov, I. (1995). Learning disabilities and social environments: Kibbutz versus city comparisons of social competence and loneliness. *International Journal of Behavior Development*, 18(3), 519–536.

Margalit, M., Tur-Kaspa, H., & Most, T. (1999). Reciprocal nominations, reciprocal rejections, and loneliness among children with learning disorders. *Exceptional Children*, 19:79–90.

Meaden, H., & Halle, J.W. (2004). Social perceptions of students with learning disabilities who differ in social status. *Learning Disabilities & Practice*, 19(2), 71–82.

Nelson, J., Lott, L., & Glenn, S. (2000). *Positive Discipline in the Classroom* (3rd ed.). Roseville, CA: Prima Publishing.

Pearl, R. (2002). Students with learning disabilities and their classroom companions. In Bernice Y.L. Wong & Mavis Donahue (Eds.), *Social Dimensions of Learning Disabilities* (pp. 77–92). Mahwah, NJ: Erlbaum.

Pearl, R., & Bryan, T. (1992). Students' expectations about peer pressure to engage in misconduct. *Journal of Learning Disabilities*, 25:582–585, 597.

Pearl, R., Bryan, T., Fallon, P., & Herzog, A. (1991). Learning-disabled students' detection of deception. *Learning Disabilities & Practice*, 6:12–16.

Pearl, R., Bryan, T., & Herzog, A. (1990). Resisting/acquiescing to peer pressure to engage in misconduct: Adolescents' expectations of probable consequences. *Journal of Youth and Adolescence*, 19:43–55.

Peplau, L.A., & Perlman, D. (1982). Perspectives on loneliness. In L.A. Peplan, & D. Perlman (Eds.), *Loneliness: A sourcebook of current theory, research, and therapy* (pp. 1–18). New York: Springer-Verlag.

Rashkind, M.H., Margalit, M., & Higgins, E.L. (2006). "My LD": Children's voices on the Internet. *Learning Disability Quarterly*, 29:253–268.

Renick, M.J., & Harter, S. (1988). *Manual for the self-perception profile for learning-disabled students*. Denver, CO: University of Denver.

Renick, M.J., & Harter, S. (1989). Implications of social comparisons on the developing self-perceptions of learning-disabled students. *Journal of Educational Psychology*, 81:631–638.

Rothman, H., & Cosden, M. (1995). The relationship between self-perception of a learning disability and achievement, self-concept, and social support. *Learning Disability Quarterly*, 18:203–212.

Schneider, B.H., Wiener, J., & Murphy, K. (1994). The giant step beyond peer acceptance. *Journal of Social and Personal Relationships*, 11:323–340.

Spekman, N., Goldberg, R.J., & Herman, K.L. (1992). Learning disabled children grow up: A search for factors related to success in the young adult years. *Learning Disabilities Research & Practice*, 7:161–170.

Stone, W.L., & La Greca, A.M. (1990). The social status of children with learning disabilities: A reexamination. *Journal of Learning Disabilities*, 23:32–37.

Tur-Kaspa, H. (2002). Social cognition in learning disabilities. In Bernice Y.L. Wong, & Mavis Donahue (Eds.), *Social Dimensions of Learning Disabilities*, (pp. 11–32). Mahwah, NJ: Erlbaum.

Tur-Kaspa, H., & Bryan, T. (1994). Social information-processing skills of students with learning disabilities. *Learning Disabilities Research & Practice*, 9(1), 12–23.

Tur-Kaspa, H., Margalit, M., & Most, T. (1999). Reciprocal friendship, reciprocal rejection and socio-emotional adjustment: The social experiences of children with learning disorders over a one-year period. *European Journal of Special Needs Education*, 14:37–48.

Valas, H. (1999). Students with learning disabilities and low-achieving students: Peer acceptance, loneliness, self-esteem, and depression. *Social Psychology of Education*, 3(3), 173–192.

Vaughn, S., & Elbaum, B. (1999). The self-concept and friendships of students with learning disabilities: A developmental perspective. In R. Gallimore (Ed.), *Developmental perspectives on children with high-incidence disabilities* (pp. 81–107). Mahwah, NJ: Erlbaum.

Vaughn, S., Elbaum, B., & Boardman, A.G. (2001). The social functioning of students with learning disabilities: Implications for inclusion. *Exceptionality*, 9:47–65.

Vaughn, S., Elbaum, B.E., & Schumm, J. (1996). The effects of inclusion on the social functions of students with learning disabilities. *Journal of Learning Disabilities*, 29:598–608.

Vaughn, S., & Haager, D. (1994). Social competence as a multifaceted construct: How do students with learning disabilities fare? *Learning Disability Quarterly*, 17:253–266.

Vaughn, S., & La Greca, A.M. (1992). Beyond greetings and making friends: Social skills from a broader perspective. In B.Y.L. Wong (Ed.), *Contemporary Intervention Research in Learning Disabilities: An International Perspective* (pp. 96–114). New York: Springer-Verlag.

Vaughn, S., McIntosh, R., Schumm, J.S., Haager, D., & Callwood, D. (1993). Social status, peer acceptance, and reciprocal friendship revisited. *Learning Disability Research & Practice*, 8:82–88.

Wechsler, D. (1974). *Manual for the Wechsler Intelligence Scale for Children—Revised*. New York: Psychology Corp.

Weissberg, L. (2000). *The non-academic world in school*. Unpublished masters thesis, Tel Aviv University.

Werner, E.E., & Smith, R.S. (1982). *Vulnerable but invincible: A longitudinal study of resilient children and youth*. New York: McGraw-Hill.

Werner, E.E., & Smith, R.S. (2001). *Journeys from childhood to midlife: Risk, resilience and recovery*. Ithaca, NY: Cornel University.

Wiener, J. (2002). Friendship and social emotional functioning of children with learning disabilities: In Bernice Y.L. Wong & Mavis Donahue (Eds.), *Social Dimensions of Learning Disabilities* (pp. 93–114). Mahwah, Erlbaum.

Wiener, J., Harris, P.J., & Duval, L. (1993). Placement, identification and subtype correlates of peer status and social behavior of children with learning disabilities. *Exceptional Education Canada*, 3:129–155.

Wiener, J., Harris, P.J., & Shirer, C. (1990). Achievement and social behavior correlates of peers' status in children with learning disabilities. *Learning Disability Quarterly*, 13:114–127.

Wiener, J., & Schneider, B. (2002). A multisource exploration of friendship patterns of children with learning disabilities. *Journal of Abnormal Child Psychology*, 30:127–141.

Wiener, J., & Sunohara, G. (1998). Parents' perceptions of the quality of friendship of their children with learning disabilities. *Learning Disability Research & Practice*, 13:242–257.

Wiener, J., & Tardiff, C. (2004). Social and emotional functioning of children with learning disabilities: Does special education placement make a difference? *Learning Disabilities Research & Practice*, 19:20–33.

Wong, B.Y.L. (1996). *The ABC's of Learning Disabilities*. San Diego: Academic Press.

Wong, B.Y.L., & Donahue, M. (2002). *Social Dimensions of Learning Disabilities*. Mahwah, NJ: Erlbaum.

SELF-REGULATION AND
LEARNING DISABILITIES

This chapter is about the thinking that effective learners do about their own learning. It is about the cognitive actions of autonomous learners who are aware of their own thinking and can regulate it within the processes of learning. It particularly concerns metacognition and self-regulation of learning and how these concepts interrelate to underpin effective academic performance. When learners are active, autonomous, and self-regulated, they have the motivation to learn and the will, or volition, to focus on learning goals and to withstand distractions to attain these goals. Such learners show initiative and independence as they maintain motivation and effort toward attaining success in school. They use appropriate attributional self-statements to explain their successes or setbacks and thus build a sense of self-efficacy that fuels their strategic approach to learning and predicts future academic achievement.

The term *self-regulation*, then, has a complex meaning, referring to students' characteristic combinations of metacognition, motivation, and volition that direct and sustain their active participation in learning. This chapter explores self-regulation through discussing the important components of self-regulated learning such as interest and motivation, metacognition, attributional patterns and self-efficacy, as well as presenting some research-based approaches to encouraging self-regulation. It will also emphasize the relevance of metacognition and self-regulation to the field of learning disabilities.

CHARACTERISTICS OF THE WHOLE LEARNER

All educators aim to facilitate the development of learners who have clear understandings of the processes of learning and who can manage these complex processes independently. Self-regulation and metacognition are not isolated cognitive processes, but they interact dynamically with other factors related to individuals' functioning (Sternberg, 1998). Because learners are not just cognitive beings, it is important to consider how their social and emotional dimensions affect their cognitive functioning and their learning. For example, a 15-year-old student named Alex recently stated that he didn't see the point in trying to learn spelling because he had been failing at it for so many years. He did not want to try anymore. Alex no longer believes he can learn to spell and said, "I can't spell and I can't do languages at school." Alex has developed these beliefs about himself based on his school experiences and early high school exposure to French and Indonesian language lessons, both of which he found difficult to engage with and master. His belief has been compounded by the difficulties he has encountered learning to spell in English. Alex has made sense of his spelling difficulties through attributing them to his inability to learn languages. He has come to believe this is an innate, immutable factor in his makeup.

The task of an educator in providing learning assistance for Alex is to target his cognitive skills as well as work on his motivation and instill some sense of self-belief through authentic success. All three of these areas—cognitive skills, motivation and self-efficacy—must be addressed for Alex to begin to learn effectively and set attainable educational goals for himself. This example reflects the need to look at the whole student when considering what is involved in fostering self-regulation of learning. It does not consist of simply teaching the student a series of cognitive strategies. Affective and metacognitive dimensions of learning must also be considered. The following section provides brief descriptions of the main dimensions of functioning that combine to result in self-regulated learning.

COMPONENTS OF SELF-REGULATED LEARNING

The development of self-regulated learners is a major goal of schooling. In general, students are motivated to develop self-regulation and independence as learners so that they can become managers of their own learning. Self-regulated learners are those who are engaged in "an active, constructive process" in which they "set goals for their learning and then attempt to monitor, regulate, and control their cognition, motivation, and behavior, guided and constrained by their goals and the contextual features in the environment" (Pintrich, 2000). Autonomous learners who are sensitive to their own thinking, the learning environment, and who are able to regulate their own behavior in relation to appropriate goals, make very effective learners. In fact, it was the recognition that although all learners may have particular self-management skills, their use of them is inconsistent and inefficient at times that led to the formulation of the concept of metacognition (Brown, 1980; Flavell, 1976). Flavell's conception of metacognition consists of two interrelated factors, self-awareness and self-regulation, which support an individual's effective learning. Brown elaborated on the nature of metacognition in her important research. She researched a model of learning with four main factors: *characteristics of the learner, nature of the materials to be learned, the criterial task*, and *learning activities*.

In the following example that illustrates Brown's model, Wong (1991) shows how good students use metacognitive strategies to study effectively. After being told that there will be a midterm examination of short-answer essay questions, the good students will begin to plan their study schedule. Three weeks before the midterm, they start reading their lecture notes and corresponding text chapters. They underline important information. In addition, they identify the parts of the text that they do not understand. Students then seek help to clarify what they don't understand from the course teaching team. After receiving the necessary help, the students then concentrate their efforts at studying the important parts of their notes and texts. Because short answers rather than multiple-choice questions will be on the exam, good students also spend time thinking about what they are studying and the implications of this information for the classroom.

In this example, it is clear how good students consciously and deliberately coordinate their efforts to study effectively. The skills they have marshaled in coordinating and regulating their efforts in studying are metacognitive skills. They have coordinated and regulated their own knowledge, notes, and texts; their own learning activities; and information they have about the criterial task. These are the factors that are key to Brown's model. Thus, it can be seen that metacognitive skills are essential for effective coordination, or orchestration, of the four factors in that model and that this coordination greatly affects students' learning.

In an influential way, Brown underscored how metacognition serves to orchestrate self-knowledge, task demands, and appropriate learning activities to result in successful learning. The work of Brown and her colleagues (e.g., Brown 1980; Baker & Brown, 1984) has served as a foundation for later models of metacognition and self-regulation. The emphasis in recent models of effective learning has shifted to self-regulation as the overarching concept within which metacognition operates alongside motivational dimensions such as attributions and a sense of self-efficacy.

Over the last decade, increasingly complex models of self-regulation have been developed. For example, Boekaerts's (1997) model proposed two dimensions of self-regulation by delineating cognitive from motivational self-regulation. Later, Zimmerman (2002) presented a three-phase model that sought to reflect the cognitive and affective dimensions of the learner, and Pintrich (2000) put forward a model with four dimensions within which regulation operates.

Pintrich's model describes the actions of an active learner engaged in complex cognition. According to his model, learners are influenced by both affect and motivation as they demonstrate behaviors and strategic functioning within a particular learning context. Pintrich's model of self-regulation integrates the concepts of metacognition, motivation, attribution, self-efficacy, planning, effort, and help-seeking behaviors under the organizing notion of self-regulation.

TABLE 5.1   Adapted Version of Pintrich's Model of Self-Regulated Learning

Phases	Possible areas for regulation			
	Cognition	Motivation/ affect	Behavior	Context
1. Forethought, planning, and activation	Target goal setting Prior content and knowledge activation Metacognitive knowledge activation	Adoption of goal orientation Efficacy judgments Ease of learning judgments Perceptions of task difficulty Task value activation Interest activation	Time and effort planning Planning for self-observations of behavior	Perceptions of task Perceptions of context
2. Monitoring	Metacognitive awareness and monitoring of cognition	Awareness and monitoring of motivation and affect	Awareness and monitoring of effort, time use, and need for help Self-observation of behavior	Monitoring and changing task and context conditions
3. Control	Selection and adaptation of cognitive strategies for learning and thinking	Selection and adaptation of strategies for managing motivation and affect	Increase/ decrease effort Persist, give up Help-seeking behavior	Change or renegotiate task Change or leave context
4. Reaction and reflection	Cognitive judgments Attributions	Affective reactions Attributions	Choice behavior	Evaluation of task Evaluation of context

METACOGNITION

A self-regulated learner sets goals and activates prior knowledge about both the content area and thinking processes. Throughout learning, the learner functions cognitively as well as metacognitively, selects cognitive strategies and makes judgments about cognition and about attribution for learning. Metacognition is the ability to "step back" from thinking and to become aware of one's own processes of thinking. Flavell's (1976) initial definition of the construct included aspects of both self-awareness and self-regulation. Later, Brown and her colleagues (Brown, 1980; Baker & Brown,1984) defined *metacognition* as consisting of a knowledge component as well as a management or control component.

Wong and her associates (Wong & Wong, 1986; Wong, Butler, Ficzere, & Kuperis, 1996) investigated how metacognitive knowledge is related to academic performance for students who have learning disabilities. Generally, students with learning disabilities have little awareness of the cognitive processes in which they engage as learners. For these students metacognition is slow to develop, tends to be less sophisticated and needs to be fostered through explicit instruction (Wong & Wong, 1986; Wong et al., 1996). Two studies conducted by Wong and her colleagues will be described to illustrate the differences in metacognition experienced by students with learning disabilities compared to their average achieving peers.

First, Wong, Wong, and LeMare (1982) investigated the importance of clear information about criterial task demands on the recall and comprehension of text for students with learning disabilities and average achieving students. In the comprehension task used in this study, students were given information that guided them to attend to prequestions about two expository passages. These prequestions modeled the test questions the students would receive later. In the recall condition of this study, students were simply told to study the passages for subsequent recall.

The results of the first part of this study showed that both average-achieving students and students with learning disabilities answered more comprehension questions correctly than those in the control condition. Findings from the recall part of the study, however, did not yield reliable differences between the experimental and control groups. This was attributed to the general nature of the instructions given to the experimental group.

In the second part of this study, Wong et al. (1982) improved the information given about the requirements of the recall task so that students in the experimental group were told to focus on important parts of the passage, while students in the control group were told to study all the passages for recall. These results clearly indicated that given specific knowledge about task requirements, both average-achieving students and students with learning disabilities were able to recall more of the passages than students in the control condition. Overall, this study showed that explicit knowledge of the task criteria can engender appropriate studying activities in students.

In a later research study also investigating metacognition in reading, Wong and Wong (1986) established that students with learning disabilities have less sophisticated metacognitive skills than students without learning disabilities. In this study, Wong and Wong focused on how metacognitive knowledge of vocabulary difficulty and passage organization affected the study time allocations made by students who were either high achieving, average achieving, or experienced learning disabilities. Wong and Wong (1986) found a significant interaction between the type of reader and the type of passage. Readers with learning disabilities were most sensitive to the level of vocabulary in a passage, whereas above-average readers were most sensitive to the organization of the text. Specifically, when discriminating between the pair of passages with either easy or difficult vocabulary, only readers with learning disabilities studied the passage containing more difficult vocabulary words for a significantly longer time. Likewise, only the above-average readers showed reliable differences in the study times allocated by concentrating on the disorganized passage for a significantly longer period of time compared to the better-organized text.

The findings of Wong and Wong's (1986) study are important because they indicate that students with learning disabilities do indeed have some level of metacognitive awareness but that it tends to be less refined than that of their average- and high-achieving peers. Readers with learning disabilities certainly demonstrated metacognitive knowledge about vocabulary difficulty and were able to employ suitable strategies to address their difficulties in this area. One reason for this finding may be related to the difficulties students with learning disabilities have with decoding and their accompanying awareness of the difficulties that challenging vocabulary words present in reading passages. Students in this study indicated that they had developed strategies to overcome this difficulty: They read slowly and studied the materials that contained the more challenging vocabulary words for a longer period of time.

Insights about the metacognitive proficiency of students with learning disabilities from these examples of Wong's research are clear. Because students with learning disabilities commonly struggle with decoding problems, they have developed the awareness that when they encounter difficult words in a passage, they must spend more time on the text to understand its meaning. However, because most of these students' cognitive resources are consumed by decoding, there are few left over to facilitate reading comprehension and the development of more sophisticated understandings about text, such as that a disorganized passage is harder to study than an organized passage. Until students with learning disabilities master decoding, they do not have the cognitive resources at their disposal to develop higher-order metacognitive skills in reading. Similarly, with regards to writing, Wong and her colleagues (e.g., Wong et al., 1994; Wong et al., 1996) again established that adolescents with learning disabilities are slow to develop awareness of their own cognitive processes and the major criterial task demands of writing (e.g., for planning and clarity of communication).

In summary, it is important to acknowledge the research-based finding that students with learning disabilities have significant difficulties with "strategic processing and metacognition" (Gersten, Fuchs, Williams, & Baker, 2001, p. 280). This perspective supports the usefulness of instruction that focuses on teaching cognitive and metacognitive strategies. Like cognition, metacognition is developmental: Both thinking itself and thinking about thinking improve with maturity and experience and can be facilitated by the explicit teaching of appropriate strategies.

MOTIVATION

Self-regulated learners are self-motivated. They are activated by interest, set realistic goals, make supportive judgments about ease of learning, about task difficulty, about self-efficacy, and attribute learning outcomes appropriately (Pintrich, 2000).

Motivation is the desire to learn and to achieve. It is a vitally important consideration for learning because students are most effective when they are active and engage with purpose and persistence in the process of learning. Human beings need to be motivated to spend cognitive and emotional energy on any activity and to persist during times of challenge. Self-regulated learners have levels of intrinsic motivation that support their need to learn and keep focused on tasks (Ryan & Deci, 2000). Intrinsic motivation, a key concept in educational psychology, refers to one's internally directed motivation for learning. It is not dependent on rewards but comes from enjoyment and interest and is related to self-satisfaction.

Although a self-motivated learner is seen to use intrinsic motivation, it is also accepted that extrinsic motivation has an ongoing role for self-regulated learners. Many effective learners manage the use of extrinsic rewards to support their effort in learning. For Pintrich this is management of motivation and affect, in which learners select and adapt strategies for supporting their learning, including activating intrinsic motivation and selecting extrinsic motivators. Motivation can vary greatly depending on the task, the learner's goals, the rewards available, and expectations of performance that teachers and students hold for themselves and each other. Although extrinsic motivators are seen to be tools to develop intrinsic motivation, they can also undermine existing intrinsic motivation and can encourage surface learning (Vialle, Lysaght, & Verenikina, 2005).

Motivation can be a problematic aspect of functioning in school for students who have learning disabilities and are likely to have experienced consistently low levels of achievement over time. Motivation decreases in the face of failure and poor achievement, irrespective of the amount of effort a student might expend or the amount of task persistence displayed. In such situations, learners can develop reluctance to take risks in learning (Covington & Teel, 1996; Quirk, 2004) or other behavioral patterns that lead them to avoid academic tasks.

SELF-EFFICACY

What students believe about their own capacities to learn is another important factor underlying self-regulation of learning. This belief in the self as a learner impacts on the choices students make regarding how much effort to expend in trying to meet their learning goals and on how much motivation there is for learning. In this way, Bandura's (1997) concept of self-efficacy has been identified as a significant factor impacting on school achievement in an Australian study into underachieving gifted indigenous children (Merrotsy, 2004). In this research, strategies to enhance the self-efficacy of primary-aged indigenous children have been employed within a camp excursion and mentoring program that aims to reduce underachievement in school learning. This intervention program appears to give modest academic gains for participants. However, school academic performance is more than just test results. Merrotsy (2004) reports that after his intervention, students participate more willingly in school, engage in classroom activities, spend considerable time completing homework, and become involved in individual learning projects.

Accordingly, the power of learners' self-beliefs can be a complicating factor in the development of self-regulation. Young children's beliefs about themselves as learners clearly affect the decisions they make about how to regulate their learning behaviors (Perry & Drummond, 2002). This process becomes very complex for students who have learning disabilities, as their self-belief and sense of self-efficacy can be fragile. There is also research evidence that connects learning disabilities to negative mental health states based on some students' beliefs about themselves as learners and, in particular, their negative attributions for failure to uncontrollable factors (Heath & Weiner, 1996; Rodis, 2001).

The well-being of students with learning disabilities is influenced by a number of variables, including the specific nature and severity of the learning disability, the level of support from family members, economic status, social support networks, the students' match with their educational program, the existence of individual competencies, and the way that students make sense of their experiences (Margalit & Levin-Alyagon, 1994). It is clear that the whole person behind the label of learning disabilities is vitally important because individual affective characteristics have significant impact on students' development as autonomous learners. Students who have a history of low achievement or failure on a daily basis can develop learned helplessness when they lose the sense of connection between their effort and any possibility of success.

Students in this situation can learn behaviors that help them cope in school and be somewhat "class wise" but that are not beneficial to them in the long term. Students may copy others' work, for example, or engage in low-level disruptive behavior that distracts their teachers from paying attention to their academic performance. Learned helplessness affects motivation and effort. It is described as "the situation in which an individual never expects to succeed with any task he or she is given, and feels totally powerless to change this outcome" (Westwood, 2007, p. 12). Learners who develop learned helplessness have great difficulty engaging in and persisting with the hard work of learning.

Going back to the example of Alex earlier in this chapter, Alex was determined that he is not going to play the spelling game. He was not engaging cognitively or behaviorally because he believed that he could not succeed. His self-efficacy and motivation blocked his cognitive engagement and limited his chances for experiencing success. As this example illustrates, experiencing learning disabilities is not just a cognitive issue, but it affects the whole person—a person with social, emotional, and cognitive dimensions who operates within a social and cultural context.

ATTRIBUTION

Self-regulated learners attribute their learning success and failure in such a way that it supports future learning. Attributions affect both cognition and motivation. Attribution theory (Weiner, 1972) is a useful framework for considering what actions can be taken to influence motivation in the classroom. Learners can attribute or explain their success or otherwise to ability, effort, task difficulty, or luck (Weiner, 1972).

Attribution theory presents a way of understanding how people make decisions about the causes of events. These decisions, or attributions, are classified according to three causal dimensions (Weiner, 1986). The first is whether the locus of control that affects the decision is internal or external, the second is whether the cause is stable or unstable, and the third is whether the cause is controllable or uncontrollable.

Students may adopt attributions for success based on their own effort (e.g., they studied hard for the test), or they may attribute failure to their own lack of effort (e.g., they didn't bother to study for the test at all). Effort as an attribution is internal, unstable, and controllable. Alternatively, students may attribute success or failure to a cause such as luck, which is external, unstable, and uncontrollable (Dweck, 1999). Attributions affect motivation, performance, and emotions, which in turn contribute to students' expectations for future success or failure (Schunk, 1991; Whitley & Frieze, 1985).

Three students eagerly waited as their teacher handed back a test. "How did you do, Jo?" asked Jamie.

"Terrible," Jo answered. "I just can't do this stuff. I'm no good at it."

    Attribution to lack of ability

"I didn't do so well either," said Jamie, "but I knew I wouldn't. I didn't study hard enough."

    Attribution to lack of effort

"Unbelievable!" shouted Harrison. "I didn't know what the heck was going on, and I got a B. She mustn't have read my paper."

    Attribution to luck

                                            Adapted from Eggen and Kauchak (1999)

FIGURE 5.1   Examples of Attributions to Explain Performance. Adapted from Eggen and Kauchak (1999).

The scenario in Figure 5.1 illustrates some of the different attributions students use to explain their performances.

Attributions that explain success or failure are connected to motivation and to an individual's ability to cope at work or at school. For example, Dweck (1999) also concluded that attribution theory connects with theories of intelligence. Likewise, Pintrich (2000) associated attribution theory with achievement goal theories, while Graham (1991) showed that attribution theories interact with theories of self-efficacy, as proposed by Bandura (1997), and self-worth, as described by Covington (1984).

To illustrate, students' attributions about the effectiveness of personal effort in underlying success may begin from a belief that intelligence is malleable. Such a belief is supported by strategies such as attempting to understand the learning context and trying harder the next time if failure occurs (Dweck, 1999). At the other end of the scale, theories of fixed intelligence generate attributions that reveal conceptions of finite ability and lead to statements such as "I'm just not smart enough." Although some theorists (e.g., Dweck, 1999) propose that attributions act as relatively stable personal characteristics that influence goal setting, other theorists suggest that the characteristics of the environment are more influential (Ames, 1990; Ames, 1992; Ames & Archer, 1988).

Overall, attribution theory suggests that teaching students to attribute their successes and failures to internal, controllable events such as effort and strategic behavior lead to students perceiving that they have more control over situations and life choices. Research also indicates that attribution retraining can be effective. For example, Dweck (1999) provided students with specific feedback that their poor performance was due to their lack of effort and appropriate strategy use. Subsequently, these learners responded more effectively to future learning opportunities by persisting longer and adapting strategies more effectively to meet their learning goals. It is vitally important to consider the types of attributional—that is, explanations for success and failure which are modeled to students by teachers through the feedback they give about classroom performance.

SELF-REGULATION AND LEARNING DISABILITIES: A SUMMARY

Before considering some ways that self-regulation can be assessed and encouraged, it is a good idea to ask how the preceding discussion of self-regulated learning and metacognition relates to learning disabilities. As a reader and as a student, what part can you suggest self-regulation plays in understanding students with learning disabilities? How does it help teachers set useful goals for students with learning disabilities as learners? Remember that self-regulated learners are those who are engaged in "an active, constructive process" in which they "set goals for their learning and then attempt to monitor, regulate, and control their cognition, motivation, and behavior, guided and constrained by their goals and the contextual features in the environment" (Pintrich, 2000, p. 453). Such autonomous learners who are sensitive to their own thinking and the learning environment and who are able to regulate their own behavior in relation to appropriate goals, are very effective learners.

Students with learning disabilities and low achievers tend to lack all of the characteristics attributed to self-regulated learners. For example, students with learning disabilities have been described as passive learners who may have developed "learned helplessness" (Torgesen, 1977) because a history of school failure eroded away their motivation and sense of self-efficacy as learners. Alternately, students with learning disabilities may have experienced too much structure and too many experiences with learning scaffolds during attempts to address their learning problems. Continuously scaffolding learning without gradually withdrawing the supports and encouraging students' ownership and independence can further disable individuals with learning disabilities. All students need to learn to value a thoughtful, strategic approach to learning that requires effort to be successful (Borkowski, Estrada, Milstead, & Hale, 1989; Harris, Reid, & Graham, 2004).

In contrast to students with learning disabilities and low-achieving students, successful students most often display all of the attributes of self-regulated learners (Butler, 2004; Wigfield, 1994; Zimmerman, 1989). Because teachers want all their students, including those with LD and low achievers to become self-regulated learners, they must focus on helping them to develop autonomy and self-direction in learning, as well as fostering a sense of self-efficacy and the motivation to learn. It should be remembered, however, that students with learning disabilities do possess certain cognitive and metacognitive strategies, but these strategies tend to be inefficient (such as word by word reading) or faulty (such as erroneous strategies in arithmetic).

What, then, is the relevance of the constructs of metacognition and self-regulation to learning disabilities? The relevance of these constructs lies in demonstrating that students with learning disabilities have less sophisticated metacognition than their peers in reading and very little of it in writing. Consequently, they need instruction in efficient metacognitive and cognitive strategies in reading and exposure to ways to enhance their awareness and understanding of the writing process and problem solving in mathematics.

ASSESSMENT OF ASPECTS OF SELF-REGULATION

Continued research into the information-processing framework of cognition has opened up alternate ways of thinking about and working with students who have learning disabilities. Some cognitive processing tests are currently available for use by psychologists and special educators to assess the cognitive processing skills of learners. For example, Swanson (1996) has developed a Cognitive Processing Test (S-CPT) based on the assumption that cognitive processing performance is modifiable. This notion is operationalized by the way the S-CPT uses dynamic testing to alter a student's cognitive processing levels during the assessment procedure. From the results of these interactive sessions, it is possible to understand how students are processing information and what instructional supports can assist them to move to more efficient levels of processing.

Das and Naglieri (1997) have also developed a specific cognitive-processing test that is used in clinical settings to investigate cognitive processing along four dimensions: planning, attention arousal, simultaneous processing, and successive processing (PASS).

These dimensions have been highlighted as a key cognitive process within A. R. Luria's (1966) seminal work on the modularization of brain function. Subsequently, J. P. Das developed the PASS theory that divides intelligence into four interrelated cognitive processes:

1. *Planning:* This is the ability to make decisions about how to solve problems and perform actions. It involves setting goals, anticipating

consequences, and using feedback. Planning also involves the attention-arousal, simultaneous, and successive processing functions and is associated with the frontal lobes of the brain.

2. *Attention-Arousal:* This involves the ability to selectively attend to stimuli while ignoring other distractions. Individuals with Attention Deficit Disorder (ADD) and Attention Deficit Hyperactivity Disorder (ADHD) have impairments in this area. The arousal functions are generally associated with the brain stem and thalamus, whereas the higher attention-oriented processes are thought to relate to the planning functions of the frontal lobe.

3. *Simultaneous Processing:* This involves the ability to integrate separate stimuli into a cohesive, interrelated whole. Simultaneous processing is necessary for language comprehension, as in "Who is the person in the following statement: My mother's father was his only son" (answer: my great-grandfather; Naglieri & Das, 1997). The occipital and parietal lobes are thought to be important for simultaneous processing.

4. *Successive Processing:* This involves the ability to integrate stimuli into a sequential order. An example of this process is the sequencing of letters and words in reading and writing. This type of processing is believed to relate to frontal-temporal lobe functioning (Das, 2002).

According to the PASS theory, information first arrives through the senses from external and internal sources, at which point the four cognitive processes activate to analyze its meaning within the context of the individual's knowledge base (e.g., semantic and episodic knowledge and implicit and procedural memories).

As mentioned previously, the PASS theory provides the theoretical framework for a measurement instrument called the Naglieri-Das Cognitive Assessment System (CAS; 1997). This test is designed to provide a nuanced assessment of individuals' intellectual functioning by providing information about their cognitive strengths and weaknesses in each of the four PASS processes. This emphasis on processes, rather than abilities, makes the CAS useful for differential diagnosis. Unlike traditional full-scale intelligence tests, the CAS is capable of diagnosing learning disabilities and Attention Deficit Disorder. It has been designed for use with children and adolescents from age 5 to 17.

The PASS theory of cognitive processing and its related CAS assessment tool have proven useful for both intellectual assessment and for guiding educational interventions. For example, the PASS theory provides the theoretical framework for the PASS Reading Enhancement Programme (PREP), which features a curriculum designed to improve the planning, attention, and information-processing strategies that underlie reading (Das, 1999). A similar curriculum has been developed to help students with difficulties in arithmetic.

Other examples of cognitive processing tests include the Learning Process Questionnaire (Biggs, 1987) that focuses on students' approaches to learning and the Active Learner Student and Teacher Questionnaires

(Minskoff & Allsopp, 2003) that aim to assist students with learning disabilities to "become more effective learners so that they can better meet the increasingly rigorous academic expectations of inclusive settings" (p.4).

INSTRUCTIONAL APPROACHES

There has been significant research into cognitive strategy instruction for students who have learning disabilities in separate and inclusive class settings (see Wong, Harris, Graham, & Butler, 2003). There has also been considerable research into the development of cognitive skills through cognitive education (Adey & Shayer, 2002). The belief that cognition and metacognition are teachable underlies the development and utility of all these instructional approaches. Because cognitive strategy instruction has been summarized in Wong et al. (2003), we focus on cognitive education.

COGNITIVE EDUCATION

There is considerable work around the world on cognitive education, in which teaching focuses on cognitive processes and strives to enhance students' cognitive processing to develop their higher thinking abilities and metacognition (Adey & Shayer, 2002). Such a focus on thinking skills in learning is reflected in curriculum documents being currently developed in Australia. For example, the first of the 26 *Essential Learning Achievements* listed in the Australian Capital Territory Curriculum Framework (ACT, 2006) is that "the student uses a range of strategies to think and learn." The development of thinking is also a central tenet of the National Curriculum for England (Adey & Shayer, 2002).

Much of the cognitive education movement has been driven by the theories of Vygotsky, who developed the influential theory of learning reflected in Figure 5.2. This model of learning presents another perspective that helps make sense of the development of self-regulation. Initially, learning is directed through the regulation of children's behavior by a more experienced person using speech, written language, number symbol systems, social rules, and value systems. This is known as mediation, and it refers not only to external behavior but also to thinking. In the classroom the teacher regulates the students' learning, and because the social learning situation is interactive, the children can also regulate others' behaviors using the same cultural tools. Learning in a social context is not a one-way transaction but rather a situation of mutual responsiveness. Teachers use strategies such as peer teaching and cooperative group work to foster the second stage of this process, in which learners regulate someone else's behavior, or thinking, using speech. The process continues through internalization until learners

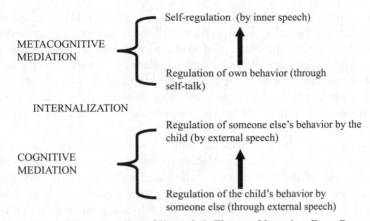

FIGURE 5.2   A Representation of Vygotsky's Theory of Learning. From Berman, 2001.

begin to regulate their own learning and thinking using self-talk. Finally, learners are fully autonomous and regulate their own thinking and learning using inner speech. Teachers aim to foster this development of self-regulation in all their students.

GENERAL CLASSROOM INSTRUCTION FOR SELF-REGULATION

Ley and Young (2001) have proposed that instruction for self-regulation can be embedded effectively within all classroom instruction. To this end, they have provided a set of four principles to guide the embedding of support for self-regulation within regular instruction. The four common instructional principles they suggest have been substantiated as significant for the development of self-regulation in "less expert learners" (Ley and Young, 2001, p. 94). The principles Ley and Young propose are (1) to guide learners to prepare and structure an effective learning environment; (2) to organize instructional activities to facilitate cognitive and metacognitive processes; (3) to use goal-setting and feedback to present the learner with monitoring opportunities; and (4) to provide learners with continuous evaluation information and occasions to self-evaluate.

CONCLUDING COMMENTS AND CONTINUING QUESTIONS

To revisit the focus of this chapter, what is the place of metacognition and self-regulation in our current conceptualisation of learning disabilities? Metacognition, defined as the awareness of and ability to regulate thinking, is important because of how it guides students' effective reading and studying. Within the broader construction of self-regulation, metacognition is combined with other dimensions of skill and will, such as motivation, attributions, and self-efficacy. Because many students who have learning disabilities have little awareness of their own thinking and do not use self-talk to regulate their learning, the consideration of metacognition and self-regulation is particularly important for this population of students. It is important for three main reasons.

First, metacognitive problems account for some of the significant performance deficiencies in academic subjects experienced by students with learning disabilities. All of the difficulties experienced by students with learning disabilities are not attributable to information processing or language problems. Some are due to affective factors, others due to motivation, and still others because of poor instruction and the cumulative effects of failure.

Second, the research reviewed in this chapter indicates that addressing students' academic learning difficulties is best attempted by combining explicit instruction in metacognitive self-awareness with strategies in reading, writing, mathematics, and spelling. In light of the research on metacognition in reading, mathematics, and writing, an exclusive focus on skill building is simply not enough. Teachers should include a self-regulating component in any strategy instruction. This can be as simple as including a form of self-monitoring to check accurate strategy use or providing an explicit procedure for self-checking one's work. For example, students with learning disabilities can check their own arithmetic calculations and answers prior to handing in assignments. Systematic and consistent inclusion of self-regulating components as part of strategy instruction would assist students with learning disabilities to behave like autonomous learners, which is one of the ultimate instructional goals for these and for all, students.

Third, because of the pervasive nature of learning disabilities, it is necessary to work toward establishing a community of learners that both encourages and facilitates the teaching and learning of self-regulation strategies across the whole school curriculum. As Perry and Drummond (2002) have identified, a community of learners exists where (1) students and teachers are engaged in complex and cognitively demanding activities; (2) students move constantly toward taking increased control of their own learning; (3) evaluation is nonthreatening; and (4) teachers provide instrumental and responsive support for student learning. Teaching children and adolescents with learning disabilities to self-regulate as they engage with learning across the whole school curriculum is the continuing challenge. To secure successful learning for all students, it is essential to have collaborative research among academics, school administrators, classroom teachers, and support teachers to develop and refine ways to inculcate self-regulation.

SUMMARY

This chapter presented research information on self-regulation and showed its cardinal role in effective learning and performance. We highlight several aspects of it.

• There is the instructive exposition on the complex meaning of self-regulation.

• The components of self-regulated learning are examined. These components include interest, motivation, metacognition, attributional patterns, and self-efficacy.

• The PASS model is succinctly summarized. Last but not least, this chapter points to the need for researchers to conduct more basic research into self-regulation in children and adolescents with learning disabilities.

REFERENCES

Adey, P., & Shayer, M. (2002). *Learning intelligence: Cognitive acceleration across the curriculum from 5 to 15 years.* Buckingham: Open University Press.

Ames, C.A. (1990). Motivation: What teachers need to know. *Teachers College Record,* 91:409–421.

Ames, C.A. (1992). Classrooms: Goals, structures and student motivation. *Journal of Educational Psychology,* 84:261–271.

Ames, C., & Archer, J. (1988). Achievement goals in the classroom: Students' learning strategies and motivation processes. *Journal of Educational Psychology,* 80(3), 260–267.

Baker, L., & Brown, A. (1984). Metacognition skills of reading. In D.P. Pearson (Ed.), *Handbook on research in reading* (pp. 353–394). New York: Longman.

Bandura, A. (1997). *Self-efficacy: The exercise of control.* New York: W. H. Freeman.

Berman, J. (2001). *An application of dynamic assessment to school mathematical learning.* Unpublished PhD thesis. Armidale: University of New England.

Biggs, J.B. (1987). *Student approaches to learning and studying.* Victoria: Australian Council for Educational Research.

Boekaerts, M. (1997). Self-regulated learning: A new concept embraced by researchers, policy makers, educators, teachers, and students. *Learning and Instruction,* 7(2), 161–186.

Borkowski, J.G., Estrada, M.T., Milstead, M., & Hale, C.A. (1989). General problem-solving skills: Relations between metacognition and strategic processes. *Learning Disability Quarterly,* 12:57–70.

Brown, A. (1980). Metacognitve development and reading. In R.J. Spiro, B. Bruce, & W.F. Brewer (Eds.), *Theoretical issues in reading comprehension* (pp. 453–481). Hillsdale, NJ: Lawrence Erlbaum.

Butler, D. (2004). Adults with learning disabilities. In B.Y.L. Wong (Ed.), *Learning about learning disabilities* (pp. 565–598). New York: Elsevier Academic Press.

Covington, M. (1984). The motive for self-worth. In R. Ames, & C. Ames (Eds.), *Research on motivation in education* (Vol. 1, pp. 78–114). New York: Academic Press.

Covington, M., & Teel, K. (1996). *Overcoming student failure: Changing motives and incentives for learning.* Washington, D.C: American Psychological Association.

Das, J.P. (1999). *PREP: PASS Reading Enhancement Program*. Deal, NJ: Sarka Educational Resources.

Das, J.P. (2002). A better look at intelligence. *Current Directions in Psychological Science*, 11(1), 28–33.

Das, J.P., & Naglieri, J.A. (1997). *Naglieri-Das Cognitive Assessment System*. Chicago: Riverside.

Dweck, C. (1999). *Self-theories: Their role in motivation, personality and development*. Philadelphia, PA: Psychology Press.

Eggen, P., & Kauchak, D. (1999). *Educational psychology: Windows on classrooms*. (4th ed.). Upper Saddle River, NJ: Prentice Hall.

Flavell, J.H. (1976). Metacognitive aspects of problem solving. In L.B. Resnick (Ed.), *The nature of intelligence* (pp. 231–235). Hillsdale, NJ: Erlbaum.

Gersten, R., Fuchs, L.S., Williams, J.P., & Baker, S. (2001). Teaching reading comprehension strategies to students with learning disabilities: A review of research. *Review of Educational Research*, 71:279–320.

Graham, S. (1991). A review of attribution theory in achievement contexts. *Educational Psychology Review*, 3:5–39.

Harris, K.R., Reid, R.R., & Graham, S. (2004). Self-regulation among students with LD and ADHD. In B.Y.L. Wong (Ed.), *Learning about learning disabilities* (pp. 167–195). New York: Elsevier Academic Press.

Heath, N.L., & Weiner, J. (1996). Depression and nonacademic self-perceptions in children with and without learning disabilities. *Learning Disability Quarterly*, 19(1), 34–44.

Ley, K., & Young, D. (2001). Instructional principles for self-regulation. *Educational Technology Research and Development*, 49(2), 93–103.

Luria, A.R. (1966). *Human brain and psychological processes*. New York: Harper & Row.

Margalit, M., & Levin-Alyagon, M. (1994). Learning disability subtyping, loneliness, and classroom adjustment. *Learning Disability Quarterly*, 17(4), 297–310.

Merrotsy, P. (2006). The Wii Gaay Project: Gifted Aboriginal students. In N. Parbury & R. Craven (Eds.), *Aboriginal studies: Making the connections* (pp. 99–110). *Collected papers of the 12th National ASA Conference*. Sydney: Aboriginal Studies Association.

Minskoff, E., & Allsopp, D. (2003). *Academic success strategies for adolescents with learning disabilities and ADHD*. Baltimore, MD: Paul Brookes Publishing.

Naglieri, J.A., & Das, J.P. (1997). The PASS cognitive processing theory. In R.F. Dillon (Ed.), *Handbook on testing* (pp. 138–163). London: Greenwood Press.

Perry, N., & Drummond, L. (2002). Helping young students become self-regulated researchers and writers: Here's how one teacher used research and writing activities to help students develop independent, academically effective approaches to reading and writing. *The Reading Teacher*, 56:298–310.

Pintrich, P.R. (2000). The role of goal orientation in self-regulated learning. In M. Boekaerts, P.R. Pintrich, & M. Zeidner (Eds.), *Handbook of self-regulation* (pp. 451–502). San Diego, CA: Academic Press.

Quirk, M.P. (2004). Do supplemental remedial reading programs address the motivational issues of struggling readers? *Reading Research and Instruction*, 43:1–19.

Ryan, R., & Deci, E. (2000). Intrinsic and extrinsic motivations: Classic definitions and new directions. *Contemporary Educational Psychology*, 25:54–67.

Schunk, D.H. (1991). Self-efficacy and academic motivation. *Educational Psychologist*, 26:207–231.

Sternberg, R.J. (1998). *In search of the human mind*. (2nd ed.). Orlando: Harcourt Brace College Publishers.

Swanson, H.L. (1996). Individual and age-related differences in children's working memory. *Memory and Cognition*, 24(1), 70–82.

Torgesen, J.K. (1977). The role of nonspecific factors in the task performance of learning isabled children: A theoretical assessment. . . . *Journal of Learning Disabilities*, 10(1), 27–34.

Vialle, W., Lysaght, P., & Verenikina, I. (2005). *Psychology for educators*. Victoria: Thomson.

Weiner, B. (1972). Attribution theory, achievement motivation, and the educational process. *Review of Educational Research*, 42:203–215.

Weiner, B. (1986). *An attributional theory of motivation and emotion*. New York: Springer-Verlag.

Westwood, P. (2007). *Commonsense methods for children with special educational needs*. London: Routledge.

Whitley, B.E., & Frieze, I.H. (1985). Children's causal attributions for success and failure in achievement settings: A meta-analysis. *Journal of Educational Psychology*, 77(5), 608–616.

Wigfield, A. (1994). Expectancy-value theory of achievement motivation: A developmental perspective. *Educational Psychology Review*, 6(1), 49–78.

Wong, B.Y.L., Butler, D.L., Ficzere, S.A., & Kuperis, S. (1996). Teaching adolescents with learning disabilities and low achievers to plan, write, and revise opinion essays. *Journal of Learning Disabilities*, 29(2), 197–212.

Wong, B.Y.L., Butler, D.L., Ficzere, S.A., Kuperis, S., Corden, M., & Zelmer, J. (1994). Teaching problem learners revision skills and sensitivity to audience through two instructional modes: Student-teachers versus student-student interactive dialogues. *Learning Disabilities Research & Practice*, 9(2), 78–90.

Wong, B.Y.L., Harris, K.R., Graham, S., & Butler, D.L. (2003). Cognitive strategies instruction research in learning disabilities. In H.L. Swanson, K.R. Harris, & S. Graham (Eds.), *Handbook on learning disabilities* (pp. 383–402). New York: Guilford.

Wong, B.Y.L. (1991). Learning about learning disabilities. New York: Academic Press.

Wong, B.Y.L., & Wong, R. (1986). Study behaviour as a function of metacognitve knowledge about critical task variables: An investigation of above average, average, and learning disabled readers. *Learning Disabilities Research*, 1:101–111.

Wong, B.Y.L., Wong, R., & LeMare, L.J. (1982). The effects of knowledge of criterion tasks on the comprehension and recall of normally-achieving and learning-disabled children. *Learning Disabilities Quarterly*, 12(4), 300–322.

Zimmerman, B.J. (2002). Becoming a self-regulated learner: An overview. *Theory into Practice*, 41(2), 64–72.

Zimmerman, B.J. (1989). A social cognitive view of self-regulated academic learning. *Journal of Educational Psychology*, 81(3), 329–339.

6

ASSESSMENT *FOR* LEARNING

This chapter examines important aspects of assessment. Specifically, we begin with the rationale of assessment. Then we discuss two major and broad assessment approaches: conventional and alternative assessments. The various alternative assessment procedures subsumed under alternative assessment are summarized. We close the chapter by addressing the importance of assessment feedback for students.

Assessment is integral to any teaching and learning situation. Good assessment procedures are particularly crucial for providing effective teaching for students with learning disabilities. Assessment is carried out for a range of purposes and in a range of situations. The move toward response to instruction (RTI) as a key framework for the assessment and identification of learning disabilities has broadened the focus of assessment because it removes the emphasis on factors inherent in the learner. Assessment practices now include consideration of the learner's environment and how well the learner responds to instruction in the classroom. This emphasis on *how* students respond to instruction means that ideally instruction can be tailored to their learning needs. Assessment for students with learning disabilities, then, has a focus on these students' responses to instruction to more effectively inform classroom instruction for all students. As teachers focus on how students respond to teaching and what factors hinder or support their learning, they develop a greater understanding of students' instructional needs and potential ways of supporting their successful learning in classrooms.

A CLASSROOM FRAMEWORK FOR ASSESSMENT

Teachers have available to them a wide range of assessment strategies that can be used in a complementary way to access comprehensive information about student learning and also to support targeted feedback about task performance. It is important for teachers to use frequent assessment that draws from the range of conventional and alternative assessment procedures so that assessment truly supports learning (Popham, 2006). Assessment can then become a powerful tool in teachers' hands to enhance teaching and learning in the classroom (Jochum, Curran, & Reetz, 1998).

The selection of appropriate assessment approaches and the valid interpretation of the resulting information are even more important when managing the learning of students who have learning disabilities. These students have learning needs that are often very complex and require careful investigation and close monitoring to make certain that their learning needs are targeted effectively.

Every time teachers choose a form of assessment to use in their classrooms they base that choice on *why* they are assessing as well as on *what* they plan to assess. Both of these factors influence teachers' choice of *how* to assess. This process of choice of assessment practices is illustrated in Figure 6.1.

No one form of assessment fits all situations. The complexity of learning has to be acknowledged. Learning depends not only on the inherent ability of each learner but is an interactive process that is influenced by factors within the student as well as within the student's learning environment, such as the curriculum and the teaching program. The elements of the model depicted in Figure 6.1 will be discussed in the following sections.

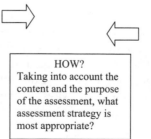

FIGURE 6.1   A process for selecting assessment strategies.

WHY ASSESS LEARNING?

Assessment supports educational decision making. Assessment in special and inclusive education supports a range of varied educational decisions ranging from placement to instructional design (Lidz, 2003; McLoughlin & Lewis, 2001; Salvia & Ysseldyke, 2001; Spinelli, 2002, 2006). In particular, four types of educational decisions that arise most consistently from the literature can be clearly identified. These four purposes of assessment are (1) determination of achievement levels of students, (2) selection and screening of students, (3) evaluation of systems and programs, and (4) informing instruction (Berman, 2001).

Classroom assessment practices can be chosen to meet each of these purposes. However, it is fundamentally important that teachers are explicit and thoughtful about the type of educational decisions that can be supported by any assessment procedure (Lidz, 2003). Teachers use assessment to determine the achievement of their students and to identify what levels of skills, knowledge, and understandings have been reached. They also use assessment to help screen and select students who may be in need of some variation to the classroom program. Another use of assessment procedures is for teachers to make decisions about the efficacy of their teaching approaches and to gather evidence of the effectiveness of their instructional programming. These are all important purposes for assessment. However, it is clear that the primary purpose of assessment for teachers in classrooms is to inform instruction. This is assessment *for* learning.

WHAT ARE WE ASSESSING?

How teachers understand the nature of learning will define what they assess in their classrooms. How learning was previously understood tended to be simple, so the assessment tools used were correspondingly simple. In the past, the products of learning and the behaviors evident in learners were most commonly assessed and usually in a summative manner. The beliefs were that learning consisted primarily of the transmission of knowledge, that teachers were there to pour knowledge into the empty vessel of the learner, and that they could measure how much knowledge the learners had gained.

Behaviorist theories are based on the philosophy that only observable behaviors can be studied. In particular, it was considered that the thoughts of individuals could not be studied because they "could not be observed by anyone except the person experiencing them, and no one, including that person, could actually measure them with any degree of confidence" (Sternberg, 1994, p. 171). For example, one early school mathematics textbook explicitly stated that "the less a pupil has to think, the more likely is it that mistakes will be avoided" (Durell, 1936, p. vii). This quote illustrates the early behaviorist perspective that thinking could interfere with behavioral performance.

The behaviorist theories of learning and the accompanying idea of transmission of knowledge are no longer satisfactory explanations of how people learn. Changes in how learning is understood have influenced pedagogical approaches as well as basic research into learning. As part of this shift, psychologists have concentrated on how individuals think and construct meaning. This focus on cognitive development rather than on behavior is the basis for current theories of learning that carry the constructivist label. The constructivist movement includes a diversity of learning theories that continue to evolve. Constructivist perspectives have differing emphases on the cognitive, social, and cultural aspects of learning (Malone & Ireland, 1996). The other major theoretical framework that has impacted on notions of teaching and assessment is information processing. The major models of learning that teachers rely on now recognize that learning involves cognitive processing and is carried out by an affective or emotional being within a sociocultural context.

Current conceptions of school learning reflect this multidimensional conception of learning. Broadly speaking, school learning is now conceptualized as including the previous behaviorist definition of skills and knowledge within a much broader discipline that sees the school curriculum as an evolving body of knowledge, skills, strategies, concepts, and processes embedded within social and emotional contexts. Learning is also defined in terms of "activity." Effective learners are expected to be active, self-reflective, and self-regulating. This is a very different characterization of a learner compared to that of the empty vessel or blank sheet of paper that behaviorist theories evoked. If we accept school learning to be represented as just described, then assessment practices need to reflect this multidimensional conception of learning.

HOW DO WE ASSESS LEARNING?

Teachers have a range of approaches and tools available in the classroom to help gather information that informs instruction. The major assessment options for teachers can be considered in terms of conventional and alternative forms of assessment.

CONVENTIONAL ASSESSMENT

As with all educational practice, a tradition of practice becomes established over the years that eventually becomes understood as the conventional paradigm of assessment (Galbraith, 1993). Conventional assessment in school learning has been aligned with general mental measurement and other established educational assessment approaches that developed over the past century. Conventional assessment is formal rather than informal, using tasks designed specifically and exclusively for assessment and presented within an "event." This kind of assessment is summative in that it provides information about prior learning. It is also terminal, usually administered at the end of a course of learning, and has generally been operationalized in the form of examinations or tests. The students' performance usually involves written responses on an examination or test with the scores marked by an examiner. The assessment can be external from the school or internal to it. External tests have been characterized as more objective and fair. Most conventional assessment uses convergent tasks designed to have only one correct response. Conventional assessment is also concerned with relating the results of an individual to the group (nomothetic), with comparing one student with another, and with understanding people in general, rather than understanding the learning needs of unique individuals (idiographic).

Conventional assessment has developed consistency in terms of procedures. The administration of written test papers, or pencil-and-paper tests, is the main procedure used in the conventional assessment of school learning. These kinds of tests have been used since at least 1845 (Kilpatrick, 1992). Such tests include a representative sample of questions selected from the defined content. The items can be selection type items (e.g., multiple choice, true-false, and matching items), short-answer closed questions, open questions, or extended response open questions (Lange, 1995). Commonly, conventional assessments involve the use of multiple-choice answer formats that are used to reduce the "demands of testing large numbers of students in short amounts of time" (Silver & Kenney, 1995, p. 43); however, "even classroom assessment is heavily dominated by a single short-answer testing format" (Webb, 1992, p. 664).

A more clinical form of conventional assessment involves individually administered oral tests. These are designed along the same lines as written tests and are administered to gather information about a student's strengths and weaknesses across topics. The format of these tests involves oral questions, accompanied by graphic or written stimuli, to which students must provide oral or written responses. Such tests are hierarchically arranged and standardized, and can be norm- and/or criterion-referenced. They are usually administered and interpreted by specialized professionals such as educational psychologists or specialist teachers.

In general, it is important to acknowledge that assessment theory developed separately from curriculum theory, the former associated with psychometricians and the latter with teachers (Graue, 1995). Psychometrics is the scientific study of the theory, development, and evaluation of measurement procedures in psychology. This paradigm began in the late nineteenth and early twentieth centuries (Galbraith, 1993; Sternberg, 1994). It has had a profound influence on perspectives of teaching and learning, which has resulted in a high level of status for psychometrically based educational assessment (Berlak, 1992; Clarke, 1992). Much energy has gone into developing and refining standardized measures of cognitive development and educational achievement. Examiners are highly trained to provide the standardization required to make results meaningful, and much money and time is invested in updating norms so that statistical meaning is retained over time. Such "well-standardized and psychometrically sound tests" are considered "indispensable for clinical and psychoeducational assessment" (Sattler, 1992, p. 4).

Thus, conventional assessment elicits behaviors and measures them, drawing conclusions about learning from the composite pattern of various behaviors. This is in conflict with how learning is now viewed. Resnick and Resnick (1992) see this as the educational community having "inherited only the tools of the routinized curriculum to meet the challenges of the thinking curriculum" (p. 41). The disquiet about the congruency of the theoretical bases of education and that of assessment was summed up by Stake's comment that the "simplicity of testing is at odds with the complexity of teaching and learning" (1995, p. 174). So in light of this discussion, what alternative assessment practices have been developed in response to the changing perception of learning?

ALTERNATIVE ASSESSMENT

Many forms of assessment have been developed as a consequence of the exploration of alternative assessment procedures in learning. Alternative assessment procedures tend to be less formal than conventional assessment. They can be continuous, not always needing an "event" to mark their occurrence. Moreover, they are generally more formative, focusing on what the procedures can do to support students' future learning. In this vein, alternative assessments focus more on the processes used by students rather than the products. More emphasis is placed on internal classroom assessment that provides space for students to demonstrate their divergence in learning. Reflecting this, alternative assessment is more idiographic (individually focused) than conventional assessment. Indeed, alternative assessment seeks to understand the educational needs of unique individuals in their school contexts. The focus is not only on factors inherent in the child but also on understanding the child's functioning as a learner and his or her individual interactions within educational settings. This kind of assessment is very appropriate to identifying the instructional needs of students with learning disabilities.

There is currently considerable interest in alternative procedures that have been developed for assessment of school learning. Herrington,

Sparrow, Herrington, & Oliver (1997) compiled a list of 23 assessment procedures that are appropriate for mathematics in K–12 classrooms at the beginning of the twenty-first century. Two of the assessment procedures listed, the pencil-and-paper test and the multiple-choice test, reflect conventional assessment. The other 21 strategies (e.g., portfolios, response journals, and self-assessments) are alternative but complementary to conventional forms of assessment.

Assessment of all students in inclusive classrooms, including those with learning disabilities, can draw on a range of approaches from highly formal conventional testing to alternative classroom procedures (Spinelli, 2006). This orientation to assessment has resulted in two strands in the development of alternative assessment. First, conventional assessment procedures may be adapted to better reflect the newly defined nature of school learning and the more focused formative purposes of assessment. Second, separate assessment approaches have been devised to replace or complement conventional procedures.

ADAPTED CONVENTIONAL ASSESSMENT PROCEDURES

One approach to developing alternative assessments has been to adapt conventional test items so that they better reflect current conceptions of learning. The rationale for the adaptation is as follows. The focus on thinking within the school curriculum has resulted in the need for alternative tasks within conventional assessment, since "tasks that provide insight into a student's understanding are often of a different form from ones typically found on tests" (Cooney, Badger, & Wilson, 1993, p. 245). A number of researchers have contributed to the development of alternative items or tasks for conventional assessment procedures. For example, Gay and Thomas (1993) asked students to explain the reasoning behind a multiple-choice response by conducting individual interviews to access the type of information needed to guide individual learning. These researchers concluded that the use of these techniques provided "accurate information about each student's knowledge and level of understanding of concepts" (p. 130). The use of open-ended questions together with closed questions was also explored by Sullivan (1997), who describes this as a way of allowing and encouraging a variety of levels of responses from students. A more formal approach to the alteration of conventional assessment has involved the development of "rich" assessment items (Beesey, Clarke, & Clarke, 1997) and "super-items" (Collis & Romberg, 1991). These broad open-ended questions provide an opportunity for students to demonstrate "the breadth of their understanding" (Beesey, Clarke, & Clarke, 1997, p. 48). Such approaches aim to extend the ability of conventional procedures to tap into the complexities of student learning.

The approach of adapting conventional assessment has been taken up by special and inclusive educators and formalized through procedures like test accommodations and alternate assessment practices for students with specific disabilities. Salvia and Ysseldyke (2001) note that they first included a chapter on test accommodations, modifications, or adaptations in their 1995 edition. Since then, it has become usual practice to consider test accommodations for students who have disabilities. When the purpose of the assessment is for screening, program evaluation, or accountability, it is particularly important to include information from all students in the results (Salvia & Ysseldyke, 2001).

Essentially, the use of assessment is to inform teachers' instruction. Teachers need to keep in mind how assessments and the feedback from them will support student learning. In this light, accommodations in assessment must be considered to provide students with optimal conditions for test performance. Teachers also need to be mindful of the *what* and *why* questions regarding assessment and determine whether the procedures will provide the information needed or whether some adaptation in assessment is required to access the information from all students.

To illustrate, a parent of a five-year-old girl recently reported that her daughter's teacher could not obtain a clear picture of the child's learning because she never finished anything. When the child asked if she could have more time, the teacher is reported to have said "No" because that would not be fair to the other children. In this situation, the teacher lost sight of the purpose of classroom assessment and did not provide optimal conditions for testing to obtain a clear picture of this child's learning. Revisiting the purpose of assessment is required so the child will get appropriate opportunities to demonstrate her learning and the teacher will then know what and how to teach that child. Part of the assessment information gathered can include what adaptations were required to access the child's learning. Such test adaptations or accommodations do not disadvantage anyone else, but the lack of them certainly disadvantaged the particular student who is the focus of this anecdote.

ALTERNATIVE ASSESSMENT PROCEDURES

Although conventional assessment procedures and instruments remain the backbone of assessment in the classroom, other less conventional models are also becoming essential to complement conventional procedures. In Figure 6.2 conventional assessment has been placed alongside three models of alternative assessment provided by Losardo and Notari-Syverson (2001). These models have emerged from the early childhood sphere, in which dissatisfaction with standardized conventional assessment has generated the development of alternatives that recognize the range of ability, variety of environments, and opportunities for development, as well as the enormous

Conventional	Alternative Assessment Models		
Assessment	Embedded Models	Authentic Models	Mediated Models
Psychometric standardized tests	Naturalistic assessment *Interpretation of learning skills during observation of everyday activities	Performance assessment *Systematic analysis of products of learning in authentic learning situations, can include self-talk, interviewing, self-assessment	Dynamic assessment *Assessment that incorporates intervention with a focus on cognition
Adapted conventional assessment	Focused assessment *Interpretation of targeted activities during classroom routines, including questioning	Portfolio assessment *Documentation and interpretation of products of learning	Curriculum-based language assessment *Using curriculum-based activities to investigate language proficiency

FIGURE 6.2   An Overview of Models of Assessment for the Classroom. Adapted from Losardo and Notari-Syverson's (2001) models of alternative assessment.

changes that occur in early childhood in response to intervention. The three different types of alternative assessment models are not seen as mutually exclusive. Rather, they are seen as complementary and, along with conventional assessment, as able to contribute to a transdisciplinary model of assessment that "uses multiple methods and sources to make a comprehensive and multidimensional assessment of children's abilities across contexts" (Losardo & Notari-Syverson, 2001, p. 25). Although this framework is developed within the context of early childhood learning, it has much to offer assessment of school learning for students with learning disabilities. Examples of alternative assessment procedures described under the three main headings of alternative assessments are provided in the following sections.

A major trend in the development of alternative assessment has been the acknowledgment of classroom learning activities as a source of information. From this perspective, every instructional activity is an assessment opportunity for the teacher, as well as a learning opportunity for the student (Chambers, 1993). Teachers use these *embedded assessment* approaches every day. The teacher plans activities that are within the immediate range of the students' development or Zone of Potential Development (ZPD) and then observes how well they respond, what supports their participation, and what hinders it. Skill in planning and in recording the information that is elicited in classroom situations is crucial to formalizing this type of assessment.

Naturalistic assessment is the process of noticing, recording, and evaluating skills within everyday activities. Observation of learners within their usual cultural context participating in familiar activities can produce valuable information about skill levels, conceptual understanding, and cognitive processing. Structured activities based on familiar settings and routines can extend the assessment to more difficult or challenging situations without removing the learner from the familiar classroom environment. *Focused assessment* is similar but uses more targeted activities and observations. The teacher is more direct in guiding the situation and in eliciting the behaviors or skills that are the focus of the assessment. Probes and think-aloud techniques are used to direct the teaching and learning interaction, which still occurs within the familiar setting and routines (Spinelli, 2006).

Observation of students at work can also be recorded and reported in structured ways so as to provide valid performance assessments. Checklists and anecdotal records contribute to this form of assessment. Significant events that are either "atypical student behavior" or a "clear illustration of new understandings or lack of understanding" (Clarke, Clarke, & Lovitt, 1990, p. 121) are recorded. Observation is thus focused and purposeful when considered a form of alternative assessment (Berman, 2001).

Teacher questioning during classroom interactions has also been acknowledged as an assessment strategy (Herrington et al., 1997; Silver & Kenney, 1995). Particular styles of questioning can elicit information about children's thinking and can inform instructional decisions (Chambers, 1993). Martin and Reynolds (1993) have observed that this kind of assessment is constantly performed by experienced teachers. Such assessment is dynamic and central to expert teaching. It is defined as "a way of looking and listening which . . . constitute[s] the basis for assessment of student understanding" (Martin & Reynolds, 1993, p. 245). The benefits of the integration of teaching and assessment are found in improved assessment for student learning as well as in ongoing learning for the teachers. This reflects the parallel drawn between teachers and researchers who are both concerned about student understanding (McLoughlin & Lewis, 2001). In fact, in action research the roles of teacher and researcher are blurred and no longer seen as mutually exclusive.

Both performance and portfolio assessment are considered *authentic assessment* practices in that they reflect the learning process and they focus on authentic products of learning rather than contrived products from assessment "events." Teachers commonly use both of these approaches in their classrooms and find that such approaches support effective reporting to students and their families. For example, portfolios can become the focus of dialogue in three-way interviews in which students and teachers report to the parents about classroom learning.

Performance assessment is the systematic analysis of learners' products of learning, usually acquired in real-life situations (Losardo & Notari-Syverson, 2003). This type of assessment procedure involves "direct judgments and evaluations of performances," such as those applied mostly in the arts and athletics (Resnick & Resnick, 1992, p. 61). Performance assessments in school learning include written essays and project reports. Such projects and open-ended problems provide opportunities for teachers to assess the "students' abilities to formulate problems, to apply their knowledge in novel ways, to generate interesting solution approaches, and to sustain intellectual activity for an extended period of time" (Silver & Kenney, 1995, p. 66). Through student documentation and work examples, a teacher can assess how students solve problems and how well they understand and can describe their problem-solving methods (Southwell, 1997).

Further examples of performance assessment include the interpretation of work samples, videoed behaviors, and anecdotal notes that have been generated during learning activities. In early childhood assessment this approach has grown out of the observed discrepancies between what children may produce in one setting in comparison to a more contrived formal assessment setting. This type of assessment is again opportunistic.

Assessment of student performance can also include interpretation of students' *self-talk* during problem solving (Lawson & Rice, 1986). From a structured analysis of students' "thinking-alouds" during problem solving, for example, hypotheses can be generated about sources of difficulty that may reside in the reading of the problem, the generation of an appropriate strategy, the computation, planning, solution, and evaluating of the approach (p. 10). This process is not only an effective assessment technique, but it provides opportunities for students to practice explaining their cognition and to review feedback on their thinking from the teacher or other students.

Another form of performance or product assessment involves ongoing collections of students' everyday classroom work. These collections of work, called *portfolios*, exhibit a student's efforts, progress and achievements. They provide a means of documenting performance as well as communicating that performance to others in contrast to marks or test scores, which tend to separate the performance from the means of communication (Clarke, 1996). Portfolio assessment is a way to document students' learning using products of learning. It is important for learners to be involved in the development of their portfolios and for them to develop self-evaluation skills and provide explanations for their performance (Losardo & Notari-Syverson, 2001, p. 101). These skills can facilitate the development of students' self-regulation. Portfolios have been advocated as a way to support the process of developing individual programs for students with learning disabilities (Carpenter, Ray, & Bloom, 1995; Salend, 1998).

Student *self-assessment* has also been advocated as a means of empowering students to understand their own learning (Clarke, 1992; Clarke, Clarke, & Lovitt, 1990). This kind of assessment can involve self-reflection of learning, interviews with teachers, and student journal writing. Such reflective activities allow a focus on the broad range of curriculum, including social and affective aspects of functioning. Journals are a form of reflection on learning that provides students with opportunities to summarize and crystallize their conceptions and to set up a useful dialogue between student and teacher (Silver & Kenney, 1995). The journal then provides the teacher with a window into a student's thinking or "an insight into students' understanding" (Norwood & Carter, 1994, p. 146). Methods of self-reporting reflect the devolution of assessment responsibility to the student.

Interviewing has also been introduced as a procedure that can be of use in assessing classroom learning. An open interview is defined as the interaction between teachers and students during a learning activity conducted with the aim to "search for the student's deeper understanding of concepts and relationships" (Herrington et al., 1997, p. 22). This type of assessment interview mirrors the clinical interview used in cognitive research. Interviews do not need to be long, can be integrated into a teaching program, and can be conducted with individuals or small groups. Such interviews may act as a bridge between formal clinical interviewing and the analysis of classroom discourse (Carr, 1994).

Mediated assessment is the most contrived of the three types of alternative assessments shown in Figure 6.2. Both mediated learning models listed are anchored in sociocultural learning theories that recognize the vital importance of language as a tool of learning and of thinking. This orientation also acknowledges the role of the more competent other, the teacher, in mediating, framing and filtering the learning environment for the student to support the ongoing development of cognitive and linguistic skills. Mediated assessment aims to explore the nature of students' learning, to enhance that learning, and to help students become self-regulated and active learners. Mediated assessment is, in essence, the close examination of teaching-learning interactions.

Curriculum-based language assessment is the "identification and analysis of potential gaps between a particular context's linguistic demands and a learner's linguistic competence" (Losardo & Notari-Syverson, 2001, p. 154). This type of assessment focuses on the learning and thinking tool of language and seeks to understand the nature of language competence for learners. It also provides a starting point for the intervention of language gaps and seeks to develop children's language competence so that they can access the curriculum more effectively.

Dynamic assessment has been developed within social constructivist theory that explicitly integrates teaching and assessment. Within this approach, learning is considered to occur through social mediation, or teaching, within a range of receptiveness that is delineated through assessment carried out by the mediator. Dynamic assessment is individualized and aims to be very responsive to the learning needs of individuals. In dynamic assessment, the assessor identifies factors that are supporting or hindering learning, teaches thinking strategies, promotes change, and becomes personally involved in the assessment interaction (Lidz, 1991). This procedure makes dynamic assessment very compatible with inclusive education that aims to individualize or personalize instruction (Sizer, 1999) by identifying the ways in which individual learners learn so that teaching can be focused on their needs.

It is generally accepted that Lev Semyonovich Vygotsky, a Russian psychologist (1894–1934), provided the foundation for dynamic assessment (Grigorenko & Sternberg, 1998). Although there have been other thinkers who independently raised the same issues that underlie the theoretical perspective from as far back as early Greek philosophy (Wiedl, Guthke, & Wingenfeld, 1995), Vygotsky postulated three key concepts that form the foundation of dynamic assessment.

The first concept is the acknowledgment of the sociocultural context of learning. All learning occurs within a sociocultural context within which humans interact. This context, or social plane, is where learning begins before it proceeds into an individual context or plane as the learner becomes more competent cognitively. The tool of learning in the sociocultural context is language and this becomes internalized as the tool of thinking within the individual. Learning involves the change of the individual and of the social environment. It is impossible to completely separate the learner from the learning environment. All teachers know that their social environment alters during a year of teaching as the students learn and grow and the teacher responds to their changing needs.

Second, mediation and internalization are proposed to be the processes by which learning occurs. Learning is initiated through the regulation of the child's behavior by a more experienced other using speech, written language, number symbol systems, social rules, and value systems. This is known as mediation and refers not only to external behavior but also to cognitive behavior, to thinking. In the classroom the teacher regulates the students' learning, and because the social learning situation is interactive, the child can also regulate others' behaviors using the same cultural tools. It is not a one-way response but rather a situation of mutual responsiveness.

Mediation produces structural cognitive changes in the learner known as internalization. During internalization, the cultural tools of learning are taken on by the learners and become qualitatively different from those used in the social situation. They become part of the learner's "independent developmental achievement" (Vygotsky, 1978) and provide the mechanisms through which the learner becomes a self-mediating agent.

Third, each individual is considered to have a zone of potential development (ZPD) within which learning occurs. This ZPD is the window of opportunity for learning that exists for every individual and within which mediation and internalization lead to cognitive development.

Conventional assessment assesses abilities that are mature and does not give an indication of maturing abilities. In contrast, dynamic assessment aims to investigate two levels of a child's development or learning, both actual and potential, as well as the nature of the learning space in between. In this way it provides much more useful information about how a student learns and what teaching approaches can enhance learning so that the child can be supported to reach a higher level of independence in learning.

Most dynamic assessment is based on the framework of pretest, mediation (teaching or instruction) and posttest. How this is operationalized has been explored in many ways (Haywood & Lidz, 2007; Lidz & Elliott, 2000; Sternberg & Grigorenko, 2002). Without consciously implementing dynamic assessment, many skilled teachers use this framework in their teaching. Skilled teachers observe what students know and can do, then teach, and then see if their teaching advances the students' knowledge and skills.

There are many applications of dynamic assessment to classroom learning, that aim to understand the learning of children with learning disabilities. Applications to mathematical learning, to reading, to speech and language skills, to science, social studies, and more generally to thinking skills across the curriculum have been developed (Haywood & Lidz, 2007). Some recent examples include the work of Moore-Brown et al. (2006), who applied dynamic assessment to understanding children's narrative skills, and that of Swanson and Howard (2005), who reported on the use of dynamic assessment to understand the modified performance of readers. Specifically, these researchers noted that poor readers were not strongly supported by procedures that "facilitated access to previously stored information" (p. 32).

Effective teachers already use the structure of dynamic assessment in their everyday interactions with learners. They embed dynamic assessment within their interactions with their students. They also adapt their verbal instructions for individuals based on their knowledge of the individual student's receptive language, memory, and organizational skills. They also alter the format of tasks for individuals based on their knowledge of the students' skills and learning strengths. In practice, most alternative assessment strategies have blurred the line between instruction and assessment. They provide opportunities not only for students to demonstrate learning but also allow for the assessment of learning to be ongoing.

INTERPRETATION OF ASSESSMENT INFORMATION

It is one process to gather information about student learning and quite another to make sense of it. However, the interpretation of assessment information gathered through a range of assessment procedures is vitally important for students with learning disabilities if they are to fulfill their educational potential.

A useful way to interpret assessment information is to consider what concepts, skills, or procedures are in need of development or of mastery. This interpretation determines the nature of the subsequent instructional goals of acquisition and mastery (Wong, 1996). Wong differentiated between acquisition and mastery to emphasize the need for the automaticity or fluency of the many skills, understandings, and processes that students with learning disabilities need to consolidate to improve their school achievement. Determining whether a student is in need of acquisition or of mastery affects the subsequent instructional decisions made by the teacher.

What teachers are assessing must be explicit and clear to facilitate the interpretation of assessment information. Teachers need to understand the concepts, skills, or procedures that are the focus of assessment so they can draw conclusions about what students' responses mean. A traditional means of explicitly defining what it is that is involved in a learning task is to carry out a task analysis. Such a process is used by teachers to produce "blueprints for instruction" (Wong, 1996, p. 177), but can also be useful to help define the nature of an assessment task and can assist in the interpretation of the meaning of the students' responses. Tasks can be analyzed temporally, developmentally, or by difficulty (Spinelli, 2002). Understanding the cognitive demands within a domain is a significant issue for the implementation of assessment practices such as dynamic assessment in which the assessor also teaches or mediates (Berman & Graham, 2002). The emphasis in dynamic assessment is on process analysis that includes consideration of the learner's attention, perception, memory, knowledge base, conceptual processing, and metacognition related to the task (Lidz, 2003). Analysis of tasks and their cognitive demands is crucial for teachers who aim to competently meet the needs of students with learning disabilities.

The importance of teachers' understandings of the content of assessment was highlighted in a recent action research project (Picker, 2006). In this project, the teacher-researcher pinpointed that her own development of a clearer understanding of the nature of phonemic awareness was vital to her effectiveness in teaching and assessing reading. This example illustrates how a strong understanding of the content of assessment is vital to underpin the meaningful interpretation of assessment information.

CONCLUSIONS

Most assessment practices are used to support teachers in designing the most appropriate teaching programs for their students. The teacher uses the assessment information to make sound instructional decisions, but what of the learner? In concluding this chapter, it is important to focus on the impact of assessment information, or feedback, on learners. The role of assessment as an information-gathering procedure that informs future teaching has already been emphasized as has how teachers use assessment information to make decisions about teaching. However, if teachers are serious about developing active learners, then they also need to consider how learners use the assessment information available to them. In classroom situations this assessment information most commonly returns to students in the form of feedback.

Weeden, Winter, and Broadfoot (2002, p. 16) argue that assessment in schools needs to not only identify what needs to be learned next but also to "focus on the use of assessment to empower [students] as learners." They also note that classroom assessment can have an impact on the student's "sense of self, on expectations, on motivation, and on confidence . . . as well as on long-term dispositions for learning" (see the anecdotal insert following). When learners are very young, they benefit from constructive feedback that takes into account their cognitive functioning, their understanding of language, and their emotional resilience. As learners become increasingly self-regulated, they continue to gain important information from their performance on assessment tasks.

REFLECTIONS ON ASSESSMENT AND FEEDBACK FROM A SCHOOL PSYCHOLOGIST

As a school psychologist I am constantly aware of the impact that everything I say to a student might have on his or her learning. I work with many fragile learners, and I use significant assessment events to help understand learning. I need to frame the purpose and content of each assessment to access as much active participation from the student as possible. I ensure that I am honest and that I explain the purpose at a level that is meaningful for the individual. I also flag an action that will result from the assessment. I want the assessment experience to support future learning, not contribute to negative self-perceptions and reluctance to learn.

Teachers must be conscious of the impact of the feedback they give. Learners make educational decisions based on the information given to them about their performance. As a result, they may increase effort and use more effective learning strategies, or they might reject and reset their learning goals. Kluger and DeNisi (1996) identified four specific decisions that learners can make after receiving feedback. Students will either attempt to reach the standard; abandon the standard or give it up; move the standard, by either lowering it to make it achievable or raising it; or deny the results of the assessment. Black & Wiliam (1998) agree that feedback has a powerful, often negative, impact on learning, particularly for students who have difficulty learning. Although the nature of the assessment indirectly affects students' future engagement with learning, the most impact comes from marks or other feedback that "emphasizes competition rather than personal improvement" (Black, 2004, p. 1).

Hattie and Timperley (2007) have produced a useful model of feedback to enhance learning. According to these researchers, the role of an effective teacher is to provide appropriate, challenging, and specific goals for their students, along with effective learning strategies and feedback (Hattie & Timperley, 2007, p. 87). Based on an extensive meta-analysis, Hattie and Timperley (2007) claim that there are four focus levels for feedback and that the "level at which the feedback is directed influences its effectiveness" (p. 90). Under this model (see Figure 6.3), feedback can be directed at either the task itself, at the processes used to complete the task, at the self-regulation level, or at the self level.

Hattie and Timperley (2007) argue that feedback directed at cognitive processes and self-regulation are the most powerful of the four levels and that feedback about task features has the most impact when it is also linked to feedback about process and self-regulation. In Hattie and Timperley's model, feedback about the self is least effective in moving learners forward to meet their learning goals.

Teachers can struggle with providing feedback to learners who experience learning disabilities. The challenge is to provide feedback about the task, learning process, and self-regulation that will motivate these learners. Feedback given to students with learning disabilities often stops them from moving forward. In particular, grades, which provide feedback about task

TASK	PROCESS	SELF-REGULATION	SELF
How well tasks are understood or performed	*The process needed to understand or perform tasks*	*Self-monitoring, directing and regulating actions*	*Personal evaluations and affective characteristics of the learner*
May direct the student to use more or different or correct information.	May direct the student to use particular processes or strategies.	May direct the student to self-evaluate or may aim to support their confidence about learning.	May be totally unrelated to task performance, such as "You are a great student!"

FIGURE 6.3   Four Levels of Feedback. Model adapted from Hattie and Timperley, 2007, pp. 87, 90.

success, can overpower other feedback and may be interpreted by learners with learning disabilities in terms of the self through such statements as "I am a failure"; "I am useless"; "I am less intelligent than the others"; and "I am dumb."

The power of feedback is evident throughout all effective teaching and learning exchanges. A significant word for teachers to use meaningfully with learners is *yet*. Teachers cannot deny their students' failures, but they can reframe them as part of the process of learning and development: "No, you can't do that sort of question *yet*, but you can learn how to do it." Effective teachers use assessment in the classroom to inform their instructional decisions and their provision of feedback to support the learning of their students. These teachers use both conventional and alternative assessment models and make meaningful interpretations of the assessment information gathered to teach to the needs of all students, including those experiencing learning disabilities.

SUMMARY

In this chapter, we examined several important aspects of assessment, including the rationale for assessment and the two major and broad approaches in assessment. Throughout, we emphasize the cardinal point that assessment serves to inform teachers' teaching.

- The threefold rationale for assessment sets the stage for the chapter.
- An exposition on the conventional and alternative assessment approaches follows.
- The nine alternative assessment procedures (Embedded, Naturalistic, Observation, Teacher Questioning, Authentic Assessment, Performance Assessment, Self-Assessment, Interviewing, and Mediated Assessment) have been summarized.
- Both the interpretation of assessment information and the impact of feedback on students are discussed.

REFERENCES

Beesey, C., Clarke, D., & Clarke, B. (1997). Making "on balance" judgements using rich assessment tasks and classroom assessment practices. In N. Scott & H. Hollingsworth (Eds.), *Mathematics: Creating the future: Proceedings of the 16th biennial conference of the Australian Association of Mathematics Teachers* (pp. 47–51). Adelaide: Australian Association of Mathematics Teachers.

Berlak, H. (1992). The need for a new science of assessment. In H. Berlak, F. Newmann, E. Adams, D. Archbald, T. Burgess, J. Raven, & T. Romberg (Eds.), *Toward a new science of educational testing and assessment* (pp. 1–22). Albany, NY: State University of New York Press.

Berman, J. (2001). *An application of dynamic assessment to school mathematical learning.* Unpublished PhD Thesis. Armidale: University of New England.

Berman, J., & Graham, L. (2002). School Counsellor Use of Curriculum-Based Dynamic Assessment. *Australian Journal of Guidance and Counselling,* Vol. 12, No 1, 21–40.

Black, P. (2004). *The nature and value of formative assessment for learning.* King's College: London www.kcl.ac.uk. Accessed June 27, 2007.

Black, P., & Wiliam, D. (1998). Assessment and classroom learning. *Assessment in Education,* 5 (1), 7–74.

Carpenter, C., Ray, M., & Bloom, L. (1995). Portfolio assessment: Opportunities and challenges. *Intervention in School and Clinic,* 31(1), 34–41.

Carr, K. (1994). Assessment and evaluation in primary Mathematics. In J. Neyland (Ed.), *Mathematics education: A handbook for teachers* (pp. 202–214). Karori, Wellington NZ: The Wellington College of Education.

Chambers, D. (1993). Integrating assessment and instruction. In N. Webb & A. Coxford (Eds.), *Assessment in the mathematics classroom* (pp. 17–25). Reston: National Council of Teachers of Mathematics.

Clarke, D. (1992). The role of assessment in determining mathematics performance. In G. Leder (Ed.), *Assessment and learning of mathematics* (pp. 145–168). Hawthorn, Vic.: Australian Council for Educational Research.

Clarke, D. (1996). Assessment. In A.J. Bishop, K. Clements, C. Keitel, J. Kilpatrick, & C. Laborde (Eds.), *International handbook of mathematics education* (pp. 327–370). Netherlands: Kluwer Academic.

Clarke, D., Clarke, D., & Lovitt, C. (1990). Changes in mathematics teaching: Call for assessment alternatives. In T. Cooney & C. Hirsch (Eds.), *Teaching and learning mathematics in the 1990s: 1990 Yearbook* (pp. 118–129). Reston: National Council of Teachers of mathematics.

Collis, K., & Romberg, T. (1991). Assessment of mathematical performance: An analysis of open-ended test items. In M.C. Wittrock & E.L. Baker (Eds.), *Testing and cognition* (pp. 82–130). Englewood Cliffs, NJ: Prentice-Hall.

Cooney, T., Badger, E., & Wilson, M. (1993). Assessment, understanding mathematics and distinguishing visions from mirages. In N. Webb & A. Coxford (Eds.), *Assessment in the Mathematics classroom* (pp. 239–247). Reston: National.

Durell, C.V. (1936). *General arithmetic for schools.* London: Bell.

Galbraith, P. (1993). Paradigms, problems and assessment: Some ideological implications. In M. Niss (Ed.), *Investigations into assessment in mathematics education: An ICMI Study* (pp. 73–86). Dordrecht, Netherlands: Kluwer Academic.

Gay, S., & Thomas, M. (1993). Just because they got it right, does it mean they know it? In N. Webb & A. Coxford (Eds.), *Assessment in the mathematics classroom* (pp. 130–134). Reston: National Council of Teachers of Mathematics.

Graue, M. (1995). Connecting visions of authentic assessment to the realities of educational practice. In T.A. Romberg (Ed.), *Reform in school mathematics and authentic assessment* (pp. 260–275). Albany, NY: State University of New York Press.

Grigorenko, E., & Sternberg, R. (1998). Dynamic testing. *Psychological Bulletin,* 124(1) 75–111.

Hattie, J., & Timperley, H. (2007). The power of feedback. *Review of Educational Research,* 77 (1), 81–112.

Haywood, C., & Lidz, C. (2007). *Dynamic assessment in practice: clinical and educational applications.* New York: Cambridge University Press.

Herrington, T., Sparrow, L., Herrington, J., & Oliver, R. (1997). *Investigating assessment strategies in mathematics classrooms: a CD-ROM resource enabling teachers to explore assessment teaching strategies in mathematics education.* Perth, Western Australia: Edith Cowan University.

Jochum, J., Curran, C., & Reetz, L. (1998). Creating individual educational portfolios in written language. *Reading and Writing Quarterly,* 14(3), 283–303.

Kilpatrick, J. (1992). A history of research in mathematics education. In D.A. Grouws (Ed.), *Handbook of research on mathematics teaching and learning* (pp. 3–32). New York: Macmillan.

Kluger, A., & DeNisi, A. (1996). The effects of feedback interventions on performance: A historical view, a meta-analysis, and a preliminary feedback intervention theory. *Psychological Bulletin*, 119(2), 254–284.

Lange, J. de (1995). Assessment: No change without problems. In T. Romberg (Ed.), *Reform in school mathematics and authentic assessment* (pp. 87–172). Albany, NY: State University of New York Press.

Lawson, M., & Rice, D. (1986). *Thinking aloud: Analysing students' mathematics performance.* Paper presented at the 11th national conference of the Australian Association of Special Education Adelaide: Institute for the Study of Learning Difficulties, South Australian College of Advanced Education.

Lidz, C. (2003). *Early Childhood Assessment.* Hoboken, NJ: John Wiley & Sons.

Lidz, C.S. (1991). *Practitioner's guide to dynamic assessment.* New York: Guilford.

Lidz, C., & Elliott, J. (2000). *Dynamic Assessment: Prevailing Models and Applications.* New York: Elsevier.

Losardo, A., & Notari-Syverson, A. (2001). *Alternative approaches to assessing young children.* Baltimore: Paul H. Brookes.

Malone, J., & Ireland, D. (1996). Constructivist research on teaching and learning mathematics. In P. Sullivan, K. Owens, & B. Atweh (Eds.), *Research in mathematics education in Australasia 1992–1995* (pp. 119–133). Campbelltown, Australia: Mathematics Education Research Group of Australasia.

Martin, K., & Reynolds, S. (1993). Veteran and rookie teachers: A stereoptic vision of learning in mathematics. *Journal of Teacher Education*, 44(4), 245–253.

Masters, G.N., & Doig, B. (1992). Understanding children's mathematics: Some assessment tools. In G.C. Leder (Ed.), *Assessment and learning of mathematics* (pp. 249–268). Hawthorn, Vic.: Australian Council for Educational Research.

McLoughlin, J., & Lewis, R. (2001). *Assessing students with special needs* (5th ed.). Upper Saddle River, NJ: Prentice-Hall.

Moore-Brown, B., Huerta, M., Uranga-Hernandez, Y., & Peoa, E. (2006). Using dynamic assessment to evaluate children with suspected learning disabilities. *Intervention in School and Clinic*, 41(4), 209–217.

Norwood, K.S., & Carter, G. (1994). Journal writing: An insight into students' understanding. *Teaching Children Mathematics*, 1(3), 146–148.

Picker, K. (2006). Phonological awareness: Prevention is better than cure! *Practically Primary*, 11(3), 17–19.

Popham, W.J. (2006). Assessment for Learning: An endangered species? *Educational Leadership*, 63(5), 82–83.

Resnick, L., & Resnick, D. (1992). Assessing the thinking curriculum: New tools for educational reform. In B. Gifford & M. O'Connor (Eds.), *Changing assessments: Alternative views of aptitude, achievement and instruction* (pp. 37–76). New York: Kluwer Academic.

Salend, S. (1998). Using portfolios to assess student performance. *Teaching Exceptional Children*, 31(2), 36–43.

Salvia, J., & Ysseldyke, J. (2001). *Assessment* (8th ed.). Boston: Houghton Mifflin.

Sattler, J. (1992). *Assessment of children* (3rd ed.). San Diego: Author.

Silver, E., & Kenney, P. (1995). Sources of assessment information for instructional guidance in mathematics. In T. Romberg (Ed.), *Reform in school mathematics and authentic assessment* (pp. 38–86). Albany, NY: State University of New York Press.

Sizer, T. (1999). No two are quite alike. *Educational Leadership*, 57(1).

Southwell, B. (1997). Learning from learners: Sources of assessment. In N. Scott, & H. Hollingsworth (Eds.), *Mathematics: Creating the future: Proceedings of the 16th biennial conference of the Australian Association of Mathematics Teachers*. Adelaide: Australian Association of Mathematics Teachers.

Spinelli, C. (2002). *Classroom assessment for students with special needs in inclusive settings*. Upper Saddle River, NJ: Prentice-Hall.

Spinelli, C. (2006). *Classroom assessment for students in special and general education*, Second Edition. Upper Saddle River, NJ: Pearson Education.

Stake, R. (1995). The invalidity of standardized testing for measuring mathematics achievement. In T. Romberg (Ed.), *Reform in school mathematics and authentic assessment* (pp. 173–235). Albany: State University of New York Press.

Sternberg, R.J. (1994). *Encyclopaedia of Human Intelligence*. New York: Macmillan.

Sternberg, R., & Grigorenko, E. (2002). *Dynamic testing: The nature and measurement of learning potential*. Cambridge, UK: Cambridge University Press.

Sullivan, P. (1997). Mixing open-ended and closed questions to enrich assessment. In N. Scott, & H. Hollingsworth (Eds.), *Mathematics: Creating the future: Proceedings of the 16th biennial conference of the Australian Association of Mathematics Teachers* (pp. 39–42). Adelaide: Australian Association of Mathematics Teachers.

Swanson, H.L., & Howard, C. (2005). Children with reading disabilities: Does dynamic assessment help with the classification? *Learning Disabilities Quarterly*, 28(1), 17–34.

Vygotsky, L.S. (1962). *Thought and language*. E. Hanfmann & G. Vakar (Eds., & Trans.). Boston, MA: Massachusetts Institute of Technology/Wiley.

Vygotsky, L.S. (1978). *Mind in society: The development of higher psychological processes*. M. Cole, V. John-Steiner, S. Scribner, & E. Souberman (Eds.). Cambridge, MA: Harvard University Press.

Webb, N. (1992). Assessment of students' knowledge of mathematics: Steps toward a theory. In D.A. Grouws (Ed.), *Handbook of research on mathematics teaching and learning* (pp. 661–683). New York: Macmillan.

Weeden, P., Winter, J., & Broadfoot, P. (2002). *Assessment: What's in it for schools?* London: Routledge Falmer.

Wiedl, K., Guthke, J., & Wingenfeld, S. (1995). Dynamic assessment in Europe: Historical perspectives. In J. Carlson (Ed.), *Advances in cognition and educational practice: European contributions to dynamic assessment* (pp. 33–82). Connecticut: JAI Press.

Wong, B. (1996). *The ABCs of learning disabilities*. San Diego: Elsevier.

7

READING

What can teachers do to address the reading difficulties experienced by students, especially students with learning disabilities? This chapter looks at effective reading instruction that can support students to improve and develop their skills in word recognition as well as for comprehending narrative and expository texts. The first section of this chapter examines the importance of word recognition as a basic reading skill for all students. The second section discusses the difficulties in reading comprehension commonly experienced by students, especially students with learning disabilities. Then, because comprehending narrative texts requires some different strategies from comprehending factual or expository texts, the final section provides examples of effective instruction for improving students' understanding of these types of texts.

READING: WORD RECOGNITION

Reading is a complex process that can be difficult for many learners. Westby's (2002) models of basic, critical, and dynamic literacy emphasize the higher-order literacy competencies that are necessary for efficient and meaningful reading in our current context. The skills required by readers have been clearly defined by research and are generally considered to be those involved in decoding or word recognition, along with those used in comprehending written text. Vygotsky's emphasis on the importance of language as the primary tool of thinking and learning is most potently evident in literacy. In fact, language, in the forms as thinking, speaking, and listening, as well as writing and reading, is a multimodal tool of learning. In its multiple modes, language "is a tool for analyzing, interpreting, and synthesizing what is heard or read in order to construct or express new interpretations" (Silliman, Butler, & Wallach, 2002, p. 6). It has been demonstrated that many learners who have reading difficulties also have had developmental difficulties in language (Lovett, Barron, & Benson, 2003). The importance of vocabulary development, as the basis for meaningful language use, is a focus of many early literacy interventions (Hoff, 2006; Sénéchal, Ouellette, & Rodney, 2006). Upon this foundation of language proficiency, the task of learning to read involves the development of skills in word recognition and comprehension.

WORD RECOGNITION

To be fluent readers, children must recognize words easily and effortlessly. As McCormick (2007, p. 225) defines it, *word recognition* refers to the "instant recall of words in which the reader resorts to no obvious mechanisms to recognize the word." When readers recognize words in this way and can say them without hesitation, they have developed automaticity—that is, the readers' brains have quickly and automatically processed the words. In contrast, word identification refers to those situations when readers slowly and carefully use one or more strategies (e.g., phonics, structural analysis, or context clues) to help them "work out" how to read words.

Decoding, or word recognition, is a necessary but not sufficient condition for understanding text. Many learners with learning disabilities find decoding or word recognition difficult and subsequently have difficulty comprehending, or making sense of, texts. Siegel (2003) outlined five processes that combine together to underpin fluent reading. These are depicted in Table 7.1. Three of these key processes, phonological processing, syntactic processing, and working memory, which are shaded, are disrupted in significant ways for children who have learning disabilities (Siegel, 2003). Assessment and intervention for literacy difficulties must incorporate a focus on these key processes involved in skilled reading. The following sections

TABLE 7.1   Five Processes Involved in Reading with the Problematic Skills for Students

Phonological processing	Sound–symbol relationship Understanding of grapheme-phoneme rules and exceptions
Syntactic processing	Understanding the syntax of the language
Working memory	Retaining information in short-term memory while accessing information from long-term memory and processing it
Semantic processing	Understanding the meaning of words
Orthographic processing	Understanding the written conventions of language, including spelling

briefly discuss each of the three basic reading processes that are problematic for students with learning disabilities.

Phonological Processing. Phonological processing is the most significant process underlying reading development (Lovett, Barron, & Benson, 2003; Siegel, 2003). Clear frameworks are available to support the effective and explicit teaching of sound–symbol relationships, particularly in the early years of school (Foorman et al., 1998; Torgesen et al., 1999). However, further work into understanding the most effective ways to instruct learners who have severe reading disabilities is continuing (Lovett, Barron, & Benson, 2003; Wagner, Torgesen, & Rashotte, 1994).

It is important to explicitly and systematically teach phonological skills in the context of reading and writing so that students' reading abilities develop in appropriate and authentic ways (Westwood, 2003). The skills that are important to consolidate include early phonological skills such as awareness of rhythm and rhyme, phonemic skills such as alliteration, the ability to isolate individual sounds, segmentation of a series of sounds, and the blending of sounds (Konza, 2003). Some principles underlying effective phonemic skill interventions for students with learning disabilities include (1) providing daily instruction, (2) ensuring that instruction is clear and intense and that basic reading skills are explicitly taught, (3) giving generous and targeted feedback about the students' accuracy, (4) arranging frequent opportunities for successful practice, and (5) making certain that the selection of texts support successful learning experiences (Westwood, 2003).

Syntactic Processing. Syntactic processing involves an understanding of how language fits together grammatically. This is an important ability because it helps readers to be able to predict the type of word that will follow and to evaluate and self-correct phrases read in terms of their grammatical correctness. A sound knowledge of language conventions is essential to this type of processing, particularly in English where there are many rules and many exceptions. Syntactical difficulties, however, have also been identified in languages such as Chinese, Portuguese, and Hebrew (Siegel, 2003).

Working Memory. Despite the wide variety of theoretical explanations for learning disabilities discussed in the literature, the processes and functioning of working memory have been identified as a common factor in all learning difficulties. For example, Keeler and Swanson (2001, p. 418) stated, "Research examining specific subtypes of learning disabilities has found that working memory deficits underlie the difficulties of students with reading and mathematical disabilities." Similarly, Miyake and Shah (1999, p. 1) described working memory as "the theoretical construct that has come to be used in cognitive psychology to refer to the system or mechanism underlying the maintenance of task relevant information during the performance of a cognitive task." Other definitions similarly describe working memory as a temporary, simultaneous storage mechanism in memory geared to hold incoming information required in the performance of a complex task (Baddeley, 1992; Hulme & McKenzie, 1992; Swanson & Siegel, 2001).

In general, poor readers take more time to decode words and have more difficulty constructing meaning from text because their limited working memory capacity is allocated almost entirely to decoding. The working memory capacity and duration of students with learning disabilities are not thought to be less than those of nonlearning disabled students, but it appears that students with learning disabilities have difficulties in efficiently coordinating processes that operate between the components of working memory (Swanson & Siegel, 2001). From this perspective fast, efficient recall, or automaticity, is a product of efficient and effective cognitive processing.

SUMMARY OF WORD RECOGNITION SECTION

Developing automaticity in basic reading skills is particularly important for students with learning disabilities because these students need to work hard to overcome their difficulties in phonological awareness, syntactic processing, and with working memory to comprehend what they read and engage appropriately with the classroom curriculum. Students are better able to focus on higher-order skills when subskills such as decoding or word recognition are less effortful. Until this time, automatic processes may have little or no effect on the processing capacity available to perform complex tasks because only the retrieval of heavily overlearned information is relatively effortless (Borich & Tombari, 1997). There is good reason, however, to expect that improving students' processing efficiency frees up cognitive capacity that then becomes available for tackling higher-order comprehension aspects of tasks.

The outcome of the effective teaching and learning of basic reading skills will be students who can "integrate their phonemic awareness skills into phonic principles (sound-symbol relationships) and . . . develop efficient orthographic word recognition that is rapid, accurate, and eventually automatic (Westby, 2002, p. 74). The automaticity of these skills frees up working memory resources and provides capacity for making sense of written text for comprehension, which is the focus of the remainder of this chapter.

READING: READING COMPREHENSION

Of all the students who are identified as having learning disabilities, the vast majority experiences problems in reading, not only in terms of decoding deficiencies but also in terms of their abilities to construct understandings

and draw inferences (Carlisle, 1999; Tractenberg, 2002). Reading comprehension is a vital academic skill. It underpins school learning and becomes increasingly important in all subject areas as students progress through the grades. Students with learning disabilities have more difficulty comprehending what they read than students without disabilities, even when their differences in decoding skill are taken into account (Englert & Thomas, 1987; Taylor & Williams, 1983).

In general, students with learning disabilities experience poor comprehension due to their failure to read strategically and to spontaneously monitor their understanding. Despite the volume of research on teaching comprehension strategies, instructing students with learning disabilities to use active and efficient reading strategies in a flexible and personalized way remains a challenge. Students with learning disabilities can experience comprehension problems for a variety of reasons, but it is mostly because of difficulties in using their background knowledge appropriately; decoding and word recognition difficulties; deficits in vocabulary knowledge; fluency, strategy use, and metacognitive skills; and problems differentiating between common text structures. A brief discussion of each of these potential sources of comprehension difficulty follows.

APPROPRIATE USE OF BACKGROUND KNOWLEDGE

The appropriate use of background knowledge is a crucial element in making meaning of text. Current research indicates that students benefit most from activities that assess, activate, and develop students' background knowledge before reading (e.g., Brownell & Walther-Thomas, 1999; Jitendra, Hoppes, & Xin, 2000; Raben, Darch, & Eaves, 1999). Structured pre-reading activities serve to make the text accessible to students and enable them to remember what they have learned.

When students are not familiar with the topic of a text, they are likely to find the concepts presented in it difficult and confusing. As Rumelhart (1980) pointed out, background knowledge and comprehension interact in several ways. The reader may simply not have the background knowledge to link to the text. The more limited students' general knowledge and vocabulary skills are, the more difficulty they have in activating appropriate knowledge to assist in comprehending text. Alternately, textual cues may not be recognized as clues to link to or activate the knowledge the reader already has, or the reader may construct an interpretation of the text that is not the one intended by the author.

Students with learning disabilities may experience difficulties in activating appropriate knowledge or in developing background knowledge when it is missing or uncertain. These students may have knowledge about a topic, but they do not necessarily bring this known information to the experience of reading and comprehending (Paris, Lipson, & Wixson, 1983).

Prereading activities, such as brainstorming, developing a graphic organizer, questioning activities, and writing related to the topic, can help activate knowledge. When students lack the background knowledge necessary to understand a particular text, decisions need to be made regarding what specific knowledge will be provided, how much time can be allocated for knowledge development activities, and what specific activities will best facilitate students' understanding. In general, the more students know about a topic, the more motivated they are to learn and the easier it is for them to integrate text information with their background knowledge, organize the new information in memory, and have it available for later retrieval.

DECODING AND WORD RECOGNITION

Decoding and word recognition skills are implicated in comprehension difficulties because they are related to the core phonological processing deficit that is assumed to underlie learning disabilities. Although there is some evidence that other factors like naming speed are also important in understanding the difficulties experienced by readers with learning disabilities (Wolf, 2002), phonological processing remains conceptualized as a core deficit at the heart of learning disabilities (e.g., Seigel, 1992; Shaywitz, Stuebing, Shaywitz, & Fletcher, 1996; Stanovich & Seigel, 1994).

When students do not decode quickly and accurately, their available cognitive resources and limited working memory capacity are consumed by identifying words and not available for constructing meaning at the sentence and text level. Some readers labor so much over decoding and word recognition that by the time they struggle to the end of a sentence, they have forgotten what happened at the beginning. Such effortful and inefficient decoding obviously affects students' comprehension and their motivation to read.

Rapid and accurate decoding seems a necessary, but not sufficient, condition for comprehension to occur. It reduces memory demands for word identification and releases limited working memory resources for the construction of meaning. However, this does not ensure that meaning will be constructed successfully. It is clear, though, that students need to establish a bank of words they know instantly by sight so that they gain confidence and enjoyment from reading.

VOCABULARY KNOWLEDGE

A lack of vocabulary knowledge or a mismatch between the reader's vocabulary and that of the text can also be a cause of reading comprehension difficulties. Text that contains many unfamiliar words leads students to experience a high error rate in reading due to their inability to link text to their background knowledge. This can impact on their comprehension and contribute to frustration and loss of motivation.

In terms of research findings, Birsh (1999) indicated that successful reading comprehension is closely related to an individual's oral language comprehension and vocabulary skills. Further, Perfetti (1984) noted that vocabulary differences contribute to reading ability because when words are not known, readers' initial understandings of text can be incomplete and the integration of ideas becomes problematic. Just as a lack of vocabulary knowledge can hamper comprehension, a lack of knowledge of the rules of syntax and sentence structure, which relate to the sequencing of words in phrases and sentences, can also interfere with comprehension. As a consequence most students with learning disabilities benefit from explicit instruction regarding how various connecting and signal words, such as prepositions, can change the meaning of text, and how pronouns relate to their referents.

READING FLUENCY RELATED TO READING COMPREHENSION

Fluency related to reading is most often considered in terms of speed and accuracy (Chard, Vaughn, & Tyler, 2002; Welsch, 2007). There seems to be an optimum reading rate that allows the smooth processing of information by the reader. Automaticity in reading is the smooth effortless decoding and word identification that frees cognitive capacity so that the reader's attention can be focused on meaning (Perfetti, 1977, 1985). Slow reading rates make it difficult for students to retain information in working memory long enough for meaning to be constructed. This restricts students to low levels of processing by focusing their attention on letters and words rather than on concepts and how these link together. In contrast, reading too fast may result in the neglect of important details in text.

Students with learning disabilities often struggle to read fluently (Meyer & Felton, 1999). Common problems are related to sight words, decoding consistently and accurately, and reading phases and sentences with meaning. A slow reading rate is debilitating because it prevents students from thinking about the text while reading. Both rapid reading of high-frequency words and the speedy application of decoding skills appear critical for optimal reading development (Chard, Vaughn, & Tyler, 2002).

As students with learning disabilities are so commonly dysfunctional readers, Wolf (2002) and her colleagues (e.g., Bowers & Wolf, 1993) have put forward the double-deficit hypothesis, which theorizes that students with learning disabilities have a core difficulty in the naming speed of words as well as in the phonological processing of letters and sounds. The implication of this hypothesis is that students who are able to decode need ample opportunities to practice reading connected text to become fluent readers.

STRATEGY USE, METACOGNITION, AND SELF-REGULATION

An area of focus in comprehension research is strategy instruction and meta-cognition, which is concerned with students' awareness of their own thinking and their ability to regulate strategy use while working to comprehend printed material. It is important for students to monitor their own comprehension and to take steps to regain clarity of understanding when meaning breaks down or becomes confused. Comprehension strategies can teach students how to draw inferences from text explicitly, summarize information, predict what will happen next in a narrative, formulate and answer questions about text, and visualize what they read in order to improve their comprehension. Table 7.2 presents a summary of some useful comprehension strategies that can be applied before, during, and after reading texts. These strategies are research-based and derived from studies conducted by Foorman et al. (1998), Gajira, Jitendra, Sood, and Sacks, (2007), Graham and Wong (1993), and Taylor and Williams (1983).

More important, in the light of findings from research investigating students' metacognition, self-regulation, and strategy use, conceptions of the nature of learning disabilities have changed. Although the notion of an underlying processing difficulty still stands, in terms of strategy use the present view is that inefficiencies rather than deficiencies characterize the difficulties experienced by students with learning disabilities (Gersten, Fuchs, Williams, & Baker, 2001). Students with learning disabilities may possess the strategies necessary to approach the comprehension of text in a planned and strategic way but fail to use these strategies at the appropriate time or apply them in an inefficient or incomplete manner.

The primary function of reading is extracting meaning from text. If students do not notice that comprehension has broken down, they will fail to take steps to fix whatever the problem is. Students need to monitor the success and failure of their attempts to construct meaning from text if they are to be strategic and successful readers. Comprehension monitoring is key in the development of this kind of independent and self-regulated reading for meaning (Forness, 1997; Gersten et al., 2000; Swanson, 1999).

DIFFERENTIATING BETWEEN COMMON TEXT STRUCTURES

Research during the 1980s and 1990s established that students with learning disabilities have difficulty recognizing the many task demands related to comprehension activities, including how to differentiate between, and strategically approach, different types of texts (e.g., Englert & Thomas, 1987; Taylor & Samuels, 1983; Wong & Wilson, 1984). Students with learning disabilities tend to be unsure of the characteristics of common narrative and factual or expository texts, and they consequently experience difficulties using their knowledge of text structures and recognition of the different purposes of texts as an aid to comprehension. As more narratives tend to be used in schools, general comprehension strategies were initially taught to suit these story-oriented texts. In recent times, however, increased awareness that specific strategies apply more to one text type than another has meant that differentiating between types of texts has become increasingly important.

Students in today's schools encounter a variety of texts such as poems, plays, stories, novels, essays, reports, descriptions, and textbook expositions that are presented through traditional book forms and electronic and Web-based media. The most common of these text structures are narrative and factual or expository. With experience, most students gradually develop awareness of the different structures used in written texts, but it is particularly important that teachers facilitate this awareness for students with learning disabilities. These students tend to be delayed in their comprehension of the different text structures used in factual or informational texts (Weisberg & Balajthy, 1989) and in their awareness of the basic elements of narratives (Montague, Maddux, & Dereshiwsky, 1990).

Gersten et al.'s (2001) review of reading comprehension research presents the following three major research findings related to students' awareness of text structure and their comprehension of factual/expository texts. From the literature it appears that (1) awareness of text structure increases developmentally (Brown & Smiley, 1977); (2) that some text structures are more obvious and easier to recognize than others (Englert & Hiebert, 1984); and (3) that skill at discerning text structures and then using knowledge about them appropriately is an important factor in comprehending factual/expository text (Taylor & Beach, 1984; Taylor & Samuels, 1983).

Acquiring an awareness of text structure is particularly important for readers with learning disabilities. It fosters an appreciation of the organizational factors that underlie factual texts and provides a way for students to remember new information. The strategy of analyzing the structure of texts may also lead to more active processing and greater effort on the part of students to understand and remember what is read (Carlisle & Rice, 2002). Although an awareness of text structure is not likely to address all the comprehension problems experienced by students with learning disabilities, it is clearly likely to make texts more understandable to them.

SUMMARY OF DIFFICULTIES IN READING COMPREHENSION EXPERIENCED BY STUDENTS WITH LEARNING DISABILITIES

Students with learning disabilities can experience comprehension problems for a range of reasons that stem from their lack of mastery of the component knowledge and skills that make up effective reading comprehension (e.g., background and vocabulary knowledge, decoding and fluency, comprehension strategies, and understanding of text types). Frequently, these reasons do not operate independently of one another; rather, there is a reciprocal causation between the component skills of reading comprehension, resulting in potentially complex and debilitating reading comprehension problems. Nonetheless, students' difficulties with reading comprehension can be ameliorated by focused and effective instruction.

Swanson's (1999, p. 522) extensive meta-analysis of the learning disabilities research indicated that the following are the most important instructional components associated with improvements in reading comprehension:

1. *Directed response questioning*, which includes the teacher directing students to ask questions, the teacher and students engaging in dialogue, and/or the teacher asking questions.

2. *Controlling the difficulty of the processing demands of tasks* so that activities are generally short, with the level of difficulty controlled, the tasks appropriately sequenced, and the teacher providing necessary assistance through demonstration.

3. *Elaboration* that occurs when additional or redundant explanations are made about the concepts, procedures, or steps in a strategy.

4. *Modeling* by the teacher of strategy steps so that the teacher demonstrates the cognitive processes involved in task completion.

5. *Small-group instruction* either with students and a teacher or collaborative study by groups of students. The teacher highlights *strategy cues* that include reminders to use strategy steps, uses "think-aloud" model to demonstrate the processing that underlies task completion, and informs students of the benefits of strategy use and its applicability to specific reading situations.

Obviously, there are no "quick fixes" for the difficulties with reading comprehension experienced by students with learning disabilities. However, well-considered instruction delivered over an extended period of time, and integrated across the curriculum, will support students to improve and develop their skills and enable them to better participate in learning at school and in the wide variety of real-life experiences that require effective and efficient reading comprehension.

EFFECTIVE READING COMPREHENSION INSTRUCTION

Before discussing the role of specific strategies in improving the comprehension of narrative and factual/expository texts, we will outline general approaches to implementing effective instructional interventions for students with learning disabilities. This is important to address because considerable progress has been made in designing, implementing, and evaluating effective interventions that target these students' performance disabilities in academic areas (e.g., Vaughn, Gersten, & Chard, 2000).

IMPLEMENTING EFFECTIVE INSTRUCTIONAL INTERVENTIONS FOR STUDENTS WITH LEARNING DISABILITIES

One of the prevailing criticisms of interventions for students with learning disabilities is "its overemphasis on the 'basics' with the exclusion of any creative or cognitively complex activities," which consequently limits these students to a sparse intellectual diet (Gersten, 1998, p. 163). This type of instruction reflects the belief that the development of basic skills precedes any complex cognitive activity. Swanson's (1999) meta-analysis of reading research, however, suggests that providing many practice opportunities can actually minimize the disabilities experienced by students with learning disabilities, as long as the practice takes place in small, interactive groups and is accompanied by direct questioning, and careful control of the difficulty level of tasks.

Similarly, Vaughn et al.'s (2000) meta-analysis, which examined the components of interventions associated with high-effect sizes, found that the strongest impact on students' learning came from interactive, small-group instruction coupled with controlled task difficulty that, together, ensured students' success. Vaughn and her colleagues (2000) also found that effective interventions focused on key learning areas and used a style of "direct response teaching," which was interactive and set up many opportunities for dialogue between the teacher and students and among peers.

In their analysis of reading comprehension research for students with learning disabilities, Mastropieri, Scruggs, Bakken, and Whedon (1996) also concluded that self-questioning strategies had a positive impact on students' learning. Similarly, Gersten, Fuchs, Williams, and Baker (2001) in their review categorized effective strategy interventions as either "comprehension monitoring" or "text structuring." In both instances, students were taught to generate questions and to think aloud about what they read before, during, and after they interact with text. Table 7.2 presents some of the self-questions students can ask as they work toward constructing and clarifying the meaning of a passage.

Overall, it is important to remember that in effective reading comprehension interventions, students are encouraged to articulate their thoughts while teachers provide feedback or ask follow-up questions based on the students' responses to text. This interactive dialogue accelerates the comprehension process and moves students with learning disabilities toward the ultimate goal of using more appropriate and sophisticated thinking skills as they read. The role of the teacher is to explicitly teach students how to apply comprehension strategies. This instruction should be overt and include multiple opportunities for students to practice under quality feedback conditions with the teacher or with able peers. Students should also be taught the subtleties of strategy instruction—that is, that there are some instances where strategies are only somewhat useful and other situations

TABLE 7.2   Self-Questions Asked Before, During, and After Reading

Before reading	During reading	After reading
What will this text be about? Make predictions based on the cover, title, context of book, prior information about the author, etc.	What is the most important information? Underline important parts of the passage to remember where the important information is.	Can I retell the story or restate the main points in my own words? Summarize the story and ask self-questions.
What do I already know about this topic? Relate and explore in terms of background knowledge.	Where does the information fit into my graphic organizer?	What connections does this text have with my life and background knowledge?
Make connections to what I already know.	Formulate an ongoing graphic overview of the text.	Make links with what I already know.
What don't I understand about this text?	Consider relationships and connections to what I already know.	What do I need to find out?
Skim to identify any words that may be difficult. Clarify their meanings.	What is the author going to say next?	Skimming for a date or name and to look for key words or a particular phrase involves knowing about text structure and layout.
What type of text is this? Get a grip on text structure to help understand the purpose of the text and to predict what to expect from it.	Make predictions based on my reading so far. What will I do if I encounter an unfamiliar word or if I realize I don't understand what I have read?	How will I answer comprehension questions after a passage?
What type of graphic organizer would be appropriate for this text?	Apply "fix-up" strategies: Sound out the word. Have I heard it before? Read ahead.	Use a strategy like the 3H Strategy. The answers are either Here, Hidden, or in my Head.
Concept map, matrix, cause-and-effect diagram, numbered steps, etc.	Reread the section that is confusing me. Vary my pace of reading to better enable comprehension (slow down) or fluency (speed up) Ask someone to help.	How can I remember information from the passage? Complete the graphic overview.

Adapted from Graham and Bellert (2004).

where strategies do not fit particular passages. Interactive dialogue is an essential component of strategy instruction. It provides ongoing and systematic feedback to assist students in understanding what they read.

IMPROVING STUDENTS' COMPREHENSION OF NARRATIVE TEXT

Although the following discussion of the strategies that are appropriate to different text structures is separated into narrative and factual/expository sections, in actuality many of the instructional procedures that facilitate comprehension of narratives can also ease the interpretation of factual texts and vice versa. There are some special features of each type of text, however, that merit separate consideration. For example, Graesser, Golding, and Long (1991) suggest that several characteristics of narratives make them easier to comprehend than factual/expository texts, mainly because the topics covered and the organizational strategies used in narratives tend to be more familiar than those employed in, for instance, textbooks. Table 7.3 contains a range of strategies that specifically support students' comprehension of narrative texts. These strategies are derived from the work of Carlisle and Rice (2002), Gersten, Fuchs, Williams, and Baker (2001), Mastropieri, Scruggs, Bakken, and Whedon (1996) and Westby (2002).

Question-Answer Relationships (QARs) and Reciprocal Teaching are two general comprehension strategies that can be applied to narrative texts. Although strategic readers attempt to visualize the action of the story and ask themselves questions focusing on narrative elements (such as setting, characters, and motives; the main events of the plot; the problem presented in the story; and its resolution), students with learning disabilities are generally not as active in processing text. QARs, then, are useful in

TABLE 7.3   Strategies That Support Students' Comprehension of Narrative Texts

Strategies that Support Students' Comprehension of Narrative Texts	
Stories	Focus on descriptive passages featuring noun groups, adjectives, and adverbs that illustrate characters and settings.
Drama	Develop understandings about story grammar.
Poetry	Explain how narratives are typically structured in terms of orientation, complication, and resolution.
Fairy Tales	
Myths	Develop appropriate graphic organizers. For example: *sociograms* to plot understandings about characters and relationships, *storymaps* to clarify the sequence of events.
Fables Legends	
	Look for nuances, hints of future events, and the implications of happenings. These are often key clues to what will happen in the narrative.
	Identify main characters and secondary characters. Consider their roles. Explore the relationships between characters.
	Consider, explore, and visualize the setting. Relate it to the characters.
	Derive meaning from figurative language. Deconstruct similes, metaphors, and descriptions.
	Verbalize and reflect on "The movie in your head": students' visualization of the narrative. How and why does it change as the text is read?
	Identify temporal words that connect happenings to clarify the sequence of events.
	Retell or recount the text using "who, what, when, where, why" questions as a guide.

engaging the student in thinking about the text during and after reading. They also develop students' understandings about different question types. QARs focus on three particular types of comprehension questions that can be asked after reading: text-explicit questions that are answered using literal information from one sentence in the passage, text-implicit or inferential questions, and script-implicit questions that rely on students' background knowledge.

The 3H strategy is an example of a QAR strategy with mnemonic and meta-cognitive features. Although many strategies direct students to reread or look back in the text if they cannot respond confidently to questions after a passage, simply rereading or returning to the text in a random way does not help students with learning disabilities improve their comprehension. Instead, these students have to learn to reread strategically. Graham and Wong's (1993) instruction of the 3H strategy compared self-instructional training to more traditional teaching of a question-answer relationship strategy. Their results indicated that instructing students with learning disabilities to ask themselves three focus questions as a strategy to guide rereading was more effective and resulted in substantially better maintenance of learning (see Figure 7.1).

The three self-monitoring questions used in Graham and Wong's (1993) 3H study were (1) How will I answer this question? (Select a strategic approach.); (2) What kind of question is this? [literal (Here), inferential

The 3H Strategy

1. Head First!

Before reading	What do I know?
During reading	What don't I understand?
After reading	What do I need to find out?

Ask for help if you need to.
Content?
Vocabulary?
How to?

2. Use the 3Hs to remind you where the answers to questions are found:

HERE In one sentence from the passage.

HIDDEN Join together. The answer is in two or more parts of the passage. Or the answer comes from joining together information from the passage and information that you already know.

In my HEAD Use what you already know to answer the question. Just you or the passage and you.

3. Check Your Answers.
Reread each question and your answer to see if they fit together. How confident are you of your answer? After you have finished all the questions, return to any answers you are not sure of. Go through the 3H strategy and check these answers again. You should have a reason for each of your answers. You do? Well done!

FIGURE 7.1 The 3H Strategy for Answering Comprehension Questions After a Passage.

(Hidden) or creative (In my Head)]; and (3) Is my answer correct? (Justify or prove the answer.) The 3H strategy has been used successfully by students in Canada and Australia as a self-instructional, comprehension strategy that guides students' rereading and answering of questions.

Another strategy that also encourages students to "relate information in the text to their own experiences" (Au, 1999) is reciprocal teaching. In this strategy, the adult and students take turns assuming the role of the teacher (Palincsar & Brown, 1986). Using a reciprocal teaching framework, the "teacher" and students interact by predicting, questioning, summarizing, and clarifying information from text. When students predict what will happen or what information the author wants them to understand from what they are about to read, they are activating their background knowledge. They also learn to use the structure of the text to help them make defensible predictions. Students are, therefore, using and consolidating their knowledge of the structure of text when engaged in reciprocal teaching activities.

The questioning part of the reciprocal teaching strategy provides students with opportunities to identify the kind of information that is the basis of a good question, to frame their own questions and then engage in asking themselves and their peers what their answers might be. In formulating questions, students learn to identify important information in a passage.

In a similar way, reciprocal teaching fosters summarizing skills. Summarizing is a difficult task for students with learning disabilities. They find it difficult to condense information and to determine which parts of a text are important and which can be omitted without losing key concepts. Teaching summarizing requires much modeling and practice before students with learning disabilities experience independent success.

Clarifying is the final component of the reciprocal teaching strategy. This component encourages students to preview difficult vocabulary in a passage and gives them practice at implementing fix up strategies to address comprehension breakdowns. This strategic approach to comprehension monitoring is of particular importance to students with learning disabilities who are less likely to have developed the habit of self-monitoring their comprehension than students without learning disabilities. Once students are taught in a structured and direct way to clarify their understanding of text through rereading, reading ahead, using pictures or structural clues, and asking for help, the conditions are set for them to read meaningfully and to engage thoughtfully with both narrative and factual texts (Gajira et al., 2007).

IMPROVING STUDENTS' COMPREHENSION OF EXPOSITORY TEXT

Compared to narrative texts, many students find factual texts less familiar and less engaging (Gersten et al., 2001). Because factual texts are written to communicate information, they are more likely to incorporate a greater

TABLE 7.4   Strategies that Support Students' Comprehension of Factual Texts

Strategies that Support Students' Comprehension of Factual Texts *Reports Arguments* *Procedures* *Descriptions Explanation* *Responses* *Discussions and Debates* *Recounts* *Personal Responses*	Build up knowledge of text types in order to understand the social purposes of text, and identify important organizational structures and features. Focus on keywords, technical terms, and their synonyms. This key strategy requires development of vocabulary skills. Develop skills in skimming, scanning, and summarizing for understanding text organization and for locating information. Read charts, graphs, pictures, headings, and other graphics. Use graphic organizers: Concept maps, definition maps, flow charts, and structured overviews are all useful organizers for factual texts. Make judgments and be critical. For example: Is this an argument or an information report? Is this a realistic procedure? How concrete are these "facts"? Use contents, glossary, indexes, dictionary, and other sources to gather information and clarify vocabulary knowledge.

variety of text structures (e.g., analysis, cause and effect, classification, comparison and contrast, definition, description, enumeration, identification, illustration, problem and solution, and sequence) and, therefore, to require the use of multiple comprehension strategies. Table 7.4 presents a number of strategies that specifically support students' comprehension of factual/expository texts. This table summarizes some of the research findings of Englert and Hiebert (1984), Gajria et al. (2007), and Gersten et al. (2001). The following section will specifically describe the utility of graphic organizers, the KWL strategy, and SQ3R in supporting students' effective comprehension of factual/expository texts.

The use of graphic organizers is a general strategic approach to teaching reading comprehension that is particularly applicable to factual/expository texts. Graphic organizers can alert students to the organization of the passage, the central concepts, and the relationships among the ideas presented in the text. Graphic organizers are also known as semantic maps, semantic webs, concept maps, frames, or thematic maps. In essence, graphic organizers are representations of what has been read. They can take various forms such as a Venn diagram of similarities and differences between two countries described in a magazine article, a matrix that organizes attributes of different minerals along two or more dimensions, or a flowchart marking the events of a significant period of history. Graphic organizers not only help to make text comprehensible, but they also assist in the memorization, storage, and analysis of information. As well, they can encourage students to engage in critical thinking activities and improve students' recall of factual information. Graphic organizers are particularly helpful to students who have limited vocabulary knowledge because they can serve as mental maps that allow students to draw and visualize the complex relationships between concepts in any content area.

Another frequently used strategy for understanding factual/expository text is the K-W-L method (Ogle, 1989). This strategy emphasizes the importance of activating students' background knowledge to assist them in constructing meaning from purposeful reading (e.g., Anderson, 1977; Steffensen, 1978). This strategy makes use of a chart divided into three sections:

What we already know (K)

What we want to learn (W)

What we learned (L)

After the teacher introduces the topic in a general way, students are instructed to complete the first column of the chart. The teacher then leads a class discussion on what the students think they already know about the topic and writes down every response the students offer. No judgment about the validity of responses is made at this time. After the brainstorming session is complete, the teacher elicits and lists comments from students about what they want to find out about the chosen topic. At the completion of the activity students can direct the teacher to cross out the things they thought they knew but that proved inaccurate during their exploration of the topic. During the time set aside to record what was learned, students can clarify vocabulary, categorize new knowledge, and reflect on the amount of learning that has occurred (Ogle, 1989).

SQ3R (Survey, Question, Read, Record, Review) is a well-known study method (Robinson, 1961) that also helps students work actively with content material. The process provides a systematic format for reading that helps students interact with the text by asking questions and then looking for answers:

1. *Survey.* Students examine the titles, headings, subheadings, captions, charts, and diagrams to get the "big picture."

2. *Question.* Formulate questions for each title, heading, subheading, caption, chart, or diagram.

3. *Read.* Students read and make notes about each section in order to answer the questions formulated from reading the titles, headings, subheadings, captions, charts, or diagrams.

4. *Record.* After reading the selection, students attempt to answer the questions without looking back at the material.

5. *Review.* Students reread to verify answers and to make sure they have understood the main points of the text.

At the introduction of the strategy, the instructor models appropriate questions and works with students to develop their own. As the students become more proficient at using the SQ3R, they formulate their own questions and guide their own study of text. The time students spend practicing and being guided to learn this strategy benefits them when they begin to use this strategic approach independently. Carlisle and Rice (2002) note, however, that "although SQ3R is often advocated as a useful comprehension strategy for poor readers, research on the technique over the years, most of which involved college students, has yielded mixed results" (p. 197). Indeed, most of the studies investigating this technique have focused on normally achieving students, not those with learning disabilities. It is clear from the current research on comprehension strategy instruction, however, that students with learning disabilities need modeling and explicit instruction to master the prerequisites of strategic reading like *how* to formulate good questions and *how* to locate the main idea of a passage. Such instruction must accompany strategies like SQ3R if they are to be of maximum use to students with comprehension disabilities.

Researchers from the University of Kansas developed a strategy called MULTIPASS, based on SQ3R (Schumaker et al., 1982) that takes into account the particular needs of students with learning disabilities. In this strategy readers are taught to make several purposeful "passes" over a passage from a textbook. The innovation Deshler, Schumaker, and team made in developing this strategy and many others appropriate to content area reading was not so much in the technique itself but in the teaching method they used. Students experienced instruction that was very explicit and intense, and they practiced on materials of controlled difficulty before applying the strategy to grade-appropriate textbook passages. Under these conditions there was clear improvement in comprehension for adolescents with learning disabilities. These findings suggest that for students with learning disabilities strategy instruction needs to be systematic and sustained over time, with many opportunities to practice and extend the use of strategies to a variety of reading situations.

In summary, explicit instruction is an essential feature of effective interventions that aim to improve the comprehension of both narrative and factual texts for students with learning disabilities. The elements of appropriate strategies should be identified and demonstrated to students through using examples and by providing models of strategy use and interactive dialogue. Ample opportunities for teachers to provide formative feedback and to shape students' habits of using comprehension strategies are necessary.

CONCLUSION

Although strategy instruction for students with learning disabilities has undoubtedly been successful in improving reading comprehension performance, considerable work still remains in order to unravel how students come to "own" and to modify, over time, the strategies they are taught. Importantly, future research will also need to grapple with how strategy instruction can be incorporated into schools and classrooms to better support students with learning disabilities.

Classroom teachers can do a great deal toward ensuring that students with learning disabilities participate meaningfully in quality teaching and learning experiences. The effective teaching of students with learning disabilities generally does not require new or specific instructional strategies but rather relies on what Westwood (2007, p. 92) calls "the tried and true basics of skilled teaching," such as that outlined in this chapter. Considered in this way, instructional strategies that enhance comprehension and other learning outcomes for students with learning disabilities should result in improved outcomes for *all* students in inclusive classrooms (Vaughn, Gersten, & Chard, 2000).

SUMMARY

This chapter focuses on the two components subsumed under reading: word recognition or decoding and reading comprehension. A brief summary is given of the key processes underlying fluent reading that are disrupted in children with learning disabilities. Additionally, an exposition is given on the various causes of reading comprehension problems followed by a presentation of an array of very useful reading strategies for the three phases of reading instruction: before, during, and after reading. We highlight several aspects of this chapter.

• Three key processes underlying fluent reading are disrupted in children with learning disabilities: phonological processing, syntactic processing, and working memory.

• There is the recurrent theme of how to structure optimal reading instruction for all students, but particularly for students with learning disabilities. Readers are informed of a research-based analysis of the most important instructional components associated with enhancing reading comprehension. These components include direct response questioning, controlling the difficulty of the processing demands of tasks, elaboration, modeling, and small-group instruction (Swanson, 1999, p. 522). Students with learning disabilities benefit from explicit comprehension instruction, interactive dialogues between teacher and students and among students, and opportunities for multiple practice of strategy use with materials gradually increasing in difficulty.

• There is the presentation of a rich array of reading strategies that benefit beginning teachers and the detailed descriptions of several that make them readily accessible for all teachers to use.

REFERENCES

Anderson, J.A. (1977). Distinctive features, categorical perception, and probability learning: Some applications of a neural model. *Psychological Review*, 84(3), 413–451.

Au, K.H. (1999). A multicultural perspective on policies for improving literacy achievement: Equity and excellence. In M.L. Kamil, P.B. Mosenthal, P.D. Pearson, & R. Barr (Eds.), *Handbook of reading research* (Vol. 111, pp. 835–851). Mahwah, NJ: Erlbaum.

Baddeley, A. (1992). Working memory. *Science*, 255(5044), 556–564.

Birsh, J.R. (1999). *Multisensory teaching of basic language skills*. Baltimore, MD: Paul H. Brookes.

Borich, G.D., & Tombari, M.L. (1997). *Educational psychology: A contemporary approach*. New York: Longman.

Bowers, P.G., & Wolf, M. (1993). Theoretical links among naming speed, precise timing mechanisms and orthographic skills in dyslexia. *Reading and Writing: An Interdisciplinary Journal*, 5(1), 69–85.

Brown, A.L., & Smiley, S.S. (1977). Rating the importance of structural units of prose passages: A problem of metacognitive development. *Child Development*, 45:1–8.

Brownell, M.T., & Walther-Thomas, C. (1999). An interview with Dr. Marilyn Friend. *Intervention in School and Clinic*, 37(4), 223–228.

Carlisle, J.F. (1999). Free recall as a test of reading comprehension for students with learning disabilities. *Learning Disabilities Quarterly*, 22:11–22.

Carlisle, J.F., & Rice, M.S. (2002). *Improving reading comprehension: Research-based principles and practices*. Baltimore, MD: York Press.

Chard, D.J., Vaughn, S., & Tyler, B. (2002). A synthesis of research on effective interventions for building reading fluency with elementary students with learning disabilities. *Journal of Learning Disabilities*, 35(5), 386–406.

Englert, C.S., & Hiebert, E.H. (1984). Children's developing awareness of text structures in expository materials. *Journal of Educational Psychology*, 76:65–75.

Englert, C.S., & Thomas, C.C. (1987). Sensitivity to text structure in reading and writing: A comparison between learning disabled and non-learning disabled students. *Learning Disability Quarterly*, 10(2), 93–105.

Foorman, B., Fletcher, J., Francis, D.J., Schatschneider, C., & Mehta, P. (1998). The role of instruction in learning to read: Preventing reading failure in at-risk children. *Journal of Educational Psychology*, 90:37–55.

Forness, S. (1997). Mega-analysis of meta-analyses: What works in special education services. *Teaching Exceptional Children*, 29(6), 4–9.

Gajira, M., Jitendra, A.K., Sood, S., & Sacks, G. (2007). Improving comprehension of expository text in students with LD: A research synthesis. *Journal of Learning Disabilities*, 40(3), 210–217.

Gersten, R. (1998). Recent advances in instructional research for students with learning disabilities: An overview. *Learning Disabilities Research and Practice*, 13:162–170.

Gersten, R., Fuchs, L.S., Williams, J.P., & Baker, S. (2001). Teaching reading comprehension strategies to students with learning disabilities: A review of research. *Review of Educational Research*, 71(2), 279–320.

Graesser, A.C., Golding, G.T., & Long, V.B. (1991). *Advances in discourse processes: Structures and procedures of implicit knowledge*. Norwood, NJ: Ablex.

Graham, L., & Bellert, A. (2004). Reading comprehension for students with learning disabilities (pp. 251–279). In B.Y.L. Wong (Ed.), *Learning about learning disabilities*. New York: Academic Press.

Graham, L., & Wong, B.Y.L. (1993). Comparing two modes in teaching a question-answering strategy for enhancing reading comprehension: Didactic and self-instructional training. *Journal of Learning Disabilities*, 26(4), 270–279.

Hoff, E. (2006). Environmental supports for language acquisition. In S.B. Neuman & D.K. Dickinson (Eds.), *Handbook of early literacy research, volume 2*. 163–172. New York: Guildford.

Hulme, C., & McKenzie, S. (1992). *Working memory and severe learning difficulties*. Hove, UK: Lawrence Erlbaum Associates.

Jitendra, A.K., Hoppes, M.K., & Xin, Y.P. (2000). Enhancing main idea comprehension for students with learning problems: The role of summarization strategy and self-monitoring instruction. *Journal of Special Education*, 34:127–139.

Keeler, M.L., & Swanson, H.L. (2001). Does strategy knowledge influence working memory in children with mathematical disabilities? *Journal of Learning Disabilities*, 34:418–434.

Konza, D. (2003). *Teaching children with reading difficulties*. Tuggerah: Social Science Press.

Lovett, M., Barron, R., & Benson, N. (2003). Effective remediation of word identification and decoding difficulties in school-age children with reading disabilities. In H. Swanson, K. Harris, & S. Graham (Eds.), *Handbook of learning disabilities* (pp. 273–292). New York: The Guildford Press.

Mastropieri, M.A., Scruggs, T.E., Bakken, J.P., & Whedon, C. (1996). Reading comprehension: A synthesis of research in learning disabilities. In T.E. Scruggs & M.A. Mastropieri (Eds.), *Advances in learning and behavioural disabilities*, Volume 10, (pp. 201–223). Greenwich, CT: JAI Press.

McCormick, S. (2007). *Instructing students who have literary problems*. Columbus, OH: Merrill/ Prentice Hall.

Meyer, M.S., & Felton, R.H. (1999). Repeated reading to enhance fluency: Approaches and new directions. *Annals of Dyslexia*, 49:283–306.

Miyake A., & Shah P. (Eds.) (1999). *Models of working memory: Mechanisms of active maintenance and executive control*. Cambridge: Cambridge University Press.

Montague, M., Maddux, C.D., & Dereshiwsky, M.I. (1990). Story grammar and comprehension and production of narrative prose by students with learning disabilities. *Journal of Learning Disabilities*, 23:190–197.

Ogle, D.M. (1989). K-W-L: A teaching model that develops active reading of expository text. *The Reading Teacher*, 39:564–570.

Palincsar, A.M., & Brown, A.L. (1986). Interactive teaching to promote independent learning from text. *The Reading Teacher*, 39(8), 771–777.

Paris, S.G., Lipson, M.Y., & Wixson, K.K. (1983). Becoming a strategic reader. *Contemporary Educational Psychology*, 8:293–316.

Perfetti, C.A. (1977). Language comprehension and fast decoding: Some psycholinguistic prerequisites for skilled reading comprehension. In J.T. Guthries (Ed.), *Cognition, curriculum, and comprehension* (pp. 20–41). Newark, DE: International Reading Association.

Perfetti, C.A. (1984). Some reflections on learning and not learning to read. *Remedial and Special Education*, 5(3), 34–38.

Perfetti, C.A. (1985). *Reading ability*. New York: Oxford University Press.

Raben, K., Darch, C., & Eaves, R.C. (1999). The differential effects of two systematic reading comprehension approaches with students with learning disabilities. *Journal of Learning Disabilities*, 32(1), 36–47.

Robinson, H.M. (1961). The major aspects of reading. In H.A. Robinson (Ed.), *Reading: Seventy-five years of progress*, Chicago: University of Chicago Press.

Rumelhart, D.E. (1980). Schemata: The building blocks of cognition. In R.J. Spiro, B.C. Bruce, & W.F. Brewer (Eds.), *Theoretical issues in reading comprehension* (pp. 33–58). New Jersey: Lawrence Erlbaum.

Schumaker, J.B., Deshler, D., Warner, L., & Denton, T. (1982). Multipass: A learning strategy for improving reading comprehension. *Learning Disabilities Quarterly*, 5(3), 295–304.

Seigel, L.S. (1992). An evaluation of the discrepancy definition of dyslexia. *Journal of Learning Disabilities*, 25:618–629.

Seigel, L.S. (2003). Basic cognitive processes and reading disabilities. In H. Swanson, K. Harris, & S. Graham (Eds.), *Handbook of learning disabilities*, 158–181. New York: The Guildford Press.

Sénéchal, M., Ouellette, G., & Rodney, D. (2006). The misunderstood giant: On the predictive role of early vocabulary to future reading. In S.B. Neuman & D.K. Dickinson (Eds.), *Handbook of early literacy research, volume 2*, 173–184. New York: Guildford.

Shaywitz, B.A., Stuebing, J.M., Shaywitz, S.E., & Fletcher, J. (1996). Intelligent testing and the discrepancy model for students with learning disabilities. *Learning Disabilities Research and Practice*, 13(4), 295–304.

Silliman, E., Butler, K., & Wallach, G. (2002). The time has come to talk of many things. In K. Butler, & E. Silliman (Eds.), *Speaking, reading and writing in children with language learning disabilities: New paradigms in research and practice*, 3–26. Mahwah, NJ: Lawrence Erlbaum Associates.

Stanovich, K.E., & Seigel, L.S. (1994). Phenotypic performance profile of children with reading disabilities: A regression-based test of the phonological-core variable difference model. *Journal of Educational Psychology*, 86:24–53.

Steffensen, M.S. (1978). Satisfying inquisitive adults: Some simple methods for answering yes/no questions. *Journal of Child Language*, 5(2), 221–236.

Swanson, H.L. (1999). Reading research for students with LD: A meta-analysis of intervention outcomes. *Journal of Learning Disabilities*, 32(6), 503–534.

Swanson, H.L., & Siegel, L. (2001). Learning disabilities as a working memory deficit. *Issues in Education*, 7(1), 1–48.

Taylor, M.B., & Beach, R.W. (1984). The effects of text structure instruction on middle grade students' comprehension and production of expository text. *Reading Research Quarterly*, 19:134–146.

Taylor, M.B., & Samuels, S.J. (1983). Children's use of text structure in recall of expository material. *American Educational Research Journal*, 20:517–528.

Taylor, M.B., & Williams, J.P. (1983). Comprehension of learning-disabled readers: Task and text variations. *Journal of Educational Psychology*, 75:743–751.

Torgesen, J., Wagner, R.K., Rashotte, C., Lindamood, P., Rose, E., Conway, T., & Garvan, C. (1999). Preventing reading failure in young children with phonological processing disabilities: Group and individual responses to instruction. *Journal of Educational Psychology*, 91(4), 579–593.

Tractenberg, R.E. (2002). Exploring hypotheses about phonological awareness, memory and reading achievement. *Journal of Learning Disabilities*, 35(5), 407–424.

Vaughn, S., Gersten, R., & Chard, D.J. (2000). The underlying message in LD intervention research: Findings from research syntheses. *Exceptional Children*, 67(1), 99–114.

Wagner, R.K., Torgesen, J.K., & Rashotte, C.A. (1994). Development of reading related phonological processing abilities: New evidence of bidirectional causality from a latent variable longitudinal study. *Developmental Psychology*, 30(1), 73–87.

Welsch, R.G. (2007). Using experimental analysis to determine interventions for reading fluency and recalls of students with learning disabilities. *Learning Disabilities Quarterly*, 30(2), 115–130.

Weisberg, R., & Balajthy, E. (1989). Improving disabled readers' summarization and recognition of expository text structure. In N.D. Padak, T.V. Rasinski, & J. Logan (Eds.), *Challenges in reading* (pp. 141–151). Provo, UT: College Reading Association.

Westby, C. (2002). Beyond decoding: Critical and dynamic literacy for students with dyslexia, language learning disabilities (LLD) or attention deficit hyperactivity disorder (ADHD). In K. Butler & E. Silliman (Eds.), *Speaking, reading and writing in children with language learning disabilities: New paradigms in research and practice*, 73–108.

Westwood, P. (2003). *Commonsense methods for children with special educational needs: Strategies for the regular classroom* (4th ed.). London: Routledge.

Westwood, P. (2007). *Commonsense methods for children with special educational needs: Strategies for the regular classroom* (5th ed.). London: Routledge.

Wolf, M. (2002). The second deficit: An investigation of the independence of phonological and naming speed deficits in developmental dyslexia. *Reading and Writing: An Interdisciplinary Journal*, 15(2), 43–72.

Wong, B.Y.L., & Wilson, M. (1984). Investigating awareness of and teaching passage organization in learning disabled children. *Journal of Learning Disabilities*, 17:477–482.

8

MATHEMATICS

In this chapter, mathematics and mathematics-learning disabilities is discussed. We describe new views on mathematics and mathematics learning and compare them to more traditional conceptualizations. As well, we summarize research findings in the area of mathematics-learning disabilities, a field that is only in its infancy.

MATHEMATICS

Development of mathematical literacy in school-aged children is increasingly viewed by policy makers worldwide as a potential source of social capital and as a means to sustain healthy technological societies. Over the past several years, mathematics curriculums in industrialized nations have expanded to ensure that during the school years, children have access to the learning opportunities necessary to attain a high level of mathematical literacy (Hopkins, 2007). This move to broaden the scope of mathematics instruction is exemplified in the principles and standards for school mathematics proposed by the National Council of Teachers of Mathematics (NCTM) in the United States (2000). In this document, mathematics is described not only in terms of *content areas* (i.e., number and operations, algebra, geometry, measurement, data analysis, and probability) but also with respect to *cognition and communication* (i.e., problem solving, reasoning and proof, communication, connections, and representations) and *emotions* (i.e., attitudes toward mathematics, confidence in being mathematical, and the emotional aspects of learning mathematics). Despite this concentrated push for increased mathematical literacy, recent research has shown that approximately 5 to 8 percent of school-aged children experience difficulty meeting the standards proposed by the NCTM (Badian, 1983; Geary, 2005; Kilpatrick, Swafford, & Findell, 2001). Reasons to account for the poor mathematical performance among children in this group are complex and not well understood (Gross-Tsur, Manor, & Shalev, 1996). One possible explanation is that for some children, the cognitive load of the expanded mathematics curricula is too high, and they fail to fully engage in the instructional activities that are optimal to learning (Woodward, 2006; Woodward & Montague, 2002). Vaughn, Klinger, and Hughes (2000) also caution that having students spend time on problems they are unable to solve may take away much-needed time for instruction to improve basic skills. Whether children in this group have specific learning disabilities is not certain, for there is no agreement among theorists and/or researchers about the criteria that should be used to identify children with mathematics-learning disabilities (Geary et al., 2007). This general lack of consensus has prompted an exponential increase in the number of studies that investigate challenges children face when interpreting and applying mathematics. In this chapter, we review what is currently known about the influences that constrain development of mathematics abilities among children who struggle in school. We begin the chapter with a discussion on the nature of mathematics and mathematics-learning for school-aged children. We then discuss the identification of mathematics-learning disabilities and how they are conceptualized from a constructivist and an information processing approach. As in previous chapters, we conclude this chapter with a summary of the important research findings.

WHAT IS MATHEMATICS?

In theory, mathematics represents a body of conceptual, procedural, and declarative knowledge and its use in communication with others to solve problems. Briefly, *conceptual knowledge* refers to the mental structures that underlie children's reasoning with mathematics. Within each structure or model, various components are linked together, and it is this linkage with previously learned concepts that contributes to children's deep conceptual understandings. For example, a basic arithmetic combination, such as 3 + 8, may initially seem overwhelming to a first grader, but when it is linked to previous knowledge (e.g., $3 + 7 = 10$, therefore $3 + 8 = 3 + 7 + 1 = 11$), the solution becomes more apparent. Carpenter and Moser (1984) suggest that the most difficult problems for children to solve are those that cannot be easily associated with an existing mental representation. *Procedural knowledge* refers to knowledge about the sequence of steps necessary to solve a mathematical problem. For example, children come to know that when multiplying any number by 10, all they must do to find the solution is add a 0 to the end of the number (e.g., $5 \cdot 10 = 50$). *Declarative knowledge* refers to mathematical ideas that are automatically retrieved from long-term memory. For example, when presented with the number 4, children may automatically think of the word *four*, or they may associate the algorithm "2 + 2" with the number or perhaps various other numerical combinations (e.g., "0 + 4"; "1 + 3"; "5 − 1"; "8/2"; etc.).

The relative importance of conceptual, procedural, and declarative knowledge on school-aged children's mathematics performance has been historically controversial. School curriculums in western industrialized countries have traditionally emphasized development of procedural and declarative knowledge at the expense of conceptual knowledge. In this view, instructional approaches stress memorization and automaticity of computation skills rather than construction of understandings of mathematical concepts in real-world situations (Montague, Warger, & Morgan, 2000). More contemporary approaches, such as those outlined in the principles and standards of the NCTM, are focused on the development of conceptual knowledge through problem solving. Evans (2007) argues that the dichotomy created by educators and curriculum developers between procedural/declarative and conceptual knowledge is illusory, for children must use all types of knowledge to fully engage in mathematics. For example, automaticity in estimation and in retrieving mental representations of arithmetic combinations is considered foundational to effective mathematics problem solving using this information (Woodward, 2006). One challenge for educators concerns finding ways to make the connections between these bodies of knowledge strong and explicit for students, without emphasizing one type of knowledge over the other. Constructing solutions to mathematical problems is a complex, multidimensional undertaking; therefore, it seems reasonable to assume that the origins of mathematical learning difficulties of school-aged children could arise from limitations in any one or combination of these knowledge areas.

Although much of the research in mathematics is concerned with the construction of knowledge within the minds of school-aged children, it is important to note that when children solve mathematical problems, they also describe, question, argue, predict, and justify their reasoning within interactive, communicative settings with others (Australian Education Council, 1991; Montague, 2006). These communicative acts, in turn, are thought to facilitate growth in children's knowledge about mathematics. In this view, mathematics is a language with its own set of *symbols and rules for their use.* For children to use "mathematics," they need to know about the *functionality* of mathematics symbols and tools, they need to engage in *social cognition* where ideas are shared, and they must *use the symbols of mathematics* in purposeful ways to problem solve and meet their own goals. (See Figure 2.1 in Chapter 2 to link these ideas to a social-pragmatic view of language acquisition.) The National Council of Teachers of Mathematics (NCTM, 2000) stated the following:

When students are challenged to think and reason about mathematics and to communicate the results of their thinking to others orally or in writing, they learn to be clear and convincing. Students who have opportunities, encouragement, and support for speaking, writing, reading, and listening in mathematics classes reap dual benefits: They communicate to learn mathematics, and they learn to communicate mathematically. (p. 60)

MATHEMATICS DEVELOPMENT AND COMMUNICATION

Adams and Lowery's (2007) qualitative study of two fourth graders "reading mathematics" is illustrative of the processes involved when children communicate mathematically. In the following discussion, we describe three observations from this study that affirm previous findings in the research on mathematics learning and set the stage for thinking about the difficulties that some children may experience while using mathematics. The two children (a boy and a girl) were asked to read and discuss mathematical problems embedded in two different reading texts: a mathematics textbook and a children's trade book. A page from a fourth-grade mathematics text, *Problem-Solving Practice* (Harcourt School Publishers, 2004), was used as the first source of reading material. The trade book used in the study was *Moira's Birthday Story* (Munsch, 1981), a story about a young girl who, against the wishes of her parents, invites all the children in her school to her birthday party and is subsequently faced with the challenge of ordering enough food for 200 children. Moira is only able to secure 10 pizzas and 10 birthday cakes, so after cleaning the house and receiving a present from Moira for their work (one of her birthday gifts), her invited guests leave the party to find more food. At the conclusion of the story, 190 pizzas and 190 cakes are eventually delivered to the party, but the guests had long gone. The researchers engaged the children in conversations and asked each child questions at different points in the story to elicit mathematics language—describe what had happened in the story or respond to questions related to the mathematics embedded in the text (e.g., "If 200 pizzas were for grades one to six, about how many pizzas were for each grade?"; p. 170). We highlight three observations from the study that have relevance to our discussion on mathematics and communication.

OBSERVATION #1: CHILDREN'S KNOWLEDGE OF MATHEMATICS BUILDS FROM THEIR PRIOR EXPERIENCES

One important observation from the study is that both children drew from their prior experiences at birthday parties to generate responses to the mathematical problems associated with *Moira's Birthday Party*. For example, when asked "if 10 pizzas were for 20 friends, how much pizza would each friend get," one child responded "about 4 pieces," which is an appropriate estimate for a medium-sized pizza containing approximately 8 pieces. No information was provided to the child about the size of the pizza, so the assumption is made by Adams and Lowery that the child used her previous experiences dividing and sharing pizzas to know that each pizza would yield approximately 8 pieces and thus used this knowledge to estimate her response. The authors use this and other examples to propose that children's lived experiences support their interpretation of mathematics problems even as their understanding of the mathematical symbols and the concepts they represent are developing. An alternative view, and perhaps a stronger interpretation, of this finding is that children's experiences in a social world are critically important for them to gain knowledge about the functionality of mathematics symbols and tools. Unfortunately, few studies are available to illustrate how children's communicative interactions with others in social environments influence their construction of mathematics knowledge, conceptions, and beliefs (for further discussion of this issue, see Thompson & Chappell, 2007).

On the other hand, educators in the field of mathematics have long recognized that school-aged children and adolescents are more likely to communicate understandings of abstract mathematical symbols and tools when they are used in meaningful ways to solve real-world problems (Bottage et al., 2007). Unfortunately, the mathematical tools that children are expected to learn and use during the school years may not always have an immediately recognizable function or a clear purpose for them. One of the many challenges facing both elementary and secondary school math educators is to find ways to make the *functionality* of abstract, mathematical concepts and language salient to students in a real-world environment. Students may not be willing to engage in meaningful communication using mathematics symbols and tools unless they are made aware of the functionality of the activity. Conversely, a student may be more willing to engage in mathematical discussions when they are interpreted as purposeful interactions. For example, learning about mathematics from a school textbook may seem less important to students in secondary school than using mathematics to accomplish goals such as calculating the amount of food and/or drink needed at a social event, rationalizing the benefits and costs of owning a car, or designing a snowboard that carves well in specific kinds of snow. Research has shown that educators can assist children to recognize purposes for mathematics by engaging in interactive dialogues with them, in which problem solving becomes a shared activity and educators and children together interpret mathematical symbols and the concepts that they represent (Butler, Beckingham, & Lauscher, 2005).

OBSERVATION #2: CHILDREN'S CONSTRUCTIONS OF COHERENT MENTAL REPRESENTATIONS OF MATHEMATICAL PROBLEMS OPTIMIZES PROBLEM SOLVING

Another observation in Adams and Lowery's study is that when asked to explain how they solved mathematical problems, the children described a schematic mental representation of the activity rather than using a symbolic mathematical algorithm. For example, when asked to determine the amount of fencing required for a rectangular playground area, one child first summed the length of the vertical sides (i.e., 66 + 66) and then summed the length of the horizontal sides (i.e., 42 + 42) on a piece of paper. In the final step, the child added the summed lengths of the vertical and horizontal sides together (i.e., 132 + 84) to obtain the estimated perimeter of the playground. This example illustrates how the child first recognized and formulated a mental representation of the problem (as one of finding perimeter) and second used his conceptual and procedural knowledge about mathematical symbols (e.g., +, =, perimeter) to solve it. A more parsimonious strategy would have been to substitute numbers into a symbolic equation [e.g., perimeter of a rectangle = $(2 \cdot width) + (2 \cdot length)$]; however, theorists have long argued that building conceptual, procedural, and declarative knowledge about mathematics is more important to children's development of mathematical literacy than memorizing complex algorithms in isolation of these understandings (Miller & Hudson, 2007). Mathematical problems that cannot be framed within an existing mental representation are known to be difficult for both typically developing children and for children with mathematics-learning disabilities (Garcia, Jimenez, & Hess, 2006).

OBSERVATION #3: ADULTS PLAY AN IMPORTANT ROLE BY MEDIATING CHILDREN'S CONSTRUCTION OF KNOWLEDGE ABOUT MATHEMATICS

School-aged children require guided support from adults to make mathematics embedded in social activity explicit. For example, both children in the study clearly grasped the main idea of the story about Moira's birthday party: Too many guests were invited, and Moira was faced with a problem about how to feed her guests. One child did not seem to recognize that when the additional food arrived after the guests had left, there was more food than people to feed. Construction of ideas about mathematical concepts through discussion of children's literature or during social activity is sometimes labeled "discovery learning," as if children are left to negotiate meanings of mathematical symbols in context by themselves (Butler, Beckingham, & Lauscher, 2005). In this interpretation, adults act as facilitators to allow children to construct their own meanings about mathematics (i.e., through inquiry, problem solving, making connections). However, as this example clearly illustrates, even when children are encouraged to make connections, mathematical ideas may not always be salient to them. More intensive forms of scaffolding and adult support may be needed for children who struggle with mathematics than is available through instructional approaches advocated by the current standards and principles espoused by the NCTM.

Another issue concerns whether collaborative problem solving with peers can be assumed to support children's construction of mathematical ideas. The idea is theoretically justified; however, empirical support to affirm its validity is lacking. Studies of peer-tutoring interventions provide some support. Peer tutoring has been successfully used across a range of content areas (Greenwood, 1991; Mastropieri, Scruggs, Spencer, & Fontana, 2003) and in mathematics with students of varying age and abilities (Fuchs, Fuchs, & Karns, 2001; for reviews, see Baker, Gersten, & Lee, 2002; Kunsch, Jitendra, & Sood, 2007). The rationale for peer-mediated mathematics instruction does not emphasize construction of children's knowledge about mathematics in social activities per se; rather, this instructional approach is viewed as a means to increase academic engagement and rates of responding of children with mathematics-learning disabilities in general-education classrooms. However, it could be argued that during peer-mediated instruction, tutors and tutees engage in a form of triadic communication in which they jointly attend to and create solutions to a mathematics task. Tutees attend to their tutor's use of mathematical language during problem solving, and they are encouraged (explicitly through the use of prompts and cues) to use these same language tools to advance their own ideas about solving the mathematics problem. One area for further research is highlighted by Kunsch, Jitendra, and Sood (2007), who report that, on average, the effect size (ES) for peer-mediated instruction in mathematics for students in secondary school is small (ES = .18) and relatively lower than the average effect size obtained for peer-mediated mathematics instruction for students in elementary school (ES = .57). It is not entirely clear why peer-mediated mathematics interventions appear to be less effective for adolescents in secondary school compared to children in elementary school. One explanation provided by Kunsch et al. is that peer-mediated interventions are less feasible in secondary schools that are organized in ways to support whole-class instruction rather than paired student learning. Another possible explanation has to do with differences in complexity of the problems and in the symbolic mathematical language required to solve problems at the elementary and the secondary school levels. Peer-tutors at the secondary level may not be sufficiently skilled in communicating the meanings of complex mathematics concepts and symbols. A third reason could be that the magnitude of severity in mathematics-learning disabilities identified among adolescents at the secondary school level may be greater than among children identified at the elementary school level, and as a result, resistance to intervention may be greater among older students. Much more research is needed to clarify these issues and to tease out the role of social communication on the learning of students with mathematics-learning disabilities.

In summary, mathematics is probably best conceived as a complex cognitive activity in which children construct solutions to mathematical problems with others in their social community. It follows that children's difficulties with mathematics can originate from multiple sources that have to do with the child (i.e., mathematics knowledge and processing abilities) or with the social context in which mathematics is used (i.e., complexity of problems to be solved; amount and type of scaffolding support available). Although the research on learning of children and adolescents with mathematics-learning disabilities is far from complete, the number of studies on the issue has increased markedly in recent years, and it is to this body of research that our discussion now turns.

MATHEMATICS AND LEARNING DISABILITIES

A model that fully explains children's construction of conceptual, procedural, or declarative mathematics knowledge (a constructivist view); the importance of the social environment on the acquisition of mathematical symbols and tools (a social pragmatic view); or relations between different types and levels of cognitive processing while solving mathematics problems (an information processing view) is not currently available to researchers. The breadth and complexity of mathematics without such a framework makes the study of children's mathematics-learning disabilities a daunting venture (Geary, 2005). It is probably not surprising that without a well-defined and comprehensive model to guide research efforts, far less is known about the association between mathematics literacy and learning disabilities compared to what is known about the relations between print literacy and learning disabilities (Gersten, Jordan, & Flojo, 2005). In the following discussion, we explore issues that concern the identification of children with mathematics-learning disabilities and what is currently known from research on mathematics-learning disabilities.

IDENTIFICATION OF MATHEMATICS-LEARNING DISABILITIES

One problem facing researchers interested in the study of mathematics-learning disabilities concerns defining the criteria to use to identify children to include for study (Barbaresi et al., 2005). As previously discussed in other chapters of this text, the validity of traditional IQ-achievement discrepancy criteria for identification purposes is questionable for a number of conceptual and statistical reasons. Another issue concerns the fact that the relations between IQ and mathematics achievement are not well understood. To avoid these problems, a more common approach used by researchers has been to identify children on the basis of a cutoff score on a composite measure on a standardized mathematics achievement test. Cutoff scores < 30th percentile is found most often in studies of children with mathematics-learning disabilities; however, in some cases, more restrictive cutoffs (< 5th or < 10th percentile) have been used. When lenient cutoff scores are used, it is feasible that the child may have strengths in some aspects of cognitive processing and weaknesses in others, but when restrictive cutoff scores are used, children have difficulty performing on a wide range of mathematics cognition tasks. Geary and his colleagues (2007) tested this hypothesis by comparing the cognitive characteristics of two groups of kindergarten-aged children with mathematics learning difficulties: One group was identified on the basis of performance on a mathematical achievement test using lenient criteria (23rd to 39th percentile), and the second group was identified with more restrictive criteria (< 15th percentile). Findings showed that relative to typically developing peers, children in the mathematics-learning disability group classified with more restrictive criteria had difficulty performing on a wide range of mathematics cognitive tasks, and variability in group performance differences was mediated at least in part by working memory and/or speed of processing. In comparison, the performance of children in groups classified with more lenient criteria was similar to that of typically developing peers on some tasks (e.g., use of backup strategies to solve simple number combination problems), but overall, children in this group were less fluent in processing arithmetic sets, in making number line estimates, and in computing simple arithmetic combinations than typically developing children. Most researchers agree that for practical purposes, lenient cutoff scores on standardized measures of mathematics achievement are necessary to cast a wide net to identify all children in the primary grades who may benefit from instruction to prevent mathematics-learning disabilities (see Gersten, Jordan, & Flojo, 2005, for a review). However, caution must be exercised to ensure that early identification procedures for instructional purposes are not confused with those necessary for a diagnosis of learning disability, for research has shown that children who score below a cutoff at one point in time on a standardized measure of achievement may perform in the average range on later occasions (Geary, Hamson, & Hoard, 2000). Although benefits accrue when lenient cutoff scores are used to identify children in need of instruction in school-based prevention programs, restrictive criteria may be more suitable for research on the learning and development of children with various subtypes of mathematics-learning disabilities (to be discussed later in this chapter).

ORIGINS OF MATHEMATICS-LEARNING
DISABILITIES

Children and adolescents who struggle with mathematics do so for a number of reasons that have been interpreted using different theoretical paradigms. Social pragmatic explanations for the difficulties that children face communicating with others using mathematics have yet to be investigated in the research; constructivist and information processing views of mathematics-learning disabilities, however, have garnered more empirical support. Therefore, we limit the discussion that follows to what is known about mathematics-learning disabilities from constructivist and information processing viewpoints.

COGNITIVE STRATEGIES AND SELF-REGULATION
(A CONSTRUCTIVIST VIEW)

A number of studies have found that school-aged children with mathematics-learning disabilities have difficulty constructing knowledge about mathematics, using cognitive strategies to solve mathematical problems, and self-monitoring their construction of understandings and solutions to mathematical problems. These abilities are highly connected and inter-related. For example, Geary, Hoard, Byrd-Craven, and DeSoto (2004) studied the development of children's *conceptual knowledge of number sets* and found that this knowledge facilitates children's use of strategies on problems that require the decomposition of number sets. For example, children who know the concept that $3 + 3 + 3 = 9$ can solve the problem $5 + 9$ by decomposing the 9 into three sets of 3 and reformulate it as $5 + 3 + 3 + 3$. Children with mathematics-learning disabilities are less likely to decompose number sets to solve problems and more likely to use unsophisticated, immature strategies where they make more errors (Geary, 2005). Other forms of conceptual knowledge that have been linked to poor problem solving by school-aged children with mathematics-learning disabilities includes *number estimation* (i.e., the ability to use the number line to compare quantities), counting knowledge (the ability to count in sequence), and number combinations (i.e., the ability to compute operations involved with adding, subtracting, multiplying, and dividing) (Desoete & Grégoire, 2006; Jordan, Kaplan, Locuniak, & Ramineni, 2007; but for a review, see Gersten, Jordan, & Flojo, 2005).

Children with mathematics-learning disabilities have also been shown to have fewer metacognitive strategies available to self-monitor their mathematical problem solving (Montague, 2007). To solve cognitive problems, children must learn how to monitor and regulate their thinking to meet their goals (Flavell, 1987). Many school-aged children who struggle with mathematics lack the ability to reflect deeply on their own cognitive processes as they engage in mathematical problem solving. As discussed previously in this chapter, some children may have difficulty identifying the problem that needs to be solved, for the problem may not be immediately salient to them (e.g., when mathematics is embedded in word problems or in children's literature). Another source of difficulty arises when children do not have a mental representation of the problem available in memory (Montague, 1997). Even when the problem is identified, research has shown that children with mathematics-learning disabilities have difficulty planning the operations and procedures that are required to solve the problem, and they are less efficient at self-monitoring their performances and self-correcting errors they make (Lucangeli, Cornoldi, & Tellarini, 1998). Children with mathematics-learning difficulties have also been shown to be less accurate in their self-evaluations of their competence to problem solve using mathematics (Desoete & Roeyers, 2006). Garrett, Mazzocco, & Baker (2006) compared groups of second graders with and without mathematics-learning disabilities on their ability to accurately evaluate their ability to perform mathematics tasks. Findings showed that children's metacognitive understandings about mathematics in both groups improved over time (i.e., from second to third grade); however, children with mathematics-learning disabilities were less accurate than their age-peers without learning disabilities in (1) predicting problems that they could solve accurately and (2) evaluating both their incorrect and correct solutions to problems. The difference between children's perceived and actual ability to problem solve may contribute to the well-documented finding that several children with mathematics-learning disabilities have low self-perceptions of their competence in mathematics (Butler, 2002). When children feel less able to perform cognitive tasks, they are less likely to engage in cognitive activity or to persist in the face of challenges they encounter during problem solving. In support, Montague and Applegate (2000) found that compared to children without learning challenges, children with mathematics-learning disabilities report that mathematics problems are more difficult, they require more time to problem solve, and they use fewer and less sophisticated strategies to solve problems.

Much of the intervention research for children and adolescents with mathematics-learning disabilities has focused on instruction to increase conceptual and procedural knowledge and to improve self-regulation during problem solving (for a thorough discussion, see Montague, 2007; Fuchs et al., 2005). Self-regulation in this sense includes self-assessment (asking questions of oneself throughout problem solving), self-recording (self-monitoring and checking accuracy of performance), and self-instruction (providing prompts and cues to oneself throughout the problem-solving routine) (Montague, 2006).

Jitendra's (Jitendra, Hoff, & Beck, 1999) schema-based instruction model is illustrative of a constructivist instructional approach to problem solving. In this approach children are taught to identify mental representations or schemas for specific problem types. Different classifications for the difficulty of word problems have been used in the research (Carpenter & Mosner, 1984; García, Jiménez, & Hess, 2006; Jitendra, Griffin, Deatline-Buchman, & Sczesniak, 2007). In these studies, *combine problems* involve two distinct groups or subsets that combine to make a new group or set: "There were 48 children on the bus: 23 girls and 25 boys for a total of 48 children." *Compare problems* also involve a discrete group or sets, but in this case, they are compared: "Shawna bought 5 pencils for school, and Miriko bought 10 pencils for school. How many more pencils does Miriko have?" *Change problems* involve an initial quantity that is either increased or decreased as a result of a direct or implied action: "Yuki kicked in one goal in the first half, and he got two more goals in the second half of the soccer game. How many goals did Yuki get in the game?" *Equalize problems* involve the same actions as in change problems, but in this case, there is a comparison of two disjoint sets: "Nima has 8 stickers. If Kaitlin gets 3 stickers today, she will have the same number of stickers as Nima. How many stickers does Kaitlin have?" Schema-based instruction encourages children to approach the word problems by identifying the underlying structure rather than focusing on the specific content of the word problem, and they are taught methods to self-monitor their success at identifying the schematic representation of the word problem (Jitendra et al., 2007). Maccini, Mulcahy, and Wilson (2007) conducted a meta-analysis of 23 studies (1995–2006) of interventions to support learning of secondary students with mathematics-learning disabilities. Positive effect sizes were found for schema-based instruction, as well as instruction of other cognitive and mnemonic strategies on outcome measures of declarative and/or procedural knowledge. Some of these strategies are helpful for students to automatically recall number combinations (i.e., declarative knowledge), whereas others are more useful for recalling the procedures to steps necessary to solve problems (i.e., procedural knowledge).

Findings from studies based on constructivist theories have been foundational to further understandings of development and construction of knowledge, strategy use, and self-regulation abilities of children and adolescents with mathematics-learning disabilities. To garner more complete understandings about the cognitive system that underlies mathematics performance of different subtypes of mathematics-learning disabilities, we turn to studies of information processing.

UNDERLYING COGNITIVE PROCESSES (AN INFORMATION PROCESSING VIEW)

There are two common subtypes of mathematics-learning disabilities discussed in the literature: children with reading disabilities in addition to mathematics-learning disabilities (MRD) and disabilities that are specific to mathematics (MD) (Fuchs & Fuchs, 2002; Fuchs, Fuchs, & Prentice 2004;

Jordan, Hanich, & Kaplan 2003). Geary (1993, 2003) suggests that the same phonological and semantic memory system that underlies the recall of number combinations also influences reading performance and accounts for the association often found between reading and mathematics-learning disabilities. Alternatively, Landerl and his colleagues (2004) suggest that semantic memory for numerical information underlies mathematics-learning disabilities rather than a general semantic memory system, for it is deficits in processing numerical processing that the affects poor learning of children with mathematics-related disabilities. To investigate this issue, Swanson and Jerman (2006) conducted a selective synthesis of the literature on the differences between samples of children with reading disabilities (RD), MD, and comorbid MRD on measures of cognitive functioning and reported that compared to children with RD, children with MD had more severe deficits on measures of naming speed (processing efficiency) and visual working memory; however, compared to children with MRD, children with MD performed better on measures of reading, visual-spatial reasoning, and memory (including long-term memory, short-term memory, and working memory). Results of hierarchical regression analyses further showed that the differences between MD and RD groups was best accounted for by differences in a general verbal working memory system, rather than a semantic deficit specific to numerical processing. In the following section, we review what is known about processing efficiency and working memory, the two components identified in Swanson and Jerman's synthesis that underlie MD.

PROCESSING EFFICIENCY

A number of studies of children's information processing suggest that children's difficulties with mathematics stem from an inability to quickly and effortlessly retrieve information from memory. Specifically, the research has focused on children's rate of processing number combinations (Goldman, Pellegrino, & Mertz, 1988). Inefficient or slow processing of number combinations has been associated with an increased frequency of procedural errors (Cumming & Elkins, 1999). Also, children may resort to using more developmentally immature strategies (e.g., using fingers to count) or to applying less resource-demanding algorithms to solve problems.

WORKING MEMORY CAPACITY

Children's slow rate of processing number combinations has also been attributed to capacity constraints in working memory. That is, children with small working memory capacities are less able than children with larger working memory capacities to formulate adequate mental representations of number combinations in long-term semantic memory (Geary, 1993, 2005; Geary et al., 1991; Passolunghi, Vercelloni, & Schadee, 2007). Creation of representations in long-term memory requires that children must simultaneously hold information about the problem and the solution in working memory (Rouselle & Noël, 2007). If the information decays too quickly, the representation created in long-term memory is less stable, and access to this information for future problem solving is less efficient and subsequent recall is less accurate (Geary, 1993).

Limitations in a working memory executive have also been used to explain mathematics-learning disabilities (Geary, 2005; Geary et al., 2007; Rosselli, Matute, Pinto, & Ardila, 2006; Swanson, 2006; Swanson & Kim, 2006; Swanson & Sache-Lee, 2001). In this account, children with small working memory capacities either due to age or individual differences perform poorly on mathematics tasks because they have fewer resources available to allocate to the processing and storage of mathematical information. That is, children have less working memory capacity available to retrieve and *update information* as illustrated here with a change word problem:

> Sital went to the market and bought five apples. He ate two apples as he walked around the market. How many apples did Sital have when he returned home?

Children with small working memory capacities also have fewer resources to allocate to the *inhibition* of irrelevant information, as illustrated with the following lengthy word problem (notice that this is also a change word problem of equal complexity to the one mentioned previously to illustrate updating of information):

> Meili took a bus 20 km to visit her grandmother, and then she walked with her grandmother another 5 km to the airport to meet her cousin, who was arriving in Vancouver on a flight from Hong Kong. Meili's aunt who lives 3 km north of the airport took a taxi to the airport, and her great uncle who lives 2 km south of the airport said that he would see her visiting cousin later in the week. Luckily, the flight that normally took 9 hours was late arriving for Meili, and her grandmother took 124 minutes to walk to the airport. Meili was not looking forward to her long trip home. How many kilometers must Meili travel from the airport to reach her home?

Although there is general agreement among researchers that many older children (i.e., over eight years) and adolescents with mathematics-learning disabilities have limitations in working memory capacity, more research on the role of a developing working memory system among younger school-aged children is needed to understand the relations between working memory and other executive functions and their influence on children's mathematics abilities.

EMOTIONS AND ATTITUDES ABOUT MATHEMATICS

Increasingly, educators and researchers are turning their attention to exploring the mediating influence of affect on mathematics performance both for children with and without mathematics-learning disabilities (Ma,

1999; McLeod, 1992). Children hold strong beliefs about the purpose and function of mathematics and about their own abilities to perform and communicate using mathematics. Educators also hold beliefs about their ability to teach mathematics and about the instructional practices that support mathematics learning. Such beliefs foster attitudes about mathematics that are considered to be relatively stable throughout the lifespan (McLeod, 1992).

Students who experience repeated failure in mathematics are vulnerable to feelings of low self-efficacy, which is predictive of ineffective use of cognitive strategies and limitations in metacognitive knowledge about mathematics (Tanner & Jones, 2003).

Moreover, anxieties about mathematics or fears, tension, or helplessness about one's ability to perform in mathematics activities have been shown to constrain student's educational goals and aspirations (Kulm, 1980; Maxwell, 1989). Mathematics anxiety can contribute to attitudes where students do not like mathematics or where mathematics causes them fear and anxiety. Attitudes of students toward mathematics assessed in middle school have been shown to be "remarkably prophetic" of student's subject choice in secondary school and whether they continue with studies at the postsecondary level (Leder & Forgasz, 1997).

SUMMARY

To summarize, in this chapter, we discussed different views of mathematics, the identification of mathematics-learning disabilities, and the cognitive and affective correlates of mathematics-learning disabilities:

• Key aspects of the definition of mathematics provided by the NCTM include a focus on content, cognitive, and language processes and emotions.
• The prevalence of mathematics-learning disabilities in the school-aged population ranges from 5 to 8 percent.
• A clear definition of mathematics-learning disabilities is not available in the research.
• To engage in mathematics, children must know and use conceptual, procedural, and declarative knowledge.
• The origins of mathematics-learning disabilities for school-aged children could arise from any one of these knowledge areas.
• Traditionally, procedural and declarative knowledge has been emphasized in instruction; more recently, conceptual knowledge and problem solving have become the emphasis.
• One way to conceptualize mathematics is as a language with its own set of symbols and rules for their use.
• Children's knowledge of mathematics builds from their prior experiences.

- Children's constructions of coherent mental representations of mathematical problems optimizes problem solving.
- Adults play an important role by mediating children's construction of knowledge about mathematics.
- Peer-mediated instruction appears to be more effective for younger, elementary school students than for secondary school students, but further research is required.
- Identification of children with mathematics-learning disabilities involves either lenient or more restrictive cutoff criteria on a standardized measure of mathematics achievement.
- For practical purposes and to identify children who may benefit from early instruction, a lenient cutoff score is advisable.
- For research purposes to investigate different subtypes of mathematics-learning disabilities, more restrictive cutoff scores may be required.
- The relation between IQ and mathematics achievement is not fully understood.
- Children with mathematics-learning disabilities may have difficulties with number estimation, counting knowledge, number combinations, and/or number sets.
- Children with mathematics-learning disabilities may have limited metacognitive knowledge to support problem solving.
- Children with mathematics-learning disabilities may also have difficulty self-monitoring their performance as they problem-solve.
- Low self-perception of competence in mathematics is associated with lack of persistence to complete mathematics tasks.
- Much of the intervention research for children and adolescents with mathematics-learning disabilities has stressed improving conceptual and procedural knowledge.
- Students who are unable to form a mental representation of the word problem (i.e., change, compare, equalize, combine) are less likely to be able to solve the problem.
- There are at least two subtypes of mathematics-learning disabilities, but many more may be found in future research.
- There are differences in cognitive processing between children with MD, RD, and comorbid MD + RD.
- The best predictors of cognitive processing among children with mathematics-learning disabilities only are rapid naming (processing) and verbal working memory.
- Children with small working memory capacities may have difficulty updating information and/or inhibiting information on word problems.
- Increasingly, researchers and educators are turning their attention to the emotional factors that are associated with mathematics-learning disabilities because a high number of students with mathematics-learning disabilities also have anxieties about mathematics.

REFERENCES

Adams, T.L., & Lowery, R.M. (2007). An analysis of children's strategies for reading mathematics. *Reading and Writing Quarterly*, 23:167–177.

Australian Education Council (A.E.C.) (1991). *A national statement on mathematics for Australian schools.* Carlton, Vic.: Curriculum Corporation.

Badian, N.A. (1983). Dyslcalculia and non-verbal disorders of learning. In H.R. Myklebust (Ed.), *Progress in learning disabilities.* Volume 5 (pp. 235–264). New York: Stratton.

Baker, S., Gersten, R., & Lee, D. (2002). A synthesis of empirical research on teaching mathematics to low-achieving students. *Elementary School Journal*, 103:51–73.

Barbaresi, W.J., Katusic, S.K., Colligan, R.C., Weaver, A.L., & Jacobsen, S. (2005). Math learning disorder: Incidence in a population-based birth cohort, 1976–82, Rochester, MN. *Ambulatory Pediatrics*, 5:281–289.

Bottage, B.A., Rueda, E., Serlin, R.C., Hung, Y., & Kwon, J.M. (2007). Shrinking achievement differences with anchored math problems: Challenges and possibilities. *The Journal of Special Education*, 41:31–49.

Butler, D. (2002). Individualizing instruction in self-regulated learning. *Theory into Practice*, 41:81–92.

Butler, D., Beckingham, B., & Lauscher, H. (2005). Promoting Strategic Learning by Eighth-Grade Students Struggling in Mathematics: A Report of Three Case Studies. *Learning Disabilities Research & Practice*, 20(3), 156–174.

Carpenter, T.P., & Moser, J.M. (1984). The acquisition of addition and subtraction concepts in grades one through three. *Journal for Research in Mathematics Education*, 15:179–202.

Cumming, J., & Elkins, J. (1999). Lack of automaticity in the basic addition facts as a characteristic of arithmetic learning problems and instructional needs. *Mathematical Cognition*, 5(2), 149–180.

Desoete, A., & Grégoire, J. (2006). Numerical competence in young children and in children with mathematics learning disabilities. *Learning and Individual Differences*, 16:351–367.

Desoete, A., & Roeyers, H. (2006). Metacognitive macroevaluations in mathematical problem solving. *Learning and Instruction*, 16:12–25.

Evans, D. (2007). Developing mathematical proficiency in the Australian context: Implications for students with learning difficulties. *Journal of Learning Disabilities*, 40(5).

Flavell, J.H. (1987). Speculations about the nature and development of metacognition. In F.E. Weinert & R. Kluwe (Eds.), *Metacognition, motivation and understanding* (pp. 20–29). Hillsdale, NJ: Erlbaum.

Fuchs, L.S., Compton, D.L., Fuchs, D., Paulsen, K., Bryant, J.D., & Hamlett, C.L. (2005). The prevention, identification, and cognitive determinants of math difficulty. *Journal of Educational Psychology*, 97(3), 493–513.

Fuchs, L.S., Fuchs, D., & Prentice, K. (2004). Responsiveness to mathematical problem-solving instruction: Comparing students at risk of mathematics disability with and without risk of reading disability. *Journal of Learning Disabilities*, 37:293–306.

Fuchs, L.S., & Fuchs, D. (2002). Mathematics problem-solving profiles of students with mathematics disabilities with and without comorbid reading disabilities. *Journal of Learning Disabilities*, 35:563–573.

Fuchs, L.S., Fuchs, D., & Karns, K. (2001). Enhancing kindergartners' mathematical development: Effects of peer-assisted learning strategies. *The Elementary School Journal*, 101:495–510.

García, A.I., Jiménez, J., & Hess, S. (2006). Solving arithmetic word problems: An analysis of classification as a function of difficulty in children with and without arithmetic LD. *Journal of Learning Disabilities*, 39(3), 270–281.

Garrett, A.J., Mazzocco, M.M., & Baker, L. (2006). Development of metacognitive skills of prediction and evaluation in children with or without math disability. *Learning Disabilities Research and Practice*, 21(2), 77–88.

Geary, D.C. (2005). Role of cognitive theory in the study of learning disability in mathematics. *Journal of Learning Disabilities*, 38:305–307.

Geary, D.C. (1993). Mathematical disabilities: Cognitive, neuropsychological, and genetic components. *Psychological Bulletin*, 114:343–362.

Geary, D.C., Hamson, C.O., & Hoard, M.K. (2000). Numerical and arithmetic cognition: A longitudinal study of process and concept deficits in children with learning disability. *Journal of Experimental Child Psychology*, 77:213–239.

Geary, D.C., Hoard, M.K., Byrd-Craven, J., & Desoto, M. (2004). Strategy choices in simple and complex addition. Contributions of working memory and counting knowledge for children with mathematical disability. *Journal of Experimental Child Psychology*, 88:121–131.

Geary, D.C., Hoard, M.K., Byrd-Craven, J., Nugent, L., & Numtee, C. (2007). Cognitive mechanisms underlying achievement deficits in children with mathematical learning disability. *Child Development*, 78(4), 1343–1359.

Gersten, R., Jordan, N., & Flojo, J.R. (2005). Early identification and interventions for students with mathematics difficulties. *Journal of Learning Disabilities*, 38(4), 293–304.

Gleason, J.B. (2005). *The development of language*. Boston: Allyn & Bacon.

Golaman, S.R., Pellegrino, J.W., & Mertz, D.L. (1988). Extended practice of basic addition facts: Strategy changes in learning-disabled students. *Cognition and Instruction*, 5(3), 223–265.

Greenwood, C.R. (1991). Classwide peer tutoring: Longitudinal effects on the reading, language, and mathematics achievement of at risk students. *Journal of Reading, Writing, and Learning Disabilities International*, 7:105–123.

Gross-Tsur, V., Manor, O., & Shavev, R.S. (1996). Developmental dyscalculia: Prevalence and demographic features. *Developmental Medicine and Child Neurology*, 38:25–33.

Harcourt School Publishers. (2004). *Harcourt Math: Grade 4*. Orlando, FL: Harcourt School Publishers.

Hopkins, M.H. (2007). Adapting a model for literacy learning to the learning of mathematics. *Reading and Writing Quarterly*, 23:121–138.

Jitendra, A.K., Griffin, C.C., Deatline-Buchman, A., & Sczesniak, E. (2007). Mathematical word problem solving in third grade classrooms. *Journal of Educational Research*, 100(5), 283–302.

Jitendra, A.K., Hoff, K., & Beck, M.M. (1999). Teaching middle school students with learning disabilities to solve word problems using a schema-based approach. *Remedial and Special Education*, 20:50–64.

Jordan, N.C., Hanich, L., & Kaplan, D. (2003). A longitudinal study of mathematical competencies in children with specific mathematics difficulties versus children with co-morbid mathematics and reading difficulties. *Child Development*, 74:834–850.

Jordan, N.C., Kaplan, D., Locuniak, M.N., & Ramineni, C. (2007). Predicting first-grade math achievement from developmental number sense trajectories. *Learning Disabilities Research and Practice*, 22(1), 36–46.

Kilpatrick, J., Swafford, J., & Findell, B. (Eds.) (2001). Conclusions and recommendations. In Mathematical Learning Study Committee, National Research Council, *Adding it up: Helping children learn mathematics* (407–432). Washington D.C.: National Academies Press.

Kulm, G. (1980). Research on mathematics attitudes. In R.J. Shumway (Ed.), *Research in mathematics education* (pp. 356–387). Reston: National Council of Teachers of Mathematics.

Kunsch, C., Jitendra, A.K., & Sood, S. (2007). The effects of peer-mediated instruction in mathematics for students with learning problems: A research synthesis. *Learning Disabilities Research and Practice*, 22(1), 1–12.

Landerl, K., Bevan, A., & Butterworth, B. (2004). Developmental dyscalculia and basic numerical capacities: A study of 8–9 year-old students. *Cognition*, 93(2), 99–125.

Leder, G., & Forgasz, H. (1997). Looking back towards the future: A case study in mathematics. In F. Biddulph & K. Carr (Eds.), *People in mathematics education: Proceedings of the twentieth annual conference of the Mathematics Education Group of Australasia 1*, (pp. 302–309). Waikato: Mathematics Education Research Group of Australasia.

Lucangeli, D., Cornoldi, C., & Tellarini, M. (1998). Metacognition and learning disabilites in mathematics. In T.E. Scruggs & M.A. Mastropieri (Eds.), *Advances in learning and behavioural disabilities* (pp. 219–244). Greenwich: JAI Press.

Ma, X. (1999). A meta-analysis of the relationship between anxiety towards mathematics and achievement in mathematics. *Journal for Research in Mathematics Education*, 30(5), 520–540.

Maccini, P., Mulcahy, C.A., & Wilson, M.G. (2007). A follow-up of mathematics interventions for secondary students with learning disabilities. *Learning Disabilities Research and Practice*, 22(1), 58–74.

Mastropieri, M.A., Scruggs, T.E., Spencer, V., & Fontana, J. (2003). Promoting success in high school world history: Peer tutoring versus guided notes. *Learning Disabilities Research and Practice*, 18:52–65.

Maxwell, J. (1989). Mathephobia. In P. Ernest (Ed.), *Mathematics teaching: The state of the art* (pp. 221–228). Barcombe, UK: Falmer Press.

McLeod, D. (1992). Research on affect in mathematics education: A reconceptualization. In D. A. Grouws (Ed.), *Handbook of research on mathematics teaching and learning: A project of the National Council of Teachers of Mathematics* (pp. 575–596). New York: Macmillan.

Miller, S.P., & Hudson, P.J. (2007). Using evidence-based practices to build mathematics competence related to conceptual, procedural and declarative knowledge. *Learning Disabilities Research and Practice*, 22(1), 47–57.

Montague, M. (2007). Self-regulation and mathematics instruction. *Learning Disabilities Research and Practice*, 22(1), 75–83.

Montague, M. (2006). Self-regulation strategies for better math performance in middle school. In M. Montague & A. Jitendra (Eds.), *Teaching mathematics to middle school students with learning difficulties* (pp. 89–107). New York: Guilford.

Montague, M., & Applegate, B. (2000). Middle school students' perceptions persistence, and performance in mathematical problem solving. *Learning Disability Quarterly*, 23:215–226.

Montague, M., Warger, C., & Morgan, T.H. (2000). Solve it! Strategy instruction to improve mathematical problem solving. *Learning Disabilities Research and Practice*, 15(2), 110–116.

Munsch, R. (1981). *Moira's Birthday*. Buffalo, NY: Annick Press.

National Council of Teachers of Mathematics (N.C.T.M.). (2000). *Principles and standards for school mathematics*. Reston: Author.

Passolunghi, M.C., Vercelloni, B., & Schadee, H. (2007). The precursors of mathematics learning: Working memory, phonological ability, and numerical competence. *Cognitive Development*, 22:165–184.

Rosseli, M., Matute, E., Pinto, N., & Ardila, A. (2006). Memory abilities in children with subtypes of dyscalculia. *Developmental Neuropsychology*, 30(3), 801–818.

Rouselle, L., & Noël, M. (2007). Basic numerical skills in children with mathematics learning disabilities: A comparison of symbolic vs. non-symbolic number magnitude processing. *Cognition*, 102:361–395.

Swanson, H.L. (2006). Cross-sectional and incremental changes in working memory and mathematical problem solving. *Journal of Educational Psychology*, 98:265–281.

Swanson, H.L., & Kim, K. (2006). Working memory, short-term memory, and naming speed as predictors of children's mathematical performance. *Intelligence*, 35:151–168.

Swanson, H.L., & Sache-Lee, C. (2001). Mathematical problem solving and working memory in children with learning disabilities: Both executive and phonological processes are important. *Journal of Experimental Child Psychology*, 79:294–321.

Swanson, H.L., & Sherman, O. (2006). Math disabilities: A selective meta-analysis of the literature. *Review of Educational Research*, 76(2), 249–274.

Tanner, H., & Jones, S. (2003). Self-efficacy in mathematics and students' use of self-regulated learning strategies during assessment events. In N. Pateman, B. Dougherty, & J.J. Zilliox (Eds.), *Proceedings of the 2003 Joint Meeting of PME and PMENA*. International Group for the Psychology of Mathematics in Education. Volume 4 (pp. 275–282).

Thompson, D.R., & Chappell, M.F. (2007). Communication and representation as elements in mathematical literacy. *Reading and Writing Quarterly: Overcoming Learning Disabilities*, 23(2), 179–196.

Vaughn, S., Klinger, J., & Hughes, M. (2000). Sustainability of research based practices. *Exceptional Children*, 66:163–171.

Wheatly, G.H. (1993). The role of negotiation in mathematics learning. In K. Tobin (Ed.), *The practice of constructivism in science education* (pp. 121–134). Washington, D.C.: AAAS Press.

Woodward, J. (2006). Developing automaticity in multiplication facts: Integrating strategy instruction with timed practice drills. *Learning Disability Quarterly*, 29:269–289.

Woodward, J., & Montague, M. (2002). Meeting the challenge of mathematics reform for students with LD. *The Journal of Special Education*, 36:89–101.

9

WRITING INSTRUCTION

Writing is a complex skill and involves recursively several cognitive processes. The latter processes include planning, drafting, and revising that draw heavily on an individual's working memory (Flower & Hayes, 1980; Hayes, 2000; Hayes et al., 1987). Good writing is a prized skill that requires not only much practice but also a cultivated awareness of what constitutes good writing—in short, possession of metacognition of good writing (Wong, 1999). To help individuals develop good writing skills, we need to lay the foundation in elementary school children. Specifically, we need to teach them the process approach to writing, writing strategies, and self-regulation in the use of strategies and effort expenditure in writing. Sustained effort at learning to write on the part of the children results in their mastery of the writing process and strategies. Consequently, they would improve in writing skills across time as they continue to write. In turn, discernible improvements in writing bring about enjoyment of writing in the children. Buoyed by success in use of both writing process and strategies, children will continue to invest effort at writing. Such a learning and motivational cycle ensures that the children will hone their writing skills to good effect.

But let us return to the important rider in the development of good writing skills, which is instructing elementary school children in the knowledge and use of the writing process, writing strategies, and self-regulation in writing. We are all very familiar with the writing process approach to teaching writing that remains popular in elementary and middle schools. It was developed by Donald Graves and subsequently promoted by his associates such as Lucy Calkin and others like Nancy Atwell. Because numerous textbooks cover the writing process approach to writing instruction, there is no need for us to cover it here. Rather, we will concentrate on writing strategies and the role of self-regulation in writing instruction. To this end, we now turn to describe the quality writing research of Karen Harris and Steve Graham.

Harris and Graham developed the Self-Regulated Strategy Development (SRSD) model in writing as a direct response to the instructional needs among students with learning disabilities (Graham & Harris, 2003; Harris & Graham, 1996, 1992). The model specifically addresses one's needs in writing, but the SRSD is grounded first and foremost in the premise that the development of expertise involves three necessary and sufficient factors: domain-specific knowledge, strategic knowledge, and motivation (Alexander, Graham, & Harris, 1998). In the context of writing, domain-specific knowledge refers to knowledge of genres, strategic knowledge refers to knowledge of writing strategies, and motivation in writing refers to goal-setting, sustained effort expenditure, self-efficacy, and self-reinforcement in writing.

Ensuing from this premise and recalling the model's purpose, Harris and Graham conceptualized two focal components in their SRSD model: direct instruction of writing strategies and inculcation of self-regulation. The former component comprises the design and empirical validation of strategies that promote good writing. The latter component comprises cognitive and metacognitive behaviors that result in successful learning. Specifically, students show self-regulation when they approach tasks in a planful and mindful manner; when they spontaneously deploy task-appropriate strategies; when they self-monitor and self-check their ongoing performance and progress toward learning goals set by themselves; when they evaluate the quality of end products (e.g., essays written) and revise texts and attend to mechanics (e.g., spelling errors); and when they give themselves self-reinforcement for a task well done (e.g., by patting themselves on the back, by praising themselves for work well done). One may say with an element of truth that the picture painted here is that of an idealized student. Nevertheless, we have met and seen demonstrations of such behaviors in good students. More important, Harris and Graham and their associates have demonstrated repeatedly in their intervention research that students with and without learning disabilities could successfully be taught to be self-regulated learners in their writing.

Describing the stages and reporting the ample empirical base of the SRSD model is very straightforward. But textbook authors' tendency to become engrossed with describing the model's stages and its numerous validation studies may inadvertently omit addressing the important relevance of the SRSD model in writing instruction to students with learning disabilities. Let us therefore pause and consider this point.

The relevance of the SRSD model lies in the match between the model's emphasis on cultivating self-regulation in students and the notorious characteristic of passivity in learning among students with learning disabilities.

How do students with learning disabilities demonstrate this passivity in learning? They do so by their constant need in teacher or researcher *prompting!* To elaborate, in the context of writing, students with learning disabilities need to be prompted to continue to exert effort in generating more ideas in writing (Graham, 1990). They need to be prompted to activate extant genre knowledge; to self-monitor ideas generated for the two opposing sides of an argument for a balanced opinion essay (e.g., Have I got ideas down for both pro and con sides to the argument or does my essay contain only pro ideas?); to self-check progress in their writing; and to reread what they have written with a view to revising the text and edit problems in mechanics (Wong et al., 2006). In contrast, students without learning disabilities rarely need the same extent or amount of prompting in these different aspects of writing.

The SRSD model consists of seven steps in implementation: preskill development, initial conference—instructional goals and significance, discussion of the strategy, modeling, strategy mastery, collaborative practice, and independent practice (Graham & Harris, 1992, p. 51). Graham and Harris (2003) elaborated on these steps. Using the SRSD model, Harris and Graham and their associates have generated innumerable intervention studies on writing strategies that they had designed. The efficacy of the validated writing strategies is clearly demonstrated in the meta-analysis of the studies (Graham & Harris, 2003). Moreover, Graham and Harris ceaselessly provide workshops to teachers on how to implement the validated writing strategies in inclusive classrooms. They have also written a teacher manual on those strategies (Harris & Graham, 1996).

The writing strategies based on the SRSD model substantially increased both quantity and quality of writing in students with learning disabilities. They also benefited students without learning disabilities (Graham & Harris, 2003), but the increases assume more significance with students with learning disabilities. Why is that so? For an explanation, we turn to the nature of the writing problems in students with learning disabilities. In describing and enabling understanding writing problems in students with learning disabilities, we choose to use the context of comparison with students without learning disabilities because it puts their writing problems in perspective.

In what ways are students with learning disabilities like their normally achieving peers in writing? Devoid of instruction, students with and without learning disabilities engage in little planning or revising when they write. Thus, both students with and without learning disabilities need instruction on the writing process involving planning, drafting (sentence generating), and revising. Moreover, both kinds of students need to learn to be aware of or sensitive to the readers' needs. In short, to facilitate readers' reading comprehension of their writings, students with and without learning disabilities must learn to evaluate their writings for clarity and genre-specific qualities such as cogency in opinion essay writing.

In what ways are students with learning disabilities unlike their normally achieving peers in writing? To begin with, students with learning disabilities write very little. They have an unmistakable production problem, of which some of them are painfully aware! While they do not appear to lack ideas, they have much difficulty forming sentences to express their ideas. They also have poor vocabulary that forces them to resort to using a peculiar and unprofitable strategy, "stepping down" (coined by Steve Graham). When students with learning disabilities cannot find the appropriate choice of word to express themselves, or cannot spell the words, they substitute with words they know and can spell. However, these substitute words usually do not match their communicative intent. So the words obscure the meaning of their communication or blunt its forcefulness, rendering the communication ambiguous or ineffectual. Moreover, the writings of students with learning disabilities typically contain many more spelling errors than the writings of students without learning disabilities. They also tend to require more practice in writing to master a writing strategy (Wong, Butler, Ficzere, & Kuperis, 1996, 1997). Last but not least, they have an erroneous conception of good writing. To them, a good essay is one without spelling errors (Graham, Schwartz, & MacArthur, 1993; Wong, Wong, & Blenkinsop, 1989).

How do students with learning disabilities differ from students without learning disabilities when they write? As mentioned in conjunction with the relevance of the SRSD model for students with learning disabilities, these students need teacher or researcher prompting to activate their incomplete knowledge of story structure and to continue generating ideas for writing. More important, when students with learning disabilities write, they typify what Scardamalia and Bereiter (1987) dubbed "knowledge telling." Specifically, they write in a piecemeal fashion. When they think of an idea, out it comes onto the paper. Then there would be a pause or lull before the next idea comes and so on. It is a case of "ideas in, ideas out" without much crystallization of ideas or elaborations of them. Needless to say, the cohesion of the writing suffers from such a disjointed manner of idea generation and writing. Curiously, despite the aforementioned writing problems, in self-reports, students with learning disabilities have shown unwarranted confidence in the quality or goodness of their own writing!

The writing problems among students with learning disabilities point to where and in what they need instruction. Clearly they need to be taught the writing process, but that is not enough. In addition, they need to be taught writing strategies and self-regulation. Specifically, they need to learn writing strategies that guide them in planning, evaluating, and revising their writing. They also need to learn self-regulation so that they can regulate their own writing process and monitor how well they are doing.

As mentioned earlier, the writing process approach to writing instruction was spearheaded by Donald Graves and promoted by Lucy Calkins and

Nancy Atwell in primary, intermediate, and middle schools. This particular writing instructional approach is commonly practiced in schools and does not need any introduction or elaboration. Readers can read up on it in numerous textbooks. But the conditions that produce effective implementation of the writing process bear highlighting.

CONDITIONS THAT PROMOTE EFFECTIVE IMPLEMENTATION OF THE WRITING PROCESS

1. *Teachers set up routines in writing.* Teachers must attend to establishing routines in writing for the whole class. Specifically, teachers must set aside time that is designated exclusively to writing—for example, from after recess to lunch break. Thus, children come to expect that they should be engaged in writing during that time and nothing else. Moreover, for children to learn the writing process well, they must write frequently, preferably every day.

2. *Teachers create safe environment for feedback.* Teachers make it a point that feedback from teacher to student and from student to student is a constructive process. Teachers model the giving of feedback. They help peers see praiseworthy aspects of a student's writing and enact the role of helper to improve his or her writing through feedback that addresses ambiguities and weaknesses in the writing. Teachers also ease the writer into accepting comments and questions from his or her peers. In sum, teachers make students feel at ease with peer and teacher feedback because they explicate the purpose of the comments given in feedback, which is to enhance the quality of the student's writing. Through teacher modeling and monitoring, students become comfortable in assuming positive roles as constructive critics of one another's writings and helpers in one another's revisions.

3. *Clear standards for good writing.* Teachers set clear standards in good writing and enable students to reach them. Teachers inform students of their expectations of good writing: clarity and good organization (*organization* in writing refers to sentences being written in a logical order within any paragraph). They remind students that if their writings are unclear and disorganized, readers will be confused and will not understand what they wish to communicate. Hence, the quality of clarity and organization are hallmarks of good writing and demand close attention. They also remind students that they should carefully reread their writings before handing them in so that they can revise the writings should they find ambiguities or misplaced sentences (disorganization). Afterward, students check for spelling, grammatical, and punctuation errors. Notice that teachers emphasize higher-order cognitive processes of clarity and organization in revisions and put first to last, revisions of mechanical errors. Then, through individual conferencing with students, teachers teach students to revise and improve their writings and deal with mechanical errors.

4. *Student autonomy regarding topics and genres in writing.* Students should be given a choice on topics and genres in writing during their regular writing periods. This point relates to motivation in learning in general and writing in particular. Choice in writing topics and genres impacts on students' motivation to write. Hence, teachers should attend to giving students such choices in writing. However, on occasions of instructions of specific writing strategies—for example, opinion essay writing—teachers do restrict the genre. But within the genre, they give students choice in essay topics. For example, the students may write on one of the following: Should public schools have uniforms? Should children be paid to do house chores?

5. *Authenticity of writing tasks.* This means teachers should assign writing tasks that are meaningful to students. Writing tasks that hold little personal meaning or significance to the students will not lead to motivation to write, resulting in little generation of good and interesting ideas for writing. In our current multiethnic and multicultural classrooms, teachers should ensure that writing tasks are meaningful to the students.

6. *Opportunities for students to share their writings.* To cultivate interest and motivation in writing, teachers can provide opportunities for students to share their writings. There are various ways of doing this: from the author's chair, taping one's writings for others to listen to, posting them on cork boards in the classrooms, putting them on notice boards in the school's corridors, producing a book of students' writings that is kept in the library, or printing them like a newspaper for the school. The aim is to provide a way for students to share their writings. Except for some shy students, students generally enjoy sharing their writings. For shy ones, they can resort to taping their writings and allowing only specific students, usually their friends, to listen to the taped recordings of their writings.

7. *Teachers also write.* This is a condition that seems to be ignored by many teachers. If we want to develop good writers in our students and the concomitant enjoyment of writing, then we, teachers, must also write with our students! What would students think when they are expected to write daily for a certain time block while their teachers flit about doing their own chores? They may well think that the teachers are just creating work for them to do! Hence, we can't emphasize enough the importance that teachers also write during the writing periods! More important, through thinking aloud, teachers can demonstrate to students how they plan their writing and how they can change their writing plans while they are writing so that students realize writing plans are always modifiable and not set in stone. Additionally, it benefits and amuses students to see that, like themselves, teachers can have a hard time finding the right words in their writings and stymied in spelling particular words! Students learn problem solving when they see how teachers use the thesaurus in resolving their problems in choosing appropriate words in writing and the dictionary for correct spellings.

We end this section by describing a study that demonstrates the implementation of the preceding conditions in writing instruction.

Using the writing process approach to teaching writing, D'Ambrosio (1988) described how he taught his second graders to write and enjoy writing. In daily sessions of 20–30 minutes of writing, D'Ambrosio had his class write about their personal experiences that they deem important and/or interesting—for example, the child's experiences with his minibike. He also engaged in writing while the children wrote. Moreover, D'Ambrosio readily conferenced with them before, during, and after their writing. In his conferences with his second graders, D'Ambrosio emphasized the importance of their focusing on developing their ideas and not being too concerned with mechanical aspects of spelling and neatness of handwriting. Initially in the academic year, the children relied on conferencing with him for feedback on their writing plans and writings. Soon after, through reading aloud their writings in class, they learned to seek out one another for conferences in addition to conferencing with their teacher, D'Ambrosio. In such peer conferences, they mimicked the teacher's questions and style. They also frankly informed their classmates of what they liked and disliked about their writings and made suggestions for revisions of the less popular parts.

The children got to publish what they wrote after suitable revisions in which they focused first on clarity and necessary elaborations of ideas. Next, they attended to revisions on mechanical aspects of their writings, such as spelling. Through his dedicated application of the writing process instructional approach in his classroom, D'Ambrosio's second graders all became involved with and interested in writing by the end of the academic year. However, he had the typical range of individual differences in the desire to write among his pupils, beginning the year with a few who were highly enthusiastic and responsive to his writing sessions and an equal number of reluctant writers! D'Ambrosio never coerced the latter to write. He waited them out with patience and constant encouragement to write. He tried to elicit their responsiveness to write by getting them to focus and elaborate on what they said were personally interesting experiences.

The most instructive element in the preceding study lies in D'Ambrosio's success in getting his second graders to understand the importance and necessity of revisions in one's writing. He made them realize the purposes of revisions: making one's ideas clearer and making one's writing more interesting. Moreover, through repeated emphasis in individual conferences with each pupil, he underscored the importance of the child's paying primary attention to higher-order cognitive aspects of writing—namely, clarity and development of ideas—and secondary attention to mechanical aspects of writing such as spelling and neatness of handwriting. D'Ambrosio's most striking accomplishment in the study was in the children's coming to view revising as a natural part of writing at the end of the academic year.

We now suggest some writing strategies that promote planning, drafting, and revising in students' writing. We choose to focus on strategies that are useful for teachers in inclusive classrooms as well as in resource rooms. These strategies range from those collaboratively developed between teachers and university researchers to those designed and empirically validated by researchers in intervention research. Readers will find that these writing strategies are used from grade five to high school, with the bulk of them targeting students in grades five through seven. This is understandable because in grade four, the children are introduced to expository texts, and the instructional focus would be on reading comprehension.

Two strategies target story writing and are eminently suitable for grade five children. The first is by Elizabeth Short and her associates at Case Western University and it contains five self-instructional questions:

1. Who is the main character?
2. Where and when did the story take place?
3. What did the main character do?
4. How did the story end?
5. How did the main character feel?

The second strategy comes from a study by Danoff, Harris, and Graham (1993) and consists of five self-instructions:

1. Think of a story you would like to share with others.
2. Let your mind be free.
3. Write down the story part reminder (mnemonic):
   W-W-W
   What = 2
   How = 2
4. Write down story part ideas for each part.
5. Write your story; use good parts and make sense.
   The Mnemonic:
   Who is the main character? Who else is in the story?
   When does the story take place?
   Where does the story take place?
   What does the main character want to do?
   What happens when the main character tries to do it?
   How does the story end?
   How does the main character feel?

The next strategy, POWER QUESTIONS (see Figure 9.1), applies equally well to students with and without learning disabilities in higher intermediate grades (sixth to seventh), as well as high school students with learning disabilities. Carol-Sue Englert at Michigan State University designed it. The strategy consists of a series of questions that deal with planning, organizing, drafting, editing, and revising. In planning, the

---

POWER QUESTIONS

Plan:

    WHY am I writing this?
    WHOM am I writing for?
    WHAT do I know? (brainstorm)

Organize:

    How can I organize my ideas into categories?
    How can I order my categories?

Write rough draft.

Edit:
Reread & Think

    Which parts do I like best?
    Which parts are not clear?
    Did I   • stick to the topic?
               • use 2–3 categories?
               • talk about each category clearly?
               • give details in each category?
               • use key words?
               • make it interesting?

Revise/Rewrite

FIGURE 9.1 POWER QUESTIONS. Reproduced with permission from Carol Sue Englert.

questions prompt the students to consider the purpose of and audience in their writing and to brainstorm ideas for writing. In organizing, the questions prompt the students to cluster similar ideas into respective categories and to order the categories in priority for writing. Then they are prompted to write their essays. Subsequently, the students are guided by questions to edit their writings according to criteria of clarity, organization, quantity of details, and providing interest to readers. Revision or rewriting follows editing.

We have found Englert's POWER QUESTIONS very useful in teaching middle school and high school students with learning disabilities to write. Another Think Sheet that was also designed by Englert applies to fifth and sixth graders' writing compare and contrast essays (see Figure 9.2). This Think Sheet is self-explanatory and ready for teachers' use.

For guiding grades six and seven students in writing expository essays, Sue De La Paz (1999) had designed two very good strategies that are used in the context of the SRSD model. The Expository Planning Strategy (PLAN) consists of four steps:

1. **P**ay attention to the prompt. Read the prompt. Decide (a) what you are being asked to write about and (b) how to develop your essay. ["Prompt" refers to the title of the test question or assignment.]

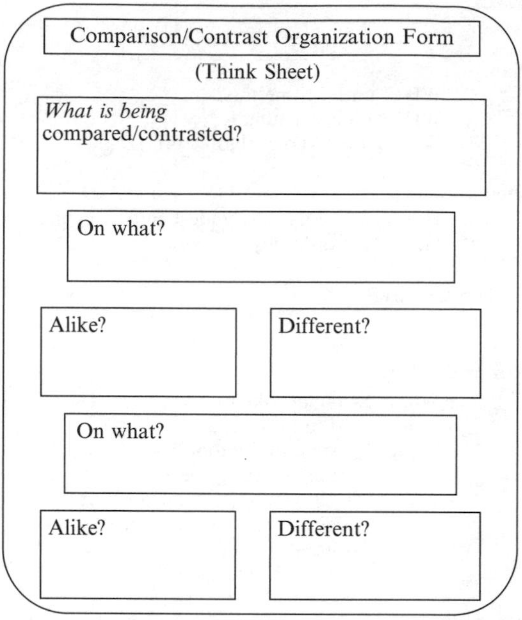

FIGURE 9.2 Compare/Contrast Organization Form. Reproduced with permission from Carol Sue Englert.

2. List the main ideas. Brainstorm possible responses to the prompt.
   (a) Decide on one topic, and then brainstorm at least three main ideas for
   (b) the development of your essay.
3. Add supporting ideas. Think of details, examples, and elaborations that support your main ideas.
4. Number your ideas. Number major points in the order you will use them.

To help students, especially students with learning disabilities, to continue generating ideas for writing, De La Paz designed a strategy with the acronym of WRITE, and it has five steps:

1. Work from your plan to develop your thesis statement.
2. Remember your goals.
3. Include transition words for each paragraph.
4. Try to use different kinds of sentences.
5. Exciting, interesting, $100,000 words.

We now come to writing strategies that promote quality opinion essay writing in grades four to high school. We begin with Deatline-Buchman and Jitendra's (2006) writing strategy that they used with fourth-grade children with learning disabilities. As shown in Figure 9.3, Deatline-Buchman and Jitendra devised a plan sheet that first focuses the children on their

Goal (What is the question I am answering?): <u>To continue or discontinue making cherry Coke</u>

Audience (Who is reading this?): <u>Coca-Cola®, my peers, and teachers</u>

Title: <u>Cherry Coke Should Be Continued</u>

Introductory Paragraph:

Attention Getter: <u>Cherry Coke is the best-tasting Coca-Cola®.</u>

What is my opinion: <u>Cherry Coke should be continued.</u>

What am I going to talk about: <u>I am going to talk about why cherry Coke should be continued and the pros and cons of the argument.</u>

Main Idea #1 (Pro Arguments):

1. <u>Coca-Cola® makes the best-tasting cherry cola.</u>
   a. _____
   b. _____
2. <u>Cherry Coke makes a lot of money for Coca-Cola®.</u>
   a. _____
   b. _____
3. <u>Cherry Coke tastes better than regular coke.</u>
   a. _____
   b. _____

Main Idea #2 (Con Arguments):

1. <u>Cherry Coke is too sweet compared to other colas.</u>
   a. _____
   b. _____
2. <u>Cherry Coke is not available in all soda machines.</u>
   a. _____
   b. _____
3. <u>Cherry Coke is artificially flavored.</u>
   a. _____
   b. _____

Concluding Paragraph:

Sum Up Your Argument: <u>I believe that Coca-Cola® should continue cherry Coke because ...</u>

CONVINCE ME: <u>Although there are a lot of sodas in the market, cherry Coke has its own special flavor, and once you taste it, you will agree that it should remain on the shelves.</u>

FIGURE 9.3 Plan Sheet. Reproduced with permission from Deatline-Buchman and Jitendra (2006) and Pro-Ed, Inc.

writing goal and audience and then on the organizational structure of an opinion essay. This organizational structure involves an introductory paragraph, followed by two consecutive paragraphs in which ideas in support of the Pro and Con arguments are considered, and finally the concluding paragraph. In the introduction, the children focus on interesting the reader with an attention-grabbing opening sentence, state their opinion, and prepare the reader on what the essay will be about. The body of the essay centers on the ideas in support of the Pro and Con arguments that are presented in two consecutive paragraphs. Children are encouraged to think of good supporting ideas and write them down in descending order of cogency in the respective paragraphs. They wrap up the opinion essays by restating their opinions and summing up their supportive arguments and finally end on a strong note to bring the reader to their side of argument.

For grade five and middle school students with and without LD, De La Paz has developed an interesting and useful strategy for planning in opinion essay writing. It has the acronym of "STOP" and has four steps:

Suspend judgment
Take a side
Organize ideas
Plan more as you write

In the first step of the STOP strategy for opinion essay writing, De La Paz urges the students not to form any opinion immediately but rather to generate as many ideas for and against the essay topic or question—for example, "Should hot dogs be banned on Sports Day?" Then having studied the lists of ideas on both the Pro and Con sides, they are to take a stand and form their own opinions in the second step of the strategy. In the third step of the strategy, students are to organize their supporting ideas for both Pro and Con so that they put them down in descending order of cogency. The last step encourages students to keep generating ideas. This step relates particularly to students with learning disabilities who find it very difficult in general to think of ideas to write.

A second strategy with the acronym of DARE is used to complement STOP, and it too contains four steps:

Develop your topic sentence
Add supporting ideas
Reject arguments
End with a conclusion

Both these strategies have been validated in intervention research (see De La Paz & Graham, 1997, 1999).

Recently, Wong and her associates have adapted a teacher-devised strategy for use in teaching fifth and sixth graders with and without learning disabilities to write opinion essays. Two teachers, Jackson and Pillow (1992, p. 79), used a schematic lined drawing of a chair to teach children to see different perspectives in a story and to write about the opposing perspectives. The CHAIR strategy described in Jackson and Pillow was originally tied to literature read in class and not specifically designed for exclusive use in opinion essay writing. Wong and her associates adapted it for the latter purpose. Wong elaborated on the drawing so that it more resembled a chair that children were familiar with (see Figure 9.4). The seat is where

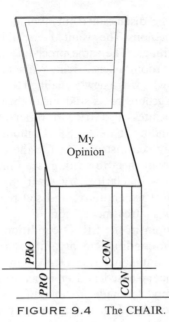

FIGURE 9.4 The CHAIR.

the child's opinion is stated, and the legs of the chair represents ideas in support of the Pro and Con arguments, respectively. The central notion in the figure capitalizes on the necessity of the chair's having balanced legs so that it won't wobble and be unsafe for anyone to sit on. Analogously, children must generate equal numbers of Pro and Con arguments in support of their positions in the opinion essay so that they have a balanced chair. Wong and her collaborative associates, the classroom and resource room teachers, and two research assistants have successfully taught 30 sixth graders with and without learning disabilities the use of this CHAIR strategy in planning to write their opinion essays. Wong taught the whole class how to use the strategy in planning an opinion essay. Her training procedures are presented in Appendix II at the end of this chapter. Subsequent to Wong's instruction, children began planning and writing the first of seven training essays. In two small groups of six, children with learning disabilities, attention problems, and English as a Second Language (English Language Learners) planned and wrote in the resource room. The remaining children did their planning and writing of the training essays in the regular classroom.

In the classroom after the children finished their writing, they shared their essays in small groups of six. Each group was attended to by an adult (the classroom teacher, Sue Agabob, Wong, or Debbie Jai, a qualified teacher serving as a research assistant). The children read aloud their essays, and the peers gave feedback. The peers commented on the strengths and weaknesses of the writer's essay and gave suggestions regarding revisions.

The adults scaffolded the discussions but avoided direct involvement on instructing children on revisions. They wanted the children to use peer feedback alone to revise their writings. The same procedure in sharing writings was followed by the resource room teacher, Kim Watson, and the other research assistant, Anne Lonthie, who was a newly qualified teacher. These two teachers met with their respective groups of six students in the resource room.

Wong and her associates also tried a different modification of the CHAIR strategy. Grounding it in the SRSD model, they devised a plan sheet plus accompanying self-instructions for the children to use as they transfer ideas from the plan sheet to writing (see Figures 9.5 and 9.6). Goal setting in the target areas of clarity, organization, and cogency of arguments, self-rating of effort expenditure, and self-reinforcement were additional features of this treatment condition. The results showed unequivocally that children in the SRSD condition surpassed appreciably those in the comparison condition in organization and cogency of arguments at posttest and maintenance test. Hence, embedding a teacher-made writing strategy in a theory-based and empirically substantiated model—specifically, the SRSD model—made sizeable differences to children's opinion essay writing. Notice that Figure 9.6 was printed on the back of the sheet containing Figure 9.5.

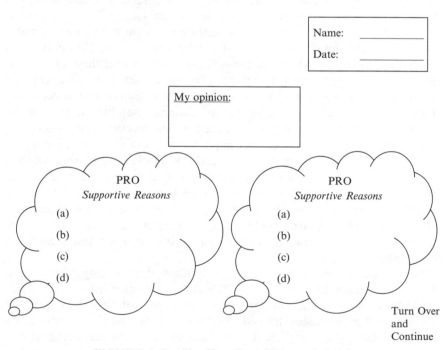

FIGURE 9.5　Plan Sheet. From Wong et al. (2006).

☞
| Self-check: |

(1) Are all my supportive
reasons (for PRO & CON)
good and strong?

Name: _____

YES	NO*

Teacher: _____

Date: _____

*Revise

(2) Have I numbered my
supportive reasons for PRO
and CON in a good order for
writing?

FIGURE 9.6   Self-Instructions. From Wong et al. (2006).

To guide the children to use their writing plans in writing the opinion essay, they were given an additional writing prompt containing four self-questions or self-instructions:

1. What's my opinion? (I write it down in the first paragraph.)
2. What are my PRO arguments? (I put them in a good order and write them in the second paragraph.)
3. What are my CON arguments? (I put them in a good order and write them in the third paragraph.)
4. Wrap up! (I write my conclusion and summarize my PRO arguments.)

For adolescents with learning disabilities, Wong, Butler, and associates had empirically validated three writing strategies in aid of their writing reportive essays, opinion essays, and compare and contrast essays (Wong, Butler, Ficzere, & Kuperis, 1996, 1997; Wong et al., 1994). All three studies were funded by the Social Sciences and Humanities Research Council of Canada (SSHRC), as was the recent CHAIR study in 2006.

PRIOR TRAINING

All students must have computer skills, and they must have sufficient keyboarding skills because all writing and revising is done on the computer. This is because teachers would want to capitalize on educational technology to show adolescents with and without learning disabilities that using a word-processing program on a computer to write alleviates physical labor in revising essays during training. Moreover, printouts of their first and final drafts always look professional and neat! These two advantages never fail to motivate adolescents to write. Imagine the contrast to the adolescents' motivation to write when teachers insist on their using pen and paper for writing and revising? How many revision drafts do you think high school students would turn in if they are told to write with paper and pen?

INSTRUCTIONAL FOCI

For the three genres that Wong and her associates taught, there were two target areas in training that cut across all three (reportive, opinion, compare and contrast): clarity and organization. It seems obvious that any piece of good or effectively written communication would be clear and organized, where organization means the sentences in any paragraph follow one another in a logical order. In addition to clarity and organization, for each genre we had one genre-specific target area in training. For reportive essays, the genre-specific instructional focus was thematic salience. In reportive essay writing, the individual describes a memorable event that has indelibly impacted him or her. The impact could be emotional or cognitive, and the individual must distill it into a theme. In teaching reportive essay writing, we emphasize to the adolescents that the theme must be prominent both at the start and at the end of the essay. Thematic prominence at the start of the essay grabs the reader's attention when he first sets eyes on it. Closing the essay with thematic repetition reminds the reader why the writer finds the event so memorable. If a student was asked to write a reportive essay on "The Most Scary Event in My Life," she states her theme forcefully at the start of her essay and repeats it at the end of it. Thus, as her theme sentence, she might write, "The most scary event in my life occurred in a game of hockey when I thought I had blinded my opponent." The bulk of her essay serves to elaborate and embellish her theme. She might close with a sentence like "I have never touched a hockey stick since that event because it was the most scary event of my life."

For opinion essays, the genre-specific target training area was cogency of arguments. In an opinion essay, the adolescent writer seeks to persuade the reader to share or support his opinion on a particular topic—for example, "Should hot dogs be banned on Sports Day?" He doesn't think so. Hence, he states his opinion and generates at least three ideas to support it. Then he must consider the PRO side of the issue and generate three ideas here as well. But he aims to show that the reasons he provides for the CON side are stronger than the PRO side so that the reader will be won over! The reader judges the writer's arguments on how convincing or compelling they are. Hence, we think cogency is a suitable target area for training regarding opinion essay writing. We want our trainees to generate good, strong arguments or reasons to support their positions on a given issue.

For compare-and-contrast essays, we chose appropriateness of ideas as the target area for training. This is because we found adolescents with learning disabilities and low-achieving students tend to be very careless and vague when they generate ideas for writing a compare and contrast essay. Very often, they put down ideas in their plan sheets that had little to do with a comparison or contrast of the topics in their compare and contrast essays! To make them more focused on what ideas they should generate and work on in the essay, we decided to target appropriateness of ideas as the genre-specific training area in compare and contrast essay writing.

TRAINING

Training consists of three phases: collaborative planning, independent writing, and collaborative revising. In collaborative planning, the trainer demonstrated planning for writing through thinking aloud her thought processes. As an illustration, for a reportive essay, she thinks aloud the sequence of events in her episode of "The Most Scary Event of My Life"; for an opinion essay, she thinks aloud the ideas contained in two opposing views in "Why high school students should not have a dress code"; and for a compare-and-contrast essay on rock versus school concerts, she thinks aloud ideas that flesh out subthemes of goals, content, and demeanor. Subsequently, trainees were randomly divided into pairs or dyads and instructed to use thinking aloud to construct a writing plan for an essay (reportive or opinion or compare and contrast). To help them in collaborative planning, each pair receives a plan sheet (see Figures 9.7, 9.8, and 9.9). Trainees choose topics provided by trainers. If they wish to generate their own topics, they are permitted with the condition that topics match genre demands.

When trainees have produced satisfactory writing plans using an appropriate word-processing program, they write their essays individually on a computer, such as a PC or Macintosh. Trainers (e.g., university researchers) or teachers must be on hand to assist trainees/students in their difficulties with word finding, sentence generation, and spelling. Subsequently, students print three copies of their first draft for the purpose of conferencing with a teacher and their dyadic partner in planning.

Collaborative revising occurs in conferencing. The trainer models for the dyadic trainees, questions to seek clarification, elaboration, and specification over ambiguities in each other's essay. Using such questioning or *interactive dialogues*, students identify ambiguities in each other's written essays. In conferencing, one student assumes the role of critic and seeks clarification from the other, the student-writer, over the latter's ambiguities in writing. When she or he has finished questioning the student-writer, the teacher points out ambiguities missed by the student-critic. Subsequently, both the teacher and the student-critic help the student-writer to revise. The process of collaborative revising is repeated with the other trainee in the dyad.

When trainees' essays satisfy the teacher on the instructional foci of each genre, using COPS strategy (Schumaker, Nolan, & Deshler, 1985), they

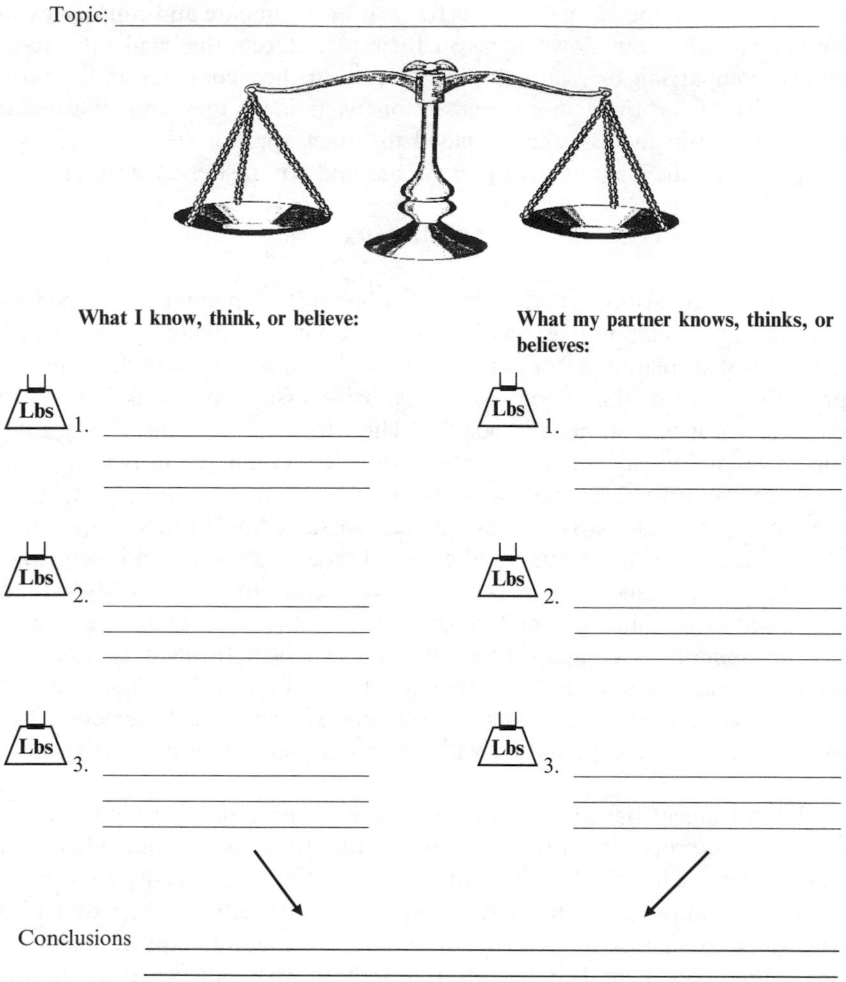

Topic: _____

What I know, think, or believe: **What my partner knows, thinks, or believes:**

Lbs 1. _____   Lbs 1. _____
   _____   _____
   _____   _____

Lbs 2. _____   Lbs 2. _____
   _____   _____
   _____   _____

Lbs 3. _____   Lbs 3. _____
   _____   _____
   _____   _____

Conclusions _____
_____

FIGURE 9.7   Plan Sheet for Opinion Essay Writing. From Wong et al. (1996). Designed by Marg Corden for use with the study. Reproduced with permission from Pro-Ed, Inc.

check for and redress with the teacher's help errors in spelling, punctuation, and grammar. Subsequently, the teacher checks their essays on the computer screen. If satisfied, she instructs trainees to print copies of their perfect (final) drafts to be kept in their individual files for scoring and record keeping.

To facilitate student learning, we use plan sheets and writing prompts that provide connection words for use in opinion essays and compare-and-contrast essays (see Figures 9.8–9.13). The writing prompts are typed on 8" × 11" paper and laminated to increase durability. Each student with learning disabilities and low achievers has one for her own use, with

OPINION ESSAY: Connection WORDS

Introductory Phrases

In my opinion,

I (dis)agree with

From my point of view

I believe

Countering Phrases

Although

On the other hand,

On the contrary,

However, someone who disagreed with my opinion might argue

Concluding Phrases

After considering both sides,

Even though

To sum up,

In conclusion,

Supporting Words & Phrases

First, Second, Finally,

Equally important

For instance,

As well,

FIGURE 9.8   Connection Words for Opinion Essay Writing. From Wong et al. (1996). Reproduced with permission from Pro-Ed, Inc. Designed by Marg Corden for use in the study.

her own name on it, kept in her own student file. Students are constantly reminded to use their own writing prompts because our goal is to make them autonomous, self-monitoring, and self-regulating students.

Figure 9.10 shows the blank form students use in planning a compare-and-contrast essay. In Figure 9.11, the plan sheet for the compare-and-contrast essay has been filled in for the purpose of modeling for students.

To motivate students' learning and performance, teachers may consider letting students' training essays contribute a certain percentage (e.g., 30 percent) of their grade in English or Modified English. Moreover, individual graphs should be kept on their writing progress that students could view daily. For example, the teacher keeps a graph showing a student's improvement on clarity of writing. The teacher can give a score on clarity first on the rough draft and a second score on the revised draft for each essay written by the students. Across training essays, the student

Prewriting

* Do I have my completed plan in front of me?
* Do I have my name, date, and title on my essay?

Rough Copy

* Does my first paragraph clearly present my opinion with supporting ideas?
* Does my second paragraph clearly express an opposing viewpoint to mine?
* Does my last paragraph include a summary statement and give reasons for my conclusions?
* Have I read my completed essay to make sure all ideas are clear?
* Have I printed three copies?

Editing

* Have I made all necessary changes?
* Have I reread my essay to make sure my ideas are clear?
* Have I printed one copy of my revised essay?

Revising

* Have I proofread my essay using COPS?
* Have I conferenced with a teacher?
* Have I made all necessary changes?
* Have I read my final draft to make sure all ideas are clear?
* Have I asked a teacher to proofread my screen?
* Have I printed two perfect copies?

FIGURE 9.9   Writing Checklist.

can readily see his or her own scores on both rough and revised drafts. Because of effective training, the student's own scores should show systematic gains on both rough and revised drafts. Hence, viewing teacher's scores of their essays motivates students' essay writing.

SOME POINTERS FOR IMPLEMENTING THE WRITING STRATEGIES FOR OPINION ESSAYS

Ensure that adolescents with learning disabilities and low-achieving high school students think aloud their planning. Moreover, ensure that they generate good, convincing ideas for opinion essays. For example, some lazy students would put down ProO ideas and then use the flip or opposite of these ideas for Con ideas. Teachers must be explicit that generating Con ideas in this manner is unacceptable. Similarly, sometimes both students with learning disabilities may say they share the same opinion and support the Pro side and then stop working! At this point, the teacher should tell them they must both put their heads together to generate ideas for the Con side and continue working!

Help students develop the routine of using plan sheets before writing their essays.

Name _____   Date _____

COMPARE/CONTRAST PLAN

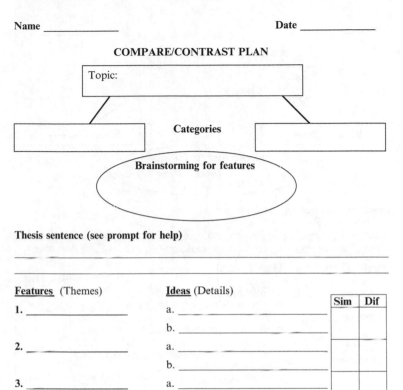

Thesis sentence (see prompt for help)

_____

_____

Features (Themes)   Ideas (Details)

		Sim	Dif

1. _____   a. _____

                        b. _____

2. _____   a. _____

                        b. _____

3. _____   a. _____

                        b. _____

Conclusion: (see prompt for help)

After comparing and contrasting _____ *and*

_____, I think I prefer _____

because _____.

FIGURE 9.10   Plan Sheet for Compare-and-Contrast Essay Writing.

*Help students model your (teacher's) way of asking for clarification and elaboration in **interactive dialogues** and collaborative revision* (see Wong et al., 1996, 1997).

Remember that adolescents with learning disabilities need help with their revisions. Specifically, they would need the teacher's help to find the right words to express their communicative intent, to structure sentences, and with spelling.

SOME POINTERS FOR IMPLEMENTING THE WRITING STRATEGIES FOR COMPARE-AND-CONTRAST ESSAYS

Teachers must ensure that adolescents with learning disabilities and low-achieving students generate ideas that concentrate on comparisons and

Name _____   Date _____

COMPARE/CONTRAST PLAN

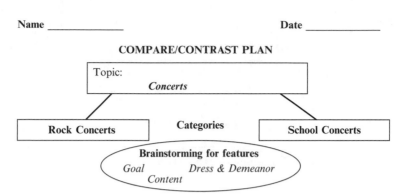

Thesis sentence (see prompt for help)

In this essay, I am going to compare and contrast rock concerts and school concerts.
I have chosen to write on three features: goal, content, and dress and demeanor.

Features (Themes)   **Ideas** (Details)

Features (Themes)	Ideas (Details)	Sim	Dif
1. *Goal*	a. *both provide entertainment*	✓	
	b. *rock concerts (pay); school concerts (free)*		✓
2. *Content*	a. *different types of music*		✓
	b. *rock concerts idols; school concerts none*		✓
	c. *both concerts need practice & rehearsals*	✓	
3. *Dress &* *Demeanor*	a. *correct attire important for rock concerts; not for school concerts*		✓
	b. *rowdy audience in rock concerts; not so in school concerts*		✓

Conclusion: (see prompt for help)
After comparing and contrasting   *rock concerts*   and
  school concerts , **I think I prefer** *school concerts*   **because**
   they are free, have my kind of music, and they don't allow rowdy behavior!

FIGURE 9.11   Plan Sheet for Compare-and-Contrast Essay Writing. From Wong et al. (1997). Reproduced with permission from Blackwell Publishing, Ltd.

contrasts. Make them self-check on ideas generated that they do match a comparison or a contrast.

   *Teachers need to explain the terms **features, topic/thesis sentence,** and **clincher sentence** to adolescents with learning disabilities and low-achieving high school students.* For example, one way to explain *topic sentence* is by asking the student to reread the ideas that she put down in her plan sheet for the compare-and-contrast essay. Then have the student summarize them. When she has finished summarizing her ideas, say, "That is your topic sentence. It tells the reader what you will be writing about. In the remaining sentences in this paragraph, you just simply flesh out what you said in your topic sentence."

   Help the adolescents with learning disabilities and low-achieving high school students develop the habit of using the writing prompt card and helpers in writing (see Figures 9.12 and 9.13)

Introduction (Thesis Statement)

In this essay, I am going to compare and contrast _____
and _____. I have chosen to write on three features:
_____, _____, and _____.

I am writing this compare-and-contrast essay on _____
and _____. I will focus on the following three features:
_____, _____, and _____.

Examples: In this essay, I am going to compare and contrast rock concerts and
school concerts. I have chosen to write on three features: goals,
content, and behavior.

Marijuana and LSD are both illegal drugs. Three important features
of each that can be compared and contrasted are effects, usage,
and appearance.

Conclusion

After comparing and contrasting _____ and _____, I think
_____ because _____.

To conclude, it seems that _____ and _____ differ
in their _____ but are similar in their _____.

Examples: School concerts and rock concerts both provide
entertainment. I like school concerts better because they
are free, they have my kind of music, and they let me wear
what I want. However, they don't allow rowdy behavior!

After comparing and contrasting Christmas and summer
holidays, I think I like summer holidays better because I
really enjoy sunbathing!

Although marijuana and LSD differ in their appearance,
they are similar in their effects and usage. Let's hope the
usage is not too high.

FIGURE 9.12   Helpers in Writing. From Wong et al. (1997). Reproduced with permission from Blackwell Publishing, Ltd.

INSTRUCTIONAL STEPS IN PLANNING FOR REPORTIVE ESSAYS

Students are instructed to search their individual memories for the event that they wish to write about. If they wish to write about the most embarrassing event in their lives, they must recall all the embarrassing events that they have lived through and choose from them, the most excruciatingly embarrassing one of all!

Relive the event in one's visual and auditory images like seeing a videotape or DVD of that segment in one's life. They are to relive this event in their mind's eye, so to speak. Because adolescents are very familiar with videotapes and DVDs, teachers could use this analogy to good vantage. Instruct them to

COMPARE/CONTRAST ESSAY
WRITING PROMPT CARD

Structure of Essay	Connection Words
Introduction (Paragraph 1)	
Purposes: Introduces the topic to the reader. Includes a thesis statement and outlines the features to be discussed.	*Introductory Phrases* When comparing and contrasting In the novel/poem/short story
Body of the Essay	*Phrases for Differences* On the other hand, However, In contrast to

1. First Feature (Paragraph 2)
    a. Topic Sentence
    b. Supporting Details with Examples
	Although
	 Whereas
	 While
	 But
	 Even though

2. Second Feature (Paragraph 3)
    a. Topic Sentence
    b. Supporting Details with Examples
	Phrases for Similarities
	 In common,
	 In the same way,
	 At the same time,
	 Similarly,

3. Third Feature (Paragraph 4)
    a. Topic Sentence
    b. Supporting Details with Examples
	Supporting Phrases
	 Furthermore,
	 As well,
	 Also,
	 Likewise,
	 For instance,
	 For example,

Conclusion (Paragraph 5)	
Purpose: To summarize the features and/or express your opinion on the topic.	*Concluding Phrases* To sum up, Thus, Therefore, In conclusion, After comparing and contrasting,

FIGURE 9.13   Connection Words for Compare-and-Contrast Essay Writing. From Wong et al. (1997). Reproduced with permission from Blackwell Publishing, Ltd.

relive the chosen embarrassing event like watching it on a video or DVD—only it is of a certain segment of their own lives with themselves as the central persons portrayed! They should see and hear "it"!

Students are to activate all the emotions associated with that chosen event. Simultaneous to reliving a particular segment of their lives, students must rekindle all the emotions associated with it. Hence, for the student who wants to write about his first date being "The Most Embarrassing Event in My Life," he should feel his face flushed, his ears burning, and his neck tingling! Last but not least, he should be tongue-tied!

In the preceding section, we described a celebrated theoretical model, the SRSD model, that has guided much fruitful writing intervention research (Graham & Harris, 2003). This research and research by other researchers, such as Englert, De La Paz, Deatline-Buchman and Jitendra, Wong and her associates, and others whose work space constrains us from reporting, have provided teachers with empirically validated strategies that promote planning, writing, and revising in students. Additionally, there are class-room-based writing activities or tasks that promote quality writing in children and adolescents such as guided journal writing (Wong et al., 2002). These writing activities or tasks are designed by teachers or collaboratively designed by university researchers and teachers. Following we present examples of such writing tasks that have been designed collaboratively between B. Wong and teachers Patty Ellis, who teaches grades five and six, and Isabel Sommerville, a resource room teacher who before her retirement, team-taught with Ellis. Several writing tasks were developed for the book *The Breadwinner* by Deborah Ellis. Other writing tasks were designed to link up language arts with social studies or science. Specifically, we used the book *Cariboo Runaway* by Sandy Frances Duncan and designed parallel writing tasks for language arts and social studies. Then we used the book *Gentle Ben* by Walt Morey and *Miracle at Willowcreek* by Annette Lebox to create parallel writing tasks for language arts and science. These writing tasks were devised as part of Wong's writing research in 2002–2004, which was supported by the Social Sciences and Humanity Research Council (SSHRC) of Canada.

WRITING TASKS FOR *THE BREADWINNER*

The story in *The Breadwinner* is set in Afghanistan, and it centers on how, with reluctance, an 11-year-old girl, Parvana, assumes the guise of a boy to be the breadwinner for the family after her father is arrested by Taliban soldiers. In the Afghan culture, only males are allowed to support the family as breadwinners. The major theme is about how Parvana changes as she adapts to her role of breadwinner.

Adaptiveness to an unexpected role is thus the key theme. The story describes new qualities that the young female adolescent develops as she adapts increasingly to her new role as the breadwinner for the family. Gradually she sheds the retiring qualities that are culture-bound for Afghan females and develops qualities totally different from the ones expected of Afghan adolescent girls such as confidence, boldness, assertiveness, adventurousness, and courage. These qualities appear to best equip her for her future as she heads into the unknown with her father in search of her mother and siblings at the end of the book.

The book has the following secondary themes:

1. The impact of war, especially a continuous war on a country's destruction (of buildings and environment; no trees).
2. Grinding and sustained poverty and brutalized people (soldiers beating people becomes a common sight).
3. Confusion for some young adolescents. Talibans are not all evil. Parvana witnessed the tears of a Taliban soldier when she read his letter to his dead wife.
4. The frustrations of a repressive government on old and young females. Young women are not allowed to go out or have fun. Older, educated women are evicted from their jobs.
5. The importance of support from friends.

After the teacher finishes reading aloud the first chapter with the children following in their individual copies of the book, the teacher engages them in a discussion on bartering. This discussion serves the purpose of familiarizing the children with the Afghan culture in which bartering is a common everyday practice. She then asks them to write about bartering with the writing task in Table 9.1. Each child was given a copy of the questions.

We think this writing task on bartering is very appropriate for the contemporary multiethnic, multicultural classrooms. The children usually get one class period to complete their writing task. Then the next day, in the language arts period, they discuss what they have written in class. If the teacher has a teaching assistant or a resource room teacher who teams up with her in classroom teaching, they can divide the class into two groups for discussions on what the children have written.

For the rest of the book, we created writing tasks that challenge bright students as well as special needs students. The research literature in learning disabilities indicates that one major reason that inclusion has been ineffectual is that regular classroom teachers do not accommodate students with learning disabilities with suitable modifications of tasks or alternative tasks. In the writing tasks that Wong and the classroom teacher and resource room teacher collaboratively created, children with learning disabilities

TABLE 9.1   On Bartering

In the market, Parvana and her father barter with customers on the price of items that she and her father sell. Have you seen your parents barter? Can you describe how bartering is done if it is something you are familiar with?

If you are not familiar with bartering, then write about what you think *and* how you feel about bartering as described in the story when Parvana and her father worked in the market and sold things.

---

are given a choice of alternative writing tasks. These alternative tasks target the same critical points/features in the novels as in the tasks assigned students without learning disabilities. Hence, Wong and her collaborative teachers have maintained learning goals and demands for quality work for students with learning disabilities. Wong has dubbed this kind of task accommodation for students with learning disabilities, "*the bendable ruler.*"

Writing Task for Chapters 1, 2, 3, and 4. Children are given seven questions, and they must choose three of them to write on. The last three questions are deliberately more challenging and are meant to interest brighter students. Students with special needs, such as learning disabilities, attention problems, and ESL/ELL, are given an additional choice. If they do not want to attempt the first set of seven questions, they can attempt a second set of four questions (see following).

Questions for Chapters 1–4

Set 1 is designed for the whole class, with the last three questions being more challenging. Set 1 questions, however, are optional for special needs children. If they do not want to answer Set 1 questions, they can answer the questions in Set 2 (see Table 9.2).

Questions for Chapters 6–11

Set 1 is designed for the whole class, with the last two questions being more challenging. Set 1, however, is optional for special needs children. If they do not want to answer Set 1 questions, they can answer the questions in Set 2 (see Table 9.3).

As an alternative to having the sixth graders write answers to guided journal questions for Chapters 4–11, ask them to write an opinion essay on "Should Parvana go bone digging?" Provide a warm-up introduction

TABLE 9.2   Writing Tasks for Chapters 1–4 of *The Breadwinner*

Set 1 questions: children choose three questions to answer	Set 2 questions: these provide additional choices to special needs children
1. Parvana and Nooria don't get along. The author gives clear instances where the two sisters bicker. (a) Find two examples from Chapters 1 and 2 to show how the two sisters don't get along. (b) Based on the examples that you have located, what words can you use to describe Nooria?	**Chapter 2: Important event: Parvana's father got taken away by Taliban soldiers**. 1. How do you feel when you read about that important event? 2. Why do you feel the way you do?

(Continues)

TABLE 9.2   (*Continued*)

Set 1 questions: children choose three questions to answer	Set 2 questions: these provide additional choices to special needs children
2. Does any part of the story in Chapter 2 or Chapter 3 leave you feeling scared, sad, angry, or frustrated? Can you locate that part? Explain why you feel the way you do.	**Chapter 3: Important event: Parvana's mother and Parvana went to the prison to try to get her father back**.
3. The author gives the impression that Parvana likes her father better than her mother. How did the author create this impression? Can you locate parts in Chapter 2 to show how the author leads you to draw the conclusion (infer) that Parvana likes her father better than her mother?	1. Do you think that Parvana's mother's decision to go to the prison makes sense to you? Give reasons for your answer. 2. Imagine you were Parvana. What were your thoughts and feelings when you were in front of the prison?
4. Do you think Parvana's mother made the right decision to visit the prison (to try to get her husband released)? Why or why not?	**Chapter 4: Important event: Parvana's mother was so upset over her husband's imprisonment that she lay down on the toshak (narrow mattress) for four days and four nights facing the wall without bothering with her children**.
5. Did Chapter 3 end the way you expect it to end (i.e., Parvana's father did not get released from prison)? If your expectation matches the ending of the chapter, explain how you made the matching expectation. If your expectation doesn't match the ending of the chapter, explain how your expectation came about.	1. Have you ever felt so sad that you hide from your family and friends? Write about your experience. 2. If you were Parvana, what would you do to help your mother so she can get up and take on her daily household chores and look after the children?
	Children choose three questions to answer.
6. What are your thoughts and feelings when you read about Parvana's mother spending four days and four nights on the toshak (narrow mattress) facing the wall and neglecting her children. Explain why you think and feel the way you do.	

to the children by discussing the reason and significance of burying the dead in most cultures and how bone digging affects that tradition.

Postreading Questions

Set 1 is for the whole class. These questions, however, are optional for special needs children. If they wish, they can answer the questions from Set 2 (see Table 9.4). After each writing task, the teacher should attend to children's sharing of their writings. Table 9.5 presents the test.

In the following section, we present writing tasks that connect novels used in language arts novel study units with research projects in social studies. We (Wong, Jai, Ellis, & Somerville, 2003, 2004) had designed such writing

TABLE 9.3 Writing Tasks for Chapters 6–11 of *The Breadwinner*

Set 1 questions: children choose two questions to answer	Set 2 questions: answer three questions
1. As the "breadwinner" for her family, do you think Parvana is a heroine? (Think of what she was doing in a country ruled by the Taliban government as the breadwinner of her family.) Why or why not?	1. Do you have a buddy? (a) Describe one time when your buddy got you into trouble. (b) Describe one time when your buddy helped you out in a big way.
2. When you read about bone digging, what thoughts and feelings run through your mind?	2. Is Shauzia a good or bad influence on Parvana? Give reasons for your answer.
3. Parvana was not keen on bone digging. Neither was her mother at first. Nooria and Mrs. Weera persuaded Parvana's mother to let her continue with bone digging. What do you think were Parvana's thoughts and feelings when her mother OK'ed her bone digging and told her to continue to do it?	3. When you read about bone digging, what thoughts and feelings run through your mind?
4. How would you describe Shauzia? (What kind of a girl do you think she is?)	4. Would you like to have Mrs. Weera as your PE teacher? Why or why not?

activities for three novels: *Cariboo Runaway* by Sandy Frances Duncan, *Gentle Ben* by Walt Morey, and *Miracle at Willowcreek* by Annette Lebox.

WRITING TASKS FOR *CARIBOO RUNAWAY*, A STORY BY SANDY FRANCES DUNCAN

The story in this book is about the adventure of two children who ran away from home in search of their father. The father had gone to seek his fortune in gold mining in Northern British Columbia. Through the children's eyes, the authoress showed the negative sides of gold mining. There were the physical hardships of gold mining, the tremendous fatigue that numbed feelings and rendered individuals incapable of helping fallen fellow miners, the greed for gold that led to murder and erosion of human trust, the lawlessness, the racism toward Chinese miners, and the deforestation from gold mining that resulted in ugly landscapes. The story had a happy ending with the reunification of father and family. But thanks to the clever authoress, grades five and six children would have learned much about gold mining in British Columbia at the end of the story.

The writing activities for the book in language arts consist of questions designed to make the children think. There are three sets of questions: The first focuses on Chapters 1–5. As with *The Breadwinner*, we provide an optional alternative writing task for children with learning disabilities or ESL/ELL in the Set 2 questions (see Tables 9.6–9.8).

TABLE 9.4   Postreading Questions

Set 1 questions: children answer all the questions	Set 2 question: for special needs children
1. What do you feel (e.g., does the story leave you feeling sad, angry, scared)? Which part of the story makes you feel sad, angry, scared?	Imagine that Parvana and her family have immigrated to your hometown and she joins your grade 6 class. Would you like to be friends with the "old" Parvana (before she became the breadwinner) or the "new" Parvana (after she became the breadwinner)? Explain your choice of friendship.
2. What do you question (e.g., do you have any questions about the story)? Do you have any questions to ask Parvana?	
3. What do you think (e.g., what were you thinking at the end of the story)? Which part of the story do you remember best? Why? Did anything in the story surprise you? Why? What's your opinion of Parvana? At the end of the story, has your opinion of her changed from the start? What caused this change if you did change your opinion of her?	

TABLE 9.5   Test on *The Breadwinner*

1. (a) Why do you think the author wrote "The Breadwinner"?
   (b) What do you think the author wants you to learn from "The Breadwinner"? (The first question is general while the second is more specific. For example, the author wants the world to know about what is happening in Afghanistan. Specifically, she wants readers to learn about the tragic impact of a continuous war and authoritarian regime on the people, especially the females.)

2. Do you think the qualities that Parvana has developed as the breadwinner are good for her living in post-Taliban Afghanistan? (Parvana used to be shy, timid, not look at Afghan men in the eye, obeys her mother. Since becoming the breadwinner of her family, she has become bold, brave, speaks her mind, goes against her mother's wishes.) Give good reasons for your answer.

3. In what ways are wars bad for people?

4. What have you learned about having helpful friends from reading "The Breadwinner"? (Think of Mrs. Weera, the two men who helped Parvana's father to get home after his release from prison, and Shauzia.)

LINKING *RUNAWAY CARIBOO* AND A PROJECT ON GOLD MINING

The teacher can initiate the Social Studies Research project after the novel is finished, or she could do it simultaneously with the novel study in Language Arts. The class of grade five or six is divided into six small groups (so if the class size is 30, there will be six groups of five children). The teacher informs the groups that each group will be researching a specific

TABLE 9.6   Writing Tasks for Chapters 1–5 of *Cariboo Runaway*

Set 1 questions	Set 2 questions
Answer three of the following questions:	Answer three of the following questions:
1. Have you ever thought of running away from home? If yes, when and why? If no, why not?	1. Is there anything you don't understand about the story?
2. Do you think Tim is a brave and clever stowaway? Why or why not?	2. (a) (for boys): Do you have a younger sister who is a nuisance to you? Why or why not?
3. (a) Why does Tim bug Elva? (b) Do you think Elva is a bit hard on Tim? Support your answers with good reasons.	(b) (for girls): Do you have a younger brother who is a nuisance to you? Why or why not?
4. Imagine yourself as Elva. How would you have felt when you cut off your hair? Long braids were the style for girls in Elva's time.	3. Imagine your father went to the Gold Rush. Would you leave home to find him like Elva? Why or why not?
5. Do you think Elva is doing the right thing to leave home to find her father and get him home? Give reasons for your answer.	4. What is a stowaway?
	5. Elva got over being mad at Tim. She said to herself, "Maybe two would be better than one." Do you agree with her? Give reasons for your answer.

topic. The six research topics are Group (1) Gold mining methods; Group (2) Mining towns—Barkerville; Group (3) Miners; Group (4) Law and justice; Group (5) Attire during the gold mining period (or what did people wear then?); and Group (6) The effects of mining on the environment.

The children are allowed to choose the research topic they are interested in and join the respective group. If the number of children exceeds the number allowed in a particular research group, the teacher mediates and encourages one of them to move to another research topic/group. When the children have settled into six groups, the teacher gives each group six file folders (8" × 11") and asks group members to write down their own names on the labels of the folders to indicate ownership. When all the children have received their individual file folders and written their names on the labels, the teacher instructs them on the meaning of research. She tells them that they are researchers whose responsibilities are to gather information in the library on their respective research topics. Moreover, they are to be collaborative with one another in their respective research groups and what *being collaborative* means. She also tells them that specific library periods have been booked with the school librarian and the timeline for completion of the project: three weeks. After three weeks, each group will present its findings in class with a speech and model building or pictures representing their research topics.

Each group is then given a list of questions to guide its research. These questions were typed on a sheet of paper and taped on the cover of each

TABLE 9.7   Writing Tasks for Chapters 6–12 of *Cariboo Runaway*

Set 1 questions	Set 2 questions
Answer three of the following questions:	Answer three of the following questions:
1. Would you like to have lived in the mining towns described in the book? (Remember, you get to eat three kinds of pies—apple, raisin, pumpkin pies, with your breakfast, lunch, and dinner!) Give reasons for your answer.	1. Why did Redbeard murder Big George McVee?
2. Elva was afraid the Indians would kill Tim and her or torture them. Did they? Where do you think Elva got those ideas?	2. Were the miners mean because they didn't help Elva over Big George McVee's murder and the dying old man? (Give reasons for your answer.)
3. Why was there so much violence (e.g., murder of Big George McVee) in the gold mining days?	3. (a) Who was Ah Sung? (b) Why was he important in the story?
4. Why was Elva worried that her father would be like the unfriendly miners she saw?	4. Why did Elva think the Indians would kill Tim and her?
5. Why wouldn't white men listen to Ah Sung and children?	5. Why did mining towns have "saloons"?

individual folder. The children are encouraged to add to the list of questions themselves. The questions for Group (1) on gold mining methods were as follows:

1. How was gold mining done?
2. What were the tools used (for example, a pan)?
3. What was used in transportation (mule, mule train)?
4. How did weather affect gold mining?
5. What is gold mining?
6. Where was the most gold found?
7. Why is gold so valuable?
8. Can people still go gold mining today?
9. How old do you have to be to go gold mining?
10. What did they do with the gold once they found it?

For Group (2) on mining towns—Barkerville, the questions were as follows:

1. What caused mining towns to develop during gold mining days? (Mining towns provided food and shelter through restaurants and hotels.)
2. Do a specific unit on Barkerville: (a) Where was Barkerville located? (b) What did Barkerville have (e.g., saloons, cafes, barber shop, etc.)? (c) Who lived in Barkerville, and how big was the population during the gold mining days? (d) Find old pictures of Barkerville.

TABLE 9.8   Writing Tasks for Chapters 13–17 of *Cariboo Runaway*

Set 1 questions	Set 2 questions
Answer three of the following questions:	Answer three of the following questions:
1. Look at page v, "Contents." You see these titles of chapters: The Runaway, The Stowaway, Murder, Redbeard, Another Death, Help, Ah Sung, and so on. When the author named her chapters that way, she was trying to help you in your reading. In what ways has she helped you understand the story by naming the chapters like that?	1. (a) Why did men join in the Gold Rush? (b) Would you have joined the Gold Rush? Why or why not?
2. How do you feel about the story? Does the story leave you feeling happy, sad, angry, frustrated? Which part(s) of the story makes (make) you feel the way you do? Why?	2. How do you feel about the story? Does the story leave you feeling happy, sad, angry, frustrated? Which part (parts) of the story makes (make) you feel the way you do? Why?
3. At the start of the story, Elva treated Tim badly (she was bossy, impatient, selfish, and sometimes mean to him). At the end of the story, Elva thought of Tim as a friend as well as a brother. What made Elva change her opinion of Tim? (See clues on page 131.)	3. (a) Think about the story. Is there anything you don't understand? (b) Do you have any questions that you'd like to ask the author?
4. Do you think Mr. Cameron Parkhurst's dream of get-rich-quick was worth it? Why or why not?	4. Pick two of these chapter titles and write down what ideas come into your head: (a) "Murder"; (b) "Another Death"; (c) "Help"; (d) "Ah Sung."
5. Make a character web of either Elva or Tim.	5. When the story began, Elva was mean and bossy to Tim. When the story ended, she started to see him as a friend. She no longer felt like bossing him or being mean to him. Why do you think she changed? (For clues, read page 131.)

3. Look in the book *Cariboo Runaway* to see how Barkerville was described.
4. Where did miners live?

The questions for Group (3) on miners were as follows:

1. From what countries did the miners come to the Cariboo for gold mining (Canadians, Americans, Chinese)?
2. Why did these men come?
3. Do a special unit on the Chinese gold miners. (a) When did they come to work on gold mines? (b) What were the restrictions put on them in gold mining? (They were not allowed to work directly in gold mines but could only mine the residues.) (c) Why were Chinese badly treated? (Prejudice) (d) Were Chinese women allowed to work? (e) How many Chinese people died while building the railroad?

The questions for Group (4) on law and justice were as follows:

1. During the gold mining days, were there policemen like ours (Vancouver Police and the Royal Canadian Mounted Police, the RCMP)?

2. There was an itinerant judge who maintained law and order. (What is an itinerant judge? How did he maintain law and order?)
3. Do a special unit on Judge Begbie ("The Hanging Judge").

The questions for Group (5) on attire during the gold mining period (or what people wore) were as follows:

1. Describe and illustrate what miners wore.
2. Describe and illustrate what women wore.
3. Describe and illustrate what women who worked in saloons wore.
4. What was Chinese people's clothing like?

The questions for Group (6) on the effects of mining on the environment were as follows:

1. Why do trees have to be cut down for gold mining to take place?
2. What does the site of gold mining look like? (Look up the book *Cariboo Runaway* to see what Elva and Tim saw.)
3. What does the loss of trees do to the environment?
4. What does the loss of trees do to the habitat of animals and birds?

To make a successful connection between the novel *Cariboo Runaway* as taught in language arts and the research project on gold mining in British Columbia in social studies, the teacher must carefully attend to certain responsibilities. To begin with, she must familiarize the children with the concept of research and clarify and emphasize the notion of collaboration within groups. Then she must work with the school librarian, not only to book specific library periods for the children's library research but also to ensure that the librarian assembles sufficient and appropriate books on the topic of gold mining. The classroom teacher should be prepared to bring in additional books from her own neighborhood libraries for the children's research project. Last but not least, she should emphasize a timeline for completing the social studies research project and expectations of the end products (class presentations per group with illustrations and model building).

LINKING *GENTLE BEN* AND A PROJECT ON SALMON

Gentle Ben, by Walt Morey, is the story of an early-adolescent boy's attachment to a brown bear, how he came to keep the bear, how he looked after it, and how the two became bonded to each other. The crux of the story is the boy's need to face reality that he could not keep the bear in the close proximity of a town. The story, however, has a happy ending in which both boy and bear manage to maintain their close ties.

Schedule of Class Activities

In the first two weeks of language arts classes (teacher works on the novel twice a week, each session lasting about one hour and 20 minutes), the teacher concentrates on building background knowledge on bears for fifth graders. They learn about differences between grizzlies and black bears, and they study handouts on information on bears (physical appearance, habitat, feeding, parenting, hibernation). The children make notes on the information in the handouts. After this, the teacher spends an entire session discussing issues in camping safety and issues that relate to bears. The children participate excitedly, sharing their camping experiences and close brushes with bears!

From the third week on, teacher begins reading aloud Chapters 1 and 2 of the novel, with the children following in their own copies. The teacher teaches and explains the concept of main idea and shows the children how to make notes on the chapters read.

At the end of reading, the children draw pictures of their impressions of what they have read (Chapters 1 and 2). A writing task follows the drawing. The children write an opinion essay on "Should Karl Anderson let his son, Mark, keep Ben the brown bear?"

Children are given one class period to write the opinion essay and are reminded to plan their essay writing, making their writing plans with either the CHAIR strategy or with webbing. In a subsequent language arts class, in groups of ten with an attendant adult (the university researcher, the classroom teacher, resource room teacher, teaching assistant), the children discuss what they have written. After the discussion, the children again write an opinion essay with the same title. But this time, they are to take the position opposite to the one they have taken previously. The two drafts of essays per child are read, marked, and returned to them with encouraging comments.

The teacher resumes reading the novel. The children continue to make notes on main ideas from the chapters read. They also begin working on the title page that illustrates the main theme of the story they read so far.

To spice things up, in the open, grassy field, the teacher plays the Survival game with the children taking roles of salmon, eagle, bear, human, and fire. This is basically a variation of the game of tag. The salmon, eagle, bear, human, and fire occupy levels of ascending hierarchy. The eagle eats salmon, the bear also eats salmon, but humans hunt both eagle and bear, and fire destroys all. Children are given cutout shapes depicting a salmon, an eagle, a bear, a stickperson, or the licking flames of a fire. The cutout shapes are looped on strings so that children can wear them round their necks. Groups of salmon, eagles, and so on are formed, and at the teacher's whistle, the tag game begins to the chaotic excitement of the fifth graders! Those who escape being tagged are the survivors!

The teacher shows a video (from the public library) on bears with questions that relate to the brown bear, Ben, in the book. She continues reading the novel with the children. The children begin work on the Salmon Research Project in their science classes while they continue to read the novel with the teacher in language arts. For the research, the children work in pairs. To facilitate the children's research, the teacher collaborates with the school librarian, who schedules two sessions in the library for the children to access relevant reading materials on salmon.

The children end their novel study unit on *Gentle Ben* by writing another opinion essay, entitled "Should we keep an exotic bird for a pet?" Again, they are reminded to plan their essay writing, using either the CHAIR strategy or webbing. The children complete their title page. Then they turn full steam in their focus on completing their Salmon Research Project (see Tables 9.9–9.15).

As part of her writing research Wong and her associates, Jai, Ellis, and Somerville, had also designed writing tasks that connect another novel, *Miracle at Willowcreek* by Annette Lebox with a science research project on the Greater Sandhill cranes.

At the heart of the story in *Miracle at Willowcreek* lies the advocacy theme of conservation of the habitat of the endangered Greater Sandhill cranes. Around this main theme, the author weaves multiple subthemes, including (1) the heroine's resentment at being uprooted from an urban setting to a rural setting (the heroine is a young adolescent girl); (2) the difficulties of an adolescent forming friendships in a new school; (3) the heroine's development of friendship and affection for a nature lover who introduced her to the Greater Sandhill cranes and how eventually she

TABLE 9.9   Salmon Research Project

Find a partner and complete your research
project on two (2) species of salmon as listed below

Types of salmon:

1. Atlantic salmon
2. Pacific salmon—Sockeye or Red
3. Pacific salmon—Coho or Silver
4. Pacific salmon—Chum or Dog
5. Pacific salmon—Chinook or King
6. Pacific salmon—Pink or Humpback
7. Pacific salmon—Cherry or Masu
8. Pacific salmon—Steelhead

Physical Attributes:

Species	Weight	Length	Other Physical Characteristics

TABLE 9.10 Draw and Color the Specific Salmon You Have Researched. Make It as Realistic as Possible

(1) Species:
(2) Species:

TABLE 9.11 Find Information on the Following Topics

HABITAT:

(1) Habitat of salmon hatchlings:

(2) Habitat of mature salmon:

FOOD:

PARENTING/LIFE CYCLE:

How do salmon spawn? Explain their life cycle. (Explain the roles of the female (mother) and the male (father) salmon.)

became involved in the advocacy of conserving the habitat of the cranes; (4) issues of bullying and racism in the rural high school; and (5) family dynamics between mother and daughter.

WRITING ACTIVITIES FOR *MIRACLE AT WILLOWCREEK*

The preceding writing tasks for *Miracle at Willowcreek* are linked up with a science research project on the Greater Sandhill crane. This research project involves much library research and writing and is presented in full in Appendix I at the end of this chapter. Teachers can

TABLE 9.12   Brain Teasers

BRAIN TEASERS:

   1. What are the differences between Atlantic and Pacific salmon?

   2. How many eggs do salmon lay when spawning?

WRITE TWO OR MORE INTERESTING QUESTIONS AND ANSWERS FOR THE
CLASS:

QUESTION 1:

ANSWER 1:

QUESTION 2:

ANSWER 2:

TABLE 9.13   Teacher Notes for Group Discussion

Types of salmon:
   1. Atlantic salmon
   2. Pacific salmon—Sockeye or Red
   3. Pacific salmon—Coho or Silver
   4. Pacific salmon—Chum or Dog
   5. Pacific salmon—Chinook or King
   6. Pacific salmon—Pink or Humpback
   7. Pacific salmon—Cherry or Masu
   8. Pacific salmon—Steelhead

Differences:

Atlantic and Pacific salmon are both "anadromous," or travel from the sea to freshwater
   birthplaces to spawn or reproduce. However, Pacific salmon spawn once and die, whereas
   Atlantic salmon may spawn more than once (several times).

TABLE 9.14   Life Cycle of a Salmon

- Female salmon returns to stream birthplace to spawn
- Lays eggs in stream bottom gravel nests called redds.
- Male fertilizes eggs with sperm.
- Females rearrange gravel to cover eggs.
- Eggs hatch into "alevin" or "sac fry."
- "Fry" develop into "pan," stay one to three years, and then, turn into "smolts."
- Body chemistry changes to adapt to salt water.
- Migrate to ocean where they stay two to three years until mature.
- Instinctively return to stream birthplace to spawn.

TABLE 9.15   Differences Between Atlantic and Pacific Salmon

Atlantic Salmon	Pacific Salmon
The Atlantic salmon has tasty flesh that is often orange-red. The fish average about 3.6 to 5.5 kg (8–12 lb) in weight, but specimens weighing up to 38 kg (84 lb) have been caught. The Atlantic salmon migrates in late spring or early summer. The female lays as many as 20,000 eggs in October or November, after which the adult salmon float downstream and return to the sea. The Atlantic salmon returns year after year and can live up to 8 years.	Pacific salmon spawn only once, dying after depositing and fertilizing their eggs. The Chinook salmon are the largest, averaging about 7 to 11 kg (15–25 lb). The Chinook migrates farther than any other salmon— 1,600 to 3,200 km (1,000–2,000 miles) inland to its spawning ground. The masu are found only in the waters of Japan. It is the smallest salmon.

have the children engage in the research individually or in small collaborative groups of about five children. For writing tasks for use in language arts, please see Tables 9.16–9.19.

SUMMARY

This chapter focuses on writing strategies for use with all students. We close by highlighting several important aspects of it.

- We have spotlighted the SRSD model developed by Karen Harris and Steve Graham and summarized the training steps of it because the model

TABLE 9.16   Writing Task #1 for Chapters 1–9 of *Miracle*

Children answer three of the following questions:

1. Have you ever changed schools? If you have, describe your experience.
   (a) Were you mad at your parents for having to change school? Why or why not?
   (b) How did you feel the first day at your new school?
   (c) How was your experience in finding new friends?
   (d) How did the new teacher and classmates compare to those in your old school?

2. Imagine you were like Tess, who moved from Vancouver to a rural town where there is no shopping mall (no fashionable clothes and shoes on sale, no video games), no theaters showing movies, and no McDonald's. Write what you would think and feel about having to live in such a rural town.

3. Tess and Sally got one week's detention for picking Wapato (Indian potato) because they went out of bounds. They broke the school's rule. Think back to the time when you got a detention with your buddy because you two had broken a school rule and got caught.
   (a) Describe this incident and recall how you felt at the time.
   (b) Then write about what you think and feel about that incident *now*. (Was it worth the detention? What did you get out of it? Would you still have done it?)

4. Clara had adopted Tabi after it got chased off the nest by its siblings. Tabi became her pet crane. Some people think it is wrong to have a wild bird or animal as a pet. They think wild birds and animals should be cared for by staff of a wildlife sanctuary, rehabilitated, and then returned to the wild. What do you think? Give reasons for your answer.

5. Rowena is not friendly to Tess.
   (a) What do you think are the reasons for her unfriendliness?
   (b) If you meet someone who behaves like Rowena toward you, how would you deal with her?

TABLE 9.17   Writing Task #2 for Chapters 10–22 of *Miracle*

Children answer three of the following questions:

1. On page 111, it reads: Tess fought back tears. "Sometimes when someone doesn't like me, I wonder if I've done something to deserve it. I think maybe there's something wrong with me. And if I keep quiet enough they won't notice. But it usually doesn't work." Do you agree with Tess? Why or why not?

2. Sally said: "I used to go home crying because someone at school would call me names. I felt like I was no good. And my grandmother would say, 'Your spirit is suffering because you've put it in a cage. You've kept it too quiet. You've told it to be too good.' She said sometimes you need to howl like a coyote and look your enemy in the eye." At the top of this page (page 111), Sally said she felt a lot better after she told Rowena what she thought of her (Rowena), even though Rowena didn't change her way of treating Sally. How would you deal with a bully? (Imagine you're being bullied.)

3. What does *imprinting* mean? (For clues, reread page 102.)

4. When Clara told Tess about her relationship with Tess's grandfather, what thoughts and feelings do you imagine would be in Tess's mind and heart? Give reasons for your answer.

5. In Chapter 22, Tess found out a terrible family secret that explains why her mother is overprotective of her. (You may reread the chapter to help you remember what that family secret was.) Do you think Tess's mother had good reasons for being overprotective of Tess? Why or why not?

TABLE 9.18 Writing task #3 for end of *Miracle*

Children answer three of the following questions:

1. Why do you think Clara, Tess, and her friends were so happy to see Miracle join the flock of Greater Sandhill Cranes and migrate?

2. Do you think it's better to conserve the habitat (polder) of the Greater Sandhill Cranes than developing a shopping mall and a golf course in the polder? Give reasons for your answer.

3. How did Tess and her mother grow closer? (For clues, reread the middle of page 256 to the top of page 257.)

4. Reread the last line on page 269 and the whole page of 270. What emotions do you think Tess felt as she released Miracle from the cage and saw it finally join the flock of cranes and fly away? Do you think she felt happy, sad, afraid, angry, frustrated? Give reasons for your answer on the emotions that Tess likely felt.

5. Tess and Sally have become buddies, and Tess has learned a lot about First Nations culture from Sally. Would they continue to be buddies? Why or why not?

TABLE 9.19 Test on *Miracle at Willowscreek*

Answer *all* the questions:

1. What have you learned from the story of *Miracle at Willowscreek*?

2. At the start of the story, Tess was not close to her mother. She resented having to move from Toronto. At the end of the story, she had become close to her mother. Why do you think the relationship between Tess and her mother had changed for the better?

3. In the story of *Miracle at Willowscreek*, Tess learned about racism, and she saw how Sally got badly treated by Rowena because she was First Nations. Tess dealt with Rowena's racism well by sticking up for Sally and being her pal. Imagine you're in the same class as Tess, Sally, Rowena, and Zak. What ideas do you have to get Rowena to see racism is bad and that she should accept and treat others of different races and cultures nicely?

with its core component of self-regulation has particular relevance for students with learning disabilities and because the writing strategies framed by the model are applicable to all students both with and without learning disabilities.

• We have devoted considerable space to delineating the conditions that promote effective implementation of the writing process. Descriptions of writing strategies for use with all students in grade five, middle school, and high school are presented.

• A presentation has been given of writing tasks for use with novels in language arts and writing tasks that connect novels used in language arts with social science and science. Although these writing tasks had been developed for specific novels, teachers can extract the ideas or principles underlying these writing tasks and develop similar writing tasks for books chosen by them for use in language arts. Similarly, they can develop writing tasks that link up novels in language arts with social science and/or science. Last but not least, they can adopt the notion of the "Bendable Ruler" in creating writing tasks that accommodate students with special needs.

REFERENCES

Alexander, P., Graham, S., & Harris, K.R. (1998). A perspective on strategy research: Progress and perspective. *Educational Psychology Review*, 10:129–154.

D'Ambrosio, V. (1988). Second graders can so write. In T. Newkirk & N. Atwell (Eds.), *Understanding writing: Ways of observing, learning, and teaching* (pp. 52–61). Portsmouth, NH: Heinemann Educational Books, Inc.

Danoff, B., Harris, K.R., & Graham, S. (1993). Incorporating strategy instruction within the writing process in the regular classroom: Effects on the writing of students with and without learning disabilities. *Journal of Reading Behavior*, 25(3), 295–322.

Deatline-Buchman, A., & Jitendra, A. (2006). Enhancing argumentative essay writing by fourth grade students with learning disabilities. *Learning Disability Quarterly*, 29(1), 39–54.

De La Paz, S. (1999). Teaching writing strategies and self-regulation procedures to middle school students with learning disabilities. *Focus on Exceptional Children*, 31(5), 1–16.

De La Paz, S., & Graham, S. (1997). Effects of dictation and advanced planning instruction on the composing of students with writing and learning problems. *Journal of Educational Psychology*, 89(2), 203–222.

Flower, L.S., & Hayes, J.R. (1980). The dynamics of composing: Making plans and juggling constraints. In L.W. Gregg & E.R. Steinberg (Eds.), *Cognitive processes in writing* (pp. 31–50). Hillsdale, NJ: Erlbaum.

Graham, S. (1990). The role of production factors in learning disabled students' compositions. *Journal of Educational Psychology*, 82:781–791.

Graham, S., & Harris, K.R. (1992). Self-instructional strategy development: Programmatic research in writing. In B.Y.L. Wong (Ed.), *Contemporary intervention research in learning disabilities: An international perspective* (pp. 47–64). New York: Springer-Verlag.

Graham, S., & Harris, K.R. (2003). Students with learning disabilities and the process of writing: A meta-analysis of SRSD studies. In H. Lee Swanson, K.R. Harris, & Steve Graham (Eds.), *Handbook of learning disabilities* (pp. 323–344). New York: The Guilford Press.

Graham, S., Schwartz, S., & MacArthur, C. (1993). Knowledge of writing and the composing process, attitude toward writing, and self-efficacy for students with and without learning disabilities. *Journal of Learning Disabilities*, 26:237–249.

Harris, K.R., & Graham, S. (1992). Self-regulated strategy development: A part of the writing process. In M. Pressley, K.R. Harris, & J.T. Guthrie (Eds.), *Promoting academic competence and literacy in school* (pp. 277–309). San Diego: Academic Press.

Harris, K.R., & Graham, S. (1996). *Making the writing process work: Strategies for composition and self-regulation*. Cambridge, MA: Brookline.

Hayes, J.R. (2000). A new framework for understanding cognition and affect in writing. In R. Indrisano & J.R. Squire (Eds.), *Perspectives on writing* (pp. 6–44). Newark, DE: IRA.

Hayes, J.R., Flower, L.S., Shriver, K.A., Stratman, J., & Carey, L. (1987). Cognitive processing in revision. In S. Rosenberg (Ed.), *Advances in applied psycholinguistics: Vol. 2. Reading, writing, and language processes* (pp. 176–240). New York: Cambridge University Press.

Jackson, N.R., & Pillow, P.L. (1992). *The reading-writing workshop: Getting started*. New York: Scholastic Professional Books.

Scardamalia, M., & Bereiter, C. (1987). Knowledge telling and knowledge transforming in written composition. In S. Rosenberg (Ed.), *Advances in applied psycholinguistics. Vol. 2. Reading, writing, and language learning* (pp. 142–175). Cambridge: Cambridge University Press.

Schumaker, J.B., Nolan, S.M., & Deshler, D.D. (1985). *The error monitoring strategy: Instructor's manual.* Lawrence: University of Kansas Institute for Research in Learning Disabilities.

Wong, B.Y.L., Jai, D., Ellis, P., & Somerville, I. (2004). Curricular research studies on *Gentle Ben* and *Miracle in Willowcreek.* This research was funded by the Social Sciences and Humanities Research Council of Canada (SSHRC) in a grant to B. Wong (grant no. 31-639400) for the period of 2002–2005.

Wong, B.Y.L., Jai, D., Ellis, P., & Somerville, I. (2003). Curricular research studies on *The Breadwinner* and *Cariboo Runaway.* This research was funded by the Social Sciences and Humanities Research Council of Canada (SSHRC) in a grant to B. Wong (grant no. 31-639400) for the period of 2002–2005.

Wong, B.Y.L. (1999). Metacognition in writing. In R. Gallimore, C. Bernheimer, D. MacMillan, D. Speece, & S. Vaughn (Eds.), *Developmental perspectives on children with high incidence disabilities. Papers in honor of Barbara K. Keogh* (pp. 183–198). Mahwah, NJ.: Erlbaum.

Wong, B.Y.L., Butler, D.L., Ficzere, S.A., & Kuperis, S. (1996). Teaching low achievers and students with learning disabilities to plan, write, and revise opinion essays. *Journal of Learning Disabilities, 29*(2), 197–212.

Wong, B.Y.L., Butler, D.L., Ficzere, S.A., & Kuperis, S. (1997). Teaching adolescents with learning disabilities and low achievers to plan, write, and revise compare and contrast essays. *Learning Disability Research & Practice, 12*(1), 2–15.

Wong, B.Y.L., Butler, D.L., Ficzere, S.A., Kuperis, S., Corden, M., & Zelmer, J. (1994). Teaching problem learners revision skills and sensitivity to audience through two instructional modes: Student-teacher versus student-student interactive dialogues. *Learning Disability Research & Practice, 9*(2), 78–90.

Wong, B.Y.L., Ellis, P., Jai, D., Watson, K., & Lonthie, A. (2006). The comparative efficacy of two instructional approaches to teaching normally-achieving children and special needs children to write opinion essays. Simon Fraser University, Faculty of Education Burnaby, British Columbia.

Wong, B.Y.L., Kuperis, S., Jamieson, D., Keller, L., & Cull-Hewitt, R. (2002). Effects of guided journal writing on students' story understanding. *Journal of Educational Research, 95*(3), 179–191.

Wong, B.Y.L., Wong, R., & Blenkinsop, J. (1989). Cognitive and metacognitive aspects of learning-disabled adolescents' composing problems. *Learning Disability Quarterly, 12*(4), 300–322.

APPENDIX I

The Greater Sandhill Crane Project

Name:_____

Grade:_____ Teacher:_____

Find information from the notes made for you and from library books to answer the following questions. Remember you are the researcher (information-finder).

Topic: Habitat of the Greater Sandhill Crane

1. What do these words mean?
   a. habitat
   b. wetland
   c. polder
2. a. What makes the best habitat for the Greater Sandhill cranes? (HINTS: Lots of food? Describe what Greater Sandhill cranes eat. Long spells of nice, dry, and warm weather? Few predators? Name the Greater Sandhill cranes' predators.)
   b. What is the size of the population of the Greater Sandhill cranes?
   c. Why has this population size of the Greater Sandhill cranes become smaller?
3. What are the threats to the Greater Sandhill cranes' habitat? Why?
4. a. Why do the Greater Sandhill cranes migrate every year?
   b. When do they migrate?
   c. How do they migrate (e.g., flight formation)?
   d. Trace their migratory routes on the given map and record them.
5. Compare the habitat of the Greater Sandhill cranes to the habitat of any 3 of the 15 kinds of cranes, and explain why only the Greater Sandhill cranes are called "the wetland bird."

Can you make up one or more questions on this topic and answer them? Bonus marks given if you do!

Illustration: Make a drawing of the habitat of the Greater Sandhill cranes.

Find the information from the notes made for you and from the library books to answer the following questions.

Topic: Mating Behaviors of the Greater Sandhill Cranes

1. Describe in detail the mating behaviors of the Greater Sandhill cranes (e.g., the unison calls, the crane dance).
2. The Greater Sandhill cranes' dance is a courtship dance. What do we mean by that?

3. a. Do you find a similar crane dance with the Whooping crane?
   b. Can you find another kind of crane that does a similar courtship dance as the Greater Sandhill crane? If you do, describe the dance so we can see the similarities and differences.
4. Do Greater Sandhill cranes mate for life?

Can you make up one or more questions on this topic and answer them? Bonus marks given if you do!

Illustration: Make a drawing of the crane dance.

Find information from the notes made for you and from the library books to answer the following questions.

Topic: Nesting and Parenting

1. Describe the size and color of the eggs.
2. Why does the female have a delay in laying the second egg after laying the first egg? (Why doesn't she lay the second egg immediately after she has laid the first egg?)
3. What happens to the second chick after it has been pushed out of the nest by the older and larger chick?
4. a. How do the male and female Greater Sandhill cranes look after the eggs?
   b. Name the predators that feed on Greater Sandhill crane eggs.
5. How do the Greater Sandhill cranes feed their chicks (e.g., do they feed the chicks whole worms or regurgitate food to feed the chicks)?

Can you make up one or more questions on this topic and answer them? Bonus marks given if you do!!

Illustration: Draw two Greater Sandhill crane eggs in a nest with attention to the proper (right) colors of the eggs.

Notes on Cranes and the Greater Sandhill Cranes

Cranes

Habitat. Habitat is the natural environment in which a plant or animal lives. Cranes live in marshy lands in many parts of the world. They have become rare as marshes are drained for farming and human settlements (new housing developments). Cranes live in large flocks and spend most of their time on the ground.

There are 15 kinds of cranes. More cranes live in Africa, Asia, and Europe than in North America. To be exact, only two kinds of cranes are found in North America: the rare Whooping crane and the more common Sandhill crane. South America and the Antarctica are the only continents with no cranes.

Africa boasts of having the elegantly crowned cranes. These cranes have ornamental tufts that make each of them look like it has a shaving brush on its head! Southern Asia has the Sarus cranes prized by Hindus, who believe that seeing a pair of these cranes in the spring brings them good luck! These cranes are found from India to the Philippines.

Physical Appearance. Because there are 15 kinds of cranes, you should expect them to differ from one another in looks. (Study the picture in your handout and look up library books to see the physical differences among the cranes!) Cranes and storks look very similar; both have long legs and long necks. Herons look like cranes, too. Herons fly with their head and neck bent into an S-shape, but cranes extend (stretch) their head and neck straight ahead when they fly.

About the Greater Sandhill Cranes. The tallest cranes are about 5 feet (1.5 meters) tall. The shortest cranes are about two and a half feet (0.8 meters) tall. Wingspan can measure up to seven and a half feet (2.3 meters).

Male and female cranes look alike. Color ranges from white to dark gray and brown. Most adult cranes have a patch of red skin on their heads.

Food. Cranes eat a variety of food: frogs, insects, and snails. They also feed on grain and other plants. Sometimes they are pests because they take grain from the farmers' fields.

Sounds. Cranes make a bugle-like sound that carries a long way. Cranes call to one another in flight, maybe to keep the flock together in migration. Look up the novel to find out more about the sounds Greater Sandhill cranes make!

Migration. Most cranes in the northern hemisphere migrate south each fall and return to nesting grounds each spring to breed. Canadian cranes migrate to Texas, New Mexico, and Mexico. In migration, cranes fly in enormous flocks, which may include more than 10,000 birds!

Cranes live mainly in wetlands. If they migrate to arid (dry) areas, they return to damp areas to breed.

Mating and Reproduction. Cranes mate after they reach their nesting grounds. The male and female perform a dance before mating. The cranes circle around each other with opened wings, bow their heads to each other, and leap into the air. (See the novel *Miracle at Willowcreek* for more about their dance.)

Nesting. Cranes build nests in shallow water in a marsh, swamp, or other wet, open area. When they build a nest, both male and female cranes help pile grasses, weeds, and other plants in a mound.

After the nest is built, the female usually lays two eggs in a season. Both parents take turns incubating the eggs, and both take care of the chicks.

APPENDIX II. TEACHING THE CHAIR
STRATEGY IN OPINION ESSAY WRITING

Suggested grades: Grades 5 and 6

Teacher says to class: "Today we're going to learn a new way of writing opinion essays: the CHAIR strategy. Look at this picture of a chair. (Shows overhead transparency of a picture of a chair on projector; make sure you have a strong light in the projector!) On the seat of the chair, you have your opinion and then you have legs supporting the chair. In any opinion essay, you are free to form your own opinion. There is no right or wrong opinion in any opinion essay. But you must support your opinion!

"Let's write an opinion essay together using this CHAIR strategy. Imagine that the Coca-Cola Company has approached your school principal and asked if it can have (or install) a Coke machine in your school. Your principal, Mrs. Claridge, being very democratic, wants your input on her decision making. You're to write an opinion essay on "Should there be a Coke machine in this school?"

"How many of you would support having a Coke machine in the school?" (In Sue Agabob's class, 19 out of 29 grade six children raised their hands. The remaining 10 indicated by a show of hands that they would *not* support having a Coke machine in the school.) The teacher continues: "All right, we'll write the essay with the majority opinion in place. There should be a Coke machine in the school. Now look at the transparency again. You see these legs supporting the chair. Let's focus on the legs with the word *PRO* on them. What does that word mean?" Teacher pauses for the children's responses. Having ascertained that they all understand the meaning of the word *PRO*, she continues. "Good! Now let's think of some PRO reasons in support of the opinion that there should be a Coke machine in this school. Remember, you must always present supportive reasons for your position. Just as in writing answers to those questions in your novel study, you always give reasons for your answers. OK, help me out!" The teacher awaits the responses of the children. She writes down their input on an overhead transparency. "Good, you have very good reasons to support having a Coke machine in the school!" When she has written down about eight responses, she stops taking any further responses despite moans from the children. She then reads aloud the children's responses: "There should be a Coke machine in this school because many students like Coke, Coke tastes good. When we come in from the playground, we are hot and thirsty, and it's good to have Coke." She praises the children's responses and then turned to the other side of the argument. "Now, let's think about the CON side. The word *CON*, as many of you know, means the exact opposite of PRO. Why do we need to think about the CON side? You see, when you write an opinion essay, your goal is to get readers of your essay to be on your side, to win people over by showing them your supportive reasons are better and stronger than the supportive reasons of the opposing side, the CON side. That's why you always need to think about the CON reasons. Understand? Now look at this transparency of the CHAIR. If you don't have the legs with the word *CON* on them, what kind of a chair would you have? You'd have an imbalanced, wobbly chair! Can you sit on such a chair? Can I (Mr. Jedsen or Mrs. Agabob) sit on it?" Teacher awaits the children's chorus of responses before continuing. "Now those of you who showed by raising your hands earlier that you support the opinion that there should *not* be a Coke machine in this school help your classmates out with supportive reasons for the CON side." The children eagerly complied and gave very good reasons for the CON side. The teacher duly writes them down on an overhead transparency and allows about eight responses from the children. She then reads them aloud: "Some supportive reasons for the CON side are 'Coke is bad for your health; it contains chemicals that can cause cancer; Coke has sugar in it; Coke is addictive; too much Coke can make you fat; if you keep drinking Coke, it can cost you a lot of money.'"

Teacher commends the children's responses. She thanks all of them for their effort and good participation. Then she says: "Now we come to the conclusion of our opinion essay. We need to wrap up what we've written. Now for those of you who hold the majority view that you *do* want a Coke machine in the school, you have a choice in how you want to conclude your opinion essay. You can change your mind and join the other side *if* you think their ideas are stronger and better than yours and make more sense to you. If so, you can write something like this:

"I have thought carefully about the PRO and CON reasons, and I change my mind. I now support the opinion that we should *not* have a Coke machine in the school because the CON reasons make more sense to me.

"But you may want to be a stick in the mud and stay with your opinion that there should be a Coke machine in the school. If so, you would end your opinion essay something like this:

"After thinking carefully about the two sides of the question for this opinion essay, I still think we should have a Coke machine in the school. The CON reasons have not made me change my opinion.

"So we have just written an opinion essay together with the help of the visual prompt of a CHAIR! I'm going to give each of you a copy of the CHAIR. Remember to use this *visual prompt* to remind you to write a balanced opinion essay, OK? By *balanced*, we mean an opinion essay that has both PRO and CON reasons. In the opinion essay that we've just written together, if you only have PRO reasons down, Mrs. Claridge would likely say: 'Mrs. Agabob has a bright group of sixth graders. But I see they have only written about the PRO side. Their supportive reasons here are real good. But where are the supportive reasons for the CON side? I can't find any in these children's papers! Ah, they haven't thought about the CON side and show me that their PRO reasons are stronger and better than the CON side. Well, they haven't thought about both sides of the question thoroughly. By omitting the CON side, they haven't persuaded me over to their PRO side! Too bad.' You've lost your chance, people! So remember, always make sure you think of the CON side in writing an opinion essay! Otherwise, you would have written an imbalanced opinion essay. Your CHAIR would be lopsided, wobbly, and unbalanced!! Your opinion essay would likely not succeed in swaying readers to your side!"

Teacher ends her talk by distributing copies of the CHAIR to the children and reminding them the purpose of this picture. She then has them write the first training essay with the title: *Should hot dogs be banned on Sports Day?*

P.S. I have used both present and past tenses in writing this CHAIR strategy for you. The past tense denotes what actually occurred in Mrs. Sue Agabob's grade six classroom.

Author Index

SUBJECT INDEX